Y0-BGT-483

Acknowledgements

I have had a fantastic team for this book—dedicated, professional, and always supportive.

I want to thank first and foremost, Victoria Weill-Hagai for her constant insistence on getting the words, punctuation, and thoughts right. She persevered on this project for a year and a half. Her support has kept me working to make this the best book it can be.

Diane Fitzgerald must be the best book designer there is. Not only did she make the words and illustrations fit the pages and look good, she actually read every word to make sure the text and illustrations went together. She designed and maintains my web site, for which I often get compliments for its clarity and good design.

Sharon Alderman did the technical editing. What a comfort it has been to know that she has checked every statement I made. We had good discussions when we had different opinions.

If you ever want a perfect team member, choose Ron Hildebrand who did the illustrations. He made my embarrassingly crude "drawings" into reality. He was always careful to put the threads exactly as I wanted and never complained when I changed my mind on things, and he made suggestions that I'd never thought of.

Without Jim Ahrens, these books would never have been written. The European techniques he taught and those he invented himself are the foundation for the series. When I teach weaving motions in workshops, even the most advanced weavers are surprised at the techniques he taught and wonder why they didn't learn them when they began to weave.

Helen Pope guided, supported, and encouraged me for over 30 years. She was truly a mentor and a person I hope to imitate. Her sharing was legendary in the San Francisco Bay Area.

Kathryn Alexander has given invaluable support for my books and has spread the word about them to her students around the country. I am honored to have her caring, her willingness to share her thoughts, and her encouragement.

My student and friend, Green, has given moral support as well as her eagle-eye as my proofreader.

Many friends have given me much support during the years it has taken to complete this series. Among them: Mary Rowe, Milton Sonday, Connie Wendell, and Ranghild Langlet.

Finally, I owe a tremendous amount to my students. I often say that the teacher is the one in the classroom who learns the most. They have been enormously encouraging.

Illustrations and Front Cover

Ron Hildebrand

Duy Ngo (Figures: 1, 2, 3, 4, 5, 8, 9, 10, 12, 13, 41, 52, 61, 83, 146, 147, 160, 164, 200, 201, 205, 209, 210, 222, 223, 224, 236, 247, 253)

Book Design

Diane Fitzgerald

Editors

Editor: Victoria Weill-Hagai

Technical editor: Sharon Alderman

Technical and Practical Advisors

Jim Ahrens

Sharon Alderman

Kathryn Alexander

Jan Doyle

Liz Gluck

Winn Kalmon

Helen Pope

Liz Williamson

Proofreader

Green

Peggy Osterkamp's New Guide to Weaving **3**

Weaving & Drafting Your Own Cloth

by Peggy Osterkamp

A guide that makes weaving fun with new techniques from European handweavers and the textile industry

Dedicated to

my mother,

Mildred Lytle

She gave me her genes, love, and determined-ness,
the tools to accomplish my dreams.
She lived in a time when she couldn't use her talents
to achieve her own dreams.

Also by Peggy Osterkamp

Peggy Osterkamp's New Guide to Weaving, Book #1:
  Winding a Warp & Using a Paddle
Peggy Osterkamp's New Guide to Weaving, Book #2:
  Warping Your Loom & Tying On New Warps
Video: *Warping the Loom Back to Front*
DVD: *Warping the Loom Back to Front*

Peggy Osterkamp's New Guide to Weaving Number 3: Weaving & Drafting Your Own Cloth
©2005 by Peggy Osterkamp. All rights reserved. No part of this book may be used or reproduced in any manner without written permission except in the case of brief quotations embodied in critical articles and reviews. For information write:

Lease Sticks Press
P.O. Box 1148
Sausalito, CA 94966

www.weaving.cc

ISBN: 0-9637793-9-7

Printed in China

Table of Contents

Introduction

I think weaving should be fun. It is the goal of my books and teaching. I show how to reach your own weaving objectives by reducing your frustration and increasing your confidence. Weavers who are familiar with my previous books will find in this book the same thoroughness and accessibility that they have come to expect.

I feel that if you are comfortable with the technical aspects of weaving, you are free to be creative. That's the reason I explain thoroughly how to weave efficiently, use shuttles properly, make good selvedges and finish your cloth. Weavers who are worried that their projects won't turn out will find this book invaluable.

Every chapter in this book contributes to my basic goals for you: to weave efficiently and fast, and to have fun.

The best weaving comes from an even rhythm. The weaving motions in this book will give you a rhythm and a speed you never knew was possible. This book answers those weavers, even the most experienced weavers, who don't know about these techniques, who ask me, "Why didn't I learn it this way at first?"

An entire chapter is devoted to shuttles—their advantages and how to use them. Knowing how to use both end-delivery and boat shuttles properly is a large part of weaving with an even rhythm.

The chapter on selvedges will explain how to make good selvedges for various situations. Questions that frustrate or intimidate weavers are carefully addressed. How and when to use tape selvedges, fixed selvedges, and selvedges on extra shafts are described so that you can make your selvedges work for you and be proud of them.

Weavers often encounter situations that are new to them with accompanying problems. The troubleshooting chapter is a resource. This chapter is divided into three sections for ease in looking up specific problems.

Finishing is a subject often glossed over in books on weaving. I've researched the literature available and incorporated information from many other sources. Again, there are sections for making it easy to look up the information needed for a particular situation.

My chapter on drafting approaches that subject from different angles. Those who have not understood drafting up until now can finally feel the wonderful pleasure of having the "power" to read drafts and to make original ones themselves. I have taught hundreds of weavers, and I'm proud of my approaches.

The 16-page index is a comprehensive guide to finding the information you want, when you need it.

All in all, the information in this book will be very useful to you. I have explained things just as I teach them, so they are accessible to you.

Weaving and Drafting Your Own Cloth is the third book in the series, *Peggy Osterkamp's New Guide to Weaving*. In the first book, *How to Wind a Warp & Use a Paddle*, you learned how to make a first-quality warp. In the second book, *Warping Your Loom & Tying On New Warps*, you learned how to put the warp on the loom, back to front, for trouble-free weaving. That book includes chapters on sectional beaming, tying on new warps, knots, and adjusting looms.

My video and DVD, *Warping the Loom Back to Front*, show the whole warping process from measuring the warp on the warping board to tying it on to the apron rod, ready to weave.

In my new book, we get to the actual weaving—no matter what method of warping the loom you use. Whether you warp back to front or front to back, these techniques work.

This book mainly addresses the weaving of cloths that are balanced or nearly balanced— that is, those in which both the warps and the wefts show equally in the finished cloth. Warp-faced weaving can generally follow these techniques, as well, with adaptations given where applicable. Rug weaving that requires hard beating is not addressed in this book. Weft-faced rug weaving is very different and is thoroughly addressed in books on rug weaving.

Two books about rug weaving are: The *Techniques of Rug Weaving*[1] and *A Rug Weaver's Source Book*[2].

---

[1] Collingwood, Peter, *The Techniques of Rug Weaving*. Watson-Guptill Publications, New York. 1970.

[2] Various authors, *A Rug Weaver's Source Book*. Interweave Press, Inc., Loveland, CO. 1984.

What I learned from Jim Ahrens, the designer of the first AVL looms, is the foundation for the books in this series. He taught the European way of warping and weaving. The classes he gave were called "Production Weaving," with emphasis on learning the efficient techniques the Europeans have used for centuries. He built looms, taught weaving, and wove huge amounts of cloth for specialty stores in San Francisco, for decorators, and for churches. He also wove art pieces on his drawloom. Efficiency was always the bottom line. That meant no frustration, broken threads, or tangles. Jim always said, "The only thread that can't tangle is one under tension—it works!"

The following quotation by Louis Pasteur is a guiding principle for me: "Chance favors the prepared mind." I think that if you know the techniques, you can be free to create your ideas.

I certainly hope that this book will prepare your mind so that your weaving is creative and satisfying.

Generic Loom

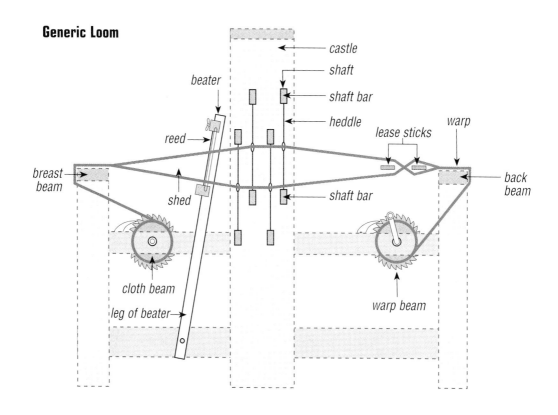

Generic Loom

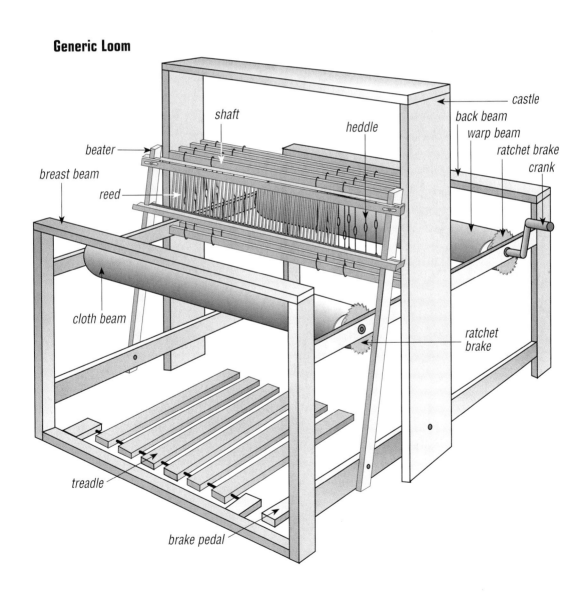

shaft

heddle

castle

back beam

warp beam

ratchet brake

crank

beater

breast beam

reed

cloth beam

ratchet brake

treadle

brake pedal

What You Need to Do
...before you're ready to weave

Tying up the treadles

Attaching the treadles to the shafts or lams is called tying up the treadles. To learn about which treadles to tie up, read the chapter on drafting on page 207. Different looms have different ways to do it–some more convenient than others. If the ties are adjustable, adjust them to the right height for comfortable weaving and a good size shed. Time spent now in adjusting the tie-up cords will be saved in the speed of weaving later. Read details about tying up the treadles for counterbalance and countermarch looms in Book #2, in the chapter on adjusting looms.

If your loom has springs underneath the shafts, undo the springs while you do the tie-ups. It will be much easier that way. Then, be sure to hook them back up before you tie the warp onto the cloth beam apron.

Jim Ahrens invented the side-tie-up for many of his looms so he wouldn't have to get all the way down to the floor to tie up the treadles. See Book #2, page 71, for how they work. Briefly summarized here, you put one treadle's worth of cords on its hook. Then, attach these cords, one-by-one, to the appropriate shafts for that treadle according to the tie-up draft.

Changing the tie-ups for some looms is easy even though you must work underneath the treadles. There's a cord hanging down from the lams or shafts with a "button" at the end. The cord slips into a slot in the treadle and that's it–the button holds the cord in place.

Some looms are notorious for the hooks they use because the hooks can fall out too easily. I've seen weavers replace the hooks with Texsolv cord. It is a strong polyester cord, machine-crocheted in two parallel rows connected at about 1/2" intervals to form a series of links or "button holes." See Figure 1. To replace the hook type connectors, loop the cord around the lam or bar under the shafts and take the tail of the cord through one of the holes to form a lark's head knot. See Figure 2. (The lark's head knot is shown in the chapter on knots in Book #2). Take the tail down through the slot in the treadle. Put one of the Texsolv "buttons" (The button looks like a small plastic arrow.) under the treadle to hold it in place. See Figure 3. You can prepare all the connectors possible for your loom in advance, and have them dangling in place at all times. Then, you can "button" them up as needed.

Fig. 1

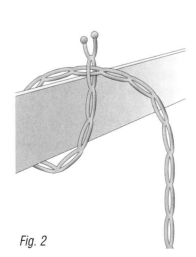

Fig. 2

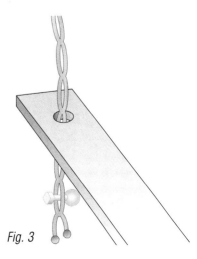

Fig. 3

Looms that require two cords, one a loop and one with two "tails," are meant to have the cords tied with snitch knots. If you use this knot, it will be easy to undo the knots when you want to change the tie-up. See Figures 4 and 5, and the chapter on knots in Book #2. Texsolv connectors can be made for these looms, as well.

Tying up the treadles on countermarch looms is much easier with Texsolv cord. Read about it in the chapter on adjusting looms, in Book #2.

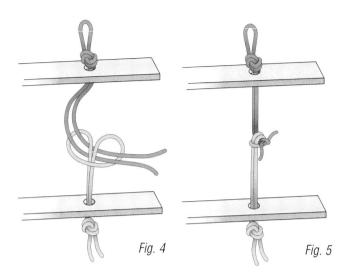

Fig. 4   Fig. 5

One tie up for four shaft looms

In my second book, beginning on page 69, I described a tie-up that never needs to be changed, for four shaft jack and counter-balance looms. You can get all the combi-nations possible with four shafts with this system. Your feet can dance over the treadles for many weaves, and if they aren't dancing, they can work very efficiently. See Figure 6. Another advantage of this system is that you can change to any weave structure you want in a project without changing the ties to the treadles.

Multi-shaft tie ups

Many multi-shaft looms don't have tie-ups at all. Dobby looms have a bar to put pegs in for each shed to create the "tie-ups." On computer-driven looms, they are typed in on the keyboard or added with a mouse, which is very fast.

On some looms it is more convenient to tie up each treadle's shafts, one shaft at a time. It's easier if you start with the back shafts first and tie all the ties for that shaft to all the treadles needed. Progress forward, so that you don't get in your own way. Many treadles won't be com-pletely tied up until the first shaft has been tied to all of its treadles. If you can, tie a treadle to a shaft and hold it down until all the treadles required have been tied to that shaft.

Treadling sticky warps

It may be difficult to open a clean shed in warps made up of hairy or sticky threads or those that are very densely sleyed (warp faced weaves). You may need to treadle by lifting one shaft and then adding one shaft at a time to create a single shed. A direct tie-up (only one shaft tied to a treadle) or a skeleton tie-up (see page 72, Book #2) lets you open the sheds one or two shafts at a time. It will slow you down, but it may be necessary to get the clear sheds you need. Read about sticky warps on page 26.

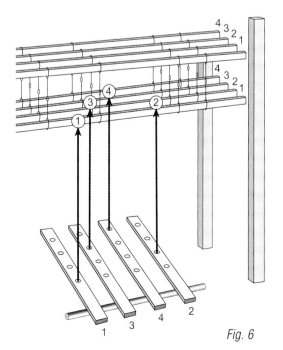

Fig. 6

3

Walk the treadles

☞ Tie up the treadles in a way that lets you alternate your feet. It's called "walking the treadles." Look at the weave draft and tie up the first treadle of the sequence to the outside treadle on the right or left side so that the appropriate (the right or the left) foot will be working that treadle.

Starting with the outside treadles makes it easy for your foot to find the first treadle without having to look down for it. The second treadle to be used should be the outside one on the opposite side from the first. The third is on the left, fourth on the right, etc., working your way from the outside to the middle treadles. Hence you are "walking" or alternating your feet. See Figure 7.

Sometimes, you'll have more than one sequence for a project, and you'll have two or more sets of treadles. Use one set for one area and the other for a second area. I like to set up the treadles I use the most often near the middle, and the ones I don't use as often near the outside, where I have to stretch my legs to reach them. To mark the beginning of the middle set of treadles, ideally, I have an empty treadle, so I can feel the outside treadle of this set. If there aren't enough treadles to "waste" like this, put rubber bands on the first treadles for the set, so you can feel it. Some people put tape on their treadles, which I don't think it is good for the wood. If you must use tape, use the blue tape that house painters use; it comes off without leaving a residue.

☞ Especially with multi-shaft weaves, it's impor-tant to walk the treadles. It may take some time to work out the actual treadle tie-ups working from the tie-up draft, but you will find the time well invested.

Your feet must be prepared to treadle. Here is the setup: while one foot is pressing a treadle down, have the other foot poised on the next treadle in the sequence. While the left foot presses its treadle (the outside one is the first

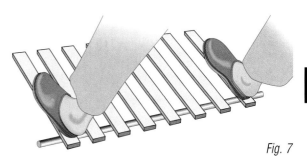

Fig. 7

one), the right foot is poised on the outside treadle on the right. As soon as the beater hits the fell, the right foot presses its treadle and the left foot lifts up and slides over to the next treadle and stays poised until it is needed.

Once you practice a bit, you'll get the rhythm and be weaving along quite fast and pleasantly. Chant: "Throw, beat, change," and when the beater swings away from the fell, say "your feet." Altogether, it goes smoothly: "Throw, beat, change, your feet"; "throw, beat, change, your feet." It is difficult to develop a smooth rhythm unless you tie up the treadles so you can alternate your feet.

The weight of your body is supported by the foot pressing the treadle.

Avoid back strain

In Book #2, in the section on threading, I tell you that the most important thing is to get comfortable. Comfort is just as important when you are treadling so you don't make mistakes.

When you walk the treadles, you avoid back strain. Think of the alternative—tying up the treadles to go in sequence from left to right. When you lift your foot off the first treadle in order to move it to the next treadle, your body has to rock backwards a bit, and, for a time, nothing is supporting your body except your back. When you alternate your feet there is always weight on one treadle to support you, and your back remains upright and unmoved.

Blocks can be attached to the treadles to make them easier to reach for weavers with short legs. Ask your loom dealer or make them yourself.

Read about body mechanics on page 9.

> If you can't get a clean shed when you begin to weave, see pages 117 and 130, in the chapter on problems, for solutions.
>
> If you find threading errors, read about fixing them in the Troubleshooting chapter, beginning on page 107.

Weaving the heading

The warp threads that were tied on to the apron rod in bundles now need to be spread out by weaving a heading. Please ignore any suggestions about headings woven with rags, toilet paper, or anything bumpy or bulgy. Instead, weave the 2-stick heading described below, which gives you a smooth, knot-free base for your cloth.

 It works for most warps except for warps with very few ends per inch (warps per inch), like those for tapestry and other weft-faced weaves.

Many weavers never learned about this heading, but it has been used for centuries. It is a great help and can be used in two different ways. First, it is used for the initial heading to spread out the warp threads. Second, it is a technique that lets you cut off lengths of your woven cloth as you go. You won't have to weave the entire warp before you can get your hands on the goods.

How to space out the warp threads

Begin weaving the heading immediately after you've tied the warp onto the apron. Weave plain weave (tabby), or as close to plain weave as you can. Use a thin weft, like carpet warp. (A color that contrasts with the warp color shows up errors fast; but don't choose a color that might make a stain when wet.) Throw 3 or 4 wefts of plain weave, but don't beat each weft. Beat the 3 or 4 wefts in together. If the warp has not been completely spaced out, throw 3 or 4 more wefts, then beat. A few more wefts of plain weave, beaten normally, will even out the selvedges. This technique will quickly space out your warp and even out any irregularities of tension in the warp.

Any loose threads will loop up and even themselves out. I tell students not to agonize when tying on. When checking that the warp tension is even, close your eyes and feel the threads. If any feel soft, they are soft, and need to be tightened. If any feel too tight, they need to be loosened. If you can't tell, they are of the same tension, and all right as is.

How to make the 2-stick heading

 You need a pair of sticks that fit on your cloth beam and won't interfere with the ratchet. They can be lease sticks, dowels, or metal rods. I prefer thin and lightweight sticks rather than thick ones because they take up less warp and aren't so bulky.

After you've woven the initial heading (or at least 1"), insert a stick in one plain weave shed; insert another stick in the next plain weave shed, and continue weaving for 1", or so. See Figure 8, which shows you the heading in detail.

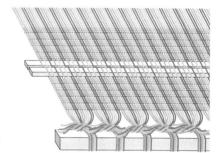

Fig. 8

How to make a smooth base on the cloth beam

Now is the time to cut off the knots in the warp bundles to make a smooth, flat, lump-free surface for your accumulating cloth to roll onto. (See below if you want fringe.)

Follow these steps:

1. Release the tension, and carefully cut between the knots and the first inch of the heading that you wove. *Leave both plain weave sections and the sticks attached to the loom!* Be careful not to cut the loom's apron cords! (If you want fringe, don't cut anything, and read below.)

If the warp is sparse or slippery, put some white glue on the cut edge to prevent the heading from unraveling or the warp threads from pulling the heading out when the warp is put back on tension.

2. Fold the first stick, with the first inch of the heading, under the second stick and the second inch of the heading. See Figure 9. *(Fold the first inch on top of the cloth if your cloth is thick, so the cloth beam will have a smoother base.)*

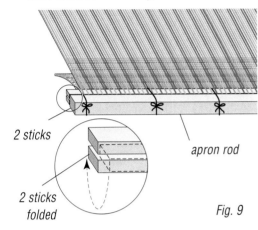

2 sticks

2 sticks folded

apron rod

Fig. 9

3. Tie the two folded sticks across the front apron rod at 3" intervals. Make the ties strong by doubling a sturdy but not fat string. Use a tapestry needle to go through the cloth and around the rod. Make the first tie in the center of the warp to hold the sticks stable. You might find it easier if you wind up the cloth apron until the apron rod is resting on the breast beam. Then pull the heading sticks (and the warp) forward to the apron rod and tie them to it, while steadying them on the breast beam. Put the knots on the front edge of the apron rod so you won't make lumps with the ties.

4. Begin weaving again. The warp tension remains unchanged; since the heading was woven on tension before the knots were cut off, all the threads remain evenly tensioned as you resume.

If you want fringe, untie the knots instead of cutting them off and fold the sticks as above. Then smoothly fold back the unknotted warp threads as well as the heading.

 After the heading, weave a few inches of the weave structure you're going to use, to get the width of the warp established. It will draw in a bit at first; then you will have a consistent width for your project.

Cutting off the cloth as you go

This is a technique I love to use. You can cut off pieces as you weave them; it's not necessary to wait until the entire warp is used up before cutting off fabric. The headings and two sticks save precious warp because you don't need to tie the warps back on to the apron rod. I always cut off a sample at the beginning of my warps to see if I like the result and to test for shrinkage.

 I don't have to worry about whether the warp tension is the same because I made the heading with the warp on tension.

When you're ready to cut off a length of cloth, make the complete 2-stick heading just like above. (Weave 1" of plain weave, or as close to plain weave as you can, insert 2 sticks into the next two plain weave sheds, and weave one inch more. That's the complete heading.)

Cut between the cloth and the first inch of the heading you wove, leaving the complete heading attached to the loom. See Figure 10. Remove the cloth from the front apron rod. Fold the two sticks, and tie them to the apron rod, as above.

Fig. 10

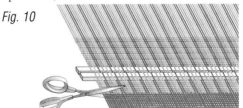

Continue weaving, knowing your warp tension remains the same.

Read what to do with the cut edges of the cloth on page 42.

What You Need to Know
...from my previous books

Sett calculations

In Book #1, there is a whole chapter that thoroughly discusses sett (ends per inch or warp threads per inch). Here is a summary of the information that I refer to in that chapter.

Making your weaving easier

In industry, a balanced looking fabric is actually a bit more warp predominant than precisely balanced. It looks balanced at a glance, but upon inspection, you will see that there are more warps per inch than wefts per inch. We handweavers can use this principle, too. The way to achieve this look is to take 80% of the maximum sett using the Ashenhurst method. (See page 7).

Why it's a good idea to weave with a slightly closer warp sett:

1. The edges of the cloth (selvedges) don't draw in as much, so the selvedges don't break. The extra warps hold out the warp width.

2. You don't have to make sure the weft is put in very loosely. The natural diagonal the shuttle makes when you throw it through, from the last row of weaving (the fell) to the beater, is usually enough slack for the weft's pathway. See Figure 11. (If the weft is put in without any slack, it will pull in the edges of your cloth.) You don't need to bubble the wefts, or make arcs to create the slack needed. More slack is taken up in the warp so the wefts can be straighter.

3. There is less trouble with warp breakage. Fragile warp threads can be used because there are more of them to pull their weight on the job.

4. There are fewer wefts (picks) per inch so the weaving goes faster.

When you don't want to use the 80% figure

It is explained in detail in Book #1, on page 94, in the chapter on sett, and briefly summarized here. Hairy yarns aren't good for the sett at 80% of the maximum. Smooth, slippery silk or rayon threads need to be sett closer than 80% (more warps per inch). Woolens are meant to shrink, so they must be sett farther apart than the 80% figure. Weft-faced, warp-faced weaves, and those with weft emphasis (e.g. overshot) can't use the 80% calculation. When you want a true plaid, and the warps per inch must be the same as the number of picks per inch, you need to use a less closely sett warp than 80%.

The percents that are recommended for specific types of fabric are given in the sett chapter.

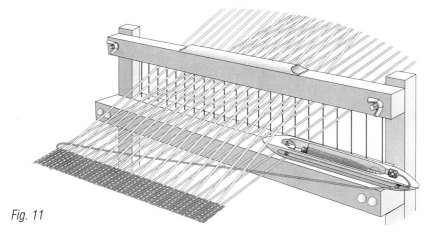

Fig. 11

Ashenhurst's Formula

The formula is explained in detail in Book #1, but summarized here.

Instead of wrapping the warp threads on a ruler to see how many there are in an inch, use this formula, which is a calculation for the number of diameters of a yarn that fit in an inch. Note: this calculation can be thought of as the number of wraps on a ruler in an inch, *but the calculation gives a larger number than the wraps on a ruler would.* "The diameters" is a way to talk about the number of threads that would fit in an inch if they were laid side-by-side.

> ### Ashenhurst's Formula
> The number of diameters per inch = .9 times the square root of the yards per pound.

It is easy to get the square root if you have an inexpensive calculator with the square root sign on one of the buttons. Multiply that number by .9 for the diameters in one inch.

The maximum sett for plain weave (tabby) is 1/2 the diameters. This is quite dense and won't look balanced.

Take 80% of the maximum plain weave sett to get the slightly closer sett discussed above that looks balanced.

The maximum sett for twill is 2/3 the diameters. To get 2/3 of a number, multiply the number by .67.

How to get the yards per pound

To find out the yards per pound of any given yarn, use a McMorran Yarn Balance (see Figure 12), which is a balance scale used to determine how many yards of a yarn are in one pound. It is described in Book #1, on page 91, in the chapter on sett, but what you need to know now is how to use it. Place a length of yarn in the "V" on the balance arm, and cut off pieces until the arm balances. Measure the length of the yarn in inches. Multiply the number of inches (and fractions) by 100 for the approximate number of yards in a pound. Measure carefully because you multiply your measurement and your error by 100.

Adjusting the height of the beater

Here are excerpts from Book #2, from the chapter on adjusting looms.

Adjusting beaters on jack and other rising shaft looms

If the warp is too high, the tension on the warp may be too great. Reduce the tension. Otherwise, raise the beater. Many beaters are adjustable. (If the beater lifts out of the loom, put a short piece of doweling at the base of each leg of the beater between the end of the leg and where the leg pivots.) The warp at rest should just touch the shuttle race.

Adjusting beaters on counterbalance and countermarch looms

Raise or lower the beater so the warp is at the mid point of the height of the reed when the shed is closed. Be sure the warp is traveling over the back beam, which is necessary for all loom types.

Fig. 12

8

Automatic warp tension system

This system is used today and has been for centuries. How it works is explained in the chapter, "The Automatic Warp Tension System," in Book #2. It maintains a consistent tension once it's set. How to beat is summarized here. See Figure 13.

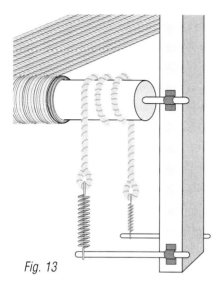

Fig. 13

Beating on looms with the automatic warp tension system

With this system you cannot beat hard. The system is for all kinds of weaving, except when the weft needs to be beaten in hard, like in tapestry and rug weaving, because the force of hard beating allows the cord to slip and the warp to come forward with each blow. You can beat with a quick bump because the force is quickly released. If you pull the beater to press the wefts into place, the warp will go soft, as well, because your beat is releasing the tension just as though you used a too-hard beat.

If you normally beat hard and can't change your ways, use another type of brake on your loom. "Regular" brakes are available for looms with the automatic system.

Weighting warps separately

This information is from Book 2, page 156, and is briefly summarized here.

The principle is: for fine threads make larger bundles of warp threads and use heavier weights, and for thick threads make small warp bundles and use lighter weights.

You can sense when to divide bundles; if the bundle is so thick that all the threads aren't being tensioned, divide the group. It's interesting that you make larger bundles for fine threads. They aren't larger in size, but they have a larger number of threads, so the bundles need extra weight to pull hard enough.

The weights need to have a strong loop of string on them, so the warp bundles can be slip-knotted into them. It makes it easy to undo the slipknot and move the weights when they climb up to the back beam and must be let down again. See how to tie the slipknot on page 82.

Warning!! Be sure to put the weights on a stool or remove them when you cut off a woven section of warp. Otherwise, the weights will pull the threads right out of the heddles.

What to do with yards and yards of warp

The bulk of the warp for each separate bundle can be wound like a kitestick onto a small stick or pencil, or it can be chained. Put each bundle in a separate baggie to keep the yarns from tangling.

Good beaming

If the warp isn't beamed on carefully and correctly, you won't have even tension on the threads during weaving which can be a major cause of selvedge trouble.

Beam on with even and tight tension. "Crank and yank." *Crank* one revolution on the warp beam then *yank* the warps in 2-inch sections all the way across to tighten up the warp. Crank another revolution and begin yanking from the opposite side of the warp. Continue, being sure to alternate sides. Detailed information is found in Book #2 in the chapter on beaming, beginning page 15.

Body mechanics

How you sit at the loom can make a big difference in how your body feels after a weaving session. It is just as important as stopping periodically and stretching. I set my timer for 25 minutes. When it rings, I force myself to stop and do some stretches or do something else for a few minutes before going back to weaving. Build in your rest periods or changes of activities. I have discovered, that just getting up, putting on the teakettle and sitting back down to work isn't enough of a shift. Real stretching or exercises are required for a couple of minutes.

Repeated motions cause body pain if they are unrelenting—in wrists, elbows, back, neck, shoulders, and hips. So, when you are doing repetitive motions for a period of time, it is imperative that you stop and stretch those muscles often.

Stress plays a part in body mechanics, too. If you are stressed, you will be straining muscles that can end up hurting. When I was stressed out about a sewing project for 4-H, I remember my mother telling me: "Put it down for awhile." I'd probably yell, "But I *have* to get this finished, now!" I should have listened to her. A little break doing something you like can set the mood for a fresh look at the task at hand. Problems look more daunting when you're under stress or have low energy. The same issue can seem very small and totally doable when you have lots of energy and low stress.

One exercise you can do is to really tense up some muscles, and hold them, and then relax. For example, tense your shoulders up; clench your fists, your jaw, your eyes. Tense up one part, and then add the rest of the parts until the whole body is tense—everyplace at once. Then, let go and relax all at once. Making a relaxing sound helps greatly. Even pretending to tense and relax can help.

Don't continuously grip anything tightly—jaw, fingers, toes, shuttles, beater.

How to sit at the loom

Sit on the front edge of your loom bench. An organist said that's what she does so she has more length in her legs to reach to the farthest pedals. Sit upright, on your sit bones. Think of the sit bones as a pivot point, and your back and shoulders, head, and neck balanced in a line on top of the pivot point. Your head should be positioned so the ears are aligned with the shoulders. This position lets your big muscles do the work, rather than asking your back alone to hold you up. Your weight is on the bench; the feet are free to work the treadles without moving your back at all. When a treadle is pressed, put your weight on it—then the other foot is free to be poised over the next treadle it will press. Some treadles aren't made to hold your weight. If you're sitting upright with your weight on your sit bones, you should be able to move your feet as needed in a gentle way. Some looms have a footrest. I don't recommend using it because it slows you down, but the configuration of your treadles, bench and body might require your using it. The main principle, just like for threading the loom, is to "get comfortable."

While you are weaving, your back should stay upright—not sway back and forth. Don't lean back on the beater; just swing it, with your body upright.

What you don't want is to sit with a slump, with your shoulders forward, spine curved, and chest caved in.

I was taught that the ideal height of the bench puts your waist at the level of the breast beam. That works unless you have a long torso or long or short legs. I've seen people in workshops pile one chair on top of another to get the right height for weaving comfortably. See the illustration on the next page. The height of your bench should be such that you don't need to raise your shoulders. Your elbows should just clear the breast beam. Your bench is too low if your hips are

10

Alexander Technique teachers help crafts people do their craft while keeping their bodies in alignment to avoid strain.

Avoiding eye strain

Avoid glare and shadows in your weaving area. Put in more lights —soft white or natural light bulbs. Remove white or other surfaces that produce glare. Try to have the light shine on your work, over your shoulder, but have lots of indirect light around, so you don't have too much contrast of dark and light. Don't face windows where a lot of light is coming in. Instead, turn your loom 90 degrees, so the light comes in sideways on your loom—and your eyes.

lower than your knees. You want your knees a little lower than your hips for more leverage.

Pressure on bony points causes pain, even inflammation. Weaver's bottom is an inflammation caused by sitting for long periods of time, especially, on a hard bench. Another problem in that area is soreness coming from the elastic in underpants! One weaver only wove in her nightgown. A firm padded bench or rounded edges on chairs can both help. Rubberized cloth for lining shelves can keep you from slipping off your bench!

Avoiding muscle strain

Stretching is a valuable tool in your arsenal to prevent pain. Stretch classes can be very helpful. Yoga techniques can be done sitting on the floor or on your bench, but did you know you could do floor exercises standing up, as well? The cat stretch, pelvic tilt, shoulder, and neck stretches can all be done standing as well as on the floor.

Remember to breathe! Breath awareness is a big part of yoga. It's the core of relaxing the body and mind.

Remember to have your eyes checked with relationship to the work you want to do. Get separate glasses for work you do at different distances. One pair of glasses for all purposes may not be helpful because you may have to tilt your head to see from different areas of the lens for different jobs. Constant tilting can cause a lot of neck and shoulder strain.

Studio lighting

Lighting in your studio should be similar to the lighting your finished work will be seen in. If it's meant for a gallery, then gallery lighting would be best. If it's to be seen in natural light, then use natural light. It is also important when making your color choices.

Getting help

Find a good exercise, stretch, yoga, or Hanna Somatics teacher: www.hannasomatics.com. You can find good information and stretches in the following article: "The Weaver's New Body," by Claudia A. Chase and Pam Altomare, *Handwoven* Magazine, March/April, 1998. Interweave Press. Loveland, Colorado.

1 Weaving

Now that the loom is set up (and the treadles tied), and you've allowed for fringe or hems, you are ready to begin weaving. The heading has been made, and the warp threads spaced out.

An even rhythm makes the best cloth

The common denominator for good weaving is a good rhythm. To get an even rhythm involves many factors: efficient weaving motions, timing, and the tie-up of the treadles. Achieving rhythm also means no broken warp ends, selvedges weaving properly, shuttles working properly, proper warp tension, avoiding treadling mistakes, and evenly woven cloth. You don't want interruptions from breakage, poorly wound bobbins, or bad weaving motions.

"Weaving itself is a rhythm, a rhythm which can carry much of the expressive feeling of dancing. For many, the highest pleasure can be attained from weaving only when the various movements of treadling, beating, shuttle-throwing and shuttle-catching are so coordinated that they flow as if to music. Each of these movements plays an important part in the full weaving cycle."[3]

Anyone can learn the theory of weaving; it is important to develop skill. If you execute efficient weaving motions, always in the same way, and in the same sequence, rhythm will become natural. Practice and become self-conscious enough to see what you're doing. If your rhythm is unsteady, slow down and concentrate on the evenness of the rhythm you're using in accomplishing the steps in the sequence.

Timing

Timing is very important. The sequence of motions needs to be done with a rhythm. If one of the steps is done too soon or too late,

problems can occur, such as poor selvedges, broken warp threads, and uneven weaving.

Weaving motions

 Basically, you want your motions to be close and short and to eliminate all unnecessary motions. To economize your motions, enter and take the shuttle out of the shed immediately at the edge of the warp. That is, the shuttle only barely comes out of the shed. See Figure 14. (You make the sheds by pressing the treadles or working the levers.

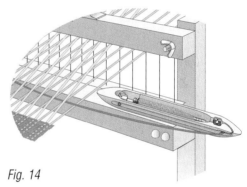

Fig. 14

 The shuttle should move as little distance as possible. The size of the shed need not be large. It is better that it opens only as high as will allow the shuttle to pass through. Any larger and it will put too much stress on the warp threads. A larger shed also takes more time to open, which will slow you down.

Weaving rapidly does not mean that you will produce a poor fabric. It is not possible to weave fast until you develop a real rhythm, a rhythm that produces the uniformity of motion required to weave top-grade fabrics. In other words, first, achieve an even rhythm and the speed will take care of itself.

---

3 Tidball, Harriet. *The Weaver's Book*, Collier Books, New York, 1976, p. 165.

The motions

It's in production weaving that you want to be the most time/energy efficient. Think of every single weft to be thrown: if you throw fewer wefts, you'll weave more cloth faster. See the excerpt from Book #1, "Making your weaving easier," in the Preliminaries chapter on page 6. If you can throw the shuttle faster, if you don't have to fiddle with selvedges or "bubble" the weft, you save time.

When beginning to learn the motions for good rhythm, don't worry about the cloth or the selvedges, just work for the rhythm by using those motions in proper sequence. For most weavers I've taught, the sequence of the motions is quite different from what they are used to, so it takes some practice first to learn the sequence of motions and then to achieve rhythm while doing them properly.

Weave very slowly at first, putting your effort into making all the motions economically. Maintain a rhythm, no matter how slow, until the speed increases naturally through the body's familiarity with the motions.

Be sure you've read the paragraph on timing on page 11.

Here are the motions for rhythmic, efficient, and fast weaving of the highest quality cloth:

1 Throw

3 Beat

3 Change the Shed

Actually, if you think of it as 4 "beats," or 4-steps, to a count of 4, you can say them to yourself as you go along getting an even rhythm. The fourth "beat" is step 3 divided into 2 beats. That would make it:

1–Throw, 2–Beat, 3–Change, 4–Your feet

Don't touch the selvedges

Notice that there's no mention of touching the selvedges in the sequence—so don't do

it. Touching the selvedges slows you down and interrupts your rhythm. There is a whole section about selvedges (See page 77). If they need help, check that section to see how to set them up for rhythmical weaving without fussing. You also may need to read the chapter on shuttles. They are very important for weaving good selvedges. See page 47.

1 Throw the Shuttle

When you throw the shuttle (boat and end-delivery shuttles), the weft thread exits the shuttle towards the weaver. In other words, the side of the shuttle facing you is the one where the weft thread comes out of the hole of the shuttle. See Figures 15 and 16.

☞ Put the bobbins into boat shuttles with the thread coming out underneath the bobbin so that the thread unwinds from under the bobbin. It cuts down on backlash. See Figure 17 .

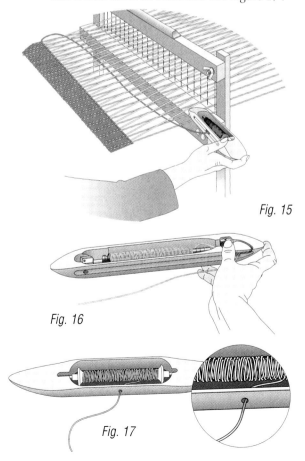

Fig. 15

Fig. 16

Fig. 17

☞ Throw the shuttle, don't push it across the warp. The shuttle should exit the shed on its own and not need to be pulled out.

☞ Throw the shuttle so it glides along on the shuttle race—the ledge on the beater at the bottom of the reed. See Figure 18. Sometimes,

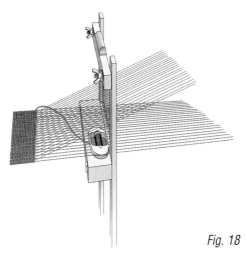

Fig. 18

people put the beater on the loom backwards so the ledge faces the shafts and isn't available for weaving. It should face the weaver. See the sidebar on page 14 for more about shuttle races and beaters. Some looms do not have a shuttle race, and the threads at the bottom of the shed must support the shuttle. Remember, the shed is the opening of the warp threads made for the shuttle to pass through. Pressing the treadles or activating levers accomplishes lifting and lowering the warp threads.

☞ The bottom of the (open) shed should rest on the shuttle race. Many looms have beaters that can be adjusted higher or lower to achieve this position Before raising the beater, however, check the tension on the warp. If the tension is too high you might not get a good shed or the warps will float above the shuttle race. Try reducing the warp tension. If adjusting warp tension doesn't put the threads on the shuttle race, adjust the beater. Check the legs of the beater to see if they can be raised or lowered. If the beater lifts out of the loom, put a short piece of doweling at the base of each leg of the

beater. You might get the warp to rest on the shuttle race if you have the fell closer to the breast beam.

Counterbalance and countermarch looms can have the height of their shafts adjusted. Read more about it in the excerpt from Book #2, "Adjusting the Height of the Beater," in the Preliminaries chapter on page 7. If your loom has no shuttle race, it is a moot point.

Always keep the shuttle on the shuttle race. The natural movement might be to swing the arm back, but this motion pulls the weft down to the fell of the cloth at the selvedge and traps it, preventing it from taking up as much as it needs to before it is beaten into place. See Figure 19. It will cause the cloth to draw in, or "neck in." If the cloth necks in too much, selvedge threads become abraded by the reed and will eventually break.

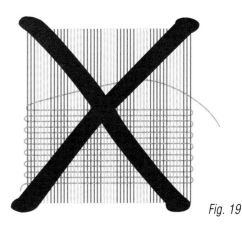

Fig. 19

Too much draw-in is prevented when there is a diagonal of weft thread placed in the shed. The diagonal is from the fell of the cloth (last weft) to the shuttle race. See Figure 11 on page 6.

 The shuttle should always touch the reed— both while it goes through the shed, and while the beater is moving back and forth. Remember, the shuttle barely comes out of the shed. As the beater moves forward and back, the shuttle does, too. Because it moves with

13

14

the beater as the beater moves toward the fell and back, the shuttle is actually on target for the next throw when the next shed is open and ready to receive it. The end of the shuttle that will enter the shed rests on the shuttle race, with the remainder of the shuttle raised a bit. See Figure 20.

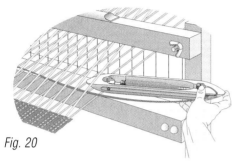

Fig. 20

The shuttle-throw has to have enough snap to take it across the warp. How you throw the shuttle depends a lot on the width of the warp and on the type of shuttle you're using. Throwing a boat shuttle (with a revolving bobbin) is different from throwing an end-delivery shuttle (with a bobbin fixed in place). See the Shuttle chapter.

The width of the warp makes a difference in your shuttle throwing. If the warp is a convenient width for you, it can be easy to get a good rhythm. It is more efficient to weave a longer and narrower cloth than a shorter, wider warp. If you must weave on a wide warp, work toward establishing an even rhythm. It takes longer for each pick (weft) of cloth to be entered because the shuttle has to travel farther.

Receive the shuttle with your hand in the same position that you use to throw the shuttle back across the other way. See Figure 21.

The shuttle is held with the index finger on the end of the shuttle, the thumb on top, and the other fingers on the bottom. Throw it through the shed so that it rides on the shuttle race up against the reed. The shuttle should be caught by your hand in exactly the same position as

Shuttle Race

Read more about the shuttle race in the section about throwing the shuttle, on page 12. Also read the sidebar: Beater Types, Shuttles, and Shuttle Races on page 20.

As I said above, the shuttle race, which is standard on most looms, is the ledge on the bottom of the beater—on the weaver's side of the beater. (Be sure you have not put the beater on backwards.) It supports the shuttle as it moves through the shed and is a huge help in saving weaving time. The surface of the shuttle race should be at the same angle as the bottom of the open shed and touching the warp. You may have read that the bottom of the shed should be above the race—but that would mean pushing the threads down with the shuttle as you throw it; and would slow the shuttle down. The shuttle throws better on a hard surface. You can adjust the height of the beater to achieve this surface. See page 7 in the Preliminaries chapter.

The race should be about the same width as your shuttles.

A shuttle race prevents the possibility of a shuttle nose-diving through the warp, especially when the warp is widely spaced.

It is most effective on two types of beaters: beaters that pivot and are attached to the loom at the base of the beater legs, and beaters that don't pivot, but move in a straight line forward and back--the articulated beater. See page 20.

was thrown—finger on the end of the shuttle, the thumb on top, and the other fingers on the bottom—so you do not need to reposition it in order to throw it back. Keep the end of the shuttle close to the selvedge and reed (on the shuttle race) to cut down on excess motions and to be targeted for the next shot.

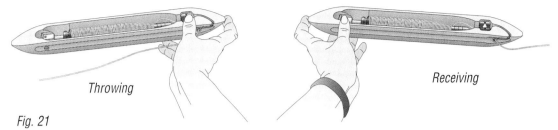

Throwing

Receiving

Fig. 21

Hand position for throwing and receiving shuttle

Don't touch the selvedge

You can control the weft with your shuttle. The weft should be snug up against the outside selvedge thread—neither pulling that thread in, nor leaving a loop on the outside of it. Placing the weft thread up against that outside thread makes good selvedges. The cloth doesn't neck in because of the diagonal of the weft from the fell to the shuttle race and because the weft is loose in the shed as it is beaten in.

Tension on the weft

How much tension should you put on the weft when you catch the shuttle?

Too much pull on the weft and the selvedges will gouge, draw in too much, or have broken threads. If the weft is too loose when it is beaten in, the selvedges will have loops sticking out, or there might be kinks or tiny loops within the cloth itself.

How to control weft tension

If you have a boat shuttle, you can control the weft tension by touching the bobbin when you catch the shuttle. In this way, with the shuttle in your hand, you can snug up the weft appropriately without touching the selvedges. Loops of weft at the selvedges are caused by not putting enough tension on the shuttle when catching it. See Figure 22. If you have an end delivery shuttle, set the shuttle's tension device very loose at first and gradually increase the tension until the wefts just snug up to the outside thread. Read more in the chapter on shuttles.

Throwing special shuttles

Throwing a flyshuttle is discussed in the sidebar on page 19. Throwing end delivery shuttles and boat shuttles will be discussed in the shuttles chapter.

Throwing 2 shuttles

Where you place a shuttle on the woven cloth while it is waiting to be thrown is discussed in the section on selvedge problems, in the section about catching the outside warp threads, on page 92.

Too much weft in the shed

Too much angle in the diagonal of the weft from the fell to the shuttle race can put too much thread into the shed forcing the wefts to loop or kink in the cloth. If this happens, decrease the angle the weft makes by keeping the fell nearer to the shuttle race.

Too much slack in the weft can also cause problems at the selvedges. If the selvedge warps begin to splay outward, there is too much slack in the *previous weft as it exited the shed*. It will continue to get worse and worse. The way I like to correct this problem

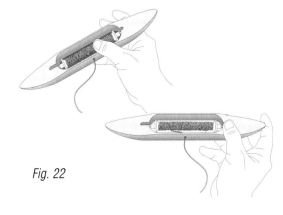

Fig. 22

is to throw the next weft, and while it is still loose in the shed, tug the previous weft at the selvedge, pulling out the tiny bit of excess weft. Then, I take up that extra weft in the new shed and beat it in as usual. The tiny bit of slack that is taken out will straighten the warps. After the warps are straightened, this procedure shouldn't need to be done again unless you see the problem developing again. Remember, the problem is too much diagonal, bubble, or slack in the previous weft at the edge where it came out of the shed. See Figures. 23a, b, and c. Remember, you are only tugging out a small amount at the selvedge, you do not pull on (or straighten) the weft that remains in the row of weaving.

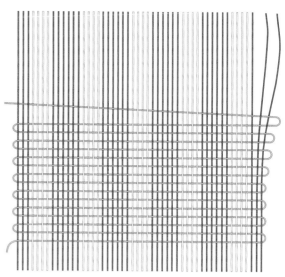

Fig. 23a

One common selvedge flaw is a characteristic ridge or ripple caused by a combination of too much weft in one shot, and too little weft in the following shot. The ridge is produced by changing the shed before the weft is beaten into place. With each shot the problem becomes worse. See Figure 24.

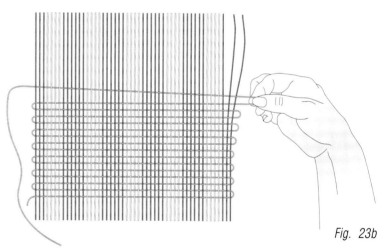

Fig. 23b

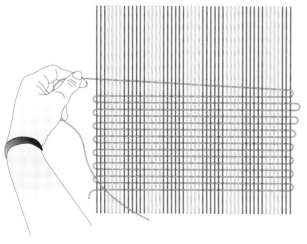

Fig. 23c

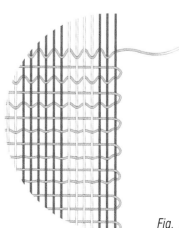

Fig. 24

The cure is the same as that for splayed selvedge warps. Read more about it in the section "When to Change the Shed," on page 27.

I've read that this problem is called purling in old books. It seems like a good word for it.

Be sure the shed is open

It may be obvious, but you need to be conscious that the shed is open when you throw the shuttle. If you throw the shuttle too soon, when the shed isn't completely open, you can break warp threads. Also, throwing too soon can cause problems at the selvedges by putting too much weft in the shed. By the way, pointed shuttles will deflect the warp threads in a partially open shed instead of breaking them.

You'll notice that if one hand is on the shuttle at all times, you'll need to beat by using the other hand, alternately, on the beater with each beat. There is more information about using the beater in the section on beat.

Bubbling the weft

What about bubbling (creating arcs in the weft) or creating a distinct weft angle? See Figures 25 and 26. If you use Ashenhurst's method of calculating sett (ends per inch in the warp), which I describe in Book #1, in the chapter on sett, bubbling isn't necessary. (His method is briefly explained here in the Preliminaries chapter on page 7.) This method of calculating makes the sett a little closer than that of wrapping on a ruler. It also keeps the cloth from necking in, which can cause selvedge threads to break. With balanced or nearly balanced weaves there is enough diagonal in the weft if it's placed into the shed on the shuttle race. The weft will go in a straight line from one selvedge to the other on a slight diagonal from the fell to the shuttle race. Bubbling or making more of a diagonal takes up time. The Ashenhurst method also gives you fewer picks per inch with more warps per inch, and it's much more efficient to make a few more warps per inch when winding the

warp than to throw more wefts per inch during weaving.

(Bubbling is necessary for certain structures and situations other than balanced or nearly balanced weaves; when putting the outlining wefts into a honeycomb weave, for example, and, of course, in weaving weft-faced structures like tapestries and rugs, which are not the subject of this book.)

Size of weft

The weaving not only goes faster if there are fewer picks per inch, but also if the weft yarns are a little larger than the warp threads. (It also keeps the cloth from necking in.)

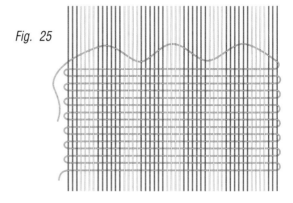

Fig. 25

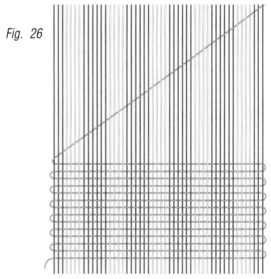

Fig. 26

② Beat

The next Step, begins on page 22.

Flyshuttle looms

" The simple invention of the flyshuttle, in the eighteenth century, was an extremely important event in the history and development of weaving…. The fly-shuttle differs from the hand-shuttle both in form and in the manner in which it is thrown and caught."[4]

It made the power loom possible. It must use an end-delivery shuttle–it cannot use a boat shuttle. It is thrown across the shed by the weaver pulling on a handle attached to a cord, attached to a device that shoots the shuttle across the warp–thus the name flyshuttle–because it "flies" along the shuttle race.

Its two advantages are: (1) the weaving can be done with increased speed. Only one hand is required to work the handle, the other being left free to manipulate the beater, thus making the beat more rapid (2) Warps of great width, which would be impossible for one weaver to weave unaided with a hand-shuttle, can, by means of the flyshuttle, be as quickly woven as narrow ones.[5]

The flyshuttle mechanism or attachment is located on the beater. The beater needs to be specially fitted both to shoot the shuttle through the shed and also to catch it. A box at each end of the beater extends out from the beater. The boxes are long enough to accommodate the length of the shuttle itself. When I see a beater with a flyshuttle attachment, I think it looks like the beater has ears or awkward extensions sticking out. (It also significantly adds to the amount of real estate a loom requires.) See Figure 27.

A cord system with a handle overhead is used to throw the shuttle. The box receives the shuttle and then becomes the staging place for the next throw. Inside each box is a "picker"(or driver or hammer block), which may be a loop of leather (traditionally, buffalo hide, which is tough). When the shuttle is to be thrown, a cord attached to the picker is jerked and the picker "bats" the shuttle out of the box, throwing it to the other box where its picker slows down the shuttle and allows it to glide in. The handle can jerk the

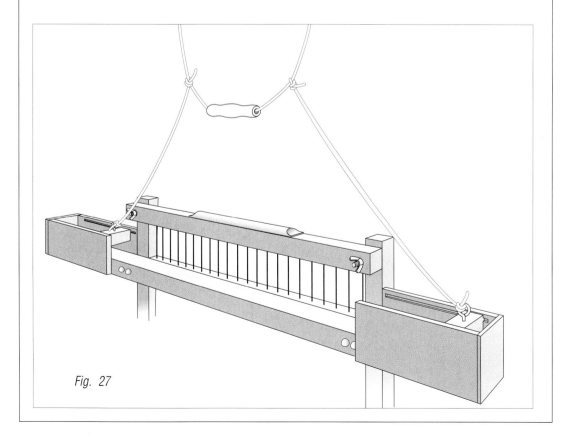

Fig. 27

cord in either direction. If you jerk it to the left, the picker will drive out the shuttle in the right-hand box. Another jerk to the right will bring it back again. Figure 27 shows one possible cord system, picker, and handle.

When using a flyshuttle, one hand usually remains on the handle and the other on the beater–often not in the center of the beater but to the side of center–in alignment with the arm as it extends from the shoulder. I know of people who change hands to even out the stresses on the muscles of the body.

The same rhythm applies as for hand throwing the shuttles: throw, beat, change, your feet.

Adjustments and practice

It takes a good bit of practice to get the hang of this system. I recommend weaving 5 yards with a flyshuttle to really get the rhythm because you have several things to think about and adjust. First, the shuttle's pirn (the "bobbin" in end- delivery shuttles) must be wound properly. It is imperative or the shuttle will fly across the warp and miss the box and hit the floor. Read about end delivery shuttles on page 48.

The flyshuttle boxes must be flush with the reed and the shuttle race so, as the shuttle goes along the shuttle race against the reed, it slides smoothly into the box. Shim the box or the reed if needed, but it is imperative that the reed is in exact alignment with the back side of the boxes and that the shuttle race is aligned with the bottom of the boxes. If the reed is too far forward it sends the shuttle off the race and onto the floor; if it is too far back, the shuttle tends to strike the box and fly out onto the floor.

It takes practice to get the jerk on the handle right. Too little force and the shuttle won't go the whole distance to the other side. Too much force, and it can bounce out of the receiving box and go back into the shed. With the warp on the loom and the shed open, you might try practicing the jerk without any thread on the pirn. The shuttle doesn't have to land with a big bang. In fact, it is better to catch the shuttle gently with the picker, allowing it to glide the shuttle into the box.

To start, place the shuttle on the shuttle race and slide it into one of the shuttle boxes so that it pushes the picker as far as it will go to the end of the box. The hole in the side of the shuttle through which the weft thread exits the shuttle should face toward the weaver.

The sequence is the same as for hand throwing the shuttle: throw the shuttle, beat, change the shed when the beater is against the fell of the cloth, and push the beater back towards the shafts to begin again. If your weaving motions overlap properly, the shuttle can be thrown so that it floats into the box and you can still get plenty of speed.

Also, you should sit just as though you were hand throwing the shuttle–relaxed, upright, with the sit-bones grounded near the front edge of the bench. Remember not to "rest" (move your body backwards) when you swing the beater toward the fell–it's wasted energy, slows you down, and affects the beat by pressing the wefts in. Read more about body mechanics in the sidebar on page 9.

There can be just one box on each side, or more than one to accommodate more than one shuttle. The single box picker handle moves sideways and if properly adjusted, can be operated with a wrist motion. The multiple box picker is usually a vertical pull handle and takes an arm motion. Some multiple box fly shuttles use a sliding device on the beater to change boxes and others use a pulling motion to change the box and then the usual flicking from side to side to propel the shuttle. Designs vary.

Remember you must leave one box empty to receive a shuttle, which determines the maximum number of shuttles that can be used.

---

4 Hooper, Luther. *Hand-Loom Weaving*, Pitman Publishing Corporation, New York and Chicago, 1920 reprint. p. 114, 116.

5 White, George. *A Practical Treatise on Weaving by Hand and Power Looms.* Whittaker & Co., London, 1866.

Beater types, shuttles, and shuttle races

Underslung and overhead beaters pivot; their paths are arc shaped, which is a consideration for the shuttle race. The articulated beater is not pivoted; it swings back and forth parallel to the floor.

Some beaters can be adjusted higher and lower. Some can be set more toward the fell, or closer to the reed.

Underslung beaters

These beaters are pivoted at the base of the loom. The shuttle race is square with the bottom of the shed and the shuttles can be rectangular in cross section, the optimum shape. No specially shaped shuttle is required. See Figure 28.

Overhead beaters

This beater hangs from the top of the loom pivoting and swinging freely. See Figure 29. The overhead beater was part of the Asiatic loom brought into Europe in the 10-12th century. There they were and still are mostly pit looms. The weavers sat on the ground or floor for anything they couldn't do standing. When they needed pedals, they dug a hole in the floor. There was no way of mounting a bottom swung beater. The overhead beater has some design problems for a shuttle

race. To locate a satisfactory shuttle race position, the shuttle race must be at an acute angle to the reed. See Figure 29.

In use, the beater is pressed back to the shafts with the knuckles of one hand. This hand is in position to receive the shuttle, which is then thrown by the other. It is about the only way to use an overhead beater and get any kind of shed. The beat is made by gravity as the beater resumes its rest position. Northern Europeans were predominately wool weavers so a soft beat was probably all they needed.

If you position the beater so it hangs vertically at the back (nearer the shafts) you don't have to push it back, but the reed is at a bad angle in the beat-up position. If you hang it at the fell of the cloth, holding it back to throw the shuttle, any kind of a smooth weaving operation is difficult; also, the shuttle race is positioned all wrong.

On multi shaft looms, when the sheds are smaller, you may need to push the overhead beater back toward the shafts to get a wider shed.

Most weavers with overhead beaters on their looms do not use a shuttle race–the shuttle is supported by the warp threads on the bottom of the shed.

Articulated beaters

Chinese looms with overhead beaters had a beater that did not pivot at all. It didn't tip or move in an arc path. The beater went straight forward and back, its path parallel to the floor. Since it doesn't pivot, the beater hits the fell squarely. See Figure 30. These beaters are available on looms today.

Articulated beater with flystuttle

With a flyshuttle on an articulated beater, there is no difficulty with the shuttle race, or advantage over the underslung type other than in particularly wide looms. With wide looms that have heavy flyshuttle box systems, it is easier to build the necessary stiffness into an articulated beater. Read more about flyshuttle looms on page 18.

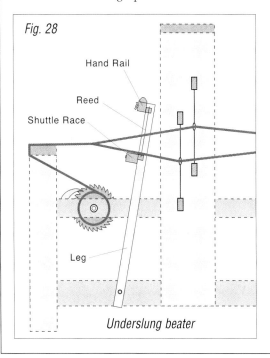

Fig. 28

Hand Rail

Reed

Shuttle Race

Leg

Underslung beater

21

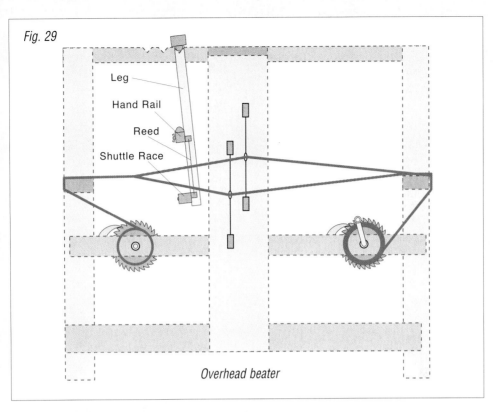

Fig. 29

Leg

Hand Rail

Reed

Shuttle Race

Overhead beater

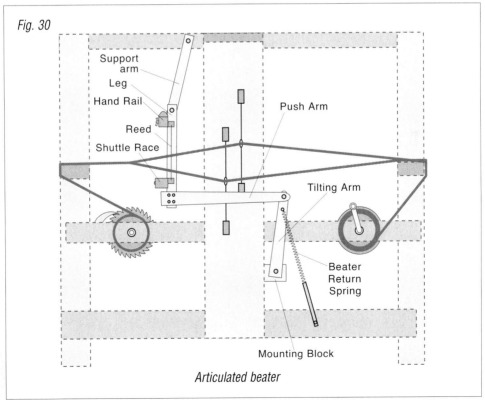

Fig. 30

Support arm

Leg

Hand Rail

Reed

Shuttle Race

Push Arm

Tilting Arm

Beater Return Spring

Mounting Block

Articulated beater

② **Beat**

All my teachers (me, too) say that "beat" is a misnomer. What you want to do, generally, is to place the weft with the beater, not beat it in. I say generally, because with upholstery and weft faced textiles and rugs, (and warp faced rugs), you must beat the wefts harder. This special type of weaving is discussed in the rug weaving books mentioned in the Introduction.

When to beat
Open or closed shed?

What is an open shed? A closed shed? An open shed means that the shed is still open when the beater hits the fell of the cloth. A closed shed means that the original shed has been closed and the warp threads are flat with no warp threads up or down.

 For efficient weaving, the timing as well as the beat is important. The beater should hit the fell just before the shed is changed, so that the reed spreads the warp out to the full width, and allows the maximum length of weft to slip into the shed. The shed is open when the beater hits the fell and the weft is loose in the shed. The shed is changed immediately after the beat, which locks the weft out to its maximum width in the reed and prevents the cloth from narrowing in (necking in).

Beat evenly

Uneven cloth with streaks will result from uneven beating. The weft will show more with more picks per inch, and the warp will show more with fewer picks per inch. This effect will be less likely if you weave with an even rhythm and use the recommendations for warp sett given in Book #1, in the chapter on sett. Read a summary of this information in the Preliminaries chapter on page 6.

Cloths requiring a very light beat are harder to beat evenly than cloths requiring a tighter beat. See Beating Very Lightly on page 25.

 Uneven cloth can also be caused by uneven warp tension, so an even beat can still result in uneven cloth if the warp tension is uneven.

Location of the fell

The position of the beater affects the force of the beat. For a gentler beat have the fell closer to the shafts. For a heavier beat keep the fell slightly farther from the shafts. This distance will make the weaving slower. A long beater swing loses time. To have the beat consistent, you must advance the warp often because you want the beater to swing the same distance each time—not sometimes soft because the fell is near the heddles and hard when it is far from them. Advance the warp every two inches. It also reduces wear on the warp threads from abrasion in the heddles and in the reed and is imperative with fragile or softly spun warp yarns. You can weave much faster the closer the fell is to the shafts. You might ask, doesn't all this advancing take a lot of time? Well, it does take time, but it's important to do it for the quality of the cloth. Some looms allow you to advance the warp more quickly than others, too. A warning: I overdid this principle once and wove with the fell too close to the shafts; my cloth was sleazy (loosely woven) because there were too few wefts beaten in. Read more about advancing the warp on page 27.

With the beater parallel to the fell, advance the warp one inch nearer to you, and then weave one inch beyond it. This method advances the warp every two inches, which is ideal.

Where you position the fell can also be determined by the angle of the diagonal formed from the fell to the shuttle race. If too much weft is incorporated into the shed with the fell at a certain location, move the fell closer to the shafts.

If you advance the warp too far, the beater can't reach the fell of the cloth, so you have to roll back the warp onto the warp beam a bit. However, if you try to weave too close to the breast beam, the wefts might not beat in straight across—they may curve up at the selvedges with unwoven V-shaped areas appearing at the edges. See Figure 31.

How to beat

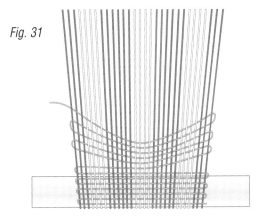

Fig. 31

Swing the beater

Swing the beater with one arm; don't pull it. Some weavers tend to "rest" by pulling the beater and rocking back with their bodies and pressing in the wefts—actually relaxing and curving the spine. This "resting" is lost time and changes the results of the cloth.

For looms with the automatic warp tension-ing system described in Book #2, on pages 140 and 141, you cannot beat very hard unless you are careful to beat with a quick bump. It works because the force is quickly released. If you beat hard and/or pull the beater with this tension system, the warp will go soft because your beat is releasing the tension. A summary of this information is in the Preliminaries chapter on page 8.

Hands on the beater

Your hand on the beater doesn't need to be in the middle of the beater, provided the beater is rigid. In fact, when you're throwing the shuttle, the hand on the beater changes from side to side. See Figures 32 and 33. The beater is like a hammer—its weight works to give an equal beat to the full width. However, if your beater is flimsy, you'll need to swing the

beater with your hand in the center of it. (For flyshuttle weaving the hand on the beater is always off center.)

Picks per inch

The number of picks (wefts) per inch does not have to be the same as the number of ends (warp threads) per inch. In fact, for a balanced looking cloth it is more efficient to weave with more ends per inch than picks per inch. Read the chapter about sett in Book #1 and the summary in the Preliminaries chapter on page 6. So, let the picks per inch be decided by your rhythm, sett, and what you want the cloth to look like.

You can tell if there are more warps or picks per inch or if the cloth is balanced by looking at the cloth, in plain weave, not under ten-sion. If the threads appear absolutely square the cloth is balanced. If they look like vertical rectangles, the cloth is warp predominant; if the rectangles are horizontal, it's weft pre-dominant. Remember to allow for shrinkage after washing (finishing) if you are aiming for a perfectly balanced weave. The threads should

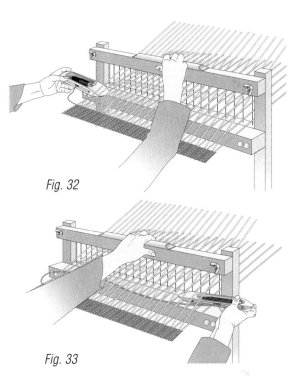

Fig. 32

Fig. 33

23

look square—after finishing.

My mentor, Helen Pope, told me that she made fabric for a sports coat for her husband. When all the cloth was woven, she said the beginning and the end didn't look like they were the same fabric because the beat had changed. After that experience her solution for keeping the beat even was to hang a card off the loom. It had 1" marked on it and the number of picks (wefts) that should be in the inch. Every "once in awhile" she would bring up the card and check the pick count. Count the picks at least 1/2" from the fell of the cloth, where all the wefts are firmly in place.

A pick glass (also called a linen tester) is very helpful for counting your picks (wefts) per inch. It's a magnifier with 1/8-inch marks, so it's easy to count the wefts. See Figure 34.

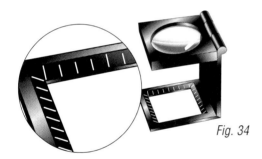

Fig. 34

Beat and warp tension

You can fine-tune the beat with a normally tensioned warp—where the warp tension is just enough to get a shed —neither extremely tight nor extremely loose. You can get a lighter beat if you loosen the tension on the warp a little bit. There's more friction in the reed with a looser tensioned warp, and that helps prevent the weft from beating in too tight. All the tension you really need is enough to get a shed. The lighter the beat, the harder it is to be consistent—loosening the warp tension will help you beat lightly consistently.

For a tighter beat, the same principle applies: tighten the warp tension a little bit, and the wefts will beat in closer.

Weaving to square

Weaving to square a pattern (for example, with overshot) can be done by adding or subtracting the number of pattern picks. Another way to adjust the rate of picks (ppi) is to beat harder or lighter. If you need almost one more pick, but not a whole one, try lightening the warp tension to beat in the wefts less tightly. Or tighten the warp, which will allow you to pack in the weft more closely, and then add your extra pick.

The squares in a plaid or pattern structure should be woven a tiny bit higher than they are wide to give a visual impression that they actually are square.

Starting to weave

When starting to weave, weave a few inches or so, just to get the rhythm and beat stabilized. Then, start to count the picks. It will be easier to adjust your beat at that point, rather than right at first.

Resuming weaving

When resuming weaving after a length of time, use your judgment about beating in those last wefts by checking visually whether they have crept away from the fell of the cloth. Give a couple of taps of the beater to put them back in place before beginning to weave again—perhaps one tap on the open shed (previous shed) and one tap on the closed shed. They still might not look identical to the others, but after a few inches, they should be as close as the rest. By the way, do not release the tension on the warp when you quit weaving—it can make a line when you start up again. See page 30.

Beating too hard

For fabric weaving, many new weavers beat too hard, so that the result is like cardboard. The cloth should be loose enough that after washing (finishing), and the threads shrink up and move closer together, the cloth will still be supple.

Beating very lightly

Here are five ways to accomplish getting fewer picks per inch in order of my preference.

1. Lessen the tension on the warp.
2. Weave with the fell a bit closer to the shafts.
3. Beat on a closed shed.
4. Beat after changing to the new shed, and even so, forget "beat" and think "nudge."
5. Increase the density of the warp (sett).

Beating on a closed shed

There are times when one would beat on a closed shed. When the wefts are very far apart, it helps to keep the wefts spaced apart by beating on a closed shed, or on the newly made shed. First try to lessen the tension, and if that doesn't cut down the count enough, then beat on the closed shed (or the newly changed shed). The closed shed's friction will help you not to beat too much. Remember to think "nudge," not "beat."

Also, weft-faced weaving, when the wefts must be bubbled, is generally done on a closed shed. The closed shed helps retain the bubbling of the weft.

Beating the wefts in closer

Double beating can be hard on the selvedge threads, takes extra time, and is not necessary for weaving ordinary fabrics. (Weft faced weaving not considered.) It may be necessary when working with warp threads that tend to stick together. The first beat is light and simply clears the shed; the next beat puts the weft in place. When the cloth you're weaving isn't beating as tight as you'd like, try beating the second time after the shed has been changed. For normally-tensioned warps, you can increase the picks per inch by tightening the warp a bit. The tighter they are the more they resemble rigid rods making it easier for the wefts to slide past them to be beaten in closer. "Normal" means warps that are not under very high or very light tension—just enough tension to get a shed.

Of course, you can beat harder if you like the look of your fabric—it just will be slower and not as efficient. Never lose track of the fact that the cloth, the end product, is the thing. If it is slower but the cloth is exactly right, so be it.

Rug weavers often put extra weight on their beaters to get a firmer beat. You can attach steel strips—the wider the warp the heavier they need to be—perhaps up to 20 pounds for a 45" warp. Another idea is to put exercise cuffs on each end of the beater and fasten them with Velcro. Re-bar, the reinforcing bar that goes inside concrete walls, is inexpensive and can work.

Upholstery fabric

Upholstery fabric must be woven tightly, and a consistent beat is very important. If the beat isn't consistent variations will show when you look at large areas of the cloth. Beat before and after the shed is changed, and that the force of the beat is important, but the speed with which the beater strikes the fell is even more critical. "Beat with a percussive motion so that you 'snap' the weft into place."[6]

Different fibers

Jim Ahrens told us, " For wool, place the weft with a soft touch. For linen, use a hard thump—you just need to drive it in—there's nothing quiet about it. With silk, if the weft pops out just keep on weaving, after 2-3 shots it stays beaten in place. When weaving tight fabrics with smooth yarns such as linen or silk, it helps to hold the reed against the cloth edge until the shed is completely changed, locking the weft into place. With wool or similar yarns that tend to cling, the beater can be pushed back as the shed is opened, making an appreciable difference in production time."[7]

---

6 Alderman, Sharon. *Handwoven Magazine*, Sep/Oct, 2003, p. 67.

7 Ahrens, Jim. See Introduction.

25

Karen Selk wrote, "When you're weaving silk, the most important consideration is its slipperiness; it must be sett and beaten closer than other natural fibers. ...Silk is very flexible and can accommodate a closer sett than other natural fibers without producing a stiff fabric. I use different setts for wool and silk yarns of the same diameter and weave structure."[8]

Beating and sampling

If you make a sample narrower than 10", it will not give you the information you need for a wider warp. The beat you can achieve with a 6" cloth will bear very little resemblance to that of a cloth 30" wide. The wefts won't beat in as much on the wider warp because there is more friction from the reed on all the extra threads. Therefore, if you plan to weave a wide warp, make a sample warp that's at least 12" to 14" wide. Make the sample warp long enough so that you can re-sley the reed if the sett needs to be changed and make any other changes necessary for the cloth design to be perfected. Then, you can usually expect the beat to be about the same for the wider warp.

I always recommend that you weave a sample on your actual warp, just to check that your cloth will really look like your preliminary sample or the way you envisioned it. It's better to know for sure now, rather than be disappointed when the whole warp is woven off. Cut off the sample, wash it and be sure it's just what you want. If not, re-sley the reed to change the sett and change anything else that you don't like. Narrow samples (6"-10" wide) can be very helpful; you just need to know that you'll have to open up the sett on a wider warp, and to check it out by sampling a few inches on the big warp. Before you cut off your sample, weave in the 2-stick heading (page 4), so you won't have to waste precious warp yarn by tying on the threads to the apron rod.

Some people omit the sampling stage; by at least sampling at the beginning of the real warp, you have the assurance that the cloth will look OK. If you didn't make a preliminary sample and no sample on the actual warp as well, you are gambling, and what you get may not be what you hoped for.

Sticky warps

At the end of the beat, when you push the beater back over the new shed, you are, in effect, combing the warps, which will help to clear a sticky shed without any special extra motion. If the warp is very sticky two beats might be necessary. The motions are: throw the shuttle, and beat, and change the shed, and beat again. The second beat is light and separates the sticky threads to completely open the shed to receive the next shuttle-throw.

Sharon Alderman says, "I have had some experiences that would curl your hair vis-a-vis sticky warps. Sometimes they have simply shredded as the sheds are made pulling themselves and their neighbors apart. What saved the day for me was a liberal application of inexpensive, mega hold (no fooling) hair spray. Spray it behind the heddles and, (bringing the reed forward) in front of the heddles each time the warp is advanced by two inches. It washes out in the finishing but during the weaving it plasters down the little fibers that make a yarn sticky. Double beating doesn't even begin to do the job in such cases."

Read more about sticky warps and sprays you might use on page 118.

---

[8] Selk, Karen. "Ins and Outs of Weaving Silk for Clothing," *Threads*, June/July 1989, p. 55. [Note that she is speaking of spun or reeled silk, not silk noil.]

③ Change the Shed

When to change the shed

Change the shed immediately after the beater has hit the fell of the cloth. It locks in the weft as wide as the warp is in the reed—preventing necking-in of the cloth and breakage of the selvedge threads.

Remember the timing: throw, beat, change, your feet. Say the last count-"your feet"-as the beater is returning toward the shafts. Work for this rhythm to achieve the four "beats," or "counts," in the timing. Change the shed just after the beater hits the fell. Thus, the beat is on the open shed, but not for long—the shed changes immediately.

If you change the shed too soon, and it is closed when you beat, you can have a selvedge problem other than breakage. You can get purling, as discussed on page 103.

How to change the sheds

To change the sheds efficiently, tie up the treadles so you can "walk the treadles." Read about this important subject in the Preliminaries chapter on page 3.

Advancing the warp

After you weave a few inches, the fell of the cloth becomes too near the shafts, and the warp must be moved forward toward the cloth beam to make room for more cloth to be woven. This process also requires that the warp on the warp beam be released or let off. It is called advancing the warp.

Advance the warp often—about every 2–3 inches. If you don't, the beat will be uneven. You can picture it yourself; if the beater travels a great distance at first and gradually a shorter and shorter distance, the effect of the beat will get less and less. In the section on beating (page 22), I explained that where the fell of the cloth is can determine whether the beat is lighter or harder. Determine where the fell should be, then, be consistent. The beater swing will be reliable, and your rhythm maintained.

If the beat isn't consistent, the color of the cloth may vary. Read the section on picks per inch on page 23.

Don't be seduced into thinking a large weaving space on a loom means you don't have to advance the warp often. In fact, it could be argued that such a space is unnecessary.

Automatic warp advance

Some looms make it easier than others to let the warp off of the warp beam and to bring it forward for winding up on the cloth beam. The most efficient looms do this operation automatically: with every beat, the warp and cloth advance a bit. This automatic warp advance device can be set so that the wefts are placed just the right distance apart by setting the distance each beat advances the warp. This system is especially useful when the wefts are spaced rather far apart and if more than one person will be weaving on the warp. See Figure 35.

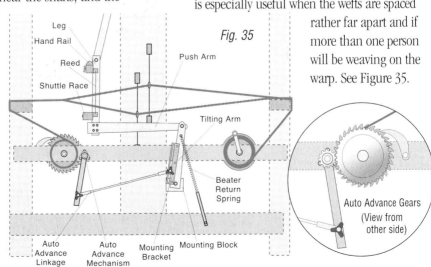

Fig. 35

Leg
Hand Rail
Reed
Shuttle Race
Push Arm
Tilting Arm
Beater Return Spring
Auto Advance Gears (View from other side)
Auto Advance Linkage
Auto Advance Mechanism
Mounting Bracket
Mounting Block

27

Automatic warp tension system

Next to the automatic advance attachment, I think Jim Ahren's automatic warp tension system allows you to advance the warp the easiest. All you do is crank the warp onto the cloth beam—there is no need to release the brake on the warp beam. It is described in a chapter in Book #2, and briefly in the Preliminaries chapter on page 8.

Too much warp unrolls

Sometimes, when you release the brake on the warp beam, the beam unrolls too much warp. You can avoid this situation by releasing the tension on the cloth beam before releasing the tension on the warp beam. You might need to hold the cloth beam as you release it so the tension is released gently. Another technique is to release the warp brake gently by a series of taps on the brake pedal, rather than pushing it down in one movement. The warp beam can unwind several yards if the tension on the warp is too great and the brake is released suddenly.

Advancing too much warp

It is also possible to advance the warp too much; then the beater can't reach the fell of the cloth. If that happens, release the tension on the cloth beam and go to the back of the loom and wind some warp back onto the warp beam. Soon, you'll know just how much warp to let off so this doesn't keep happening.

Avoid Lumps on the Cloth Beam

You must avoid lumps on the cloth beam. Knots from tying on the warp and/or lumpy apron strings on the cloth beam cause lumps that press into the cloth as it is wound up on the beam. These bumps cause the warp to be tighter in those places and make pouches in the cloth where it is being stretched over the lumps. You can also detect lumps if the fell of the cloth is wavy. The tighter warp areas will pack in more and in the areas where there are no lumps, the cloth will not pack in as much.

One way to avoid the lumps is to eliminate the knots that tied the warp onto the apron rod altogether. This method is described in Book #2, in the section on weaving the 2-stick heading. It is summarized here in the Preliminaries chapter on page 4.

Packing the cloth beam

Another solution to the lump problem is to put packing sticks around the cloth beam as the cloth accumulates or, if the cords are the problem, when the last of the cords are wound onto the beam and the cloth begins to be wound onto the cloth beam. Put in a stick every time the cords or lumps are about to touch the cloth. The sticks should be long enough to span the whole warp and all the cords, as well. How many packing sticks you need depends on how soon the lumps are eliminated. It might take 4 or 5 sticks to go around the beam once. The cloth winding up on a beam should be as smooth as the warp wound on the warp beam. Do not use paper to do this job—the bumps will still poke through and eventually destroy the tension on the warp and make the cloth very uneven. After one round of sticks, no more sticks are needed because the cloth will be building up now on a flat beam—not a bumpy one. See Figure 36. The same principle is used as when you pack sticks on the warp beam to eliminate bumps from apron cords.

Fig. 36

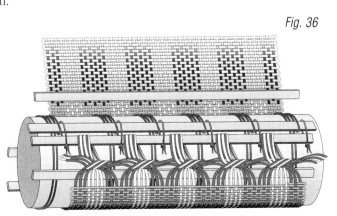

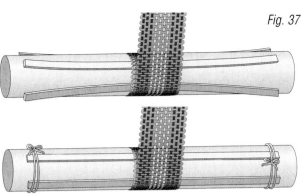

Fig. 37

Packing sticks can be any smooth, flat sticks that are as long as the width of your cloth beam, but not any longer. If they are even a fraction of an inch too long, they will jam in the brake mechanism on every turn. Lattice or lath strips from the lumberyard work fine if you sand them smooth first. Screen molding doesn't require sanding because it is nicely finished as is. Narrow slats from blinds can also make good packing sticks. If they are plastic, they can be cut with scissors. Metal ones will need metal shears.

☞ If your warp is fairly narrow, the packing sticks might curve up at the ends. Tie strings near the ends of the sticks around the whole cloth beam, including the sticks, to keep them flat. See Figure 37.

Warp tension

Even tension

☞ Uniform warp tension is essential for getting clean sheds and evenly woven cloth. To have even warp tension, the warp must be beamed onto the warp beam tightly—tighter than it will ever be during weaving when the warp in on tension. That way, the outer layers of warp threads cannot bite down into layers underneath, which causes tension on the threads to be uneven. Details are in Book #2, in the chapter on beaming.

☞ If the fell of the cloth is wavy with hills and depressions, rather than straight, it is probably from uneven warp tension. Where the warp is looser (the fell will be closer to the reed), the wefts won't pack in as much as in the areas where the warp is tighter (where the fell is closer to the breast beam). See Figure 244 in the Troubleshooting chapter.

The solution may be to cut off the cloth and re-beam the warp. If you try to weight separate areas, you might actually stretch those warp threads and increase the problem. They may

look all right on the loom, but not off tension. If the warp is long, the problem increases as you go along. If the warp is short, it may end before the problem presents itself.

If warp threads tangle on each other behind the shafts, the back shed for those threads gets shorter. The shorter shed makes those warp threads tighter, distorting the warp tension, which might make wavy lines of weft at the fell in the woven cloth. Use these wavy wefts or tight warps as signs to attend to a problem.

If you tighten the warp more sometimes and less at other times, the wefts will beat in less and more, making the cloth uneven and the pick count uneven.

The automatic warp tension system used by Jim Ahrens allows you to set the tension and maintain it throughout the warp. There is a chapter describing how it works in Book #2. Also read about the automatic warp advance mechanism on page 27.

How much tension?

Warp tension and beating are closely related. For the nuances of warp tension and beating, read the section on beating beginning on page 22. Also, note the section on beating to square a pattern on page 24.

 For weaving fabric, the tension on the warp should be just enough to get a shed. It should not be very tight. More tension than required causes more stress on the warp threads and takes more effort to make the sheds. A lighter tension makes it easier to get a light beat. Read more in the section: Beat and Warp Tension on page 24. Also, a lighter warp tension can help to hold out the selvedges because it helps keep the wefts from packing too tight. Tightly packed wefts make the warp neck in because there isn't enough weft in the sheds without bubbling. See Bubbling the Weft on page 17.

The warp tension needs to be very high for weft faced rugs and tapestries, but not for regular cloth. The higher the warp tension when weaving *balanced fabrics*, the more the threads will relax and shorten when the cloth is taken from the loom. The threads tend to revert to their former un-stretched length and may shrink even more when the fabric is washed. The result is that your fabric will be shorter than it was when you measured it on tension on the loom.

If the warp tension is too high on a jack loom, you won't be able to get a shed. The threads simply can't be forced to stretch up when raising the shafts to form the shed, or the excessive tension pulls all the warp ends up. Too-high tension might also raise the whole warp so that the bottom of the shed is above the shuttle race instead of resting on it.

High warp tension can cause the warp to narrow in too much. Severe narrowing is a drawing in of all warp ends toward the center rather than of the selvedges edges alone. Narrowing of this type also can be caused by too much tension on the weft.

Counterbalance and countermarch looms can have warps with very high tension because their mechanisms for making the sheds force the warp threads down as well as up. Thus, they are desirable for weaving rugs.

Leave the warp on tension

Don't loosen the warp tension when you stop weaving unless the tension is so great it hurts the structure of the loom. Loosening the warp tension may make a line in the weaving when you resume weaving again. The tension is not released on industrial looms when they are not turned on and shouldn't be for hand-weaving either. However, in very humid areas, you might need to release the warp tension between sessions. If you're using a temple, leave it in place when you stop weaving, as well.

One instance where you should release the tension on the warp is when you are weaving on a warp of very fine linen and you have dampened it to make it strong enough to weave. As the damp warp dries it gets tighter and threads snap all over the place.

Mixed warps

Mixing different yarns or weave structures in a warp can cause the tension to be uneven. Some threads will take up more than others making those warp yarns tighter than the others.

You can mix different types of warp yarns if they are mixed together one and one, but if you want a whole stripe of one yarn and a stripe of another, they will take up differently and cause tight and loose warp threads. It also prevents you from getting a good, clean shed. The problem will get worse and worse if the warp is long.

You can weave on such a striped warp if you tension the stripes differently by beaming them on another beam or weighting them separately. Read about weighting warps separately on page 8.

Loose warp threads

Single loose threads can be weighted separately. Use a film canister filled with pennies for weight. Tie a loop of string around the offending yarn behind the warp beam and snap the loop under the cap of the canister. The weight will slide along as the warp is advanced. See Figures 38 and 39.

Fig. 38

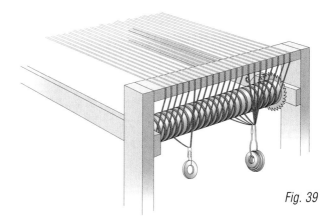

Fig. 39

Sometimes this weighting will just stretch the threads and make them looser than ever. Try weaving past the loose threads first, and then if the problem still exists, use a solution that works. Read about re-beaming the warp on page 142 in the Troubleshooting chapter.

You could use a different method. Use a hemostat—the kind of clamp used in surgical procedures to clamp off a cut blood vessel—to clamp the loose thread to its neighbors. Tighten it so it is the same tension as they are and then clamp it in place as close to the warp beam as you can. As the warp is advanced, the clamp moves forward. When it comes over the back beam, get up and re-position it. This is a way to replace a broken thread or—in the sampling process—substitute one thread color or style for another. The advantage is that the tension is just what you want it to be, the errant or added end does not twist or untwist itself because it isn't hanging free, and the clamps can be used over and over for years. Electronics supply places sell them and so does a beading catalog; you can buy them at shops for fishermen who tie their own flies, but expect to pay ten times as much!

If there is more than one loose warp, and they are all the same looseness, you can put a stick over the threads behind the back beam and hang weights from each end of the stick. See Figure 40. If there

are only a few loose threads in a group. See Figure 39.

If lots of threads are always sagging, I prefer to re-beam the warp, taking out the loose threads and weighting them separately. This method is described in Book #2, on page 156, and summarized in this book in the Preliminaries chapter on page 8.

If you use a stripe of one weave structure and another of a second weave structure, the warps in the two areas may take up differently just as different yarns do, and the above solutions apply. You can anticipate the problem before you warp the loom, and put only one structure's warp threads on the beam and weight

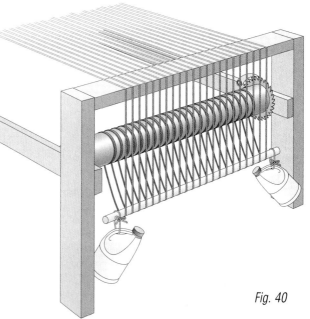

Fig. 40

Fig. 41

the other structure or put those threads on a second beam. Figure 41 shows a good knot to use when weighting warps off the beam. Read more about weighting warps separately on page 8, and how the knot is tied on page 82.

Tension that decreases

Some looms have no back beam, (the warp beam is located where a back beam would be) and the warp comes straight from the warp beam to the heddles. If the warp is very long or builds up high on the warp beam, the tension on the warp will decrease as the warp is woven off and the circumference of the beam gets smaller. This problem can happen with plain warp beams, but usually, sectional beams have a large circumference, and there isn't a significant difference as the warp gets woven off.

Changing wefts

 The fastest way to change wefts is to do it at the selvedges and to allow the new tails to hang out at the edge. It also allows your rhythm to continue uninterrupted. The weaving will not come undone, you can be assured. You can also change wefts in the middle, invisibly, but it will take much longer and definitely interrupt your rhythm. See below.

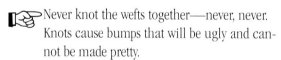 Never knot the wefts together—never, never. Knots cause bumps that will be ugly and cannot be made pretty.

Changing at the selvedges

I like to tuck the old weft into the next shed, snugging it up against the selvedge. About 1/2" in from the edge, I pull the remaining tail out of the shed and let it lie on top of the cloth. Cut this end to about 1". The shed stays open, ready for the new weft. I leave the new weft's tail, which is about 1" long, dangling outside the selvedge and cut it off later. See Figure 42.

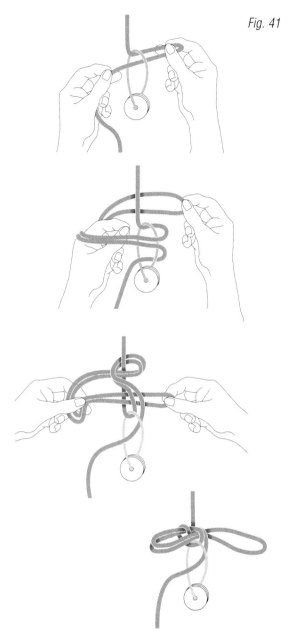

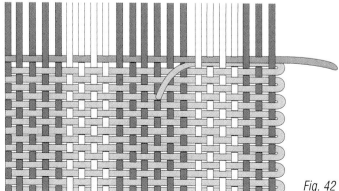

Fig. 42

☞ I find it easier to put the old weft's tail into the new shed rather than the old shed because it doesn't require taking it around the outside warp thread by hand.

The old weft might need to be put in the old shed for a change in weft color and/or if the weft is large and that 1/2" would show in the next shed. In that case, you must wrap it around the outside warp thread and tuck it back in on itself in order to put it back into the shed the weft just came out of. I let the new tail hang outside the selvedge—to be cut off after finishing. If the tails are about 1" long they won't get tangled up during washing. I usually make mine longer and trim them back to 1" just before I do the washing for the finishing. If you feel you should also tuck in the tail of the new weft, take it around the outside warp thread and place it in the new shed on itself just like you did when you put the tail of the old weft back into its own shed. Then, alternate sides

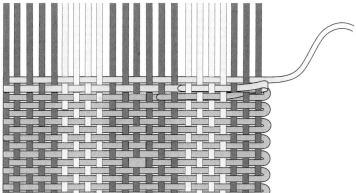

Fig. 43

where you make the weft changes so a buildup doesn't appear all on one edge. If the threads are fine, though, it shouldn't make any difference. See Figure 43.

☞ Generally, I don't recommend hanging the old weft out at one selvedge and the new weft on the other side because it changes the position of your shuttle in relation to the weave structure and can make it hard to keep your place.

Splicing wefts

Use this method when you need an invisible join in the middle of the cloth. (However, I prefer to change wefts at the selvedge instead.) Unply the last inch or two of both the old weft the new weft. Working with the tail of the old weft, put one of the plies in the shed and bring that ply out to the surface of the cloth. Put the remaining ply into the shed for about 1/2" further and then bring its tail out of the shed, so these plies are staggered in the shed. See Figure 44. Unply the new weft yarn in the same way and put it into the shed so that the unplied areas overlap those of the old weft. Bring the tails out of the shed at different places from the first tails. Where the two single plies overlap, they will

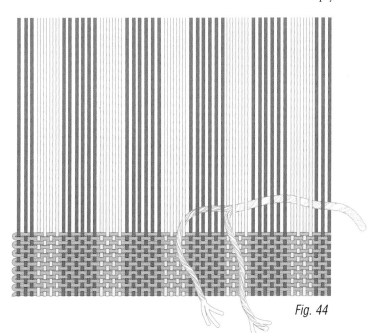

Fig. 44

add up to the size of one yarn and won't make a bump in the weft. See Figure 45. Cut the tails to 1" before washing, and cut them close to the cloth after it has been completely washed and all the finishing is done. If there are more than 2 plies in the yarns, use your judgment about how many plies to separate out for the procedure.

If an invisible weft change is needed because of a change in color, you have to make the change at a selvedge.

This unplying method works, but is time consuming. I only do splicing when I don't want to waste any weft yarn, which requires a change in the middle of the cloth, or I splice at the selvedge when there is an important-looking color change that tucking the tail into the old shed method won't suffice.

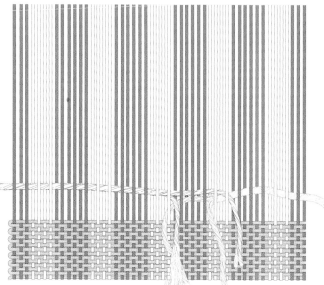

Fig. 45

Splicing thick wefts

To make the change at the selvedge, cut away all but one ply and insert it back on itself into the shed, taking it around the outside thread so it won't unweave as it is placed into the old shed. Make rough cuts as described below. See Figure 46.

Make rough cuts

After finishing (washing), the tails should be cut flush with the cloth. Try to avoid a blunt cut—especially with fat yarns— the cut end will always show. Instead, feather the cut by taking little "nips" with the points of the scissors until there is no more left, or "sawing" the yarn on the sharp edge of one half of the scissors until it is just fluff or

fibers. Then thread the tiny fibers in a tapestry needle and hide them in the cloth. To thread the tiny fibers into the needle, first "weave" the needle into the cloth with eye of the needle where the fibers are. Then put the fibers into the needle's eye and pull out the needle—the fibers will disappear into the cloth. Note: a tapestry needle has a large eye and blunt point

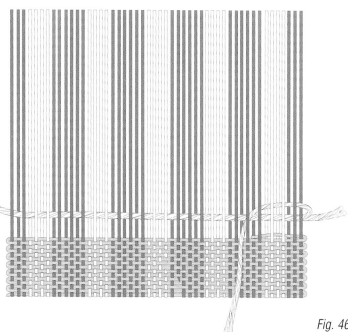

Fig. 46

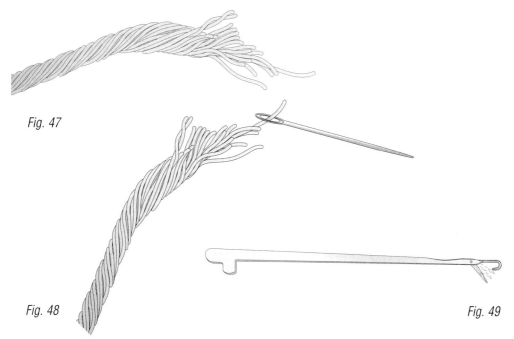

Fig. 47

Fig. 48

Fig. 49

to make the job easy. See Figures 47 and 48. You can buy a machine knitter's latch hook or a tiny hook made to mend knits; it is easier than threading a tapestry needle with something that is so short. See Figure 49.

When these methods show too much

Another way to start a new weft is to have it overlap the whole row of the old weft with the idea that a doubled thread is less conspicuous than a splice or glitch in the middle of the row. Just cut the new and the old tails off at the selvedges. This method might be a good idea for monofilament wefts in a loose weave where every thread shows a lot.

Knots in the weft

If there happens to be a knot in the weft yarn, do not weave it in—cut the yarn and continue as though you were changing wefts. If the knot is small, you might choose to weave it in and repair it later before finishing. (Knots in the warp yarn will pass through the reed and not get hung up in it if you use a reed wide enough for 2 warp ends per dent.) You can mend the knots later before washing. Read about mending in the Finishing chapter.

Frequent color changes

With frequent changes of color, the weft threads can be carried up the side, and not continually cut off and re-started. You can carry a weft up about 1/2"–1". Much more than that distance and the yarns show too much. See Figure 50.

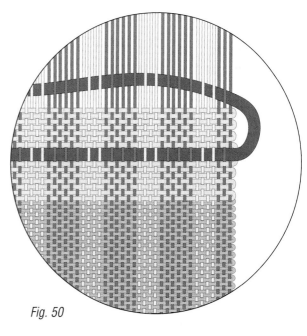

Fig. 50

Changing bobbins and pirns

It is easier to change a bobbin or an end delivery shuttle's pirn before it is entirely empty. When there is a little bit of weft still on the bobbin or pirn, attach the new yarn to the old and pull the old one with the new one attached out of the shuttle. It saves you having to re-thread the yarn through the eye or the tensioning device on the shuttle.

The last weft

Here is Harry Linder's trick for locking in the tail of the last weft shot.[9] "When you have made your next-to-last weft shot, beat it in as usual. If you have already changed sheds, go back and re-open the shed. Take a short length of yarn, perhaps four inches long, fold it in half. Insert it into the shed for about one inch leaving the loop end extended beyond the selvedge. You may now change sheds and make your last shot. Change shed and beat. Cut the weft leaving a tail some three to four inches long. Insert the tail of the weft into the loop. Grasp the ends of the inserted loop and gently pull the weft back into the weaving." See Figure 51.

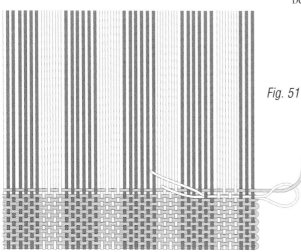

Fig. 51

Lease sticks in?

In Book #2, on pages 75 and 76, I tell you that it's a good idea to leave the lease sticks in behind the shafts during weaving to make repairing broken warp threads easier. However, I do not recommend leaving them in if they are bulky, heavy or a nuisance. Also, I wouldn't use them if there is a short distance behind the shafts, and if leaving the sticks in prevents the sheds from opening. Thin, light-weight lease sticks are easier to leave in during weaving than large, bulky ones.

Location of lease sticks

The length of the shed in front of the shafts and the length of the shed behind the shafts are both important. It's easy to picture that, as you weave along, the front shed get shorter and shorter.

When the lengths of the front and back sheds change and become very different from one another, problems can appear. To make the shed in front the same size as the shed in back, the lease sticks behind the shafts should be the same distance from them as that between the fell of the cloth and the shafts.

With normal yarns and weaves, I usually just keep pushing the lease sticks back to the back beam as they work themselves towards the shafts. See Figure 52. Many people prefer to tie them to the warp beam so they can't creep forward. The problems arise mostly with hairy or extremely fragile and fine warp threads. Read about fragile threads, below.

When weaving double cloth, you need to weave a bit closer to the shafts than usual to get a more open shed.

Lease sticks and fragile threads

Note that this section is for extreme situations that most weavers never see. If the front and the back sheds are very different in length, the warp threads may slide in the heddles every

---

[9] Linder, Harry P., *Hints From Harry*. Sun City Handweavers and Spinners Guild. 1991.

Fig. 52

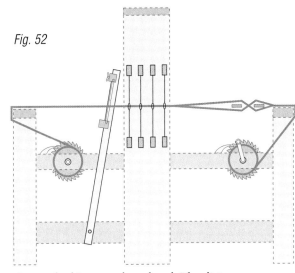

time a shed is opened or closed. The distance the threads move back and forth is small, but with fine threads it can be enough abrasion for the threads to break or to "part company," or to make lint on the threads. This fluff from warp threads can become woven into the cloth and form tiny balls, like "pills" in sweaters. On the unwoven warp these pills act like glue and often join two threads together like a knot. It is often possible to separate the threads by pulling them apart, but sometimes they must be cut. Watch out for pills or pieces of fluff on the warp threads behind the shafts. Remove them as soon as they are detected to prevent them from knotting two warp threads together.

Abrasion from unequal sheds isn't a problem with "regular" warps, say like 10/2 cotton, but it can be real trouble with fine, lightly spun silk or linen, or very dense warps. An extreme weaving situation where there are many picks per inch can contribute to this abrasion if you weave many, many sheds before advancing the warp. Use the guideline above to position the lease sticks, and advance the warp much more often than usual so the warps don't stay in the heddles in one place for too long.

Measuring

Measure the fabric while it is under tension. It gives the most consistent measurement. If you relax the warp tension, the cloth will

relax some and continue to relax. So at what moment in this relaxation process can you measure consistently? Read about relaxing of the cloth below.

It is a good idea to check that your beat is consistent by counting the picks per inch when you stop to measure the length you've woven. See page 23.

37

Use adding machine tape

I find it is the most accurate to mark my desired measurements on the edge of a long piece of adding machine tape.

Use a steel tape measure or good ruler to measure and make the marks on the adding machine tape. A cloth tape measure can be stretched or be floppy and is not as accurate. Make your mark right up to the edge of the paper, so there is no wondering about where the marks truly are. See Figure 53.

Use a fine pen and make small, fine marks. If you use a dull pencil or fat pen, the mark you make can be so fat that you won't be able to determine if you're exactly at the mark or if you need one more weft. It is especially important if you want to match two or more pieces together. It is also important to pre- serve the design you made. Once I used a cloth tape measure when weaving a wall hanging. The thick marks prevented me from changing my wefts at exactly the places I planned, so when I unrolled the completed piece, the sections were all out

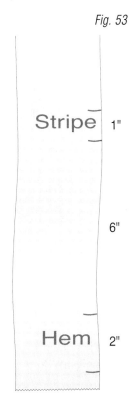

Fig. 53

Stripe 1"

6"

Hem 2"

38

of proportion. I un-wove it all and re-wove it, using my adding machine tape technique.

Check the adding machine tape a second or third time to be sure it's exactly what you want. "Measure twice, cut once."

I pin the adding machine tape on the edge of the cloth (for me, the left edge) with at least 3 straight pins. When I need to move the pin closest to me, I "leap frog" it over the other pins and place it near the fell of the cloth. Using 3 pins keeps the tape from slipping and sliding so you can be accurate. The tape does not get rolled in with the cloth on the cloth beam. I mark the entire length of the weaving, or just single repeats or sections that are repeated. I begin pinning it on when there is enough cloth woven so I can pin it with 3 pins. I don't move the paper—it just rolls with the cloth and falls away at the breast beam. If the tape is very long I'll roll the excess up and clip it with a paper clip. See Figure 54.

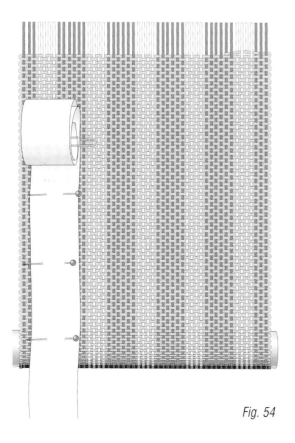

I keep the used tapes in my notebook with my records, and am surprised how many times I've gone back to check them for later projects.

For longer warps, this system might be cumbersome. Weavers have lots of ways to measure their cloth, and you might devise your own. Another good way is to put thread markers at a selvedge every yard (or any increment you want). That way, you won't need to unroll the woven cloth to know how much you've done. To do it, lark's head (Figure 55) the thread around the outside warp thread at the measurement point. Let the tails of the knot dangle outside the cloth without letting them roll up into the cloth beam so you can find them and easily see what you've woven. I suggest thread—you don't want it too fat, but it shouldn't be so fine that you can't find them, either. Be sure they are color fast so the color won't run onto the cloth during washing. You might color code the ties to coordinate with the number of yards woven. For example, use one color for marking the first 2 yards, another color for the next two, etc.

Anything you do to keep accurate measurements is important. If the measurement is critical, unroll the cloth and check to be sure you've actually woven the length you thought you had before cutting. Of course, now the cloth won't be under tension, so your measurement might not be minutely accurate, but at least you'll feel confident that a section or so hasn't been left out. Once, I wove two matching table runners for a friend. I cut the second one off a couple of inches too short—it was a disaster! Probably, it looked all right, but if I'd measured it just before cutting, I would have known it was too short.

If you unroll the cloth to check it out you need to re-roll the cloth in a certain way to retain the tension on the warp. If your warp is wide, a helper is wonderful. Put some tension on the cloth as it is being wound on the cloth

Fig. 54

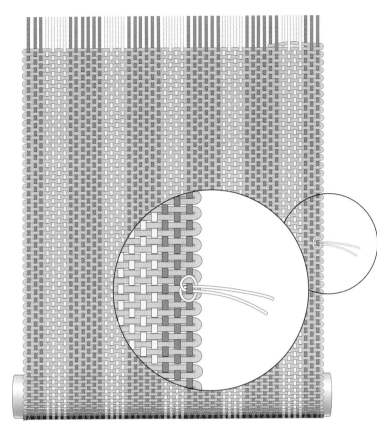

Fig. 55

If you've made your sample on the actual warp, you'll know how much relaxation took place by the measurement taken on tension and the one taken off tension when it's been cut off. You can calculate this difference along with shrinkage to know just how much longer you need to weave to accomplish your desired length.

Allow for shrinkage

After I've washed a sample piece of my fabric, I know just how much I can expect my actual piece to shrink. Then, I mark my adding machine tape accordingly. For example, if I discovered the cloth shrank 5% warp wise, I'd add 5% to each weft band's measurement. (To figure percent of shrinkage, see below.) This way I'll know the bands will turn out to be the size I want after the cloth is washed. Say, if I wanted bands of 3 inches and 5 inches, then I'd go to my calculator and do the following: 3 multiplied times .05 (or 5%) equals 0.15. Then I check to see what fraction is closest to 0.15. I see that 0.15 is a little more than 1/8" (0.125). (How to find the equivalents of fractions and decimals is explained below.) Then I'd add that to the 3" (3 1/8") and that would be the length I'd mark on the tape and how tall the band would need to be woven to have it 3" after washing. The 5" band would need to be woven 5 X .05 = .25 then 5 + .25 = 5 1/4".

Percent of shrinkage

To calculate the percent a cloth shrinks accurately, before washing, note these measurements: the width the warp was in the reed and the length of the cloth measured on the loom. Then measure when the cloth

beam by putting a stick under the loop the cloth makes between the apron bar and the fell. Pull gently on both ends to put tension on the stick while cranking. The stick should be long enough for you to tension the whole width of the cloth.

Allow for relaxation

If the measurement of your piece is absolutely critical, you need to account for the fact that the fabric will relax gradually after it is off tension. It means the piece is likely to be somewhat shorter than was measured on tension. For safety sake, measure your piece a few days after you've released the tension, before cutting it off. Some fabrics relax and shrink greatly, some insignificantly. For example, a rag rug--where the warps do a great deal of bending over and under fat rag wefts—can be much smaller after it has relaxed.

is dry after washing (finishing). Subtract the smaller (the after washing) number from the larger (before) number to find out how much the cloth shrank. Let's say a 10" long cloth measures 8 1/2" after washing. The difference is 1-1/2"—the amount the cloth shrank. We want to know what percent 1 1/2 is of 10". As my 5th grade teacher told us to do to figure out percent, "Divide the little number by the big number." That would be 1-1/2" divided by 10" which equals 1.5 divided by 10 = .15 which is 15%. These percentages tell how wide you need to make the full-sized warp and how long you need to weave it, measuring the cloth on the loom.

Decimals to fractions

I already know that .25 is 1/4, .5 is 1/2, and .75 is 3/4, but I never remember the decimal equivalents for 1/8, 3/8, 5/8, and 7/8. It's easy to find the decimals for these on the calculator when I remember what my 5th grade teacher said: "The top number is to be divided by the bottom number." So, 1 divided by 8 on the calculator gives me 0.125. Finding the equivalents for the remaining fractions gives me: 3/8 = 0.375, 5/8 = 0.625 and 7/8 = 0.875.

To determine the amount needed to add for 5% shrinkage for a 3" tall band, do this. Put 3 in the calculator and multiply times .05 (or 5 %) to get what 5% of 3 inches is. That is 0.15. To turn that into a fraction, make a fraction with 15 on the top and 100 on the bottom (15/100), then reduce the fraction to 3/20. That's an unfamiliar fraction, so I need to think about what it means in terms I know. I think of an inch divided into 20 spaces. Then I say, 1/2" = 10 twentieths, 1/4" = 5/20, 1/8" = 2 1/2 20ths. 3/20 is very close to 2 1/2 20ths, which is 1/8". Now I have converted 3/20 into 1/8—a fraction I can find on my ruler. So instead of marking the adding machine tape exactly 3" tall, I make the mark 3 1/8" tall.

For a 5" band it would be: 5 X .05 = .25, which I know, is 1/4. Mark the tape to be

5-1/4" to achieve the 5" you want after the cloth is woven.

To make pieces match

When you plan to join two or more pieces, and you want the weft bands and/or patterns to match up, use the same adding machine tape with thin marks, for each piece, so they all match the first one exactly.

Squaring a plaid

On page 24, I told you to weave the squares a tiny bit taller than they are wide to give the appearance of being square. Mark your adding machine tape to allow for both the shrinkage and the little extra to square.

How much warp is left?

I make a record sheet, like the register in my checkbook, to keep track of what I've woven and what is left to do. I measure the pieces I have cut off the loom, add 10% or so for warp take-up, and subtract them from the total warp I had before cutting the pieces off. When I near the end (or at the beginning), I subtract the back loom waste, so I know just how much warp is left. See Figure 56.

If you don't cut your pieces off and are accumulating yardage, enter the amounts you've woven by checking the measurement thread(s) you put in at the selvedges.

Another way to keep track of what's left is to make a string the length of your warp (the length of the guide string) and wind it on a tube or spool or film canister. Attach the free end of the string to the front apron rod using the same tying on technique as you use for the warp itself. Then, as you weave along, the string will unroll from the tube and what remains on the tube itself will be what's left of the warp. You will lose some length to take up, so the amount left won't be exactly the amount of warp left. Read more about take-up on page 148 in the Troubleshooting chapter.

Remember that you must allow for the back loom waste when you check what's left, and

Warp Use Record Sheet

JOB DESCRIPTION:

ACTUAL AMOUNT TO BE WOVEN:

Total Warp Length:	inches
– Front & back loom waste:	inches
= Amount to be woven:	inches
– _____% lost to take-up:	inches
= Actual woven length:	inches

NOTES:

Loom Allowances:	Front:	Back:	Total:
Loom #1:	in.	in.	in.
	in.	in.	in.
	in.	in.	in.
	in.	in.	in.
	in.	in.	in.
	in.	in.	in.
Loom #2:	in.	in.	in.
	in.	in.	in.
	in.	in.	in.
	in.	in.	in.
	in.	in.	in.
	in.	in.	in.
Loom #3:	in.	in.	in.
	in.	in.	in.
	in.	in.	in.
	in.	in.	in.
	in.	in.	in.

Balance:

DATE:	PIECE No.	WARP USED FOR:	Length Woven: Inches:	Yards:	Inches:	Yards:

NOTES:

Fig. 56

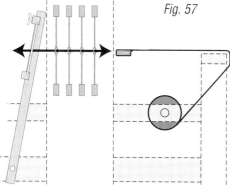

Fig. 57

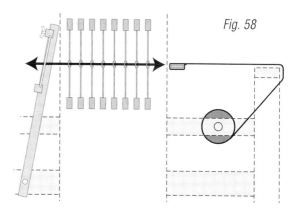

Fig. 58

that you won't be able to actually weave that amount. Figures 57 and 58 show how to predict the loom waste for your loom. Measure from the fell of the cloth to the back of the shafts. Notice that 4-shaft looms will have less back loom waste than looms with more shafts because the shafts themselves take up more space.

Marking cutting lines

Often, I want to keep weaving, and I mark places where I intend to cut the cloth later, when it's off the loom. Cutting the cloth along a line of thread that is woven in is foolproof for cutting straight. Use a contrasting color thread (colorfast) and put it into the same shed with the last pick woven. That way if you change your mind and don't want to cut there, you can pull out the thread and it won't leave a space in the cloth or a skip in the weave structure. Your cutting line reflects where to cut between pieces, including the hems, if needed. If you are just cutting the pieces apart, stitch

on the sewing machine on either side of the line. See Figure 59. Then, cut on the line and neither piece will unravel. Otherwise, cut and overcast the cut edges by hand (Figure 60).

Removing the cloth

The weaving is completed when you can no longer get a shed. There will be some warp left which is un-weaveable—the loom waste. You can predict where you will have to stop when you see the endstick approaching the shafts. When the endstick is very close to the back shaft, it prevents the shaft from moving, which means you cannot weave anymore on that warp.

Removing the lease sticks near the end will let you weave another inch or so.

 Of course, you can cut off the cloth before the very, very end of the warp, and you can cut pieces off and continue weaving, as well. Read "Cutting Off As You Go" on page 5.

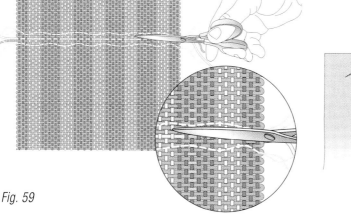

Fig. 59

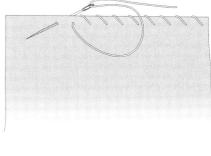

Fig. 60

Weaving the last wefts

Whenever possible, try to make the last few wefts in plain weave (also sometimes called tabby). It can give you a nice base for tying fringe or to make a straight edge when the pattern doesn't. Another good reason to end with a few rows of plain weave is to protect the last good rows of weaving so those wefts cannot come out or spread out. You can take the tabby rows out little by little as you tie fringe or finish the edge. I suggest using your "good" weft for this purpose, not some other yarn because you may want to use it—for example, for a hem. Allow for all the options you can, but you must do something to protect the final wefts from raveling. If I can't get a true plain weave because the weave structure doesn't allow it, I weave those rows as close to plain weave as I can using sheds where most of the threads cross. Then, I make sure to weave enough rows so that all the warp threads are woven in.

Even if the end of the warp prevents you from getting perfectly made sheds, try to weave these few wefts anyway—even if there are a lot of skipped threads. It is better than no plain weave at all. If your shuttle is too big to squeeze in those last wefts, use a spoke from an old umbrella to make a good-enough long needle "shuttle".

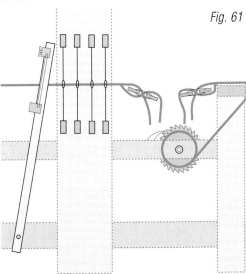

Fig. 61

If I don't plan to have fringe, I often machine stitch the edge as soon as I can after taking the cloth off the loom. Then I know the last wefts will stay in place. I like a zigzag stitch that stitches a few stitches for the "zig" and a few for the "zag." Sometimes I make the row of stitches a bit wavy just so the stitches don't always hit the same wefts all across the cloth. If they do, all the stitches plus the wefts can simply fall off the cloth during finishing. See Figure 59 on the previous page. Sergers can do this job well.

You may choose, instead, to hemstitch the end of the cloth. Do it before cutting while the warp is on tension. Read about hemstitching at the beginning and end of the cloth on page 159.

Preparing to tie on a new warp

It may be that you want to tie a new warp onto the old one. Read details of how to do it in the chapter beginning on page 99, in Book #2. I recommend tying the two warps together behind the shafts.

Here's an overview of the technique: While the old warp is still threaded in the heddles and the reed, knot together one end from your new warp to its matching end in the old warp. Work at the back of the loom after the new warp has been beamed on to the warp beam. After the knots are tied, pull the warp forward and ease the knots through the heddles and the reed. Then the weaving can begin. Ideally, the old cloth is still on the cloth beam, but you can use this method even if it has been cut off.

Before you cut off the warp, read the chapter in Book #2, so you'll know how to prepare the old warp to make the job convenient and accurate. See Figure 61 for an idea of how this process works.

How to cut off the cloth

Reduce the tension on the warp a bit, not so it sags, but so it is not taut anymore. Then, at the back of the loom, cut one-inch worth

of warps at one edge as far back as you can.
 Make sure you do not cut the apron cords that belong to the loom—just cut the warp threads at the endstick. I like to cut as far from the heddles as possible—just so I have flexibility when determining the fringe length, etc. You may not plan on a very long fringe, but you never can tell what creative thoughts might come up when you see the cloth off the loom, so allow for any possibility by cutting the yarns so they are as long as they can be. Working now at the front of the loom, pull that inch-worth of threads towards the cloth—pulling them through the heddles and reed. Then tie the threads in a temporary knot, so the last wefts cannot come out. I use a half-knot, which is the beginning part of a shoelace knot.

Continue the process by cutting the next inch-worth at the opposite edge of the warp. Work from the edges toward the middle in this way, alternating from side to side. The final group of threads should be the center warp threads.

Unroll the cloth and untie the knots at the beginning of the warp so you can remove the cloth from the loom. When I was a student, we put the cloth out on the floor to admire it. I still do sometimes, and it never fails that my cat comes along and sits on it and maybe even rolls over on it. Then, I know it's done and ready for the next steps—finishing and finishes: hems, fringes, mending, washing, deciding how to hang it, and how to cut it or sew it.

Measuring loom waste

Now is a good time to measure the amount of yarn that was un-weavable, the loom waste for your loom. Knowing the amount for your loom makes planning your warp calculations more accurate.

What to do with the cut edges of the cloth

Something must be done as soon as the cloth is removed from the loom to prevent the last wefts from unraveling. Depending on the purpose of the cloth, I either overcast the edge by hand or machine stitch it.

Often, if I'm not sure where hems and/or fringes will go, I temporarily hand sew the edges with an overcast stitch. See Figure 60 on page 42. I use a contrasting thread (not red, navy or black because they might run), so if I need to later, I can remove it easily.

I machine stitch the cut edge if I think the stitching will be permanent—taking it out
 would damage and pucker the edge and force wefts out of the cloth. This stitching is *never* to show in the finished project; it just keeps the edge secure during finishing. I usually use a row or two of straight stitching and make the 2 lines wavy so they catch wefts at different depths. See Figure 59 on page 42. Sometimes, I use a zigzag stitch that uses 3 or 4 stitches for each zig and zag. I stitch these in wavy lines, too, to vary the depth. If all the stitches follow along one weft, the whole stitching can come off in the washing process. A serger makes this job much easier.

If I think I might want fringe, I keep all the loom waste attached to the cloth (I have overcast the final wefts in place) until it has been finished. Then, I decide how long and how I want the fringe to look. To keep the fringe from tangling terribly in the washing machine, enclose them in socks and secure the socks closed with rubber bands.

Now you are ready to "finish" the cloth. See the chapter on finishing, beginning on page 157. The cloth isn't finished until it's "finished," which usually means washing and dealing with hems, fringes, etc.

Weaving tips

Using a mask

When you weave a lot and/or fast, you may create lint. The style of mask I like is shown in Figure 62. It's comfortable for me even with eyeglasses. If your nose itches or if you begin to cough (tow linen is a prime offender),

probably there's too much lint around, and you don't want to be breathing it. Another place to look for lint is under the shafts and under the loom itself.

Fig. 62

Extra heddles

Extra heddles won't bounce around when you're weaving fast if you use these ideas: hold them in place at the sides of the shafts with twist ties. Paper clips or small refrigerator magnets on the heddle bars can hold them away out to the side, too.

Scissors

I like to keep blunt scissors in my apron— there are no points to do any damage. Buy good ones, not "kindergarten" scissors. Nurse's blunt scissors are good, especially to carry in a pocket. Many weavers hang their scissors around their necks—blunt ones would be nice!

A small cutter can be made and hung near your bobbin winder:

1. Cut a piece of cardboard the width of a single edged razor blade and twice its height.
2. Score the cardboard and fold it in half.
3. Cut a very small notch in the center of the fold.
4. Insert the razor blade so its sharp edge is in the fold.
5. Tape the other 3 sides. Use the tiny edge of the razor that is revealed by the notch to cut.

Keep shears handy at the loom by taping an empty yarn cone on a front leg where it joins the breast beam—or any other convenient place. The open end of the cone will be ready to receive your shears.

Handy place for a tapestry needle

Put a strong magnet on an unused area of the reed to keep a tapestry needle handy.

I made a "sort of" pin cushion by winding a strip of handwoven cloth several wraps around a board on the castle of my loom and stitching the cloth to itself. I put tapestry needles and pins there and slide my S-shaped sley hook between the cloth and the wood and the little Allen wrench (hex wrench) for adjusting end feed shuttles, too.

Traveling looms

Unless your loom is very heavy, you need to anchor it to keep it from sliding. Anchor it in any way that makes sense in your set-up. Possibilities include: fastening blocks of wood to the floor, placing rubber mats under the loom, even putting a board across the far side of an open doorway or window and tying the loom to it. You can put boards (2x4) between the back loom legs and the wall. (It might dent the baseboard.) Nothing's too farfetched if it works.

Slippery loom bench

Cover the bench with the rubber "cloth" sold for lining shelves.

Weaving shoes

People have all kinds of ideas for weaving shoes—or bare feet. I think it depends a lot on the width of your treadles. Socks with moccasin soles or socks with non-slip treads that hospitals give out are the closest to bare feet that I can think of. Since my feet get cold, I don't like bare feet, but many weavers weave that way. One person suggested that if you have sore feet, wear jogging shoes for comfort. If your treadles aren't wide enough, try to leave an empty treadle between each treadle that you're using.

Keeping track of your place

One clever convention is to have your shuttle on the left when the left treadle is to be used, and on the right when the right one is needed. It is particularly useful when weaving tabby. This method can't be used for all weaving sequences, but when you can, it's a big help.

Another convention people use when you stop weaving, is to leave the weft on a diagonal in the shed—then you can tell where you left off. Of course, stopping at the end of a sequence is ideal, but sometimes you can't—when the shuttle runs out, for example. See Figure 63.

Balancing the shuttles

It's hard to balance the shuttles at the beginning when there isn't enough cloth woven on which to set them. Helen Pope pinned a washcloth or small hand towel over the apron cords to provide a place to put the shuttles down. This method is especially helpful when more than one shuttle is used. She used the washcloth on very narrow warps for bookmarks, as well. She also kept her scissors there—the terry cloth was rough enough to keep them from slipping off. See Figure 64.

Storing lease sticks and reeds

Pairs of lease sticks will stay matched up if you rubber band them together at one end. Make that end the visible end sticking out of your sticks container. You can store them inside towel racks attached to a wall, umbrella stands or old golf bags (check thrift stores). I made wonderful stick containers out of plastic drain pipe about 6" in diameter. I put a cover on the bottom end (the drain cover made for the pipe). I had them cut—one for shorter and one for longer sticks. A cylindrical waste basket around 10" in diameter works as well.

Good ties

Keep different lengths of shoelaces handy for different jobs. Dying them odd colors can

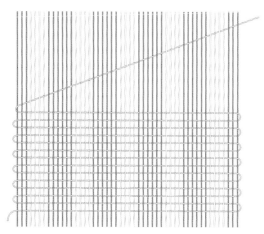

Fig. 63

prevent family members from using them! Use them to tie the lease sticks in place behind the shafts and for many of your tying jobs.

One weaver uses the drawstrings that come in pants when there's elastic already in the waist to hold the pants up. They are soft to the touch and usually longer than a shoelace.

String box

I always have lots of strings for ties, and I keep them in a small box about 3" square and 2" high, with a cover. I cut a round hole about 1–1/2" in diameter in the top and tape the cover closed. Then, I can easily reach in for a string and can stuff used strings back inside, as well. You could also use an empty tissue box.

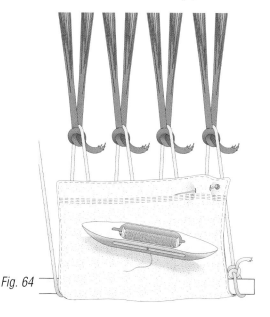

Fig. 64

2 *Shuttles*
and winding bobbins, pirns, cones, and balls

Why shuttles are important

Half the cloth is the weft, even if, by the numbers, it's not a balanced cloth. By understanding how to put the weft in place, you can avoid surprising stripes, embarrassing selvedges, and unintentional seersucker puckers.

The tension of the weft is at least as important as the tension of the warp, because the quality of a piece of woven cloth depends considerably on the evenness of these two tensions. The wefts should lie easily in the cloth. That ease depends on four things:

1. How you throw the shuttle
2. How evenly the shuttle releases the weft
3. How you take the shuttle out of the shed
4. How you wind the bobbins (pirns in end delivery shuttles.)

After the loom itself, the shuttle is the most important piece of weaving equipment. A well-designed shuttle lets you develop a rhythm that coordinates all the weaving motions; and rhythm leads to both speed and high-quality woven fabric.

Most of my students are familiar with revolving-bobbin shuttles, or boat shuttles, (Figure 65) and know that they can cause lots of trouble. The complaint I've heard most often is that the weft yarn seems to jump off the bobbin and tangle itself around the shaft on which the bobbin revolves. These shuttles can be used efficiently, on warps of less than 36 inches in width, if you know how to use them. Read how to use them beginning on

page 60. However, the weaving will be slower than using the shuttles I recommend: end-delivery, (end-feed or fixed-bobbin) shuttles. See Figure 66. Read about stick shuttles, rug shuttles, and ski shuttles in the sidebar on page 66.

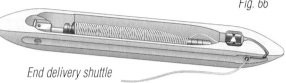

Fig. 66

End delivery shuttle

What is the difference between hand shuttles and flyshuttles?

End-delivery shuttles can be thrown by hand or by a flyshuttle beater. Those made for use as flyshuttles have pointed metal tips. See Figure 67. Those made for use as hand-shuttles have blunt tips. The sharper points on the flyshuttle deflect the warp threads, and reduce the chance of breaking them when

Fig. 67

End delivery shuttle with metal tips

the weaver accidentally throws the shuttle before completely opening the shed. For this reason, I often use metal-tipped shuttles for handweaving. The metal points are not sharp enough to hurt my fingers, and I don't have to worry about broken warp ends when I'm weaving very fast.

Fig. 65

Boat shuttle

End-Delivery (End-Feed) Shuttles

Why use end-delivery shuttles?

First, speed: the weft yarn never tangles or jerks, so you can throw the shuttle as hard and as fast as you want, and you don't have to stop weaving to unsnarl a backlashed bobbin. Second, the selvedges: they are even, not loopy and not indented from wefts being jerked or snagged. The shuttles are easy to use. The "bobbins" are called pirns. See Figure 68. The trick is to know how to wind the pirns, because when the pirns are properly wound, the shuttle does all the work of positioning the weft yarn for you. No bubbling or making an arc by hand is necessary for most weave structures! See Figure 25 on page 17. (Remember that honeycomb and some other structures will require an arc or bubbling.) They are more complicated to make, so they are more expensive than boat shuttles, but well worth the investment.

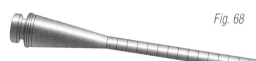

Fig. 68

What makes them work?

First of all, only the *weft thread* moves—not the pirn. (That's important because it's the momentum of the revolving bobbin in a boat shuttle that creates problems.) Second, end-delivery shuttles have a tensioning device that regulates the tension on the thread, so the weft can snug itself up to the selvedge threads perfectly on each shot (weft). The weaver never has to touch the selvedges. If you see an end-delivery shuttle without a tensioning device, avoid it, because the shuttle can't do this important task.

When you throw the shuttle, the yarn reels out, and when you catch the shuttle, the yarn stops. Weaving is more efficient because you don't have to fuss with the yarn at the beginning or the end of the throw. Boat shuttles need special motions. See the section about boat shuttles beginning on page 60.

What kinds of yarns work?

Most wefts can be used in these shuttles: cotton, wool, mohair, silk, slippery yarns, novelties, thick and thin.

What kinds of yarns don't work?

Really thick wefts, such as rags and heavy rug yarns, can't pass through the tensioning device. You need to use rug shuttles or ski shuttles for those wefts. Read about them on page 66.

Wefts that are flat strips such as ribbon or metallics do not work in end-delivery shuttles because the yarn twists as it comes off the pirns. A boat shuttle must be used or the ribbon will twist and twist. Monofilament also will kink (over-twist) if taken off the end of its package. You might find other unsuitable wefts, as well. You'll know if you're putting too much twist in if the weft kinks on itself. Conversely, if your weft becomes untwisted and pulls apart, you've taken out too much twist. Read why this happens, below, and about adding and subtracting twist in the sidebar on page 50.

Pirns and twist

As the yarn is unwound from an end-delivery pirn, its twist is changed by a small amount, usually about 1/5th of a turn per inch of yarn because the yarn comes off the end of the pirn. If the yarn is somewhat overtwisted, adding even that much twist can make it more difficult to handle. With most yarns the extra twist is not noticeable. This twist change occurs when yarn is taken off the end of any pirn, bobbin, spool, or cone. When yarn is taken off the side of a pirn, bobbin, spool, or (not likely), a cone, the twist is unchanged.

I demonstrate this effect to students with a roll of toilet tissue. See Figures 69a, b, and c. If I pull the tissue off the top end of it, everyone can see that the paper comes off twisted. (Then I ask them to tell if the twist in the paper is in the S or Z direction.) It is easy to see the

48

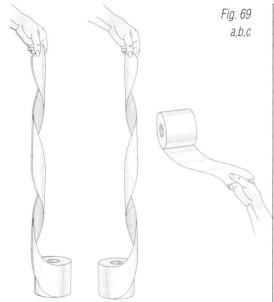

Fig. 69
a,b,c

diagonal lines in the paper to determine the direction of the twist. Read about identifying S & Z below. Then, I turn the roll of toilet tissue upside down and pull off some tissue. Of course, it is twisted again, but in the opposite direction from the first example. The last part of the demonstration is to pull the paper off the side of the roll. Voila! No twist!!

You can change the twist by how you put the pirn onto the bobbin winder's spindle—that is, with the base facing the motor, or away from it. Try both ways and examine which way your winder adds and which way it subtracts twist. Read the sidebar on page 50, and check the twist as you take the yarn off the pirn. Differently wound pirns can create a noticeable difference in the woven cloth. See Figures 70 and 71.

Fig. 70

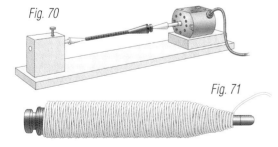

Fig. 71

For consistent cloth, you want the wefts to be totally consistent as to twist. However, a novelty cloth can be woven using different twists.

S & Z Twist

Yarns have two directions of twist: S and Z. To see the direction of twist of a yarn, look for the diagonal lines, just like the diagonal lines seen on the toilet paper demonstration. See Figure 72. To tell the direction, hold a length of the yarn taut. Look at it closely. Use a linen tester, also called a pick glass (Figure 34 on page 24), if necessary. It's a magnifying glass to count threads per inch. You'll see that the surface of the yarn spirals (note the diagonal lines). If the diagonal slants the same way as the line forming the middle of the letter S, then we say it has S twist. If it slants the same way as the line forming the middle of the letter Z, then we say it has Z twist. That's all there is to it and why the twists are named as they are.

No matter which way you turn a yarn or look at it, the twist will always look the same.

An easy way to identify S & Z

The diagonal lines you see on a yarn indicate the twist put into the yarn when it was made. Here's a quick way that always works to tell if the twist is S or Z. Knowing that most yarns are twisted in the S direction, and that the right hand is the dominant hand for most people, swing your right hand across your body. Start the swing with your hand at your side and swing it towards your left shoulder. That is the same diagonal of S twisted yarn! So, if the yarn in question has the same diagonal as you do when you swing your right hand, it's an S-twist yarn. Swinging your left hand across your body gives you the diagonal for Z twisted yarns. When I'm in a yarn shop I don't actually swing my arm-I just swing my hand across my chest-right for S direction and left for the Z direction.

Fig. 72

S Z

49

End-delivery shuttles, boat shuttles, and twist

Almost every yarn has twist (among the few that don't are flat yarns like ribbon, reed, and metallics). Twist is what makes natural fibers hold together as yarn. It's what makes the plies of thread hug together in a strong yarn. Even man-made fibers benefit from the twist. See the twist in the yarns in the figure.

The amount of twist in a yarn can affect the feel, drape, durability, water-repellence, light-reflectivity, even the color, of a finished fabric.

Three major truths about twist to keep in mind:

1) In general, adding twist makes a harder, stronger yarn.

2) In general, subtracting twist makes a softer, more easily abraded yarn.

3) Twist has two directions-S twist and Z twist.

Adding and subtracting twist

You can add S or Z twist when you unwind yarn from the end of a spool. When the yarn, as seen from the end of the spool, moves in a counter-clockwise direction as it unwinds from the spool, S twist is added. By turning the spool end-for-end, the yarn will move in a clockwise direction as it unwinds, adding Z twist to it. Look at the toilet paper illustrations. (This option is not available with cones which are made to stand only one way up.) To understand S & Z twist, read the sidebar on the previous page .

Repeating the principle: which end of the yarn package the yarn comes off from dictates the direction of the twist put into the yarn-because the yarn is coming off the end. You can add or subtract twist not only by how you wind the pirn, but also by which end of the spool of yarn you take the yarn off of.

Now, every time you wind or unwind yarn, you can slightly add twist, subtract it, or have no affect on it. Here's how: An S twist yarn can have twist added if more S twist is put into it as it leaves the yarn package. Its twist can be taken out if you turn the package upside down because then you'll be putting in the opposite twist (untwisting the yarn). You can make no change in the twist if you take the yarn off the side of the package (as in boat shuttles).

If you put in S twist on an S twist yarn, you'll be adding twist. If you put S on a Z yarn, you'd be subtracting twist. Z on S would subtract, too, and Z on Z would add. So you need to know both what you're working with and what you're doing with it. Tightening the twist would make the yarn slightly harder, and loosening the twist would make it slightly looser and softer.

Note that for consistent cloth, you want the wefts to be totally consistent as to twist. A novelty cloth can be woven using different twists, however.

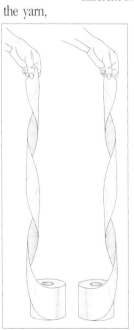

Taking the yarn off the end of a package is usually preferable, because it can be taken off fast. Taking the yarn off the side must be done slowly or the yarn will overspin and tangle on the spindle holding the package.

If you set up your yarn source on a horizontal spindle, and wind on to a boat shuttle bobbin, you have not changed the twist in the yarn one whit. In weaving, the boat shuttle bobbin also feeds off the yarn with no change in twist. In both situations, the yarn feeds off the source horizontally-not vertically (as in end-delivery shuttles).

If your yarn source is a spool or a cone, and you set it on the floor, and you wind on to a **boat shuttle bobbin**, you will have added or subtracted twist by taking the yarn off the top of the package.

The twist won't be affected further, however, in weaving, because the bobbin feeds the yarn off its side. Set on its spindle, the yarn feeds off **untwisted** in either direction. But set on its base on a flat surface, the yarn feeds off the end of the package in a spiral: one spiral for every circumference's worth of length.

If you set your cone on the floor, and wind on to an end-delivery shuttle's pirn, you will have added or subtracted twist-once in winding, and again in weaving, because the yarn is coming off both the end of the yarn package, and the end of the pirn, as well. Of course you could **add** coming off the package and **subtract** by how you put the pirn on the bobbin winder—ending up about the same as the yarn was originally.

You can use twist to your advantage. A yarn that's too hard for your purpose can be softened quite substantially by winding "against the twist." A yarn that's too soft can be toughened (slightly) by winding "with the twist." You can change these directions when you wind pirns by putting either the base or the tip of the pirn on the winder's spindle first. You can't change the direction while weaving with a boat shuttle bobbin. You can change the twist by how you take the yarn off the end of its package. Also, you can *negate* the twist off a cone by reversing it on the pirn. See how to wind the pirns on page 56.

How much yarn will these shuttles hold?

They hold a lot. When wound under tension, the pirns can be packed tightly with a great deal of yarn. Winding pirns under tension also makes a better wound pirn, which will feed off smoothly.

How heavy should your shuttle be?

 In general, use the lightest shuttle you can find. Lighter shuttles can be thrown easier and faster, and the smaller the shuttle is, the smaller the size of the shed needs to be. 6 to 7-ounces shuttles are ideal for handweaving with or without a flyshuttle system. Many end-delivery shuttles available today are made for power looms and are too heavy. Nevertheless, if the shuttle is too light for the tension needed for very heavy yarns, it can be pulled off the shuttle race-and, in the case of a flyshuttle, can prevent the shuttle from entering the box properly.

Can large power loom shuttles be used?

Industrial shuttles are available at antique shops, but are big and much too heavy. In industry, if the shuttle lightened up too much as the thread was used up, it would bounce back into the shed from the force of the flyshuttle picker. They made the shuttle just heavy enough so that the weight of the weft wouldn't be significant in comparison to the shuttle weight. Full or not has no effect, and the force of the flyshuttle picker can remain constant. The handweaver can adjust the power of the throw as the shuttle lightens up, so a heavy shuttle isn't needed. Read about flyshuttles on page 18.

You can use these heavy shuttles, but they take more work to throw, which makes them slower to use. Also, the bigger the shuttle, the bigger the shed needs to be, which slows down the weaving, and is harder on the warp threads. Throwing such a heavy shuttle might cause wrist problems and shorten the time you can weave in a day, because they are tiring.

How to modify a power-loom shuttle for hand throwing

If you want to use a power loom shuttle, you can make it easier to use by cutting its weight: pull out the heavy metal tips and replace them with wood plugs, and drill the shuttles full of holes to lighten them.

51

How to choose the right tensioning device

There are specific shuttles made for standard, thick, and thin wefts. The main difference is the type of tensioning device used in the shuttle. To make a good selvedge, some yarns need more tension, others require less.

There are shuttles with interchangeable tensioning systems, so you can change the tensioning device depending on the weft thread you're using. The easiest tensioning mechanisms to thread are those that allow you to lay the weft thread into a slot. Others use a more convoluted threading method.

Shuttles manufactured by Bluster Bay have a unique tension system. See Figure 73. There are two parallel rows of upside-down L-shaped brass hooks facing away from each other in the nose of the shuttle. They are threaded by hand (or crochet hook), so that the weft passes from side to side around as many hooks as it takes to provide the desired tension. It takes a little more time to thread, however. See "How is the shuttle threaded" on page 56 for a quick way to change threads on any shuttle.

Fig. 73

Fur, bristles, or thread

An excellent way to tension heavy or wiry yarns is to line the inside of the shuttle with a strip or two of fur, fake fur, or plush fabric. See Figure 67 on page 47. This fur pile can also be used for fine yarns. It creates the "main drag" on the thread, so you can use the shuttle's internal tensioning device for fine-tuning. Fur also helps to control slippery yarn from unwinding too fast. Read more about controlling the weft's unwinding in the section on winding pirns, on page 58. Fur for shuttles used to be Australian opossum belly fur. It was

used because it doesn't mat down which other furs do in time. A few years ago in Japan, I bought strips of fur backed with adhesive; both cat fur and fake fur strips were available.

The tensioner may take the form of a simple bunch of bristles, like a miniature horse's tail, that brush the yarn near the tip of the pirn as it exits, creating drag. See Figure 74.

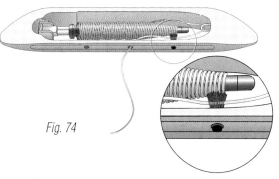

Fig. 74

Fine yarns

With fine yarns, when the edges are important, you need to have good tension on the weft. The more slippery the yarn the tighter the tension needs to be to hold it. That's one reason fur is used in shuttles. The fur puts some tension on the thread at the start, then the tensioning device gives you the variation you need for fine-tuning. Shuttles intended for silk and other fine yarns use a system of hoops and posts inside the tip of the shuttle, which allows you to produce excellent selvedges with the finest and most slippery yarns.

There are several varieties of this kind of tensioning device, but the principle in all is similar to that of a tension box: the thread goes up and down, over and under posts. This system creates friction, or drag, on the yarn as it leaves the shuttle. To get the thread positioned in the tensioning device, you push up a series of hoops, guide a small hook through them, hook the weft thread, draw it through the hoops and out a ceramic eye. As the yarn comes out of the shuttle during weaving, these hoops, or more properly "gates," cause the yarn to bend more or less sharply over the posts. You adjust the gates by turning a screw to tighten or loosen a spring, the sharper the bend, the greater the tension. See Figure 75. Some shuttles have a rubber band that you wind up on a little rod to increase tension. Replacing the rubber band when it wears out is

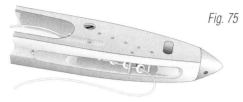

Fig. 75

easy: just cut a piece of ordinary rubber band on a long, tapering slant. Thread it in and use a tweezer to catch it in place. In choosing a shuttle that has this tensioning device, be careful to see that the hoops inside are free to move. If they're not free to move, you can't increase the tension beyond what is already set.

Heavy yarns

Heavy yarns don't need such delicate treatment—or much tension—they create their own friction, by simply passing in and out of a few holes on the outside of the shuttle. See Figure 76. Again, the effect is similar to carrying a thread over and under the dowels in a tension box. The more holes you use, the more tension you put on the weft thread. It may be that just the exit hole itself is enough. I've seen shuttles where a little plug of thread was pushed into the exit hole to create a simple and effective tensioning device. (It must be glued in place.)

Heavy yarns have more tension on them by nature and may need a heavier shuttle. If the shuttle is too light, the yarn tension pulls it off the shuttle race. The weight of the shuttle is most important when a flyshuttle is used, because it won't enter the box properly if it is pulled off course by too much tension on the exiting weft.

Fig. 76

Medium yarns

A shuttle for medium-size yarns may have a spring-loaded tensioner. Springs press against two small plates through which the yarn passes. See Figure 77. This pressure tensions the yarn and can be regulated with a tiny screwdriver or Allen (hex) wrench. The spring-loaded tensioning device can work for a wide range of yarns-from a fine, 20/2 cotton to medium-size to fairly heavy yarns-and may be your best all around choice.

53

Fig. 77

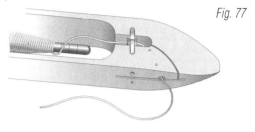

Slippery yarns

Fur keeps slippery yarns from sliding off the pirn, or unwinding too fast. You may also need to put more tension on with the tensioning device. Read about controlling slippery yarns from slipping off cones on page 65.

How is the Tension Adjusted?

Consult the instructions that come with your shuttle for how to regulate the weft tension. Then, to regulate the tension for the cloth you're actually going to make, place the shuttle on the shuttle race with the weft thread coming out of the hole on the side facing you. Now weave a few shots (wefts) to determine how much tension you need. Start to weave with very little tension at first-so little that the weft makes loops at the selvedges. Then, increase the tension, just enough, until the loops disappear. If the tension is increased too much, the selvedges will pull in. Use the least amount of tension needed.

As the pirn empties, more drag is put on the weft thread, so you may need to decrease the tension on the device slightly because of the increase of tension on the weft as it finds its way off the pirn. When the pirn is full and fat near the tip, the yarn can freely balloon off; but when it's empty, the weft can't balloon anymore because there is much more of the pirn exposed; the yarn has further to travel and is flatter on it. So, the perfect tension you made with a full bobbin may need to be reduced when the bobbin empties.

You may never need to adjust the tension as the pirn empties—depending on the situation.

How much tension is too much?

You know there's too much tension on the thread if you find that throwing the shuttle forces the selvedges to pull in, or, if the shuttle curves off the shuttle race and toward you, or, if the yarn can't feed out of the shuttle at all. In the last case, check to see that the pirn isn't so full of thread that it's braking against the sides of the shuttle cavity, or that the yarn is not too heavy for the shuttle you're using and the exit hole too small to accommodate it.

Another shuttle adjustment

The position of the spindle on some shuttles can be adjusted. I've found that on some new shuttles, the spindle points down toward the shuttle race making the filled pirn project out from the bottom of the shuttle. There is an easy adjustment that really needs to be done or the shuttle can't slide along on the shuttle race. Over time, you may need to adjust the spindle again. Find the spindle-adjusting screw on the bottom of the shuttle. It is inside the hole directly beneath the pivoting end of the spindle. Raise or lower the spindle by turning the screw clockwise or counterclockwise, respectively, using the Allen wrench which came with your shuttle. See Figure 78.[10]

Fig. 78

What weaves are best?

Balanced or warp face weaves are ideal for production weaving. When a balanced appearance is required, the sett has more warps per inch than wefts per inch to allow the weaver to throw the shuttle without bubbling or making a special angle in the weft. The natural diagonal achieved from the fell of the cloth (the edge made by your most recent weft shot) to the path the shuttle takes on the shuttle race (the ledge in front of and at the base of the reed) is sufficient, and speeds up the weaving. See Figure 79.

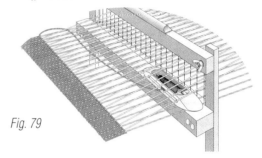

Fig. 79

For weft faced weaving, the weaver needs to stop to bubble the weft and/or to use a temple so these shuttles aren't recommended because the shuttle alone won't put enough slack into the shed. Read about temples on page 94.

How do I throw the shuttle?

With a snap. It can be thrown as hard and fast as you like, and the weft will still come off beautifully. Don't turn the shuttle end-to-end on every pick (weft). It doesn't matter whether the exit hole of the shuttle goes into the shed first or last, as long as the exit hole is facing you as you weave. Beat the weft on the open shed, and then change the shed as the beater hits the fell of the cloth. This procedure allows the maximum weft to enter the shed and prevents the weaving from drawing in too much. Read all about weaving motions in the chapter on weaving.

---

[10] Schacht Spindle Company Instruction Pamphlet for End-Delivery Shuttles, 1997.

What About Narrow Warps?

If your warp is narrower than 12 inches, and you use a "normal length" (14-15" long) end-delivery shuttle, one selvedge will probably be ragged. If the exit hole for the thread is on the right of your shuttle, the right selvedge will be ragged; if the exit hole is on the left, the left selvedge will be ragged. Why? Because the thread feeds out of the exit hole at the far end of the shuttle. So as the shuttle exits the shed it must release more than enough yarn for the next pick, just to clear the shed. See Figure 80. Shorter (11"–13" long) shuttles are readily available. They are a great advantage over modifying a too-long shuttle. I found tiny end-delivery shuttles in Japan. They are about 5" long, but they don't hold much yarn because the pirns are also tiny.

You can modify your shuttle to weave narrow warps. Drill a hole in the middle of the shuttle on the same plane as the original exit hole. This is hole "A". Drill a second hole, "B", about one inch from the original exit hole between "A" and the original. Thread out from the original hole, into "B", and then out again through "A". This puts the yarn at the middle of the shuttle. See Figure 76 on page 53. (Note that threading the yarn through these extra holes creates more tension. You may have to loosen the shuttle's tensioner to compensate. With some yarn, very thick ones for example, you won't be able to loosen the tension enough, and either will have to use a shorter shuttle or a boat shuttle.)

For very narrow warps I might simply use a small revolving bobbin shuttle (boat shuttle) if a short shuttle is still too long.

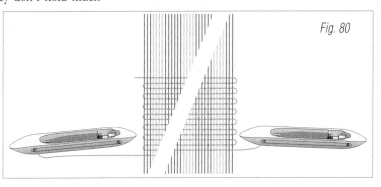

Fig. 80

How is the shuttle loaded?

To put the loaded pirn onto the metal shaft in the shuttle, first pull up the shaft at its tip. (The shaft pivots at its base, but may be stiff at first.) Push the pirn completely down onto the shaft so the groove at the pirn's base fits around the little metal retaining pin in the bottom of the shuttle. (Some shuttles do not have this pin.) Pull a bit of the weft off the tip and push the pirn down into place in the shuttle with the retaining pin seated in the groove at the base of the pirn. See Figure 81. Place the weft into the shuttle's tensioning device.

Notice that there is a difference between the top and the bottom of the shuttle. The top is the side where the spindle lifts up. You want the exit hole facing you and the bottom riding on the shuttle race. Each shuttle has a way to

prevent the pirn from falling out of the bottom of it. It's also a way for you to determine the bottom of the shuttle.

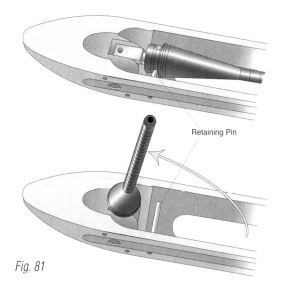

Retaining Pin

Fig. 81

How is the shuttle threaded?

No matter what kind of shuttle you have, you can make changing the pirns faster if you don't weave the last few inches of yarn. Tie the thread of the new pirn to the end of the weft still in the shuttle-and pull the old and new thread through the tensioner.

You may need a small hook for threading the tensioning device. You can make one with a flexible wire by bending its end into a hook. A latch hook from a knitting machine works if it's thin enough. See Figure 49 on page 35.

Why is winding the pirn important?

With pirns properly wound, the weft yarn will be positioned by the shuttle alone. When the pirn is not properly wound, the shuttle may fly off the shuttle race or pull and yank at the selvedges. Winding pirns is different from winding boat shuttle bobbins. It takes some practice, too, but once you master it, you will be able to make pirns that feed out the weft as smooth as butter. Read about bobbin winders on page 71.

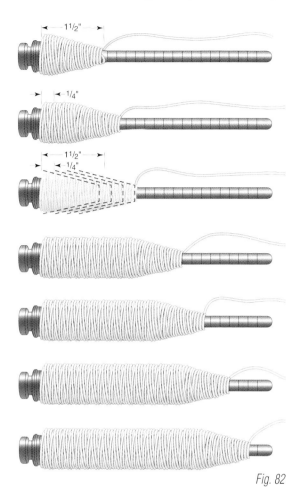

Fig. 82

How do I wind the pirns?

Read about winding equipment on page 71.

 The outside of the filled pirn will look like a long, slender cylinder, tapered at the tip. Inside, the shape of the filled pirn will be like a stack of dunce caps, or highway cones, on their side. Read how to accomplish this configuration below. See Figure 82.

 Your hand will only *guide* the thread-it should not put tension on it, because that would burn your fingers. To put tension on the thread while winding the pirns, use a tension box of some kind. See Figure 83. By running the weft yarn through the tension box over and under the pegs, sufficient tension can be placed on the weft yarn to pack the pirn firm and tight. Read more about tension boxes and their substitutes on page 75.

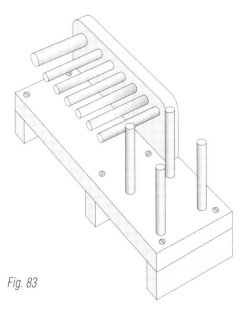

Fig. 83

The point of winding the pirn under tension is that the thread will release smoothly because the yarn cannot "bite" into the cylinder burying itself in a spongy mass of thread. It also allows you to get as full a pirn as possible. The filled pirn should feel hard, not spongy.

There are two motions going on at once while winding pirns. One motion is the overall movement from the base of the pirn toward its tip. See Figure 82. The second movement is a swinging of the yarn, back and forth for a distance of about an inch to an inch and a half. See Figure 84.

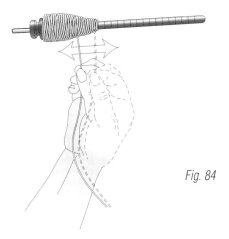

Fig. 84

The shape you are making is a cylinder with a cone-shaped tip. To secure the weft yarn to the pirn at the beginning, start by wrapping the yarn a few times on itself around the flat part of the pirn, not where you will form the base of the cone shape. See Figure 85. Do it before putting it on the winder. The yarn won't "hold" if you start it on the cone-shaped part. Then put the pirn onto the winder. Remember, how you put the pirn on the winder will determine the twist that will be put into the yarn as it leaves the shuttle. See Figures 70 and 71 on page 49.

Hold the weft yarn in your fingers close to the pirn, say, about 2" away from it. Guide the weft onto the pirn by rapidly "swinging" your hand back and forth. The

width of the swing should be about an inch or a bit more. This motion is crucial because it crisscrosses the yarn and keeps the pirn wound tight and held together and is very important because it makes the yarn feed off the pirn smoothly. The turns of yarn will be crisscrossed so they cannot cut into themselves. The yarn will collapse on the pirn if you don't swing continuously. If there is a hollow in the shape of your pirn don't go back to fill it in. Just go on and do a more uniform job with the next pirn.

Begin winding at the base-where there is a built-in cone-shape. Wind on some weft to make a small hump, which immediately begins to establish a cone shape. This initial hump should fill only an inch or so on the shaft of the pirn. Even though the base of your pirn is already shaped like a cone, you'll want to retain this shape and build it up a bit higher right at the beginning.

Remember to swing the yarn back and forth right from the start. At its base, the diameter of your starting cone of yarn should be just as big as the diameter of the finished filled pirn. See Figure 82. This diameter is determined by the size of the shuttle's cavity.

Continue winding and swinging the yarn as you guide it, maintaining the cone shape. This cone shape advances along the pirn as it is being wound with the base of the cone always the same size. As you swing the yarn, do not swing it over the high part of the cone as it advances, but keep working the cone shape down the pirn toward the tip. Don't wind these pirns in sections as the manuals often suggest. Rather,

Fig. 85

keep gradually progressing toward the tip. It's like the stack of dunce caps, or highway cones, on their side I mentioned at the beginning of this section. See Figure 82.

The angle of the cone can control how easily the weft runs off the pirn. A steep angle gives no drag on the weft as it feeds off the cone shape and allows the weft to whip off the pirn freely. See Figure 82. A shallow angle will add a little drag (Figure 86). Certain yarns, because of their nature and/or twist tend to run off the pirns with more than one coil at a time. For those yarns, use a shallow angle on the cone to put a little drag on the yarn, so it won't whip off so easily. Fur inside the shuttle helps, too, as you read in the section on tensioning devices. See Figure 67 on page 47.

The steeper the angle of the cone, the more yarn you can wind onto the pirn. See Figure 82. A

long taper is all right, but you will get less on the pirn, because you won't have a thick cone all the way down to the tip (Figure 86).

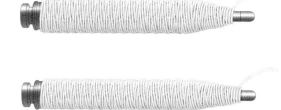

Full cones from Figures 82 and 86 shown for comparison

The completely filled pirn should be quite firm and end in a cone shape about 1/2" from the pirn tip. See Figure 82. You can fill many pirns at one sitting.

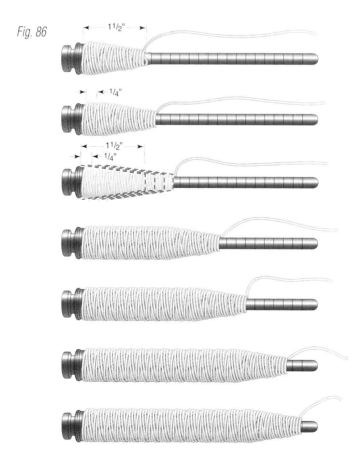

Fig. 86

If you make a pirn so big that it won't fit into the shuttle, it's easy to unwind. Just point the tip of the pirn toward a spool or another pirn and wind the new one from the old one. See Figure 87. If you wind the pirn too loosely, and it slides off the pirn (or you want to save yarn leftover from a pirn), remove the cone of yarn from the pirn. Then pull the yarn from inside the cone. See Figure 88. This unsupported cone of yarn is called a "cop," and unwinds nicely. If the yarn is still on the pirn, take the end of the yarn off from the tip.

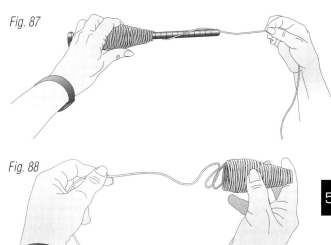

Fig. 87

Fig. 88

59

What is a cop?

A cop is a package of weft yarn that looks similar to a filled pirn except that there is no pirn inside. See Figure 88. They were used in a special kind of end feed shuttle called a cop shuttle. A cop shuttle is an industrial shuttle. It has no spindle in the cavity, but the sides of the cavity are jagged to hold the cop in place. A steel band goes over the whole cop to hold it in the shuttle.

Cops are used for heavier yarns. The inside of the cop is hollow so more yarn can be gotten into the shuttle. I've seen these cops sold as mill ends, and if you know how to unwind them they're easy to use. If not, you get a tangled mess. To unwind, take the yarn from the inside of the cop at the large end-the base, not the tip. See Figure 88. The yarn comes out freely without tangling, and the cop holds its shape.

A cop is wound the same way a pirn is except that it's wound on a spindle, not a pirn. After it is wound (cone shape and all, just like a pirn), it is pulled off the spindle, so there is nothing supporting it in the middle.

In Summary

- *Why use end-delivery shuttles?*
  Speed and superior selvedges.

- *When should they be used?*
  From balanced to warp oriented weaves.

- *When shouldn't they be used?*
  With flat wefts such as ribbon or metallics, for materials like monofilament or metal filaments which kink with the added twist, and for weft faced fabrics.

- *What makes them work?*
  Sett, timing of beat and changing the shed, tensions on warp and weft, and winding the pirns.

- *What is the effect of the angle of the slope on the cone shape?*
  A steep angle gives less drag on the weft as it feeds off the pirn and allows the weft to whip off the pirn freely. A shallow angle will add a little drag. Certain yarns tend to run off the pirn very fast and require the shallower angle.

- *What does fur do?*
  It can prevent the yarn from slipping off the pirn too fast and it can be used to create some tension on the weft.

Revolving-Bobbin Shuttles (Boat Shuttles)

These shuttles must be used for ribbon wefts, any other flat weft, or a weft that suffers when twisted, because they do not put twist in the weft. They can be used for any type of weft yarn. They are slower to use than end-delivery shuttles (Figure 89).

Fig. 89

When you use a shuttle with a revolving bobbin (Figure 90) or quill (Figure 91), the speed with which you throw the shuttle is very important.

Fig. 90

Fig. 91

Too much speed means the shuttle hits your receiving hand with the bobbin still spinning at a good rate, extra yarn flies off, and you have a mess to untangle. Even if extra yarn doesn't jump off the bobbin, it may spin back onto the bobbin in the opposite direction—which causes a jerk on the next throw when the bobbin suddenly changes direction back again (backlash). It takes force or energy to get the shuttle and bobbin moving, and they will tend to continue to move and spin (inertia) unless stopped or slowed down in some way. The heavier the shuttle or the harder the shuttle is thrown, the harder it is to stop the bobbin from spinning.

Too little speed means the shuttle slows to a stop in the middle of the shed. Not an efficient way to weave!

 Perfect speed means the shuttle and its bobbin are both slowing to a stop as they exit the shed. To overcome the inertia problem with boat shuttles, *you must throw the shuttle gently so that it is not moving at a good clip when it reaches the other side with the bobbin spinning rapidly*. If you don't, backlash and overspinning of the bobbin will occur. Your weaving will be slower than with an end-delivery shuttle, but you can achieve the rhythm you need.

Shuttle specifics

Matching the bobbin to the shuttle is important, too. The cavity in the shuttle where the spindle is mounted has either squared-off corners or oval, rounded corners. You need to fit the bobbin to the cavity in your shuttles or the bobbin's flanges will jerk and jam when they hit the corners. Squared-off corners of the cavity are for bobbins with flanges at the ends—similar to those on the ends of spools of sewing thread. (Figure 92). In a

Fig. 92

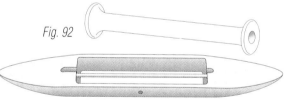

round-cornered cavity, this type of bobbin will hit the side of the cavity and get hung up there and jerk the weft. A bobbin with extensions sticking out from the flanges will keep them from hitting the rounded areas (Figure 93). Bobbins with extensions are readily available and can be used in either type of shuttle. You

Fig. 93

can put a small bead or sewing machine bobbin on the spindle at each end of the bobbin if your bobbins rub at the corners and don't have the extensions. The beads and bobbins do the work of the extensions (Figure 94).

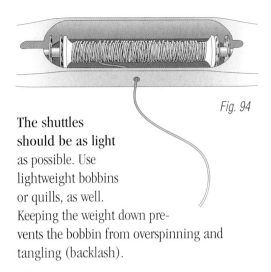

Fig. 94

The shuttles should be as light as possible. Use lightweight bobbins or quills, as well. Keeping the weight down prevents the bobbin from overspinning and tangling (backlash).

The larger and heavier the shuttle is, the more trouble it will give you: the bobbin jerks more to start and unwinds more when stopping. The heavier the shuttle, the more momentum it has. It takes more force to throw it and more force to stop it.

Use this principle about lightness wisely. If you have a heavy yarn it will naturally take a larger (and heavier) shuttle.

Smaller shuttles don't require large sheds—the smaller the shed, the less time it takes to open it and the faster the weaving can go. Smaller shuttles weigh less, as well.

Shuttles that are mostly open on the bottom allow you to stop the bobbin with your fingers underneath the shuttle to control the weft tension as you receive the shuttle from the shed (Figure 95). If the shuttle is closed on the bottom, your only choice is to tension the weft by touching the bobbin on the top of the shuttle (Figure 96).

Fig. 95

The spindle rod should be thin, to keep down friction. However, sometimes you

Fig. 96

need to slow the bobbin down and increase friction by putting a fuzzy yarn on the spindle, inside the bobbin (Figure 97).

The exit opening should be a round hole (rather than a slot) right in the middle of the shuttle. A hole produces the best angle—90 degrees—for the yarn to come off the bobbin (Figure 98).

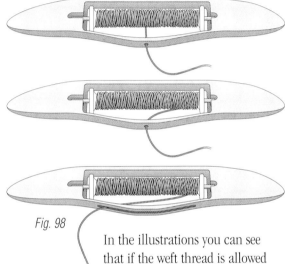

Fig. 97

Fig. 98

In the illustrations you can see that if the weft thread is allowed to come out of a slot, or the bobbin is very long, the angle of the weft as it leaves the bobbin to the exit position is not consistent. The principle is that the optimum angle of the weft leaving the bobbin and going to the exit hole should be 90 degrees as *consistently* as possible.

A shuttle with a bulge on the weaver's side, and an exit hole, combine to produce the optimum angle for the weft.

The exit hole should face the weaver (just like end-delivery shuttles). The bobbin should travel as little as possible from side-to-side. That is, you don't want the bobbin to travel on the spindle much inside the shuttle because the velocity of the bobbin is the lowest in the middle. Having an exit hole rather than a slot and putting beads on each end of the bobbin

62

prevents the side-to-side movement, and keeps the bobbin in the center of the spindle.

How to throw the shuttle

To overcome the problem of inertia which causes backlash follow these guidelines.

1. Don't try to weave fast.
2. Throw the shuttle gently. If the shuttle is thrown harder than necessary it comes into the receiving hand with the bobbin still spinning: extra yarn is unwound, creating a snarl with backlash. Throw the shuttle with just enough force to carry it across. The shuttle and its bobbin both slow to a stop as they reach the other side.
3. As you catch the shuttle, put your thumb or a finger on the bobbin to stop it from continuing to spin to prevent backlash. If your shuttle is open on its bottom, your fingers can touch the bobbin easily (Figures 97 and 98).

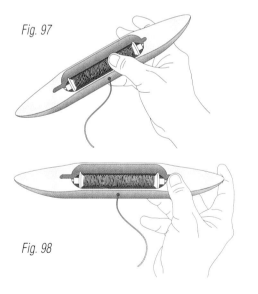

Fig. 97

Fig. 98

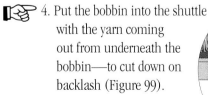

4. Put the bobbin into the shuttle with the yarn coming out from underneath the bobbin—to cut down on backlash (Figure 99).

Fig. 99

5. Fur in the cavity of the shuttle can help slow the bobbin down and reduce backlash.
6. Remember, the exit hole should be on the side of the shuttle facing you.

Add these techniques to the weaving motions given in the chapter on weaving.

I've seen professional weavers draw out a length of weft from the shuttle before entering it into the shed to prevent the weft from being too tight in the shed and cutting in at the selvedge. I teach my students not to do this, but it might be a good idea for certain (wide) warps. Stopping the bobbin with your thumb or a finger also takes time and energy. These motions aren't necessary with end-delivery shuttles.

Winding the bobbins

How the thread comes off the bobbin creates the angle for the slack in the shed and makes the selvedges even. You want to wind bobbins for boat shuttles so that the bobbin rotates at as constant a speed as possible. Remember, a sudden change in speed causes backlash, and if the shuttle stops with a jerk because the yarn has buried itself in the bobbin, the selvedge threads are stressed and weakened or broken.

Read about bobbin winders on page 71.

Start winding bobbins (and pirns) by winding a turn or two by hand before you begin the main winding so that, when the last of the yarn unwinds, there is no sudden jerk on the bobbin.

Wind the bobbins tight. Read how to do it using a tension box on page 74. The tightly wound bobbin makes the tension on the weft change more gradually during weaving, because the change in the bobbin's diameter occurs more slowly. There is less tension on the weft when the bobbin is full and more as the bobbin unwinds because more revolutions are required to get the same length of weft.

The weft should lie easily in the shed without being under tension. This ease depends on the way the shuttle is thrown and drawn out of the shed and how well the bobbin is wound. Uneven weft tension causes poor selvedges, puckers, streaks, etc. Some of these problems won't show up until the cloth is off the loom and finished.

By winding the bobbins tightly, the outer layers of threads are prevented from cutting down into the under layers, and you can get more yarn on them. However, don't fill the bobbins too full—they must not touch the walls of the shuttle cavity for obvious reasons.

How you wind depends on whether you use bobbins with flanges, or quills of paper, cardboard, or light wood. Either of these can be used with equal success on warps of up to 36 inches or so. On wider warps, however, the longer traveling distance means more yarn has to be unwound with every throw. Bobbins with flanges have larger capacities, which is more efficient on wider warps.

Quills

A quill is simply a tube. It can be made of paper, cardboard, or wood. First, I'll tell you how to make a paper quill, and then I'll explain the important things to know about winding them to reduce backlash and prevent the weft from spilling over the ends and tangling.

I use ordinary binder paper and start by folding it into quarters. The folding lets me cut the paper for 4 quills at once. I cut an oval as big as it can be on the folded binder paper. The ovals don't have to be perfectly shaped (Figure 100). Starting with one of the short ends of one of the paper ovals, begin winding it up on the winder's spindle, as tight as you can, to start the tube. Just before the paper is completely wound into a tube, take the end of the weft thread and tuck it into the paper as the last few rounds are made (Figure 101). then, continue winding tightly so the yarn

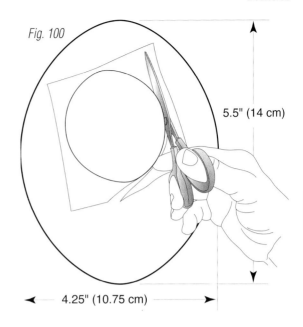

Fig. 100

5.5" (14 cm)

4.25" (10.75 cm)

holds the quill's tube shape (Figure 102). For good selvedges and to reduce backlash, the way you shape the weft yarn on the quill is crucial. The length of the quills is important, too. They should never be so long that they almost fill the shuttle cavity. Make them no more than 2/3 of the length of the cavity, so they will unreel smoothly and not get hung up on the ends of the cavity and jerk the thread. The size of the paper oval at its mid-section is the length the quill will be.

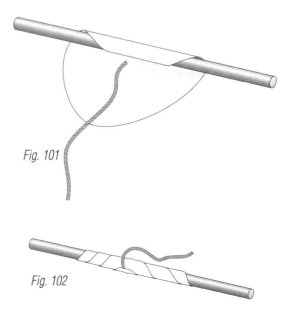

Fig. 101

Fig. 102

First, ***don't*** make lumps on either end as you may have seen recommended (Figure 103).

Fig. 103

The lumps cause the quill to spin too fast, and we know sudden changes in speed of the bobbin causes backlash. Also, a lump forces the bobbin to hit one side of the shuttle cavity and keeps it there until the lump is unwound. If the bobbin is forced to one side it can bind there, hanging up against the end of the shuttle cavity and causing a serious jerk in the weft, which cuts into the selvedge and/or prevents the shuttle from making a complete trip leaving it somewhere in the middle of the shed.

 Instead, wind the layers ***flat***. Make each layer shorter than the previous one. The first or bottom layer should ***only*** extend to within 1/2" of the ends of the quill to keep the yarn from falling off at the edges. The final layers will be short and in the middle, making a cigar or football shape. While winding the layers, crisscross diagonally each successive layer by moving the hand holding the yarn back and forth across the quill (Figure 104). Keep the spirals compact—like a slinky that is very slightly stretched (Figure 105). Too much stretch in the spiral will increase the lateral movement of the quill in the shuttle, which can make the quill jerk or get hung up. Too

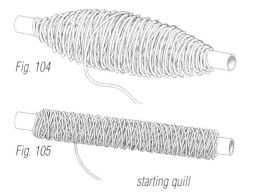

Fig. 104

Fig. 105

starting quill

little stretch in the spiral, and you won't get stable edges for the quill, and the yarn could cut down into previous layers. Remember never to wind yarn closer to the ends of the quill than 1/2". If you do, you can be assured the yarn will slip off the ends and make huge tangles. See Figures 106.

Fig. 106

 Think of a commercially-wound spool of yarn. It has no flanges or other supports except the center tube, just like a quill, yet the yarn doesn't spill over and tangle. The secret: it's wound under very firm tension (the package is hard, not even remotely spongy). Tight quills and bobbins unreel smoothly when they are as full as possible. The criss-crossing helps, too.

Bobbins with flanges

The familiar plastic or wooden bobbin that has a flange on each end should also be wound under firm tension. The well-filled bobbin should be very hard, just like a quill. You don't need to crisscross the layers as much as with quills, because the flanges hold the thread at the edges. By winding on like a spool of sewing thread (or a slinky almost at rest), you'll be able to get more yarn on each bobbin for smoother weaving and less stopping during weaving. Generally, you can get more thread on a bobbin with a flange than on a quill, because you don't need to shorten the winding length every layer—you can wind yarn the full length of the bobbin—from flange to flange.

 If you don't wind your bobbins under tension, then you must make wide crisscrosses—that is, like a slinky that is stretched out—to prevent the outer layers from biting down into lower layers.

Problem yarns

Jumpy or wiry yarns

For really jumpy or wiry yarns, fasten a small piece of fuzzy yarn inside the shuttle and thread it out through the exit hole to slow down the discharge of weft. You can also slow down the rate at which the bobbin turns by winding some masking tape around the spindle. Read more about slowing down the bobbin below.

Slippery yarns

Fig. 107

To keep slippery yarns such as rayon from sliding off cones, put the cone in a sock. I use a "knee-high stocking" so I can see the yarn inside. The sock keeps the yarns from falling down on the cone and tangling underneath it (Figure 107). Read about other ways to handle slippery yarns in the Troubleshooting chapter.

Hairy yarns

Hairy weft yarns such as mohair and brushed wool tend to get caught on the shaft of a boat shuttle or to build up fuzzy fibers on the bobbin itself preventing the yarn from unreeling. It really slows you down if every so often you have to stop and cut away the hairs to free the bobbin.

A ski shuttle can be used—not a regular stick shuttle—to deal with these yarns. With a stick shuttle the mohair yarn would touch the warp every time you put it through the shed and would fuzz up. With a ski shuttle, the yarn doesn't touch the warp. It is slower to use than a boat shuttle, but faster than stopping to free up the bobbin frequently. (See Figures 109 and 110 in the sidebar on page 66.)

To keep the yarn from fuzzing up in the first place, try this method devised by one of Margaret Gaynes' students. Fold an index card into a flattened cone with a small opening at the tip (Figure 108). Feed the hairy yarn through this opening and hold it firmly in

Fig. 108

the folded index card to smooth the hairs on the yarn while winding the bobbin. Then the hairs don't get caught on each other. She recommends using a boat shuttle with the bobbin not filled to its maximum.[11]

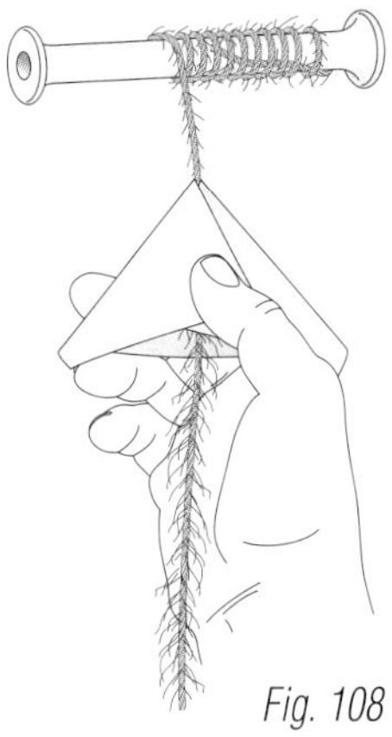

If you have to ***unweave*** mohair wefts, take care. Don't bring the beater forward because the fuzz left in the shed will be beaten in and appear as a line across the cloth. Pull out the weft, and clear the shed by hand. Be careful as you pull the wefts out because they tend to catch on some warps making them fuzzier, too, making the problem with fuzz worse. If you have more than a few shots to remove, it's often easier and a better idea to cut the weft first.[12] Read about unweaving on page 133.

Summary: Ways to slow down the bobbin's speed

- Add some drag by touching the bobbin with your thumb or a finger as the shuttle exits the shed.

- Put a bit of fur or fake fur inside the bobbin cavity—especially when using slippery yarns.

- Put a bead, or sewing machine bobbin, on the spindle at each end of the bobbin. They keep the bobbin in the center, where the velocity is lowest.

- Put a piece of fuzzy yarn or a bit of tissue paper on the spindle, under the bobbin, to slow its speed.

- Fasten a small piece of fuzzy yarn inside the shuttle and thread it out through the exit hole to slow down the discharge of weft.

- Wrap masking tape on the spindle to create extra friction between the bobbin and the spindle.

[11] Gaynes, Margaret, "Weaving with Sticky Yarns," *Handwoven Magazine*, Jan/Feb 1990, p. 49.
[12] Ibid.

Stick, ski, and rug shuttles

These shuttles have no bobbins, and the weft yarn is wound directly onto them. They are slow to use, but necessary for very heavy weft yarns or rags.

Stick shuttles are the simplest—just a thin flat stick with notches in the ends. They need to be smooth so they don't snag in the shed. They can be homemade or purchased. Don't use ordinary cardboard—the pressure of the yarn on the shuttle makes it bend. When it isn't flat anymore, it won't go through the shed. Illustration board or mat board works well. You want the shuttle to be thin but sturdy enough to hold the yarn.

The length of the stick shuttle you use is determined by the width of the warp. You want the shuttle to be a couple of inches longer than the warp width to make unwinding them easier.

Unwind just enough yarn for one weft by turning the shuttle end-for-end. You'll get a rhythm and the right "flick" to undo the yarn, soon. You can also tension the weft at the selvedge by tugging slightly on the weft yarn as you draw the shuttle out from the shed. If you unwind too much, the process will be very awkward. If you unwind too little, you will be forced to reach into the shed with your hand to retrieve the shuttle, which stretches the warp yarns, slows you down, and breaks your rhythm.

You want to get as much yarn onto the shuttle as possible but not so much it won't pass through the shed. First, wind the yarn on the edges, not across the flat part of the shuttle. There are two edges; wind figure-eights of yarn on one edge until it's full, and then on the other. You will still have some room to wind yarn onto the flat part in the middle. See Figure 109.

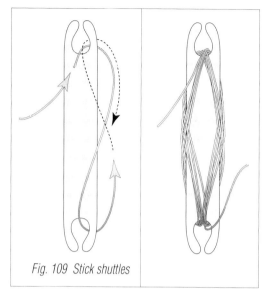

Fig. 109 Stick shuttles

Ski shuttles are a variation of the stick shuttle. The bottom of the shuttle looks like a ski—flat with the tips curved upward. On the top are two prongs around which the weft is wound. The advantage of this type of shuttle is that it will slide cleanly along the bottom of the shed. Another advantage is that it can hold a lot of thick yarn or rags.

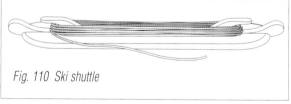

Fig. 110 Ski shuttle

Rug shuttles are another variation, which can hold a large amount of rag or heavy wefts (Figure 111).

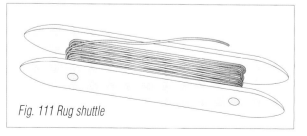

Fig. 111 Rug shuttle

Doubling wefts on prins or bobbins

Have you ever wanted to combine two or more yarns as one weft? Have you discovered it doesn't work very well because, no matter what you've tried, one yarn always loops up so they don't lie flat together in the shed? The answer is: use a doubling stand to double up weft yarns so they come out of the shuttle together and evenly.

Doubling stands

☞ *Warning!! Do not double warp yarns* because the upper and lower yarns will be of different tensions when they leave the doubling stand. It isn't a problem with weft yarns.

Doubling stands can be homemade or purchased. Figure 112 shows a commercially made stand. (Note the optional tension box for winding tight weft packages.)One or more yarns are put on vertical posts with the yarn ☞ guided exactly up from the centers of the posts, just like an ordinary vertical creel. Read more about creels on page 76.

Above these yarns is a single cone or spool of yarn supported by a vertical tube instead of a post. The yarns below are guided up through their respective thread guides and then up through the tube and the center of the extra cone. Then, the lower yarns plus the upper one are taken together up through a guide above the center of the top cone. You can see what happens: The yarn from the upper cone encircles the yarns coming up through its center. This encirclement

keeps all the yarns together without any of them looping up during weaving (Figure 113). To guide the bottom threads up through the cone on top, fashion a long hook from a coat hanger or use a long heddle.

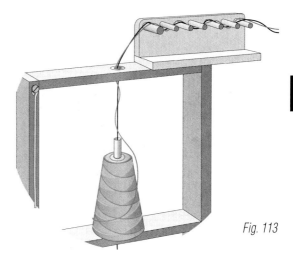

Fig. 113

67

The three keys to keep in mind when setting up a doubling "situation" or in making a homemade stand are:

1. The thread guides for the lower spools **must** be exactly over the center of the pins or dowels that hold the spools or cones.
2. There must be enough space between the tops of all the packages and their thread guides to allow the yarn to whip off the packages freely.
3. The top cone or spool must have a way for the lower yarns to pass up through its center.

A tube to hold the top cone is the hardest thing to find—try hobby shops. You could use a short length of copper tubing with the sharp ends sanded. However, there are many other ways to accomplish the job. I've seen one cone underneath an upside-down "milk crate" with another cone sitting on top and the thread from below coming up a hole in the crate and through the top cone. There are many ways you might make (or rig)a doubling "stand"

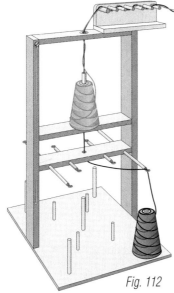

Fig. 112

yourself. Figure 114 shows a commercially made stand with 5 positions on the lower level. There will always be only one yarn on top—that's the one that spirals around the others—no matter how many there are below.

You can design your own wefts using this doubling technique.

Twist is a consideration when doubling up yarns because the yarns come off the tops of the packages. You can turn a spool end-for end to change the direction of the twist of the yarn as it comes off the spool. You can also rewind a cone of

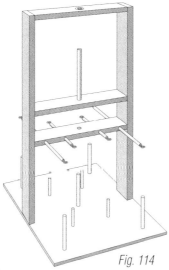

Fig. 114

yarn onto an empty cone to reverse its twist as it comes off the top of the new cone (or spool). Read about twist and end-delivery packages in the sidebar on page 50. See how to wind cones on page 73.

There are twist considerations both for the bottom and the top layers. If you are doubling two dissimilar yarns of opposite twists, it is usually better to soften (subtract twist) the thicker and harden (add twist) the thinner yarn[13]. The direction of the twist can be used to create interesting effects in your weft yarns or in your weaving. Useful as these guidelines are, in my experience, I've never needed to use them. I have just put the cones and spools on the doubling stand and used what happened. Actually, not much twist is added or taken away, so unless the yarn is very loosely or very highly twisted, you needn't consider it. If your yarn kinks up, it is a sign that it is highly twisted, and you are adding more

twist—better to turn the spool upside down and take out a little twist—the kinks will make the yarn difficult to use. On the other hand, if the yarn seems to come apart, you should add twist to strengthen it. See the sidebar on page 50 for information about how to add and subtract twist.

Winding Equipment

Swifts

A swift is a piece of equipment that helps you unwind skeins. The wooden ones are often called umbrella swifts (Figure 115). They are good for unwinding skeins, but not for winding or making skeins. A metal skein winder is best for making skeins because all of the rounds of yarn in the skein will be exactly the

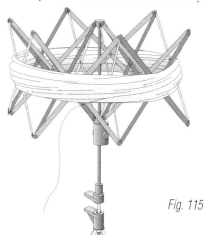

Fig. 115

same length unlike those on umbrella swifts. An umbrella swift's circumference changes because of its shape. The metal skein winder can be used to unwind as well as wind. Both of these are rather expensive, but very time saving. (Figure 116).

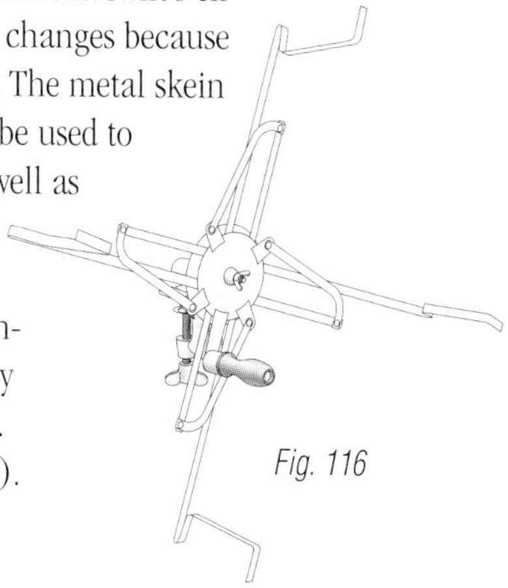

Fig. 116

---

[13]Tovey, John, *The Technique of Weaving*, B.T. Batsford Ltd., London, 1965, p. 71.

Anything that makes skeins with the yarns all the same length can be used, such as a yarn blocker that spinners use, or a warping board.

☞ Swifts and skein winders work best if the axle is horizontal, not vertical as you might expect.

Fig. 117

The yarn comes off more smoothly that way.

A squirrel cage swift looks nice in your studio, but doesn't work as smoothly as those above. It is a stand that has two barrels (cages) one on top of the stand and one that slides up the post of the stand to adjust to the size of the skein. The cages hold the skein open while you wind off the yarn (Figure 117).

Unwinding skeins

A skein is a mass of yarn in a large ring (Figure 118).

Fig. 118

You must open skeins carefully so the yarn doesn't tangle as it's being wound off the swift. If the skein is twisted (Figure 119) carefully untwist it. Even though it might not look carefully wound, it is. See the ties around the yarn? There usually are two or three ties that encircle the skein, often in a figure-8 (Figure 120). Another tie or two hold the beginning and the end of the yarn itself. Usually, there is one tie for this purpose with the two ends of yarn tied together and also encircling the skein itself.

Fig. 119

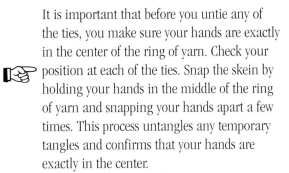

Fig. 120

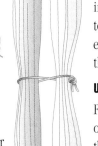

It is important that before you untie any of the ties, you make sure your hands are exactly in the center of the ring of yarn. Check your ☞ position at each of the ties. Snap the skein by holding your hands in the middle of the ring of yarn and snapping your hands apart a few times. This process untangles any temporary tangles and confirms that your hands are exactly in the center.

Before untying anything, put the skein on the swift, a friend's hands, a chair back or whatever you are using to hold the skein open while you wind off the yarn. Check again that you have found the exact center of the skein. Untie the figure-8 ties first and the ends of the yarns last. Be sure to keep track of the ends! One end will likely be on the outside of the skein and is the one to use to start unwinding. You might have to twist the skein some to get this end on the outside. I tuck the end I don't want to use into the swift and loosely tie it to a spoke so that it doesn't tangle while I'm unwinding the other end.

☞ Never take the yarn over and under other yarns in the skein—never! Always take the yarn as it comes—that way the skein can unwind smoothly. If you come to a tangle, it's probably just a temporary snag. Snap the skein or strum it, and you'll find that the yarn isn't really tangled and comes off smoothly again. If you feel you must take the yarn over and under another thread because of a real tangle, remember that you'll have to do that over and under process throughout the unwinding. It will be annoying, but may need to be done if you haven't found the exact center of the skein before untying the ties.

Unwinding fine yarns

Fine yarns need some special attention or they will break as you pull them off the swift. Wind the yarn onto a spool, pirn, or bobbin—not a ball, and use a hand-operated bobbin winder—not an electric one. The electric winder goes too fast, and the force of its pull snaps the thread. I had a skein that was so fragile that I wound the yarn from one swift onto another swift with a smaller diameter. Then, I wound it from the second swift onto the spools. This method reduced the force on the yarns needed to take it from the original skein. The new skein's yarns were looser so it was easier to unwind. I also used the swifts with their axles in the vertical position rather than the normal horizontal position. You may need to get the skein started by winding it by hand onto a spool or bobbin. Patience is important because it's a slow process requiring great care.

Ball winders

These are usually made of plastic. Balls are wound around the winder's core, by hand, with a crank. The resulting package isn't ball-shaped, or round. It forms a flat cylinder, wider than it is high (Figures 121 and 122).

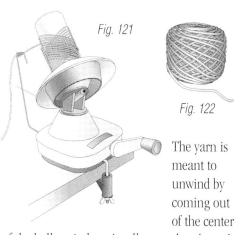

Fig. 121

Fig. 122

The yarn is meant to unwind by coming out of the center of the ball, so it doesn't roll around and tangle. However, these balls aren't very sturdy, and near the end (the outside) the yarn often tangles a bit because the ball collapses on itself.

When yarn comes out of the ball vertically, as it does when it comes out of the center of the ball, it has added a twist just as though it were coming off the end of a pirn or spool. See side-bar on page 50. Turn the ball over to reverse the twist direction if you find that the yarn

kinks on itself. If you unwind the ball starting at the outside of the ball, the amount of twist being added (or subtracted) increases as the circumference of the package gets smaller and smaller. However, if you begin to unwind a ball from the center of the ball where the circumference is small, you'll be putting in the most twist at the beginning. It will gradually get less and less as the circumference of the inside of the ball gets bigger as it is unwound, because one twist is added for each time the yarn traverses the circumference of the ball, making more twists per inch where the circumference is small—in the center. These situations aren't common, but may occur with over-twisted or single ply yarns. Irregularities might not show up until after the cloth has been finished. You

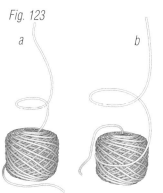

Fig. 123

a   b

will probably notice the problem when you are winding bobbins, etc. from the ball (Figures 123a and b).

If you have this problem of increasing or diminishing twist as you unwind balls of yarn, make the balls by hand and let them roll around on the floor as you wind. Then any twist will work itself out before it gets to the winder.

Fig. 124

For spools or cones, taking the yarn off the side of the package won't change the twist at all. Remember, however, that yarns come off smoother and faster if taken off the end of a package (Figure 124).Because it is less convenient, side delivery is used where there are extreme problems. By putting a cone on a lazy Susan, you can take yarn off from the side of a cone (Figure 125).

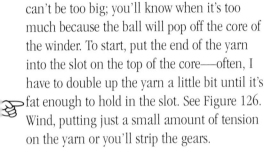

Fig. 125

Balls of yarn are usually made on the winder directly from a skein on a swift. They can't be too big; you'll know when it's too much because the ball will pop off the core of the winder. To start, put the end of the yarn into the slot on the top of the core—often, I have to double up the yarn a little bit until it's fat enough to hold in the slot. See Figure 126. Wind, putting just a small amount of tension on the yarn or you'll strip the gears.

Fig. 126

The gears are often not very sturdy and can wear out rather quickly.

Bobbin winders are usually more substantial than ball winders, but if ball winders aren't abused, they are very helpful in the studio because skeins must always be made into useable packages.

Slippery yarns

Slippery silk or rayon yarns can be wound on a ball winder, but they tend to slip off the ball onto the core of the winder and into the gears. A paper towel tube slipped onto the core can help somewhat with this problem. If the silk slips off, at least it goes onto the tube rather than into the gears. It would be better to wind these yarns onto spools with flanges.

Bobbin winders

It seems I'm always winding bobbins, pirns, or spools, so I consider a bobbin winder to be a major piece of equipment for all weavers. Bobbin winders are a big investment; so choose what is best for you and your budget. There are basically two types, single-ended and double-ended. The double-ended winders support the pirn, bobbin or spool on both ends with conical-shaped pieces that fit into the center holes of the spool. There is no long spindle for the bobbin. See Figure 127. Single-ended winders have a spindle, with only one end of it supported. See Figure 128.

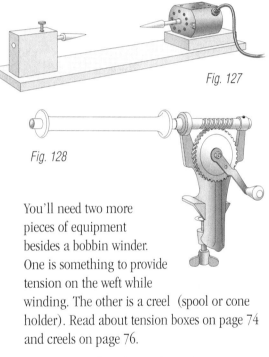

Fig. 127

Fig. 128

You'll need two more pieces of equipment besides a bobbin winder. One is something to provide tension on the weft while winding. The other is a creel (spool or cone holder). Read about tension boxes on page 74 and creels on page 76.

Most weavers don't know about the existence of a doubling stand. Read about this very helpful tool on page 67.

Electric bobbin winders

Electric winders are expensive, but they are ideal if you are weaving a lot because they work fast. A double-ended electric bobbin winder is best for winding spools and pirns, so your hand can be guiding the thread rather than turning a crank. See Figure 127. They

71

work wonderfully for bobbins, as well, but you can easily get by with a hand-operated winder for them. It will just take a bit longer to wind each bobbin.

Most electric winders have a sewing machine motor and a variable speed pedal. Often, they go too fast and are hard to control. One solution is to plug the electric winder into an outlet controlled by a rheostat (dimmer switch). Then, you can reduce the winding speed overall and still fine-tune the speed with the foot pedal. Hardware stores carry dimmer switch boxes with electrical outlets built in (Figure 129).

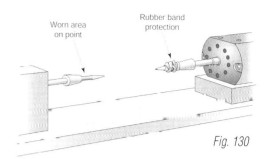

Worn area on point

Rubber band protection

Fig. 130

Hand-operated bobbin winders

There are winders operated by a crank with a spindle attached to the winding mechanism (single-ended), and there are double-ended winders—that is, the spindle is supported at each end (Figures 131 and 132).

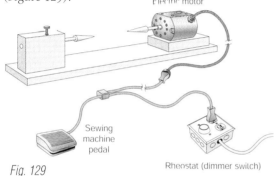

Electric motor

Sewing machine pedal

Fig. 129

Rheostat (dimmer switch)

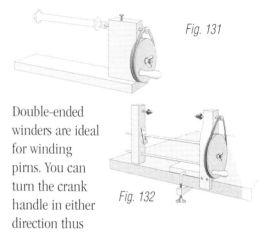

Fig. 131

Fig. 132

A good homemade bobbin winder is simply a motor firmly screwed to a board and a spindle or double-ended set-up to hold the bobbins or pirns. Any size motor is fine, even a large one. The important thing is that it gives you 1800 RPM, the perfect speed for winding (a 1/4 horsepower induction motor is ideal). You don't want a lot of speed. Adjust the motor speed, so you can just slide the bobbin onto the spindle while it's running, and so that if there is a jam, you can slip the bobbin off the spindle. That way the thread won't be drawn into the winder itself.

Sometimes, with a lot of use, the conical points that support the pirns show wear, with grooves near the tips. Then, the pirns won't hold firmly for winding. To prevent this wear, use rubber bands on the tips where the pirn contacts them (Figure 130).

Double-ended winders are ideal for winding pirns. You can turn the crank handle in either direction thus winding the pirn in the S or Z direction. Watch that you crank all the bobbins for a project in the same direction or there may be noticeable changes in the look of the cloth where the twist direction was changed. It is especially important to remember if more than one person is weaving the same cloth. Read more about S & Z beginning on page 49.

A regular, single-ended, hand-operated winder is ideal for winding bobbins for boat shuttles, and they are less expensive than the double-ended. The Swedish metal winders (Figure 128) have been used traditionally, but wooden ones are now available and may be less expensive (Figure 133). If the

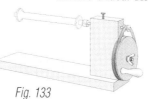

Fig. 133

spindle is too small to hold the pirn or bobbin, shim the bobbin onto the spindle with a soft piece of yarn or wind masking tape around it to increase the diameter (Figure 134). Another way to make the spindle fatter is to put shrink tubing on it and heat the tubing with a hair dryer. The tube will shrink up snugly on the spindle. When you don't want the tubing anymore, just cut it off.

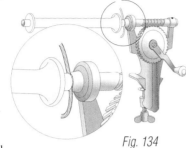

Fig. 134

Double-ended winders are needed for winding spools and pirns, because both ends of the spools and pirns need to be supported. You can get away with winding pirns on single-ended winders with some practice and patience. You may need to put something like tape on the spindle to hold the pirn firmly.

"Make-do" winders

People have modified other tools for winding bobbins. Use them with extreme caution and only if you are sure you can control the speed and wind safely at the same time.

Electric hand mixers can work if you put a chopstick into one of the openings made for the beaters. Make sure the chopstick fits in firmly. Note that the two beaters rotate in different directions, so you can choose which opening works best for the yarn you're using. One hole will turn the chopstick-spindle in the S direction and the other, in the Z direction. Hold the beater in one hand and guide the yarn with the other. Both pirns and bobbins can be wound if they fit firmly on the spindle (Figure 135). Read more about S & Z beginning on page 49.

Fig. 135

Electric hand drills can be used in a similar manner. Use a chopstick for the spindle and secure it in the opening where a drill bit is meant to go. Practice and make sure you can make the drill go slowly enough that you can control your winding. Also, be sure the pirn or bobbin fits onto the spindle firmly. One hand holds the drill pointing away from you, and the other hand guides the thread, or hold the drill in a vice (Figures 136a and b).

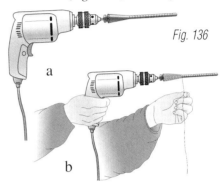

Fig. 136

a

b

Cone winders

Cones unwind more smoothly than spools. There are commercially made cone winders, both electric and hand-operated, that guide the thread in the special way needed to wind the cone shape.

You can adapt your double-ended winder to wind cones. First, get the wooden base from a large roll of butcher paper. Ask your butcher—they throw them away. It is about 2" high, and the diameter at the bottom is about 3". The top of this cone-shaped piece has a diameter just slightly less than its base, and there is a hole through its center (Figure 137).

Fig. 137 Wooden end of paper roll

Fit your cone on this base and put the base onto one pointed end of the winder. The other pointed end fits into the top of your empty cone. Note that if the holes in your cones are too big at the top to fit firmly against the winder's pointed tip, you will need to put another empty cone with a smaller hole on its top inside the first cone (Figure 138a). That smaller hole at the tip of the inside cone should fit onto the winder's point. Cardboard cones usually have small openings at the tip (Figure 138b). Plastic ones often have larger openings (Figure 138c).

Fig. 138

a   b   c

If you use the two cones in this way (Figure 139), wind only onto the plastic cone, so you can use the cardboard cone over and over as a base (Figure 140).

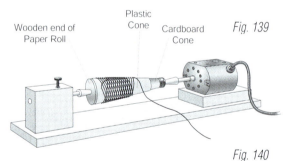

Wooden end of Paper Roll   Plastic Cone   Cardboard Cone   Fig. 139

How to wind cones

Peter Collingwood explains the special way to wind cones: "Begin by passing the yarn once round (in the direction the cone is going to turn), so that it is caught under the part coming from the hank [skein] (Figure 141). Then as soon as the cone starts to revolve, move the hand that is guiding the yarn quickly backwards and forwards, so that the yarn does not build up in any one place. This is to ensure that the first few turns of yarn grip the cone securely. Thereafter the guiding hand can move more slowly.

Fig. 141

"Never bring the yarn nearer than 1 inch from the top of the cone and nearer than 1/4 inch from the bottom of the cone. These furthest extremes of the yarns traverse should be reached almost as soon as winding begins, and each succeeding traverse should be shorter. The pear-shaped outline is a good one to aim at. Do not try to save time by overfilling cones."[15] See Figure 140.

Pirn winders

Industry manufactures machines that wind pirns perfectly, many at a time. They are costly. Olympic Pirn Winder Company makes a single pirn winder for handweavers. It automatically winds the pirns perfectly so you can spend more time at the loom. See the list of sources on page 247.

Fig. 140

Tension boxes

You want all pirns, bobbins, and spools to be wound tight, tight, tight. This tightness prevents the outer layers from biting down into the lower layers, puts the maximum amount of yarn on the package, and makes them unreel smoothly. However, you don't want to burn your hands in the process. Using a regular tension box or something similar supplies the tension, so your hands don't get burned.

---

[15]Collingwood, p. 73.

Tension boxes can look very different from one another, but they all have a series of dowels—sometimes 3 and sometimes more—over and under which you thread the yarn (Figure 142). This threading puts drag (tension) on the yarn. If there are not enough pegs, you can always wrap the yarn around one of the existing pegs a second time (Figure 143). Some of the 3-dowel models have an adjustable middle peg for creating the amount of tension required.

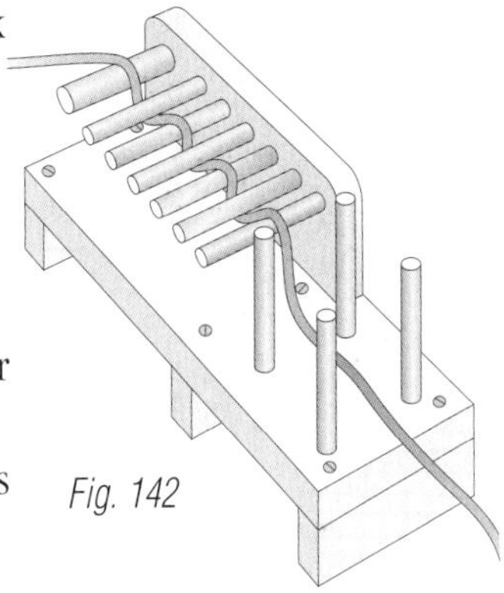

Fig. 142

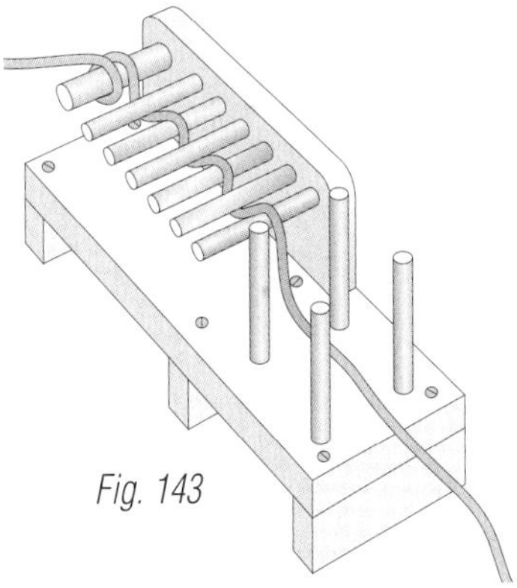

Fig. 143

A tension box, invented by Crystal Cunningham, can be made of PVC parts found in the plumbing section of a hardware store. The one in Figure 144 is made of 4 tubes, 3 elbows, and a central part shaped like a "T" with an opening in its top. The path of the yarn goes under an outside tube, then over the top tube, back under the middle tube on the bottom and finally over the tube on the other side.

If you don't have a tension box, you can use your warping board, a spindle-backed chair, or the posts of the lazy Kate located on your spinning wheel. What you need is a series of dowels or pegs that the thread can alternately go over and under to put tension or drag on the weft as you wind.

Some people use a leather glove, piece of leather, or a piece of paper to protect their fingers while creating tension on the weft thread. I prefer just to guide the thread with my fingers and depend on the tension box for tension.

75

Placement of the tension box

The PVC version mentioned above had the tension box clamped to a board, but I prefer it to be portable because I use it in so many different situations. The yarn needs to come from the creel and be guided to go over and under the pegs. I sometimes rig a guide for the yarn using a C-clamp, or reed, or the guide from the creel, or a doubling stand. If your yarn is to come off the top of the spool or cone, there needs to be enough space between the cone and the guide that the yarn can whip off the cone freely. In the illustration the cone is on the floor, the yarn is guided up over the C-clamp then taken to the tension box. The yarn exiting the tension box goes to the bobbin or spool to be wound on your winder (Figure 145).

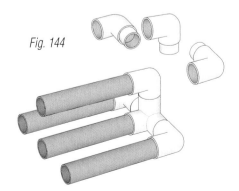

Fig. 144

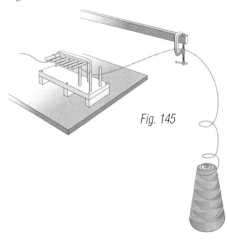

Fig. 145

Creels

You need something to hold the ball, spool, or cone of yarn while you're winding. A coffee can or small bucket can sometimes work, but a yarn holder or creel is less cumbersome, and the yarn comes off more smoothly without jerks.

Vertical creels

Basically, the yarn comes off faster and without jerks if it comes off the top of a cone, or the end of a spool. You need to set up something so the cones and spools sit upright. See Figure 146. You might be able just to set the spools or cones on the floor without using a creel. To keep them from toppling over and rolling away, be sure that you take the yarn straight up from the center of the spool or cone.

It is important for vertical creels to have enough space above the yarn package so the yarn can whip freely off the cone. That is to say, the thread guide

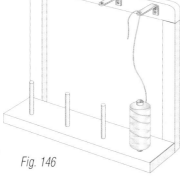

Fig. 146

above the cone needs to be a few inches away from the top of the package. Very large packages require more room. Be sure the thread guide is directly over the pin holding the package. If it isn't directly centered above the pin the yarn won't come off freely. Curtain rings or screw eyes can be used as thread guides.

 A doubling stand (shown in Figure 144 on page 68) can be an excellent creel or yarn holder. Read more about this enormously useful tool on page 67.

A vertical creel can be as simple as a reed supported by two chairs. (Figure 147.)

An end-delivery shuttle or a boat shuttle placed on the floor can be used as a yarn holder. Put a filled pirn on the spindle with the spindle pointing vertically up from the floor. Hold the shuttle down with your foot, and the yarn feeds off fast and smooth.

Horizontal creels

If your creel has horizontal rods to hold spools of yarn, you need to start and stop unwinding the spools slowly to keep the yarn from jumping off the spools and tangling. Read about this inertia problem in the section on boat shuttles on page 60. A lazy Kate from your spinning wheel can be used as a creel.

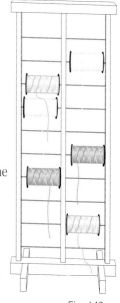 Put the spools on the creel so the yarns all come off the bottom of the spools to minimize backlash and to keep the threads from tangling on one another (Figure 148).

A knitting needle poked through holes in the sides of a shoe box works well for a horizontal creel. In a pinch, I put a spool or bobbin on a dowel or pencil and hold it in one hand near the winder.

Balls can be kept from rolling away and tangling by putting them in bowls or coffee cans. You can use a plastic gallon jug to

Fig. 148

make a container for controlling balls. Cut a large hole in the side of the jug, and leave the original top hole intact. Put the ball or spool of yarn in through the new opening and bring the yarn through the original top hole.

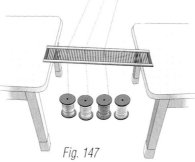

Fig. 147

76

3 *Selvedges*

Selvedges are the edges of the cloth where the wefts turn around the outside warp threads. See Figure 148. In commercial fabric, they are usually firmly woven. (However, many commercially woven fabrics today don't have selvedges because they are woven on shuttle-less power looms, so there are just raw edges at the sides of the cloth.) Handwoven edges that look nice are even, without notches or loops or broken warp threads. The warp and weft, the loom, yarns and shuttles work together with you to make good selvedges.

Fig. 148

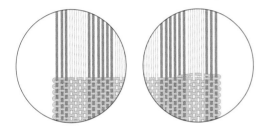

Draw-in is normal and natural

Woven cloth is narrower than the width the warp is in the reed. This narrowing is called draw-in. During the normal weaving of fabrics, even with the best techniques, the cloth will draw in. However, there are big selvedge problems if the cloth narrows in too much.

If the cloth draws in too much, the selvedges will be abraded by the reed and break. Look at the edges of the warp at the fell. Is the reed stretching out the warps way beyond the width of the cloth? If so, can you see why the reed is abrading and breaking the selvedges? See Figure 149.

To understand why the cloth draws in and how to control it so the selvedge threads don't break, you need to

understand how the warps and wefts bend in the cloth.

 Stop now, and be sure you understand the information in the sidebar, "How Warps and Wefts Bend," on page 78.

Fig. 149

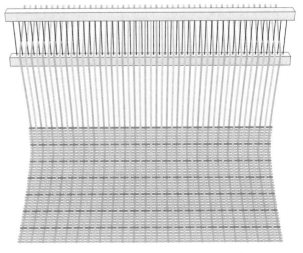

How warps and wefts bend

Yarns in woven textiles bend. In some cases, both the warp and weft curve; in others, just the wefts, as in weft-faced fabrics and rugs, or only the warps, as in warp-faced fabrics and rugs.

To avoid too much draw-in when you ask the wefts to bend a lot, you must put in extra weft in each shed, because the extra bending takes up more weft. You can put in the extra weft by bubbling or making a big diagonal with the weft. You can use a temple to keep the selvedges from breaking, but the draw-in will still occur. Read about temples on page 94. All of these suggestions work, but they are slow. You can weave fast and still allow enough weft in the sheds. Read about sett on page 6, and in Book #1 for details.

Here's how the bending works in different situations and how it affects your cloth's draw-in.

Balanced plain weave is shown in Figure 150. "Balanced" means there are the same number of warps per inch as wefts per inch. You can see that both the warps and the wefts bend or curve. However, in Figure 151, the warps are bending and the wefts are straight. In this case, the warp ends are much closer together for a warp-faced plain weave. Warps that close force the wefts to be straight. These warps take up much more than those in balanced weaving because they have to curve so much over and under the wefts. In weft-faced weaving, the warps are straight and the wefts do all the bending, and they are close together. See Figure 152. Many rugs are woven this way. With the wefts bending so much, there needs to be much more weft in the shed to allow for the yarn to take up.

In the weaving chapter, you read that for speedy weaving, you don't want to take the time to bubble each weft or place it on a distinct diagonal. If the warps are close enough together, there is enough diagonal for the weft from the fell of the cloth to the shuttle race. The cloth will appear balanced even though in reality it is slightly denser in the warp than

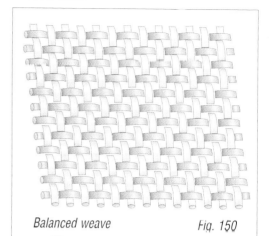

Balanced weave   *Fig. 150*

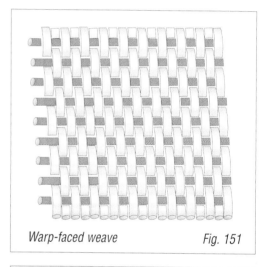

Warp-faced weave   *Fig. 151*

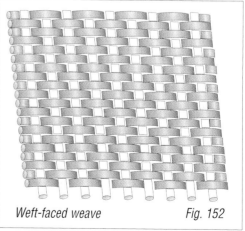

Weft-faced weave   *Fig. 152*

weft. Using Ashenhurst's rule and 80% of the maximum sett, you can achieve this goal of fast weaving and good selvedges. See page 7.

Allowing for normal draw-in

With precautions, normal draw-in won't cause the selvedge threads to abrade in the reed and break. The selvedge threads crowd together naturally, and we all know, having read the sidebar on page 78, that the closer threads are, the more they will bend. Good selvedges require selvedge threads that bend enough but don't get too tight and break.

My beginning students are surprised to see that the twill sections in their samplers are narrower than the plain weave sections. The reason is that plain weave has more intersections of warp and weft than twill, which makes the cloth wider there. Weaving both structures in a piece could cause problems at the selvedges if some areas draw in a lot more (e.g., the twill). Twill weaves are sett differently from plain weaves. The number of warp threads per inch should be determined by which weave structure you will be weaving. Read more about sett on page 6 and about different setts for different weaves in Book #1 in the chapter on sett.

There are other draw-in problems that don't occur naturally and some solutions given in the section about selvedge problems on page 97.

Selvedges tend to get tight

As the cloth is woven, it becomes somewhat narrower than the warp in the reed. This draw-in is normal, but it's the selvedge threads that become closer together rather than the threads in the middle of the warp. Because the selvedges threads get closer they tend to become warp faced, and warp threads take up more in warp faced weaves than in balanced weaves.

Tight selvedge threads can make the selvedge threads break or the cloth pucker at the selvedges. They may also prevent the shed from opening cleanly at the edges.

Avoiding tight selvedges

When selvedge threads become warp-faced, they draw closer together and take up more. The problem of take-up difference is solved by winding and weighting the selvedge threads separately and sleying them closer in the reed. Information about winding selvedges separately begins below, and sleying them closer in the reed begins on page 84.

More than anything, you want to keep the selvedge warp threads from tightening up. When they can weave at their own tension, you won't ever have to cut them off because of puckering. One selvedge thread will hold the weft, but the first 1/2 dozen or so threads will crowd and shorten, so all of these first few (4 or 6) threads need to be weighted separately. Selvedges should be about 1/4" wide. Commercially woven fabrics that have real selvedges have wider selvedges to hold a stretcher, or temple. I usually use 4 threads for my selvedges.

Wind selvedge threads separately

The reason for winding and weighting selvedge threads separately is to allow them to take up more than the main warp. I recommend making and weighting separate selvedge threads for warps that are over 3-5 yards. It isn't hard to do, and it ensures good-looking selvedges that weave without problems. It is more efficient to start with them as separate, rather than to find out mid-warp that your selvedge threads are breaking because they are too tight, or that they are becoming so close together that the shed can't open, or that the wefts are beating down too much.

In order to weight the selvedge threads separately, they must be made separately from the main warp. Four threads are often used for each selvedge. Because they will take up more than the main warp, measure them out longer, say, 10% longer. If you repeat a project, you can tell exactly how much longer the

79

selvedges need to be, but 10% should be a good starting amount.

Make a thread-by-thread lease (cross) at one end; no group lease is necessary.

You can wind your little selvedge threads on a pencil, bobbin, or small tube, or make a chain. Figures 153a and b show how the threads can be secured to prevent the warp from unwinding.

Fig. 153a　　　　　　　*Fig. 153b*

You can also wind the threads on a 2" to 3" square piece of cardboard with a slit in two of the edges. The cuts work like the tiny slit on the end of spool of thread. One cut is to anchor the ends of the selvedge threads before wrapping the supply of threads onto the card. The second cut is to secure the threads so they don't unwind too much. See Figures 154a and b.

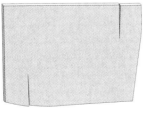

Fig. 154a

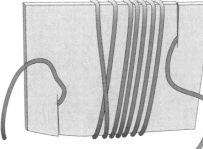

Fig. 154b

They will not be beamed onto the warp beam with the main warp, but will hang over the back beam behind the loom with weights providing the tension on them. Put each little selvedge warp in a plastic "baggie" to keep it from twisting and tangling during weaving. See Figure 155. Sometimes, I do it the other way round—I put the weights in the baggie and the threads outside.

Fig. 155

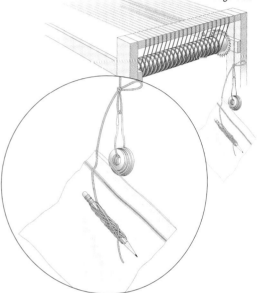

Weighting selvedge threads

In industry, the selvedges are always separate from the main warp and are wound on smaller spools—one at each edge of the warp. Selvedge spools for handweavers are available with the apparatus for attaching them to the loom, but I found the "baggie and pencil" way to be satisfactory. For very long warps, selvedge spools or rollers do save a lot of interruptions (because you have to stop periodically and release some of the warp from the baggie or pencil) and allow you to maintain your rhythm.

See Figures 156 and 157 to see the separately weighted selvedge spools for industry and handlooms.

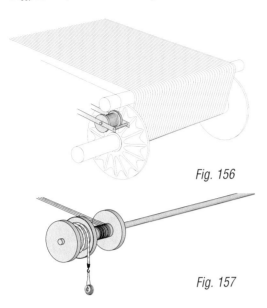

Fig. 156

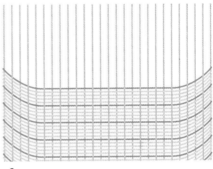

Fig. 157

one selvedge takes more weight than the other. Do whatever is needed so the fell is straight. See Figures 158a, b, and c.

It's better to have the selvedge threads too loose than too tight. If too tight, the body of the fabric may pucker into the selvedges. It might not be noticeable until the cloth is washed. You may have cut off selvedges on commercial fabric to avoid this puckering. If your weight is adjusted correctly, you shouldn't ever have to cut selvedges off your handwoven cloth.

Fig. 158

81

The weights

I like to use nuts, washers or fishing weights for my selvedges. These "weights" are small enough that I can add or subtract them in small increments to adjust the tension. You can use plastic bottles filled with the amount of water needed for the weight. As the selvedge threads get woven, the weights and their supply of thread rise up and need to be let down to just above the floor when they reach the back beam. A small bag of weights is more convenient than a bottle because it doesn't have to be let down so often during weaving. The advantage of weighted spools is that the yarn unrolls automatically, so you don't need to get up from the loom and move the weights to let out more thread. See page 83.

How much weight?

Ten to fourteen ounces of weight are needed. I start with 10 ounces and add or subtract, as necessary. The way to know if you need more or less weight is simple. The fell of the cloth will be straight if the weight is correct. If it curves up at the edges towards the shafts (making a "smile,") it means there isn't enough weight. If the cloth curves down at the edges towards the breast beam (a "frown"), it means there is too much weight. Sometimes,

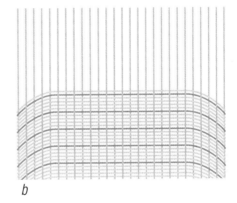

a

b

c

When to attach the weights

The weights can be attached after the selvedge strands are threaded in the heddles, sleyed in the reed and tied on to the cloth apron bar. Ways to sley the threads in the reed are discussed on page 84. Tie the threads onto the apron bar, keeping them separate from the body of the warp's bundles. Often, just weighting the selvedges separately is enough, and no special threading or weave structure is needed for them. However, you can read about different threadings and weave structures for selvedges on page 85.

Attach the weights

Most weights need a loop of some kind so you can attach the selvedge threads. It can be a loop of string or a metal shower curtain hook. See Figure 159.

There is a wonderful knot to tie the weights to the threads. It's easy to undo, which is necessary every time you need to let down

Fig. 159

the weights for more thread. This is the same knot I tie for weighting supplementary warps, described in Book #2, on page 156. Here it is again along with the steps to tie it. See Figure 160. The steps sound more complicated than they are, but if you learn it well, you'll save yourself a lot of time and aggravation in your future weaving life because the knot comes undone quickly.

1. Hold the selvedge supply taut through-out the procedure. With the well-secured selvedge threads hanging off the back beam (or warp beam) at the back of the loom, pull a very big loop of the selvedge threads warp through the loop of the weight. This big loop is the worker "thread" used to tie a slipknot around the threads hanging from the loom.

2. Take the loop over and then behind the selvedge threads.

3. Bring the loop back under the "worker thread" but over the selvedge threads.

4. Grasp the "worker thread loop" with your left hand.

5. Now, tighten down on the slip knot you have made keeping both the loop in your left hand and the end loop of the "worker thread" in your right.

To undo the knot, simply pull the "tail" loop, drop the weight down, and retie.

For the cardboard system on page 80, put weights on each end of a short cord and hook it over the dangling selvedge threads at the card.

Fig. 160

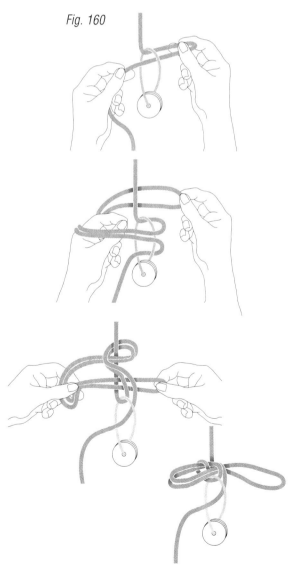

Automatic tension

You can use the principles of the Automatic Warp Tension System some looms have to weight selvedge spools. I've summarized the system in this book on page 8. The details are in Book #2, on pages 140-142. This spool system works especially well on looms with no back beam that have the automatic tensioning system. (It would be worth exploring if this system could be used on a loom with a back beam and a brake on the warp beam. I've read that it can work, but haven't seen it myself. The problem might be with the regular warp and the selvedge threads advancing evenly.)

Each selvedge spool is divided so that there is space for the threads and another area for the weight system cord. See Figure 161. The cord goes around the spool one or two times. (You may have noticed in Book #2, on page 140, that the cord goes around 3 times to tension the whole warp, but since the selvedges are so tiny, fewer turns around the spool are needed.)

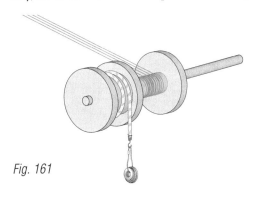

Fig. 161

There are several variations to setting up the cords and spools, but basically, one end of the cord is attached to the loom and the other end to a weight. Instead of weights, the cord can be attached to the loom with a spring. See Figure 162. The cord provides the friction needed to put tension on the selvedge threads. The number of times the cord is wound around the selvedge spool is important. Winding fewer times around the spools lets the cord slip around the spool more easily and lets

the weight do its work to tension the threads. If the cord is wound around too many times, the weight can't operate because the cord can't slip. The cord leading to the spool from the loom should be taut. If it is slack, it won't slip enough.

The spools, or selvedge rollers, need to be on their own rod, and they need to turn freely on the rod with as little friction as possible. It takes some engineering to put on the rods, depending on your loom. Where you place the tension system is important. The selvedge warps should not go over the loom's back beam touching the beam—the roller must roll freely, and the back beam would prevent this. If your loom has a back beam, the rod with the spools can be in front of the warp beam or behind the loom and a little above the warp beam. The selvedge threads should be at about the same level as the regular warp. If your loom has no back beam and has the automatic tension system, you don't have to worry about having the warp going over a back beam and preventing the spools from rolling—just put them on about the same level as the warp beam, or a little below it.

83

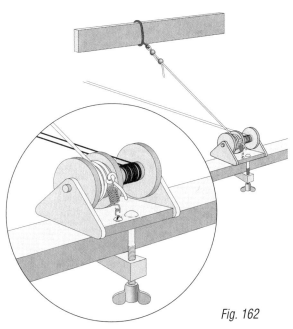

Fig. 162

Selvedges draw in too much

Selvedge threads naturally migrate toward each other, becoming warp faced, and so are closer together than the rest of the threads in the body of the warp. The problem of too much draw-in can be addressed in several ways. If it isn't addressed, the warps could abrade against the reed and eventually break. No one strategy is "right." You'll know if the solution you choose is successful if the selvedges build up at the same rate as the body of the cloth, and if they don't get tight or break, and if they have a good appearance. Weight them separately, and then do what's convenient. You might need to experiment with each project to see what works best.

Reeds

In Book #1, I suggest you use a reed that allows two threads per dent. This size reed allows any knots that might be in the warp threads to pass through without hanging up, letting you continue your weaving rhythm. It is a good idea regarding the selvedges, too, because the wider-spaced dents will allow you to sley the selvedge threads more densely, or to make them heavier. By the way, sometimes you want even larger dents, say with double weave, because there are so many ends to be threaded in a dent, and they need to pass freely to make the sheds.

Selvedge strategies

Here are several strategies for selvedges, in order of preference. Note however, that sometimes the warp yarn itself dictates the strategy. For example, a soft warp yarn might need doubling up in the heddles, and a fine, hard yarn might need to be sett singly in the heddles, but doubled in the reed.

There are many variables: the yarn used for the selvedges, its density (denting in the reed), its relationship to the warp and weft yarns, and the weave structure. Read about weave structures and yarns for selvedges on page 85.

Adjust size and density of selvedge threads

There are several strategies relating to whether you adjust the size of the selvedge threads or their density.

Strategy 1: Sley selvedge threads more densely.
Since the warp will naturally draw in a bit, it is a good idea not to fight it, and sley the selvedge threads more densely than the body of the warp to keep the threads from breaking. Thread the ends one per heddle, but put more in the reed. I double the sett for the 4 selvedge threads in the outside dents of the reed. However, if the selvedges build up faster than the rest of the fabric, the threads may be too close together. Threads sleyed too closely may keep the weft from packing in. (Remember, the selvedges may build up faster than the rest of the cloth if they aren't weighted enough.)

If the warps are too thick to double up, use thinner threads for the selvedge threads. With thinner threads you can get them closer, and the selvedges look almost machine made.

Don't make the selvedge threads so dense that the sheds won't open cleanly, or the weft won't beat in easily.

This strategy is the first choice for finer, harder yarns.

Strategy 2: Make selvedge threads heavier.
Many weavers make the selvedge threads heavier by doubling them up in the heddles. Jim Ahrens recommended this method as a second choice if sleying the selvedge threads more densely didn't work.

It is a good strategy for soft yarns. Double a soft warp yarn in the heddles, but keep the sett in the reed the same as for the body of the warp.

For weft-faced rugs, the selvedge threads need to be both thickened and sleyed closer. If the body of the rug is threaded 2 ends as one working end, at the selvedge, try 3 ends as one working end (thickening the warp yarn) and putting the three ends in one dent (sleying them closer).[16]

If the warp itself is already rather dense, the selvedge threads may not need to be any denser, so you might use a slightly heavier yarn for the selvedges.

Strategy 3: Sley threads farther apart.

If the selvedges are building up faster than the body of the cloth, consider sleying the threads farther apart or increasing the tension on them.

For thin fabrics, try having an empty dent between the main body of the fabric and the selvedges or, in some cases, an empty dent in the middle of the width of the selvedge. The empty dents won't show, but they will improve both the weaving and the appearance of the cloth.

Summary

If adjusting the tension (weight) isn't enough to keep the selvedges weaving together with the main cloth, that is, the selvedges lag or weave ahead of the body, adjust the size and density of the selvedge threads.

Selvedge yarns

Selvedge yarns or threads should be strong and smooth. You can use selvedge yarns that are different from the main warp yarns. Thus, your warp can be made of a soft or fragile yarn or even a singles yarn, and you won't have to worry about the selvedges abrading or break-ing. I like the selvedges to be inconspicuous, so I would make the special yarns blend in with the main warp ends. Do what looks good.

If your warp threads are singles or rather frag-ile, use a smooth, plied yarn for the selvedges. The plied yarn is stronger and will stand up to the abrasion of the reed. I usually use 4 or so of these threads. Read about sleying them on page 84.

16Collingwood, pp. 88-89.

My first thought is to use yarns of the same grist (size) as the regular warps. However, if the regular warps are rather thick, I use a smaller size for the selvedge threads.

Read the strategies above for information about thinner and thicker selvedge threads.

Selvedge threadings

With plain weave and simple twills, it's usually sufficient to continue using the same weave right through the selvedges, simply sleying the reed twice as densely. However, there are several reasons why you might use a different weave structure at the selvedges. The threads may be too dense and prevent the sheds from opening. The wefts may lag or weave ahead of the main weave structure. The main weave structure of the warp may not make good enough selvedges to turn the weft on. The borders of Bronson lace weaves, for example, can be threaded alternating shafts 1 and 2 to achieve good selvedges.

A simple and effective threading for the selvedges uses all the shafts used in the main weave in the outside dent or two. The weft should catch often, if not on each shed.

Floating selvedges

Floating selvedges are commonly used when the outside warp thread doesn't weave into the cloth and is left dangling, or when it isn't caught often enough because of the structure of the weave. Read about selvedges for twills on page 90.

On each edge of the warp, sley one thread in the reed, but not through a heddle. See Figure 163. These floating threads move neither up nor down when the sheds are made, but stay in the middle of them. See Figure 164. Since they don't interlace with the wefts like the main weave, they are likely to get looser as you weave along. You can hook a weight on each one and let it slide along as the warp is

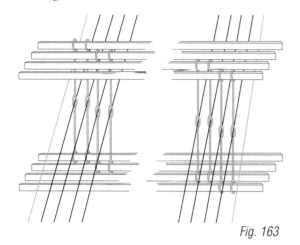

Fig. 163

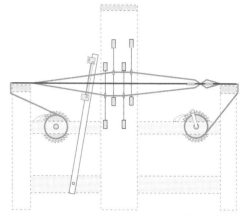

Fig. 164

advanced. See Figure 165. Because they don't get tighter as a rule, they can be beamed on with the regular warp ends. If your selvedge threads are dense, put the floaters in their own dents, next to the outside selvedge threads to keep them from sticking to the other selvedge threads.

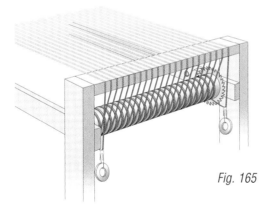

Fig. 165

Floating selvedges give a thread for the weft to go around. You can enter and exit the shed in a variety of ways, and they will work. You just need to do it the same way all the time. Here's the method I prefer. Enter the shuttle into the shed *over* the floating thread and exit the shuttle *under* it. See Figures 166 and 167. You can do the reverse, but it's easier to push the warp end down with the nose of the shuttle when entering the shed, and it naturally leaves the shed at the opposite side going under the floating selvedge. With floating selvedges, the weft cannot fail to catch around the

selvedge thread at both sides. You can also place the shuttle *under* both selvedges when weaving one direction, say right to left; and on the return always take the shuttle *over* both selvedges. Of course, for the *over* rows, you'll have to push the floater down with the shuttle on the way in—easy—but also push it down on the other side before catching the shuttle—not so easy. As I said, all will work, but be consistent.

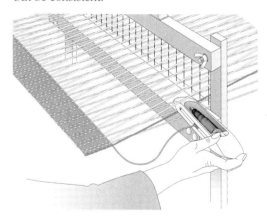

Fig. 166

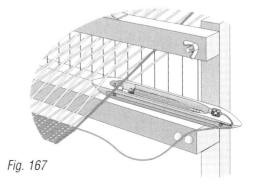

Fig. 167

Harry Linder made this discovery when weaving with a pattern weft followed by a tabby weft (e.g. overshot, summer and winter). With floating selvedges, you will get a much better edge if the tabby shot is made opposite from the pattern shot. That is, pattern shot, *over-under*, tabby shot, ***under-over***.[17]

I never use a floating selvedge unless it's needed because it slows down the weaving. If a twill weave doesn't catch the outside thread, I might just cut off the un-caught warp and forget it. In some weave structures the weft will skip outside warp threads periodically. If I were to sew the cloth into a garment whose selvedges wouldn't show, I'd just leave the not-so-nice-looking selvedges alone.

Twills that only weave in one direction do not need floating selvedges. Read about selvedges for twills on page 90. Only twills that change directions need them.

You can use floating selvedges for basket weave. Because, in this weave, the shuttle must go into the same shed twice, the floating selvedges prevent the wefts from unweaving on the second throw. Read other ways to catch the outside thread on page 92.

A floating selvedge cannot be used with a flyshuttle.

If the floating selvedge isn't high enough in the shed for the shuttle to go under it easily, raise it on the back beam with a short piece of wood or anything you can find in your studio or the hardware store. Another way to raise the threads is to tie loops of string around them and attach the loops to the castle of your loom. Adjust the loops so the floating selvedge threads float in the middle of the open sheds.

Usually, the floating selvedges are simply the outermost threads of the warp. However, they can be a different type of thread from the body of the warp. See page 85.

Selvedges on two shafts

Regardless of what structure you use for the body of the cloth, you can make a neat selvedge by putting the selvedge threads on their own shafts. Two shafts will make plain weave selvedges. Four shafts can make tape selvedges (2/2 basket weave), which are described on page 88.

Plain weave selvedges on two shafts are ideal for two-tie weaves.

Plain weave selvedges look less machine-made than tape selvedges, on placemats, for example.

 Use the two-shaft plain weave selvedges when the main weave structure's warps and wefts don't intersect enough. The plain weave makes more intersections, which will make neat edges to turn the wefts around on.

 Use the four-shaft tape selvedge when you need fewer intersections in the selvedges, or the selvedges build up too fast, or the wefts don't pack down as much as in the body.

Selvedge threads carried on their own two shafts, will always weave plain weave at the selvedge. They will be caught when the shed changes for the pattern or main weave structure. They should be weighted separately, of course, because they will take up differently from the ends in the main cloth. Plain weave takes up the most of all weaves, which might make it weave too far ahead of the main weave. If that happens, and you have two more shafts, switch to a tape selvedge, (see page 88) or abandon the idea and use a floating selvedge.

Which shafts?

I usually put the selvedges on the back two shafts. However, if the warps are sticky, putting them on the front two shafts will force them to open better when making the sheds. For

[17] Linder, p. 25.

very long warps, and for the best balance, put the selvedges on the middle shafts; they won't get lifted as high as on the back ones, so they won't get so much wear and tear.

Thread the body of the warp according to your plan, but on each edge put four or so threads onto two shafts. If the body uses 4 shafts, then alternate the threads of each selvedge on shafts 5 and 6. The threading for each selvedge is: 5,6,5,6 or 6,5,6,5, depending on which edge you are threading and which shafts the threads in the main part start and end on. If your main warp is to be a weave on 5 shafts, then the selvedges would be on shafts 6 and 7. If the main warp uses 8 shafts, then the selvedges go on shafts 9 and 10, etc.

 Remember, since they will be weaving plain weave, they will take up differently from the main warp so, of course, they must be weighted separately.

The tie-up

Tie up the treadles so every other shed lifts shaft 5 and the alternate sheds lift shaft 6. See Figure 168.

It's the tie-up that makes the selvedge and the main weave integrated, so be sure that the selvedge shafts alternate with each treadle in your sequence. See the draft.

It's desirable to have the main structure of the cloth weave with an even number of treadles. Then, both the main body and the

Fig. 168

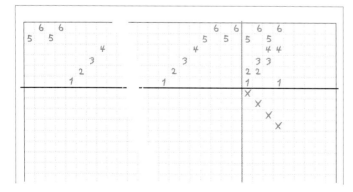

selvedges will take an even number of sheds. An odd number of shafts in the body, such as a 5-shaft weave, would need 10 treadles to tie up to achieve the 5 sheds for the body and the 2 sheds for the selvedges. In other words, you would have to go through the weave sequence twice to complete a cycle, because the plain weave structure requires two sheds. Or, you can use two feet at once: one for the selvedge treadles and the other for the cloth structure.

My loom has ten shafts so that I can weave 8-shaft weaves and still have two shafts for the selvedges.

Tape selvedges

A tape selvedge is also called basket weave or 2/2 hopsack weave. Use it when you can't sley the selvedge ends close because the threads are too sticky to make clean sheds. Or use it when the selvedge warp ends are too dense to open for a plain weave in every shed. It can also be used when the weave structure doesn't make a neat selvedge. The warps and wefts will intersect less (or more) often than they do in the body's weave structure, so you can get clean sheds at the selvedges. It makes a very neat selvedge, which can look as if it were commercially made. It is nice for rugs as well as for fabric. The selvedges will not pucker as they do sometimes in commercially woven fabrics. When the edges pucker they must be cut off before you sew with the cloth. However, if they make your cloth look too machine-made, use two-shaft, plain weave selvedges.

This technique requires four shafts—two on each edge of the cloth. Four or six ends per selvedge work just fine. The reason machine-woven selvedges are wider is to accommodate the temple which holds the cloth out to its full width. Read about temples on page 94.

The selvedge ends that are raised change only on one edge with each weft. At the other edge, the selvedge ends are raised or lowered as they were in the previous shed. See Figures 169a and b where the two shafts on the right are 1 and 2, and the two on the left are 3 and 4. Note that the side that changes is the side where the shuttle enters the shed. (The X's indicate the warp ends lifted over the weft.) Figures 170a and b show four selvedge threads at each edge.

Fig. 169

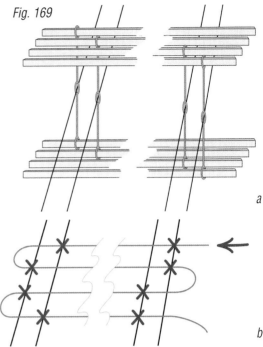

a

b

Fig. 170

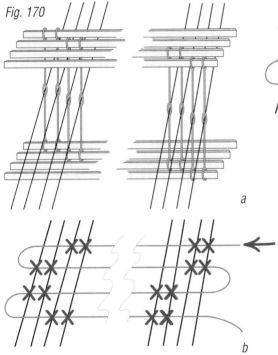

a

b

Figure 171 shows how the tape is a true 2/2 weave with two warps threaded on one shaft, alternated with 2 threaded on the other shaft. The principle remains the same: to catch the weft, enter the shuttle on the side that has just changed.

One weaver uses a tape selvedge when three shuttles are used, with two threads per selvedge. See Figure 172.

You may have to adjust the density in the reed and the weight on the selvedge threads to get them to match the tension of the main warp. Of course, they will be weighted separately from the main warp. The take-up of the selvedge threads is usually less with a tape selvedge because it has fewer intersections of warps and wefts. The wefts should weave straight across the body, and at the selvedges, neither lag nor weave ahead. By the way, don't make the tape super dense or use a sticky, hairy, or loopy yarn.

Fig. 171

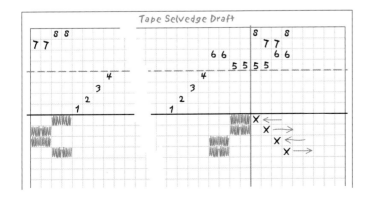

Tape Selvedge Draft

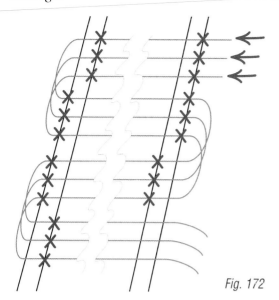

Fig. 172

This edge works perfectly with 8-shaft satins. The tape selvedge threads will intersect more often than the satin weave itself. The warps are usually very densely sleyed for satin, and there aren't enough intersections in the weave to interlace at the edge to make a good-looking selvedge. A tape selvedge with half the inter- sections of a plain weave selvedge works better than a two-shaft selvedge because the plain weave has too many intersections, which causes it to build up faster than the satin. The tape's sequence used twice equals one sequence of the satin. (Remember to add four shafts to the eight needed for the satin.)

A tape selvedge can prevent the edges of warp and weft faced weaves from curling when they are taken off the loom.

It would not be easy to use a tape selvedge for overshot patterns. Just think of the nightmare of keeping track of the four sheds of the selvedge along with the treadling for four overshot blocks. Of course, a computer driven loom could do it easily.

Selvedges for twills

Twills that only weave in one direction do not need floating selvedges, or special threading. Their outside threads can be caught if the threading of the warp has a thread on an even shaft at one edge and one on an odd shaft at the other. See Figure 173. (Start your shuttle on the even side.) Read about catching the outside warp thread in the sidebar on page 92.

Reversing the direction of the twill at the sel- vedges can keep the edges from curling. At the beginning of the selvedge, (at the point of the reversal) make a break in the twill. That is, skip one shaft and reverse the twill threading. See the draft in Figure 174. If the twill hadn't been broken, the reverse threading would not have skipped shaft 3 and would be 3,2,1,4 instead of 2,1,4,3.

A broken twill may also be used to thread selvedges for a four shaft twill. A broken twill is threaded with two threads going in one direc-

Fig. 173

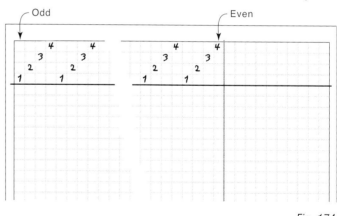

Fig. 174

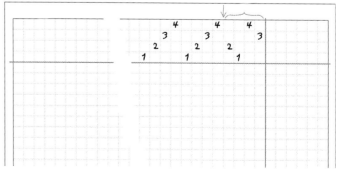

tion (for example in the Z direction), a break (skipped shaft), and two threads in the other direction (S direction). For example: 1,2,4,3. Note the skip between shafts 2 and 4. For comparison, a straight twill is threaded 1,2,3,4. To make a break at the reversal, skip shaft 3. See Figure 175.

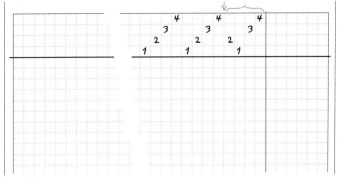

Fig. 175

Fixed selvedges

This technique uses fishing line (monofilament) at the selvedges during weaving, but the fishing line doesn't remain in the cloth. It holds the warp out like a temple, preventing the weft from drawing in at the edges. It works with looms that have an automatic cloth advance, and might work with looms that don't. Braided fish line works well. Read about temples on page 94.

At the back of the loom, have a spool with some monofilament wound on it attached at each edge of the warp. Put the monofilament through the last heddle along with the last end of each edge. In the reed, put it in its own dent next to the last thread on each side. See Figure 176. Bring it over the breast beam on the loom and put some weight on it. See Figure 177. When you have woven about 2 feet of cloth with the monofilament, cut off the weights at the front. There will be enough friction along the monofilament that is woven in the cloth to keep it taut. Keep weaving; the cloth slides forward on the monofilament, but the fishing line doesn't unwind more. It just stays stationery, with the back attached and the front, inside the edges of the fabric, slipping off as you wind the cloth on the cloth beam. It makes nice little loops on the edges when the monofilament is gone.

There needs to be enough monofilament woven in the fabric to create enough drag, or tension on it. Weave in plenty before cutting off the weights. If there is too much drag it's easy to remove some of the line that's in the cloth.

(continued on page 94)

Fig. 176

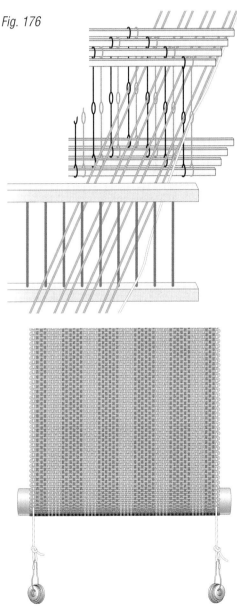

Fig. 177

Ways to catch the outside warp threads

There are several instances in weaving when the outside warp thread doesn't "catch" or get woven in. If you don't want to cut those threads off or to ignore them, use the following solutions.

Twills that don't change direction

 Selvedge threads can be caught, or woven in, each time if the twill doesn't change directions in the treadling, and if the threading is a straight draw—1,2,3,4, etc. Which side of the warp the shuttle enters relates to which shed is made in the twill sequence. If one side's outside warp end isn't catching, here's how to know which side the shuttle should enter.

If the threading of the warp starts on one edge with an even shaft and ends on the other with an odd shaft (Figure 173 on page 90), always start the sequence with the shuttle on the even side.

Another way is to start the shuttle from the side where the edge thread is on 1 by lifting shafts 2 and 3 instead of 1 and 2.

Sometimes my students miss a thread or make an extra one. When they do, the outside warp threads on both sides are on either an even or an odd shaft. They need to make floating selvedges or to remove one warp thread, so there will be a thread on an odd shaft on one edge and a thread on an even shaft on the other (Figure 173 on page 90).

A special selvedge threading for twills that don't change directions always catches the outside threads. Skip the shaft the outside thread is on and put it on the shaft of the next thread in the sequence. If the right hand edge threading ends, 1,2,3,4—skip the last shaft (4), and thread the last thread on shaft 1, (1,2,3,1). The left edge thread of a straight-draw threading is normally on shaft 1 (the thread on shaft 1 being the outside thread). So, skip the 1 and put the thread on shaft 4, (4,2,3,4). See Figure 178.

A quick fix

 I find it easier to simply cut the weft thread and insert the shuttle at the opposite edge of the warp. In other words, if the shuttle is on the right when it's about to enter the shed, cut the weft and enter it from the left. You may have to do it a couple of times, but eventually both outside warp threads will be woven in. Don't skip any rows of the twill order; just change the side which the shuttle enters. (The threading must start on an odd shaft and end on an even, as usual. See Figure 173 on page 90). Usually, you only do this process once—it might take a second time, but you don't have to do it over and over.

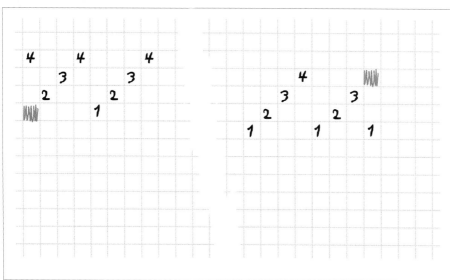

Fig. 178

Point twills and fancy treadlings

Sometimes, there is no way your weft will catch both the edge threads because the twill changes directions (from S to Z and vice versa). In that case, use a floating selvedge.

Floating selvedges

Read the section on floating selvedges on page 85. Basically, these are extra warp threads, usually only one for each edge, that go through the reed but not through the heddles. Pass your shuttle over the floating selvedge as it enters the shed and bring it out under the floating selvedge on the opposite edge as your shuttle exits. (You can enter and exit the shuttle in various ways. See page 86.)

When two shuttles are used

Regardless of the threading, you can always catch the outside thread if you lay your shuttles down on the web (cloth) just right. It's not difficult to do once you get used to it.

If the shuttle comes out of the shed *under* the last warp thread, place that shuttle closer to the reed (*away from you*). If the shuttle comes out *over* the last warp, put the shuttle *near* you, or toward the fell.

See Figure 179. In the illustration, the shuttles are lying on the cloth with shuttle A closer to the reed, or away from you. Shuttle B is closer to the weaver. When you put down the shuttles this way, the wefts interlock around one another at the edges and enclose the outside thread on every shed. Sometimes the shuttle is required to go in the same position (near or away) two sheds in a row—no problem. Just place it where it belongs and move the other shuttle out of its way. So, if the weft came out of the shed under the last thread, you should put it in the position of shuttle B. If the next shed requires the shuttle also to be in the B position, put the shuttle down near you pushing up the shuttle that is already there to the A position.

Plain weave selvedges

Read "Selvedges on two shafts" on page 87.

Tape selvedges

Read about these interesting edges that take four shafts on page 88.

Use two or three shuttles

You can use two shuttles on purpose to catch the outside warp threads even though one shuttle is sufficient for the weave structure itself. One shuttle goes right-to-left and the other, left-to-right. (Eventually, they both end up on the same side.) Using three shuttles can be even easier. Read about a neat selvedge for three shuttles on page 94.

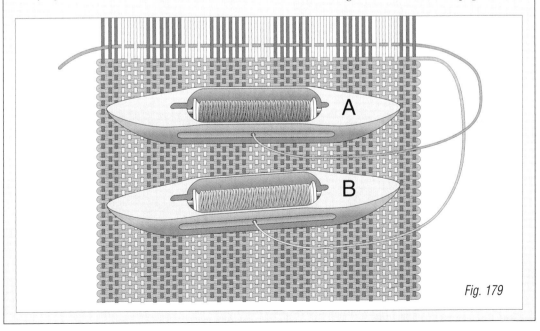

Fig. 179

It will wear out in the reed, and eventually, you'll have to let out some of the mono-filament on the spool at the back of the loom. Each day, for example, you might pull it forward and cut off the excess, so it doesn't wear in the same place all the time. The rate at which it wears out is dependent on the number of picks per inch. The higher the p.p.i., the fewer yards it takes to wear the fishing line.

The technique can be used to make fringe beyond the selvedges of a cloth. Some regular warp ends are needed out by the monofila-ment to anchor it at the front of the loom. That is, the monofilament needs to be woven into something. See Figure 184 on page 97 for how to weave fringe at the selvedges with regu-lar warp threads.

Two or three shuttles

When weaving with two shuttles, the outside warp thread often doesn't weave in unless effort is made to catch it. Read the sidebar, "Ways to catch the outside warp threads," on page 92 to learn how to lock the two wefts together at the edges.

When using three shuttles, a tape selvedge arrangement can be used with 2 selvedge threads at each side. See Figure 172 on page 90.

Another neat selvedge for 3 shuttles depends upon where you place the shuttles when they are taken out of the shed and the order the shuttles are used. If you alternate the three shuttles, begin by throwing shuttle 1 from the left when the left selvedge thread is up. Place shut-tle 1 on the woven cloth. Throw shuttle 2 from the right and place it behind shuttle 1, (closer to the fell which is away from you, or closer to the reed). Throw shuttle 3 from the left again, and place it behind shuttle 2 (closer to the fell [reed]). Pick up the shuttle closest to you, which should be shuttle 1 and continue. Never throw twice from the same side. Before the weft

enters the shed, it should go around the other weft on the same side automatically.[18]

Rug weavers use special techniques to keep multiple shuttles in sequence and make neat selvedges, but they are outside the scope of this book.

Using a temple

A temple is a stretcher that holds the cloth out at the selvedges. See Figures 180 and 181. It could be just a stick with a pin taped to each end. It allows you to pull the wefts tight up to the selvedge threads without breaking them. It may be made of wood or metal. The wooden ones don't rattle, but they obscure the last few inches of the weaving. The metal ones are slimmer and let you see more of the cloth. Any temple needs to be strong. They are available in many widths for weaving wide rugs or narrow placemats. Read where to place them below, in the section, "Positioning the temple."

Temples can slow you down, but in certain situations they are necessary. Rug weavers use them. They are helpful for weft-oriented weave structures that tend to draw in more, such as overshot. Some weavers say that if the sett and everything else is right, there is no need for a temple. I would like to encourage you to use

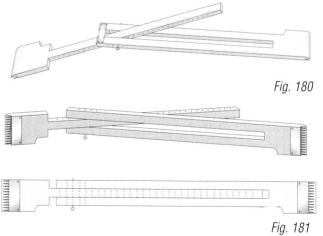

Fig. 180

Fig. 181

[18] Hoykinpuro, Anja, *Handwoven Magazine*, Nov/Dec 1994, Interweave Press, Loveland, CO, p. 56.

one whenever your weaving is drawing in so much that your selvedge threads keep breaking. Before buying an expensive temple, read how to reduce draw-in, beginning on page 84.

The metal or wooden bar is adjustable for the width of the warp and has teeth at the ends, which poke into the selvedges and hold them firmly out to the width the warp is in the reed. There are actually two bars, which lock and unlock together. Unlocked, they allow the bars to pivot and release the "stretch" so you can unhook the teeth from the selvedges and move the temple to its new location. When in place, the bars are locked, with the teeth properly gripping the selvedges and spreading out the warp. See Figure 182.

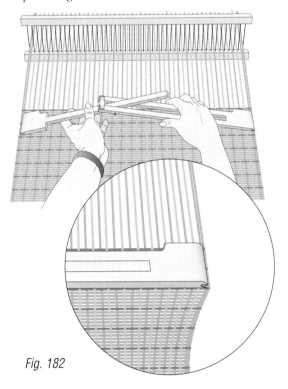

Fig. 182

 Since the temple needs to be moved frequently, it's a good idea to choose a type that opens and closes easily. The method for locking the two bars together should be quick to use, such as a collar that slides back and forth. Some temples are unwieldy, which slows you down and interrupts your rhythm.

 The teeth should be set at an angle to grip the cloth firmly—avoid temples with the teeth sticking straight out from the ends. Be aware, too, that those teeth are, necessarily, very sharp!

The temple works more to help with the beater than to preserve the selvedge threads, although it does that, too. It eliminates the drag on the beater and keeps the fabric open for the beater to hit the fell. With a dragging beater, it's difficult to maintain an even beat. You are not stretching the cloth itself, but holding out the crimp in the weft (the slack needed for the weft to go over and under the warp threads). It's the crimp of the weft that makes the fabric neck in (draw-in).

With the reed in the beater moving without resistance, the selvedge threads are protected from abrasion, and therefore, breakage.

With a temple, you can weave your cloth with more draw-in. The draw-in still takes place in the woven cloth itself, but at the fell, the temple holds the warps stretched out, so there is no friction on the reed or abrasion on the selvedge threads. If you like the appearance of the cloth with the wefts drawing in the cloth, use a temple. That way, your selvedge threads won't always be breaking from abrasion from the reed.

For fragile yarns, use minimum tension on the weft, so the draw-in is less, and there is less stretching for the temple to do.

Positioning the temple

Keep the temple on the woven cloth as close to the fell as possible, not more than 1/4"– 3/4" from the fell. It shouldn't hit the shuttle race, which will determine how far from the fell to put the temple on your loom. Since the fell will be changing, you need to change the temple often, perhaps every 1/2" in rug weaving, or every 1"– 2", or each time you advance the warp, for fabric weaving.

95

The teeth catch close to the outside selvedge threads. To adjust the length of the temple for your warp, lay it upside down on the warp and adjust the length so that the base of the teeth lines up with the space between the last warp threads. You want the cloth to be spread out to the same width as the warp ends are in the reed. The warp threads should be in a straight line from the reed to the fell. See Figure 183. Be sure the teeth are securely imbedded before locking the temple bars.

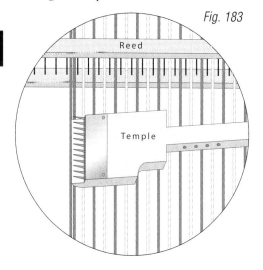

Fig. 183

Points to remember

The width of woven cloth is narrower than the width of the warp ends in the reed because the wefts curve over and under the warps and take up. Weft take-up is normal and can't be eliminated, which means, naturally, there will be some draw-in or necking in of the fabric. Remember, you can't widen the cloth with the temple—just the fell at the point when the weft is beaten in—the cloth itself will narrow in according to the amount of slack there is in the weft.

Some weavers take great pains to bubble the wefts, laying them in arcs, to eliminate any draw-in at all. This technique may work, or it may simply make weft loops at the selvedges. What the temple does is let you weave without bubbling the weft, which means you can weave faster. With it, the warp threads come straight out from the reed. The selvedge threads are held out to the width in the reed at the time the wefts are beaten in, and the reed does not abrade the selvedge threads because they are not rubbing in it, and the beater swings freely with no drag.

I once wove a wide fabric in overshot. Since this weave is weft oriented, I was not able to sett the warp ends more densely to eliminate too much draw-in, as I prefer. (See page 6 in this book and find details in Book #1, in the chapter on sett). Since the sett had to be for a balanced weave, draw-in was an issue. Using a temple, I wove with an end-delivery shuttle, the diagonal of the weft from the fell to the shuttle race being enough, and no bubbling needed. The beater swung freely, no selvedge threads abraded and broke, and the weaving rhythm was quite pleasant.

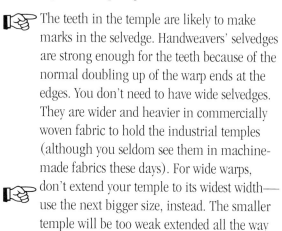 The teeth in the temple are likely to make marks in the selvedge. Handweavers' selvedges are strong enough for the teeth because of the normal doubling up of the warp ends at the edges. You don't need to have wide selvedges. They are wider and heavier in commercially woven fabric to hold the industrial temples (although you seldom see them in machine-made fabrics these days). For wide warps, don't extend your temple to its widest width—use the next bigger size, instead. The smaller temple will be too weak extended all the way out. You don't want to extend it more than one-half again its length when it's closed.

Alternatives

Rotary temples like those used in industry are now available for handweavers. They are rollers with pins that are attached to the loom at selvedge-width. During weaving, the cloth rolls along as the pins hold out the warp threads at the fell of the cloth.

I've seen a variety of homemade and commercially made appliances used to act like temples. Basically, they hook onto the outside threads, close to the fell, with weights hung on them over the edges of the loom to hold out the selvedges. "Crocodile clips" are available at building supply stores. They are made to clip tarps and are very inexpensive.

Selvedge fringe

You can "weave" fringe along the selvedges. Determine how long the fringe should be and stretch a cord on each side of the warp the fringe-length distance from the selvedges. Put the cords through the reed and attach them to the breast beam and the back beam. When you weave, you must weave some wefts only the width of the cloth and some, out to the width where the cords are. If you don't weave some wefts just the cloth width, the outside warps will splay out at the selvedges. See Figure 184. Cut the weft fringe from the string when they reach the breast beam.

You can weave fringes by taking the shuttle around the cords with every pick, but you'll need to hemstitch the edge of the cloth as you weave so the outside warps won't splay out.

Fig. 184

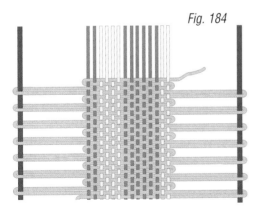

Selvedge problems

Even with good weaving techniques, there may still be selvedge problems. The remainder of this chapter is devoted to such problems. Other weaving problems are in the chapter on troubleshooting, beginning on page 107.

Selvedge threads break
Too much draw-in

The most common reason for selvedges breaking is too much draw-in. See page 84, "Selvedges draw in too much." If the draw-in isn't too great, try weighting the selvedges separately (See page 80) and sleying them more densely (See page 84). If it is extreme, read about the causes and solutions to the problems, below. Selvedge threads can break if the woven cloth draws in or necks in too much. Then, every time the weft is beaten, the warp is forced by the reed into a straight line, which stretches the edge warp ends out to the width in the reed and causes excess wear on them and breakage. In other words, the reed is chafing the threads as it goes from the narrow width of the cloth to the wider width in the reed. See Figure 185. You can either eliminate the draw-in (see Cause #3, below) or use a temple if you like the appearance of the cloth as it is. See page 94.

Fig. 185

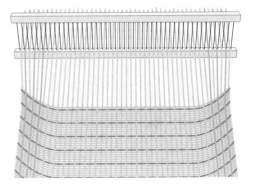

Cause #1: Sett not dense enough. If the sett isn't dense enough to prevent too much draw-in, you'll have to bubble the weft or use a temple. Bubbling the weft will put the necessary amount of weft into the shed. See Cause #3, below and read, "How warps and wefts bend," on page 78. The temple won't help to get enough weft into the shed, but it will hold out the selvedge threads at the fell so the reed can't abrade them. Read about temples on page 94. Read about sett on page 6.

Crowding the selvedge threads in the reed a bit can give selvedge threads the extra strength they need and allow for the natural draw-in of the cloth. See page 84.

Cause #2: Too much tension on the weft. If your warp sett was calculated according to Ashenhurst's rule, at 80% of maximum, and the draw-in is still so great that selvedge threads are breaking, it may be that you're putting too much tension on the wefts as you draw the shuttle from the shed. If you like the appearance of the cloth and don't want to incorporate more weft in each shed, you can use a temple (See page 94). Adjusting the tension on the weft thread in end-delivery shuttles can reduce too much draw-in. With boat shuttles, don't pull the weft too tight as you take the shuttle out of the shed.

Cause #3: Not enough weft in the sheds. If the sett isn't dense enough to prevent too much draw-in, you'll have to bubble the weft or make more of a diagonal to put the necessary amount of weft into the shed. Read, "How warps and wefts bend" on page 78. A temple won't help get enough weft into the sheds, but it will hold out the selvedge threads at the fell so the reed can't abrade them. Read about temples on page 94.

Cause #4: Warp tension too tight. Too much draw-in and subsequent breakage can be caused if the warp tension is too tight. Too much tension doesn't allow the warp threads to bend enough and requires the wefts to do the extra bending. If you don't allow extra weft in the sheds, the cloth has to draw in. Read about bending and take-up on page 78. See Cause #3 above, for ways to incorporate more weft into the sheds. Reduce the tension on the warp to reduce necking in.

Other solutions to breakage caused by too much draw-in

A weft that is a little heavier than the warp threads will tend to pull in the warp less. For fabric weaving, beating on a closed shed can cause the warp to draw in too much. Beat on the open shed. See page 22.

Be sure the shuttle stays on the shuttle race when it leaves the shed to allow more weft to go into the shed during the beat. If you don't, and pull the shuttle down to the fell, you'll be making an arc of the weft that will be trapped in the shed. See Figure 186.

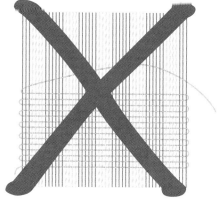

Fig. 186

Changing the shed too soon can cause draw-in. Be sure to change the shed just after the beater hits the fell of the cloth, when the warp is stretched out to its full width, to allow all the weft needed into the shed. See page 27. If you change the shed too soon, so that the beat is on a closed shed, the weft can draw in too much, and the selvedges abraded by the reed, break. Read about temples on page 94.

Fixed selvedges, described on page 91, might keep the selvedge threads from breaking, but they won't solve the draw-in problem. See page 97.

Other reasons for breakage

A beaming problem. Beaming the warp on the warp beam narrower than it is in the reed can cause selvedges to break. Beam the warp on the warp beam a bit wider than it will be woven to help keep the selvedge threads from being abraded by the reed. The warp threads are naturally narrower in the cloth than in the reed. Making the warp wider in the back enhances this natural angle of the selvedge threads. Just remember, never beam the warp narrower than the width it will be in the reed.

Fragile selvedge threads. Some threads may be just too weak to use for selvedge threads. Also, some threads are naturally susceptible to abrasion, such as singles linen, softly spun cottons, and some woolen yarns. Use different threads for the selvedge, say, plied threads when the rest of the warp is singles or a worsted yarn with a woolen warp. See page 85. Try using one thread of pearl cotton at each edge of a woolen warp and remove them just before finishing (washing). A fine silk yarn at the edges of fine fragile warps can help. These special threads may need to be weighted separately. Read about weighting the selvedges on page 80.

Strengthen cotton and linen threads with bees wax, available from sewing stores, in the quilting section. The plastic holder makes it easy to rub the wax onto the threads.

Advancing the warp often doesn't let the threads stay in one place long enough for the reed to cause serious abrasion. You might need to do it even more often for fragile threads.

Weaving too close to the shafts can cause broken ends, because the width of the warp in the reed is greater than the width of the woven cloth, and there isn't enough distance between the shafts and the fell to accommodate this difference.

Breakage can occur when the weft is much heavier and less pliable than the warp, for example, rags or very heavy yarns.

By the way, don't crowd fragile threads in your reed for the main warp. Use a reed that allows you to put two threads in a dent rather than one per dent. There will be more room for the yarns to move past each other during weaving without being abraded by the wires of the reed. The sett doesn't change, only the reed. If you want 20 ends per inch (epi), use a 10-dent reed sleyed two per dent to give space for the threads, while maintaining the number of ends per inch. There is more room in the outside dents to crowd the selvedge threads a bit, too.

Excess heddles. It may be that excess heddles riding on the ends of the shafts are abrading the outside threads. See the tip on page 45 for ways to keep them away from your warp threads. If there is no room on the shafts to keep them apart, you'll have to remove them. Next time, when you have too many heddles, space them between the heddles used in the warp, if you can. See Figure 187. If your warp threads are very close together, the extra heddles could get in the way, so you're better off removing them.

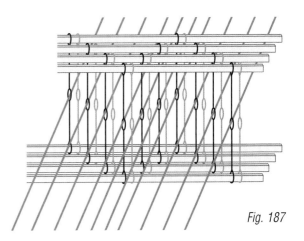

Fig. 187

Fell is concave

There are several causes for this problem, and they tend to relate to the bending of the threads. Read about how warps and wefts bend on page 78.

When the selvedges are too loose, the fell builds up at the sides because that part of the weft can't be beaten down. The main part of the warp packs in more, causing the fell to curve up like a smile. If you're weighting your selvedges separately, add more weight. If the selvedge threads are beamed onto the warp beam along with the main warp, hang weights on the loose selvedge threads as in Figure 165 on page 86. Read about loose selvedges below.

If the main warp is too tight when weaving balanced weaves, you are probably not putting enough weft into the sheds for the amount of tension on the warp ends. Remember, if the warps are too tight, they are forcing the wefts to do all the bending. If you don't put in enough slack in the wefts for all this extra bending, the cloth will draw in. The draw-in happens at the sides and edges—not in the middle of the cloth. That means that the warps are closer together at the sides than they are in the middle of the cloth. When the warps in the middle of the cloth are wider apart than those at the sides, the wefts will pack down more in the middle.

The middle of the cloth will build up slowly, and the selvedges will build up too fast. The solution is: don't weave balanced weaves with the warp tension too tight. All the tension that is needed is enough to allow the sheds to open cleanly. You can also use a temple if you like the appearance of the cloth as it is. See page 94.

When there is **too much draw-in**, the selvedge warps get closer together, so the sheds can't open enough, and the wefts can't be beaten in enough. Then, the selvedges build up more than the body of the warp. See, "Too much draw-in" under "Selvedge threads break," on page 97. Read about sleying the selvedges on page 84. Also, see Figure 185 on page 97.

Not enough draw-in can happen when the selvedge threads are too far apart, so they don't bend and take up enough, and the selvedges get too loose. Read about loose selvedges

below and on page 99, and selvedges that splay out on page 102.

Fell is convex

When the fell is lower at the selvedges, it usually means the selvedges are too tight. Read about it on page 101.

Loose selvedge threads

With good weaving techniques, the selvedge threads will tend to tighten. However, many weavers find their selvedge threads getting looser and looser. There are several possible reasons that this happens. If you ignore the reason and add weight to the selvedge threads as shown in Figure 165 on page 86, you are still not addressing the cause of the problem.

If the warp draws in or necks in too much, the pulling in of the wefts can stretch the outside threads and cause them to get loose. Remember, the wefts should just snug against the outside threads—not pull them in. Try sleying the selvedge threads more densely to tighten them up. See page 84. Read about cloth drawing in too much on page 84. Sometimes, yarns will stretch and not go back to their original length. Silk, for example, will stretch but not return to its original length. Some weavers report this phenomenon with cotton and linen yarns, too. Be especially vigilant about cotton and linen yarns that are softly spun and/or weak.

Sometimes, there's not enough draw-in from the weft (too much slack in the weft), so the selvedges don't interlace and don't take up and become loose. Ridges can form when there is too much slack in the weft as it exits the shed. See page 16.

If there is too much slack in the wefts at the edges, the warps will splay out and become too far apart to interlace properly with the wefts. The selvedge threads won't take up, and they will get longer and looser. (See "Edges splay out" on page 102.)

Poor beaming of the warp could make the selvedges loose if the edges of the warp on the beam have a larger diameter than that of the middle of the warp. The warp needs to be beamed on tight, and some paper is needed to support the edges so the whole warp is the same circumference. If the tension on the warp during beaming is less in any area (e.g., an edge), those threads will be longer and will be loose in the shed. Beam on with an even and tight tension. Read a brief summary on page 7, and for details, see page 29, in Book #2.

One side is looser

If one side of the warp gets looser and nothing is done about it, that side of the cloth will be longer than the other making the cloth a trapezoid shape. The reverse is also true— if one side is tighter, the other will be looser. The warp can become tighter with too much draw-in from the weft on one side. It might be, however, that the warp beam apron rod wasn't parallel to the warp beam during beaming. Peter Collingwood has a good solution. "Hang a strong metal bar half-way between the back beam and the warp beam. Attach a thick cord to each end of the bar and bring these cords forward and tie them to some upright of the loom frame. Then, if the warp is slacker towards the right side, shorten the right-hand cord."[19] See Figures 188 and 189.

Tight selvedge threads

This problem can happen naturally with good weaving techniques and is discussed at length on page 79 in this chapter. If the warp threads slip off the warp beam during beaming, they become shorter than the rest of the warp and tight during weaving. Wefts that are pulled in too much may cause the problem: they may not interlace equally with the selvedge warps. Those wefts are pulled straight, so they cannot bend as they should. If the selvedge threads are

spaced too far apart, as well, the wefts just lie in the sheds without bending over and under the warps. If the wefts are not bending, then the selvedge warps have to do all the bending, and they become tighter. See the sidebar, "How warps and weft bend" on page 78.)

Loops at selvedges

Some yarns are more apt to make weft loops than others, for example, stiffer, finer yarns or those with an unstable twist. These yarns can loop or twist on themselves in the body of the cloth or at the selvedges. When you use them, put more tension on the weft or wind the bobbins or pirns tighter. Read about twist and selvedges on page 106, "One side is better." If you can't prevent weft loops, you'll need to cut them and weave in the ends before washing (finishing) the cloth. See page 164.

101

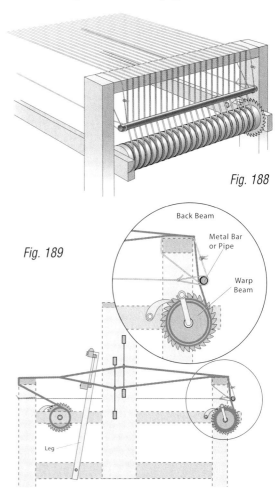

Fig. 188

Fig. 189

Back Beam

Metal Bar or Pipe

Warp Beam

Leg

---

[19] Collingwood, p. 82.

If you are using a regular length end-delivery shuttle on a narrow warp, loops might form on one edge. You need to use a shorter shuttle or a boat shuttle. Read about narrow warps on page 55.

Weft loops can come from the weft not being snugged up against the outside selvedge threads during weaving. Beginning weavers think that they can prevent draw-in if they leave loops at the edges as they throw the shuttle. The slack in the warp needs to be within the body of the warp, not at the selvedges. So, snug the wefts up! If there is not enough tension on an end-delivery shuttle for your weave, it will make loops at the edges. Increase the weft tension on the shuttle.

If you are using a boat shuttle, put some tension on the weft thread as it leaves the shed by putting your thumb or a finger on the bobbin. Then, you can snug the weft up to the outside thread. As the bobbins in boat shuttles get empty, they weigh less and unwind more easily, so you will need to change the tension you put on the bobbin with your fingers, or you may get loops at the selvedges. See Figure 190.

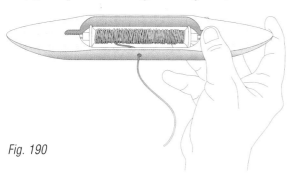

Fig. 190

If the bobbin unwinds too quickly, as it some-times does with wiry singles, wrap the shuttle spindle with masking tape. Read how to slow down bobbins on page 65.

If there is too much weft in the shed, loops can form. Decrease the angle of the weft by weaving closer to the shafts. That way, there is less diagonal from the fell of the cloth to the shuttle race.

Notches in selvedges

If the shuttle is drawn out of the shed too suddenly, the weft will be too tight, and besides causing a pucker across the cloth, it can jerk the selvedge thread and make a dent in the edge.

If the pirn is not wound properly, it will jerk suddenly, pulling in the selvedge. See page 56. If the bobbin in a boat shuttle is wound so it is spongy, the weft may bite into the mass of yarn and stop part way across the shed, pulling in the selvedge.

If a boat shuttle is thrown or caught too fast, it can cause the bobbin thread to tangle and jerk the selvedge. See page 62. The weft can tangle, also, if it is wiry, a singles linen, for example, and unwinds too fast. Try slowing down the bobbin. See page 65.

Soft selvedge threads or too much tension on the weft thread can cause the shuttle to pull the outside threads into the shed and notch in the edge.

Edges splay out

If the selvedge warps begin to splay outward, there is too much diagonal, bubble or slack in the weft where the shuttle exits the shed. Working at the edge where you want the selvedge threads to get back into alignment, change to the next shed and throw the shuttle, but don't beat the weft in. The weft is in the new shed and the shed is open. Now, at the offending edge, with your thumb and index finger, tug the excess weft out of the previous shed to align the selvedge warps. Then, with the other hand at the other edge of the warp, take up that *small amount* of slack in the new shed. What you're doing is taking out a *tiny* amount of excess weft from the previous shed and transferring it to the new weft by pulling slightly on the new weft. Then, beat in the new weft to keep the slack from going back to the offending edge. It might need to be done a couple of times, but after this tiny bit of slack has been taken out for a weft or two, the warps will be straight and stay in alignment. After the warps are straightened, this procedure shouldn't need to be done again unless you see the problem developing again. See Figures 191, 192, and 193.

You may need to do this operation on both sides of the warp. Remember, the problem is caused by too much slack at the edge where the shuttle exits. Loose wefts can also cause the selvedges to bulge out.

Ridges at selvedges

A ridge, or ripple, at the edge is caused by too much weft where the shuttle exits the shed and not enough weft in the shed at the side where the shuttle enters. It can happen when you change the shed too soon. Remember, you want to change the shed just after the beat. It continues to get worse as you weave along and must be addressed.

Eliminate the ridge by gently pulling the weft at the offending edge after it has been beaten and before the next shed is opened. It will take out the small amount of excess weft in the shed at the edge. You can use this technique with the shed closed or still open. The solution is similar to that of curing splayed selvedges described above. After a few shots (perhaps 4), the problem should be solved, and you can continue weaving, but remember to be sure to beat in the weft first, then, change the shed. See Figure 191.

Smooth silk and wiry linen are more susceptible to making ridges at the selvedges. The weft tension on these threads needs to be tight enough. Increase the friction on the weft thread by increasing the tension on an end-delivery shuttle or slowing down a boat shuttle bobbin. See page 65.

This problem is also called purling and can happen if the flyshuttle is thrown too hard

and bounces back into the shed. It can also be caused if the flyshuttle hits the box instead of sliding into it. It will make the weft loose in the shed just as if the shuttle had bounced back into it.

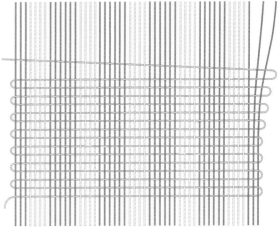

Fig. 191

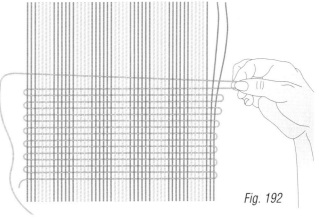

Fig. 192

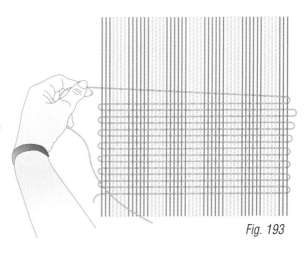

Fig. 193

Selvedges curl

The edges curl in satin, damask or 1/3 and 3/1 twills. Often, ironing them flat during finishing will make them stay flat. You can avoid the curl by using a special selvedge threading. See page 85.

Another solution for damask weaving is to thread small blocks at the edges (alternating A and B blocks) and treadle them in a checkerboard pattern. Weave them so that one of the blocks weaves warp-faced and the other, weft-faced. Reverse to weft-faced and warp-faced blocks in the treadling to weave little checkerboards at the edges.

A tape selvedge eliminates curling, too. See page 88.

Selvedges build up too fast

Read about tape selvedges on page 88. Also read about the problem, "Fell is concave," on page 99.

Edges bow in and out

If you notice that the edges bow in and out every few inches, it's that you waited too long to advance the warp. Remember to advance it often (every 2"–3") to maintain a consistent weft angle. When the fell of the cloth is far from the beater, there is more weft in the diagonal from the fell to the shuttle race, which can let the cloth weave wider. If you continue to weave too close to the beater, there will be less weft in the diagonal, and the cloth will draw in more.

Not advancing the warp often enough ensures that the beat won't be consistent. See page 27.

The tension on the weft thread can increase slightly as pirns empty, which could cause the selvedges to bow in just before a pirn is changed. This bowing-in would most likely occur when the tension on the weft thread is also high to start with. The added tension

is noticeable at the selvedge, especially after finishing. Read how much tension to put on the weft when using end-delivery shuttles, on page 53.

One side is better

Whatever you do, one selvedge tends to be better than the other. I learned that this phenomenon occurs because one is right or left-handed. Usually, the side opposite your dominant hand turns out better, but it is not always the case. The answer is to observe what you're doing and work toward making both hands work consistently and alike. I also think another reason should be considered. See the sidebar on page 106. It may be a small issue, and the selvedges are not actually disfigured, just different from each other. If they don't bother you, let them be slightly different.

I've changed end-delivery shuttles to ones with the exit hole at the opposite end to improve a bad edge. I have a large collection of these shuttles. You can make the exit hole be at the opposite end by turning the shuttle you have upside down.

Unsightly selvedges

In overshot, the blocks at the edges might not make good enough selvedges. Try putting one thread from each shaft in the outside dent, so with every shed some threads will catch.

Stiff linen wefts

To help stiff linen yarns fold smoothly over the selvedges, soak the wound bobbin in water for half an hour or lightly mist it. Squeeze out the excess moisture in a thick towel. If you use this method, be sure to wet all your bobbins. If you weave with some wet and some dry, the wefts won't turn around the selvedges the same, and the edges will be inconsistent. (If you are weaving in a humid place, be sure that the cloth is dry before it wraps around the cloth beam. Use a hair dryer , if necessary.)

Selvedges impede sheds

You might try weaving closer to the shafts where the shed is bigger to force the selvedge threads to open sufficiently for the weft to lie in the shed.

Your selvedge threads are too close together if the sheds can't open at the edges. Try skipping a dent in the middle of the selvedge, putting 3 instead of 4 threads in a dent, etc.

Edge threads fall off warp on beam

If the edge threads aren't supported on the warp beam, they will slip off the rolled up warp supply and ruin the warp tension. It could be that you tried to wind a warp that was too wide for your loom. It's never, never a good idea to make warps the full width of the loom. You need at least a couple of inches of empty warp beam on each edge for the outside threads to be supported. It's true whether you're using sticks or paper to pack the warp.

Also, it could be that the warp wasn't beamed on (wound on) the warp beam in precisely flat layers. It is an absolute must for every single warp end to be the same length and therefore, the same tension. If your warp beam looks like a football— thicker in the middle than on the edges, your edge threads won't be uniformly tensioned. The edges of the warp on the beam should look like cliffs. See Figure 194.

Hairy threads

Put mineral oil (a light oil) on selvedge threads to keep the hairs down. Or spray the warp with hair spray or gel to keep them down. See page 129 for other ideas of sprays. Opening the sheds one shaft at a time is another solution.

To open the sheds in the body of the warp, you also may need to lift one shaft at a time. When you plan the warp, mix other non-hairy yarns all across the warp to help separate the hairy ones from one another. Putting the hairy yarns all on the same shaft will allow you to raise that shaft by itself before adding the remainder of the shafts needed for the shed.

Replace the hairy threads at the selvedges with smooth yarns.

105

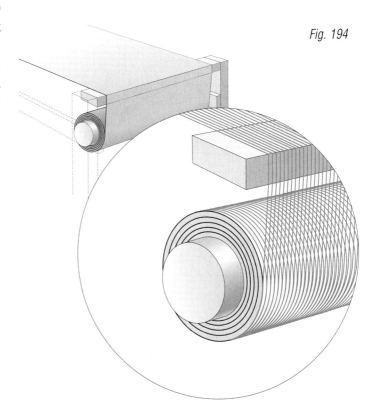

Fig. 194

One side is better and twist

It may be that the twist of the weft yarn has something to do with one selvedge being better. Tiny loops can form on one edge because as the shuttle changes direction it can slightly add twist to or take it out of the yarn. In Figure 195, see that the weft yarn has a S twist. (Read how to quickly determine if a yarn twists S or Z, on page 49.) When the shuttle exited the shed and entered the next one, a little loop occurred on the right edge because the direction of the weft yarn when it entered the shed opposed the natural lie of the S-twist weft yarn. On the left edge the shuttle direction is the same as the twist of the yarn, and a smooth turn of the weft occurs around the outside warp end. Figure 196 shows the reverse. With an Z-twist weft, the loop occurs on the left edge.

You can solve the problem yourself by taking out or putting in a little twist on your weft yarns. You can add or subtract a little twist when you take the yarn off cones or spools from the top and when you wind pirns. It may be that you are putting just enough twist into the weft yarns during winding to *cause* the problem! Read about adjusting the twist in the sidebar on page 50.

Remember, when you add or subtract twist from pirns and taking thread off the ends of yarn packages, you only change the twist slightly. Yarns with high or hard twist are more apt to contribute to this problem than soft yarns with only a little twist.

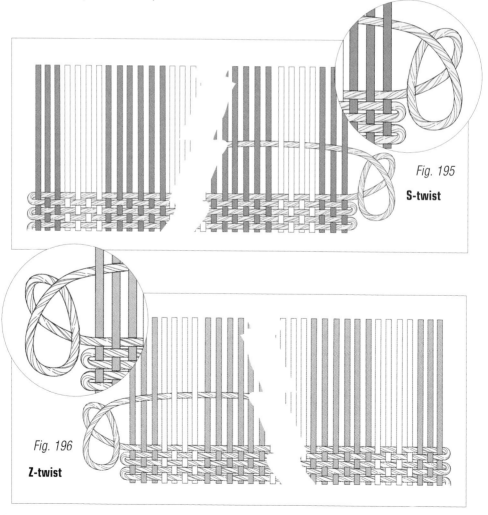

Fig. 195

S-twist

Fig. 196

Z-twist

4 Troubleshooting
...When You Begin Weaving

Chapter 4 has three sections to help you correct any problems that may occur during the weaving process. This section discusses how to recognize various mistakes and how to fix them when you begin your weaving.

Checking for Errors

If you've worked methodically when you were threading and sleying, and you checked your work frequently—after each section—you might never have to spend time re-doing instead of doing.

Once you've tied on the warp to the cloth apron rod, you can open the sheds to check for errors. If you find one, you may have to re-thread from the place of the mistake to the nearest selvedge, but many mistakes can be corrected without all that work.

Mistakes in threading usually don't appear until you have woven a little. A good way to see them easily is to weave the heading, or first inch or so, with a contrasting color weft in plain weave (tabby).

Errors are listed in the order of the most often found. Most mistakes need to be repaired in a way similar to that of broken warp threads, so that information is given first, and referred to when relevant problems are discussed.

Repairing Warp Threads

Whether repairs are due to errors in threading or to broken warp threads, the process is basically the same. There are two ways to make repairs: by replacing the warp thread completely or by making a splice. I make a replacement thread if the repair is near the end of the warp. Otherwise, I prefer to make a splice. In either case, having the lease sticks

in behind the heddles greatly speeds up the repair.

Making repair heddles

There are times, when making repairs, that a heddle is not in the place where you need it, and you will need to make your own heddle. Although commercially made repair heddles are available, it's easy to make one. Loop a length of string (I like to use cotton "carpet warp.") around the bottom heddle bar of the shaft; tie a square knot level with the base of the heddle eyes of the regular heddles on that shaft. To make the eye of your new heddle, tie another square knot above the first one, even with the tops of the regular heddle eyes. Tie the top of the new heddle to the top heddle bar of the shaft. See Figure 197. Be careful to tie the repair heddle onto the correct shaft on the top, as well as on the bottom. Be alert when making corrections—I can repeat the mistake instead of correcting it if I'm not careful.

Make a few repair heddles to have on hand, with safety pins at the top and bottom for easy insertion on the shaft bars.

If you have a lot of repair heddles to make, make a jig on a board, with finishing nails

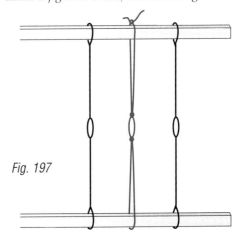

Fig. 197

positioned for the length of the heddle eye. Cut the strings longer than needed (more than twice the distance between the heddle bars on

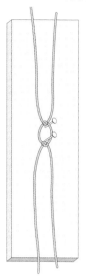

Fig. 198

the shafts) so there's enough length to tie the new heddles onto the bars as needed. Just tie the eyes, leaving the tops and the bottoms of the heddles untied—ready to put into place on the shafts later. See Figure 198.

Metal heddles can be cut and then used as repair heddles. With wire cutters, cut the loops that are at the top and bottom of a heddle. Cut the loops carefully and close to the center area of the loop—not at the tops or ends of the loops. This cut will give you enough loop to put the heddle onto the shaft like a hook. Be careful of the sharp edges. See Figure 199.

Unwanted heddles can be left on their shafts and remain empty during weaving. They will not be noticed in the cloth or interfere with the weaving in any way.

Fig. 199

Lease sticks make repairs easier

Ideally, the lease sticks stay in the warp until the warp comes off the loom, mainly because they are the key to repairing broken warp threads quickly and efficiently. See Figure 200.

 The lease sticks help you find and repair broken ends *faster*. With the sticks in place you can easily find the broken end and trace its

position through the lease to exactly where it belongs on the warp beam, in the heddles, or in the reed. It is a lot faster than hunting in the shafts for the empty, hard-to-find heddle, especially with very fine threads and many shafts. If you don't find the exact position in the lease when you repair a thread, you get crossed warp threads behind the heddles, which can make tangles in the warp.

Separate lease sticks

If it's too difficult to push the lease sticks back as a pair during weaving, you can separate them and work them back one at a time. Remember to secure the threads by tying a string on each stick from one end to the other, so you don't risk losing the lease (cross). See Figure 201.

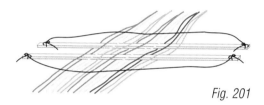

Fig. 201

A comb helps make repairs

Often, when making repairs, you need to hold the warp threads apart to make a repair heddle or re-thread one or mend a broken warp thread. A hair comb spreads out the threads and holds them apart while you work. Put the comb between the reed and the heddles if you're working at the front of the loom. Put it behind the shafts if you're working at the back.

Fig. 200

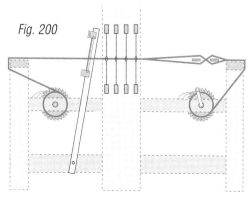

Repairing an error

Trace the problem threads back to the heddles. It's easier if you push the heddles, apart, away from the threads.

After discovering which threads need to be corrected, follow them back into the cloth from the fell as far as you can see—with any luck, only a few inches into the woven area—and cut them there carefully. See Figure 202. Pull the threads out from the cloth. See Figure 203. If there hasn't been any cloth woven yet, untie the bundle of warp threads containing the offending threads and pull them out of the bundle. Now, with the threads free, you can take them through the reed and heddles and make the correction. If there are only a few offending threads, and your warp is all nicely tensioned, you can cut the ends at the knot bundle, without untying any knots, and then make the corrections.

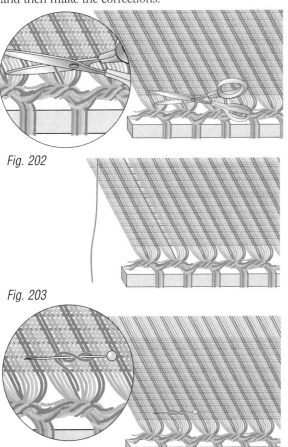

Fig. 202

Fig. 203

Fig. 204

☞ Use a pin like a cleat to re-tension the threads and anchor them to the woven cloth or a warp bundle tied onto the apron rod. See Figure 204. If the cut ends aren't long enough to wind around a pin, tie extensions to the warps with short lengths of the warp yarn. Secure a pin in the woven cloth or the warp bundle's knot. Tighten the thread to the correct tension and wind the cut end around a pin (like a cleat on a boat or a flag pole). You won't have any trouble knowing how much tension to put on the thread—do whatever feels right—just not too tight. If it's a tiny bit looser than the other threads, it will loop up and even itself out. You could darn it in later.

Repairing a broken warp: the splice method

Cut a piece of warp yarn that matches the broken end, about the length of the loom's depth, maybe a little longer if the loom is small. Whether I begin working on a repair at the front of the loom or at the back depends on where I noticed the break.

If I'm working at the front of the loom (the broken end is in front of the shafts), I first isolate the offending thread and tie the splice thread to the end of the broken end (I like to use an overhand knot—Figure 205). Anchor the other end of the splice thread to the woven cloth with a pin like a cleat (Figure 204).

Fig. 205

Then, pull the splice though the dent in the reed and heddle to the back of the loom. You can avoid manually threading through the reed and/or heddles by pulling the original warp end with the splice connected to it through them.

Fig. 206

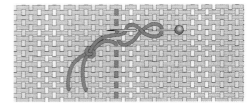

Pull the splice toward the back of the loom as far back as you can—through the lease sticks and close to the warp beam. With the splice and the original warp still connected, tie a slipknot at the back of the loom as shown in the the box below. See how to tie the special slip knot and how to un-do it. Go to the front of the loom and re-adjust the tension of the warp thread on the pin in the woven cloth. See Figures 206 and 207. The reason to tie the slipknot is that it will be easy to undo when it appears just behind the heddles. See Figure 208. At that time, undo the slip-knot and pull the splice connected to the original warp thread through the heddles and reed to the cloth and tension it on a new pin used like a cleat. You'll be winding the original thread on the pin, and the splice thread will no longer be used. See Figure 211.

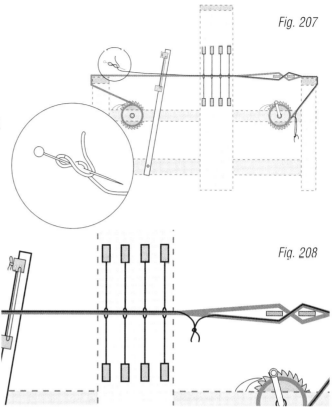

Fig. 207

Fig. 208

110

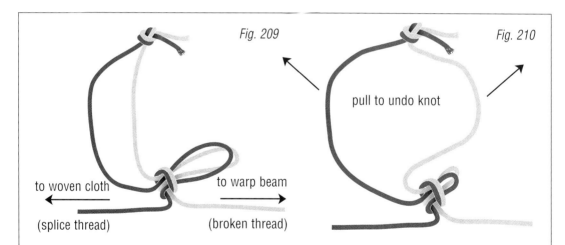

Fig. 209

Fig. 210

pull to undo knot

to woven cloth ←

to warp beam →

(splice thread)

(broken thread)

Tie a slip knot to take up the slack in a spliced thread

Pinch the splice thread and the broken thread to form a loop of the excess thread. Use the two threads in the loop together as one thread (the tail) to tie the slipknot. See Figure 209. Make a loop in the excess thread by crossing the tail on top of the pinched threads. Reach through the loop and grasp the tail pulling it to form a second loop. Tighten the knot by pulling the second loop away from the pinch. To loosen the slipknot, pull the two threads in the tail in opposite directions. See Figure 210. In order for the slipknot to hold, it is important to tie the slipknot using only the excess thread you've pinched off.[20]

[20] Halsey, Mike and Youngmark, Lore, *Foundations of Weaving.* David & Charles Ltd. England, 1975.

working the separation up toward the shafts. I drape the splice thread on top of the warp at right angles to the warps so I can easily see it from the front of the loom, and then I thread it through its heddle while I'm sitting at the front of the loom. See Figure 213.

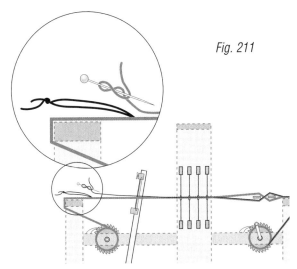

Fig. 211

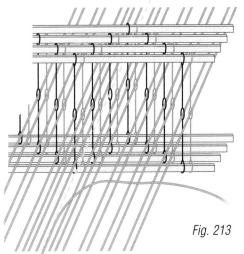

Fig. 213

Instead of using the slipknot, you can replace the overhand knot with a big bow. It works fine, but won't be as easy to undo as the slip-knot.

Another method is to weight the splice thread and let it dangle behind the back beam as you weave. When the original thread is long enough to go through the heddles and reed, attach it to the woven cloth on a pin. See Figure 212. Read more about this method in the replacement warp section.

With the same separating motion at the front of the loom, you can quickly find the correct dent, pull the thread through the reed, and anchor the splice thread in the cloth with a pin like a cleat. See Figure 214.

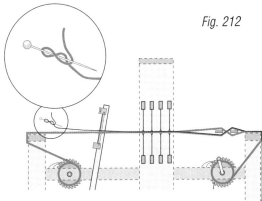

Fig. 212

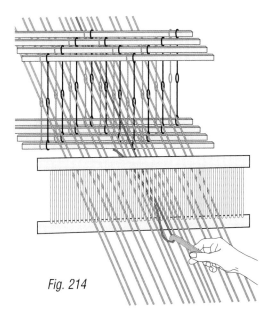

If the break is behind the heddles, connect one end of the splice thread to the broken warp end with an overhand knot (Figure 205 on page 109.) and tie the slip knot (see above) as close to the warp beam as you can. Then, it's quick and easy to find the empty heddle by pushing the threads on either side of the broken thread apart at the lease sticks and

Fig. 214

111

When the slipknot advances, continue weaving until the slipknot has moved forward to the back of the shafts. See Figure 208 on page 110. Then, stop and undo the slipknot as shown in Figure 210. By then, the original thread will be long enough to be pulled through the heddle and reed, and pinned like a cleat into the cloth Figure 211 on page 111. Resume weaving and never think of that warp thread again.

Instead of knotting the threads together behind the heddles, the splice thread could simply be clamped to the warps on either side of it as far back from the heddles as possible. A good clamp is a hemostat, a clamp-like instrument that surgeons use.[21] See where to order them in the Sources section at the end of this book. See Figure 215. When the hemostat advances to just behind the heddles, you can unclamp the warp and draw the original thread through the heddles just as though you had done the slip-knot procedure. Use small hemostats that are about 6" long or so.

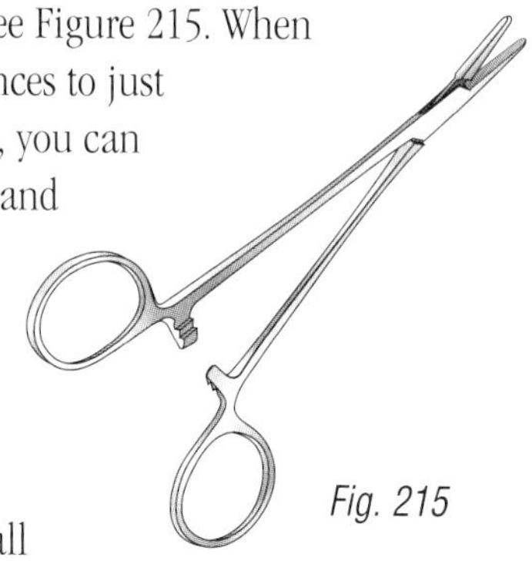

Fig. 215

Repairing a broken warp: the replacement warp method

Measure out a warp thread a bit longer than the original warp (refer to your project records for the correct length). You can work at the front of the loom or at the back, depending on where the break is located.

From the front, attach the replacement thread with an overhand knot (Figure 205, page 109) to the broken warp thread and draw it through the reed and/or heddles to the back of the loom. Then, cut the replacement thread apart

from the broken warp thread so that it can be weighted. Attach the free end of the replacement warp thread to the cloth by cleating it in place, (Figure 211) and weighting the replacement thread (Figure 216). You can use a film canister as shown below.

From the back, thread the replacement warp through the empty heddle and the reed. It is easy to find the empty heddle if the lease sticks are in the warp during weaving. Attach the new thread to the woven cloth or to the warp bundle at the apron rod using a pin like a cleat (see Figure 212). Wind the extra warp length at the back onto a spool and hang it over the back beam with a bit of weight to give it the same tension as the rest of the warp. Instead of a spool and a weight, you can use a 35-mm film canister. It makes a good weight, and you can put coins inside if more weight is needed. You can stuff the excess yarn inside (or wind it around the outside) and snap the cap onto the yarn to keep it from unwinding. See Figure 216. The thread needs to be unwound periodically as you weave when it reaches the back beam. Read more about weighting the threads in the sidebar opposite.

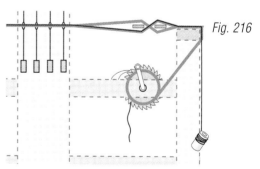

Fig. 216

Repairing a broken warp: the white glue method

You might be able to glue the ends of a broken thread with white glue. Wait 10 minutes for it to dry and see if you can weave past the break. I think it might be quicker to repair the thread as usual and continue weaving—unless the yarn seems right for gluing and you need a 10-minute break from weaving.

[21] Alderman, Sharon and Wertenberger, Kathryn, *Handwoven*, Tailormade Interweave Press, Loveland, CO. 1982. p. 56.

Weighting Repair and Loose Warps

Weavers have invented many ways to weight a single or a few warps. Harry Lindner adapts clothespins by boring holes near the ends where you pinch and tying on a fishing weight.[22]

Put a paper clip through the hole of a sewing thread spool; at the bottom of the spool, hook on a fishing weight, and at the top, hook the loose, or repair, thread.

To weight a single thread coming from a cone sitting on the floor below the warp beam, take the thread around the back beam one or two times then take it to the heddles, etc. These two times around provide the tension on the thread. You can also just hang a spool of thread off the back of the loom. See Figure 217 for how to loop the thread around itself to keep the spool from unwinding.

Sometimes, just hooking a paper clip over the loose thread with some weight on it does very well. See Figure 218. It moves along as the warp is unwound and never needs any more attention. Place the clip on its warp thread below the back beam. Instead of a paper clip, you can make a loop of smooth thread and encircle it around the loose warp and attach the ends of the loop to a film canister securing them by snapping them in the lid. Use a weight for each loose thread.

Old-fashioned shower curtain hangers are good for attaching the weights. They are available in hardware stores. See Figure 219.

Instead of weighting a yarn, it can be clamped with a hemostat (Figure 215) to a neighboring warp thread as far back toward the warp beam as possible. You have to unclamp it periodically so the threads can go through their separate heddles. The extra yarn can be wound on a pencil used as a small kitestick (Figure 220) or wound on a spool. The extra yarn can rest on the floor.

The weights

What you use for weights can vary, but they should be relatively small, so you can add and subtract weight in small increments. The first ones I bought were one-pound fishing weights! If I wanted to add a little bit of weight, I was stymied. I soon began using washers that I found at a garage sale. Tire weights, small stones, coins, etc., can work. Bleach bottles filled with water work and can be adjusted, but they are big so they would need to be re-adjusted more often than small weights.

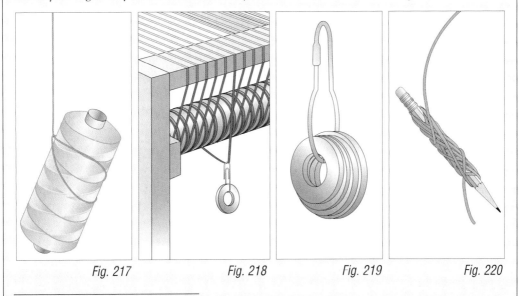

| Fig. 217 | Fig. 218 | Fig. 219 | Fig. 220 |

[22]Lindner, Harry. ibid., p. 44.

Threading Errors

Thread stays in the middle of the shed: Warp threads crossed

When you make a shed, you may see one or more threads sitting in the center of the shed, and you can't tell whether they belong in the top or bottom layer of warps. Check first to see if it's a loose thread sagging into the shed. See how to correct loose threads below and on page 132. It might be that the thread missed its heddle completely. More than likely, it's a crossed warp thread.

You can quickly tell if a crossed thread is the problem by reaching into the open shed and feeling for any tight warp threads, which indicate crossed threads. If the threads are crossed in any way, they won't weave and eventually, will impede your weaving. They must be corrected; the problem won't go away.

It's most likely that two threads have been crossed between the heddles and reed or among the heddles. Look behind the reed to see if a thread is crossing over an adjacent thread. See Figure 221. This problem results when you sley the reed with two or more threads in improper order. Threads may be

Fig. 221

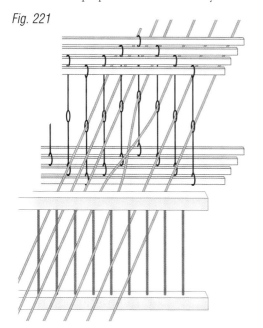

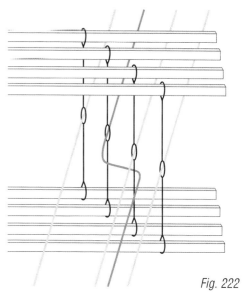

Fig. 222

crossed in the heddles, too. Look carefully, because it's harder to see crossed threads in the heddles. See Figure 222.

To correct the problem, untie the knot on the apron rod or cut the crossed threads and rearrange them in the correct order. If there is a little bit of cloth woven already, you're in luck and don't have to untie the knot on the apron rod. Follow the threads you are going to rearrange as far back into the woven cloth as you can and cut them at that point. See Figures 202 and 203 on page 109. It will give you enough thread to put on a pin like a cleat to re-tension them after repositioning. See Figure 204 also on page 109.

A thread sags into the shed: A loose warp thread

If a thread is very loose, it will sag into the shed. Cut it as far back into the cloth as possible (Figures 202 and 203), pull it towards you and re-tension it on a pin like a cleat in the woven cloth. If it's not long enough to wind on the pin, make an extension by tying a thread onto the warp thread. If you don't have any cloth woven at that point, undo the bundle on the cloth apron rod, re-tension the thread and re-tie the knot. If you don't want to untie the bundle, you can tie a short piece of warp thread to the warp and tie it onto the apron rod beside its bundle.

The cause of loose threads might be careless warping, beaming, or tying onto the apron rod. Remember, when beaming, the threads should go on the beam tightly.

Warp loops in the cloth:
Warp a little loose

If there are a few loose individual threads, they will soon loop up in the cloth and tighten up as needed, and you don't need to do a thing to tension them. When you tension the warp at the beginning by tying onto the cloth apron rod, don't agonize. If a bundle feels soft, it is. If it feels tight, it is. But if you are unsure, it's probably all right the way it is, and the tension is even and any individual loose ends will loop up and re-tension themselves.

One thread isn't weaving in:
Warp threads crossed

One thing you might not notice at first is a thread not woven in underneath the cloth. It is just floating. It is another symptom of crossed warps. See above.

Warp not in heddle eye

See page 116.

Two or three threads weave together:
Warp threads crossed

If you see two or more threads weaving along next to each other, all weaving in the same way, it probably is a crossed warp threads problem (see above), or it could be a threading error. Read on.

A thread is left out

If a thread is missing, you may find an empty heddle and dent space for it. The thread may have broken. Make a replacement warp thread as above. When you come to the loose end of the broken thread when weaving, tie the replacement to that end, and pull the original warp through the heddle and reed just like

for splicing. Remove the leftover replacement warp after winding the original end around a pin for warp tension. Read about the splice method of fixing a broken warp, above.

A thread was left out if you found threads on shafts 1,2,and 4 instead of 1,2,3, and 4. A thread on shaft 3 is missing. If you counted out all the threads and the heddles for each repeat as you threaded, the needed warp thread and heddle are near one another, and you only need to re-thread within the repeat. If they aren't in the repeat, you may have to insert a brand new thread on shaft 3 by making a new warp thread and a repair heddle for it. See how to make a replacement warp on page 112. Read how to make repair heddles on page 107. You probably also need to re-sley the reed from the error to whichever edge is nearer. It is not as daunting as you might think. Read how to do it easily in the sidebar on page 116.

A thread is on the wrong shaft

Threads threaded in the wrong sequence could be the problem. Trace the strand(s) in question to the heddles. If it's just a thread or two arranged out of order, all the threads are there and all the heddles. In other words, you want 1,2,3,4 threading and you have 1,2,2,4. There are the four threads needed, but there isn't a heddle for shaft 3 at that location. Check around the area for an empty heddle on shaft 3. If you find it nearby, re-thread all the threads in the group, and you'll be done. However, if no heddle is available on shaft 3, make a repair heddle in the place where you need it. See page 107. After getting the threads in their proper order, sley them in the reed. Since you're not adding or subtracting any threads, you shouldn't have to re-sley any other threads in the reed.

Two threads in the same heddle can cause them to weave together. If one of the threads is extra, remove it and hang it over the back of the loom and just leave it out during weaving. If one thread is needed for a heddle, put it into a nearby correct heddle.

Two threads through adjoining heddles on the same shaft will weave together, too.

Extra thread

An extra thread in the heddles, or an extra thread in an extra heddle, can be eliminated, hung off the warp beam, and never woven in. You can leave the empty heddle in place—it won't bother anything. However, the order of threads in the reed might need to be corrected, and you'll have to re-sley it to the nearest edge. It isn't difficult. See the sidebar below.

Three threads weave together

If three threads weave next to each other in plain weave (also called tabby), the middle thread has probably been threaded on the wrong shaft. In this case, tie a repair heddle on the correct shaft and take the thread through this new heddle.

A thick or thin line appears:
An error in the reed

You're weaving along and see that you have a thick or a thin "line" in the warp direction of the woven cloth. It may look like tight threads or loose ones. A thick line means too many ends were sleyed into a dent. Thin lines are from skipped dents or too few ends in a dent. If either occurs there's only one solution: re-sley the reed from the point of the error to the nearest selvedge. It is easy and quick using the method in the sidebar. Sometimes, you don't notice it until you are well into weaving the cloth, and then you have a dilemma: you can undo all that you've done and correct the mistake, starting over at that point, or leave it alone. I know I must fix it when I feel it disfigures the cloth. It's better to make the correction on the loom. Mending it in after the cloth is off the loom can be tedious, and may not provide a perfect look.

A broken warp

If a dent in the reed is empty or incompletely filled, it might be that a warp thread has broken, and that there is a corresponding heddle without a thread. Read how to repair warp threads, beginning on page 109.

A space in the warp

If a dent has been left empty in the reed, a space will show along the length of the cloth. Correct it as you would a sleying error discussed in the sidebar on re-sleying.

A thread slays stationary:
Thread not in a heddle

When an end stays stationary and doesn't take part in the shedding action, it isn't threaded into a heddle. You might not spot it at first because if it isn't being lifted, it will lie below the woven cloth. Your first clue may be a slack

---

A Fast Way to Re-sley Errors in the Reed

There's an easier way to re-sley the reed than un-threading all the ends that need to be moved at once. Instead, before un-threading anything, insert your sley hook into the new reed position for the incorrectly sleyed thread. Hook the thread to be moved behind the reed and draw it and the sley hook through the dent. In effect, you are "de-sleying" and "re-sleying" in one movement. See Figure 223.

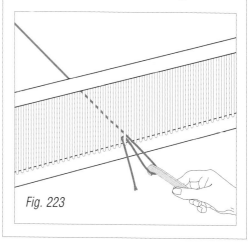

Fig. 223

end or, if you are paying close attention, an anomaly in the structure. If there is an empty heddle in the right place and on the right shaft for this end, cut the thread, take it through the heddle and attach the end by cleating it to a pin on the woven cloth. You might find the heddle near, but not exactly in the place where you need it. In this case, you will have to re-thread a group of threads to get the heddle into its proper position. If there is no heddle nearby, use a repair heddle. See page 107.

A crossed warp thread

It also could be a crossed thread. See page 114.

A thread floats above or below the cloth

It could be that the thread is not in a heddle or there are crossed warp threads. See above.

A warp thread rises higher or not at all:
The warp thread missed the heddle eye

An end that rises higher than the other ends is threaded into the top half of a string or Texsolv heddle instead of through the eye.

A warp thread floats under the cloth:
Missed heddle eye

An end that won't rise at all is threaded into the bottom loop of the heddle, below the eye or not threaded through the heddle at all.

Crossed threads could also be the problem. See page 114.

Extra or crossed heddles

After making your repairs, you might have a heddle here and there that are no longer going to be used on this project. They can stay on their shafts even though they are empty and won't show in the cloth or do any harm.

Crossed heddles can ride along empty on the shafts, too. They can never be used, however, so you might as well cut them out so they don't get in the way or cause mistakes in counting heddles on future warps.

Shed Problems

Your loom may need adjusting, which is covered in Book #2 in the chapter: "Adjusting Looms." Here are other shed problems.

Warp not over back or breast beam

If the warp isn't over **both** the back beam and the breast beam, you won't be able to get sheds. Check Figure 224 to see that your warp is going on the correct path over both beams. If the warp isn't over the back beam, you might be able to remove the beam and place it under the warp. If it's not possible, unroll the whole warp to the front of the loom (threads stay in heddles and reed), and re-tie the end stick to the warp beam apron rod with the warp going over the back beam. Then, beam the warp onto the warp beam.

If the threads are fragile or sticky and can't withstand going through the heddles and the reed, you'll have to take them out from the heddles and thread them all over again. Be sure that your lease sticks are in the warp; if you have taken them out, you can make one plain weave shed—or the nearest thing possible—and insert a stick. Make the opposite shed—lift what was *down*—and insert the other. Getting the two sheds for the lease sticks may take some engineering

117

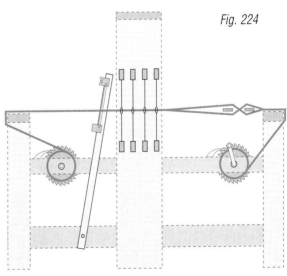

Fig. 224

because the reason you're doing all this is that you can't get a shed. Try making one shed and get a helper to step on the treadle while you guide the lease sticks into the shed.

If the warp isn't over the breast beam, the easiest thing to do is to untie the bundles of warp threads on the cloth apron rod, re-route the warps over the breast beam and re-tie the bundles.

Lease sticks impeding

If you suddenly find that you can't open the sheds after you've advanced the warp, it's probably that the lease sticks have moved up too close to the back shaft. When you weave with the lease sticks in, as I recommend, because it makes repairs much faster, the lease sticks will advance toward the shafts. Many people tie them to the back beam so they don't move forward, but I prefer to let them move freely and to move them back periodically. This job gives me a reason to pause and stretch and also to check behind the heddles to see if there are any knots in the warps or bits of fuzz that need to be repaired or removed. Figure 224 shows where the lease sticks should be during weaving.

If the lease sticks are difficult to push back, before taking them out, tie each one separately, so you can push one at a time. See how to tie them separately in Figure 201 on page 108.

Many table looms, because they are so small, have a very short space between the shafts and the back beam, and there may not be room at all for the lease sticks during weaving. With the sticks in, it's not possible to get a shed because the sticks prevent the warps from moving up and down. Remove the lease sticks, even though they can be helpful; getting sheds is more important.

Warp tension too high

On jack looms, the sheds can't open if the warp tension is too high. Reduce the tension and see if the sheds improve.

Warp tension too low

Maybe you don't have enough tension on the warp to get a good shed!

Sticky warps

Sometimes, threads stick together and prevent the warp from making a good shed. The warp may be too slack. The sticking might stop after weaving the first foot of cloth (where the warp threads were handled when threading). They might be so sticky that the beater won't move.

Hairy threads

Usually, the threads that cling to one another are hairy ones. Beside preventing the sheds from opening, they can be the cause of weft skips, that is, some warp threads stick together and don't go up or down with the rest of the threads on the shafts forming the shed. Some yarns just might be too hairy for warps, mohair, for example, might not work as a warp unless the threads can be spread far enough apart that the sheds can open.

Sometimes, the sample weaves perfectly, but the full width cloth is hopelessly sticky so that the shed won't open. The application of a warp dressing is messy and damp (slow drying) at this point in the process, but a liberal spraying with heavy-duty hair spray (use "mega hold") will slick down the hairy bits and make the weaving go more easily. Spray on the heddle side of the reed and behind the shafts and repeat each time the warp is advanced. The beauty of hair spray is that it dries quickly and washes out during finishing; the down side is that it isn't pleasant to breathe.

Static electricity

Static electricity can cause warp threads to cling. With low humidity fine silk warps are likely to build up a static electrical charge as the sheds are changed. Synthetic yarns are likely to do so, as well. If your heddles and reed won't rust, mist the threads with water. Hair spray dries quickly and won't rust the heddles. Sprays that eliminate static in the clothes dryer will work. Don't use much and read the label to make sure nothing in the can will harm your loom or your threads. Sizing the yarns works, too. There are a lot of suggestions in the sidebar on page 128. Many preparations are found around the house (see Spray the Warp, below). Read more about humidity on pages 131 and 132.

Solutions

Raise just one shaft at a time when making the sheds. Here is a clever way to set up your treadles for weaving plain weave (tabby) on four shafts. If the loom doesn't have a direct tie-up, tie the treadles this way using 4 treadles. From left to right: shaft 1 on treadle #1, shaft #2 on treadle #2, shafts 2&4 on treadle #3, and shafts 1&3 on treadle 4. Here's the sequence so you can walk the treadles (alternate your feet):

> Treadle #1 (lifts shaft #1)
>
> Treadle #4 (completes the 1 and 3 shed by lifting 3)
>
> Treadle #2 (lifts shaft #2)
>
> Treadle #3 (completes the 2,4 shed by lifting 4)

Raising the shafts one at a time to make the sheds can be done the same way on a dobby loom or on a computerized loom.

Strum the warp with your fingertips on the top of the shed before entering the shuttle into the shed to help separate the sticky threads.

Weave with the fell closer to the shafts. See pages 120 and 124.

Advance the warp often, so no areas on the threads get too much abrasion from the heddles and reed, making the threads even stickier.

Beat twice. See page 26.

Mix sticky threads with non-sticky ones.

Put sticky threads on one shaft, so they are easy to lift separately.

Watch out for pills on the yarns; see page 128.

The threads may have been sett too close if the warp continues to stick. Also, read about heddle density, below.

Spray the warp. Spray when you advance the warp. Spray behind the heddles and in front of the reed, and let it dry with a shed open before beginning to weave. It can slow you down a lot, but if you've already tried advancing the warp very, very often, it might be your only solution to saving the warp. Protect the loom by placing plastic over the breast beam. Read more about hairy yarns on page 118. See the sidebar about sizing on page 128.

Here is a list of things to spray on the warp that might be found around the house—fabric finish, spray sizing, hair gel or conditioner, Static Guard, spray starch, hair spray, "No More Tangles," water, oil (not yellow oil which might stain the yarn), hair conditioner, white glue, skim milk. When you choose a spray, remember that wool is weaker when wet, so be sure it is completely dry when you begin to weave. (Cotton and linen are stronger when wet.) Whatever you use, be sure it will wash out completely. Read the sidebar about sizing on page 128 for more solutions you can put on the yarn to smooth down hairy fibers on warp yarns.

Warps are too close
Heddle density

Sometimes, the threads are just sett so close together that the threads can't pass one another in the shafts. A rule of thumb is never to have more than 20-25 ends per inch (epi) on one shaft—no matter how fine and strong the warp threads are. If you have extra shafts, you can re-thread the warp threads so they are not so dense in the heddles but are the same density in the cloth as originally planned. For example, you can weave plain weave (tabby) on just two shafts. If you use four shafts, you'll be spreading the threads out more in the heddles—there are 1/2 as many threads on each shaft, now. You can use six or eight shafts to spread them out even more. Another way to spread the warps apart in the heddles is to thread them on shafts 1 and 5 instead of on shafts 1 and 3.

Try opening the sheds one shaft at a time. See page 119. On future warps, use the heddle density rule

Besides not being able to get a shed, there is more friction and abrasion on the warp threads in the heddles when the threads are very dense in them. Abrasion leads to breakage.

For similar reasons, with a close sett warp, put several ends per dent in a larger reed rather than a fine reed. It will reduce abrasion on the warp threads. They will be able to pass one another in the reed without scraping up and down against the reed wires. You may get reed marks with many ends in a dent, which might come out in the wash, but they might not, too. Wash your sample before weaving your entire project, so you know what will happen, and see if you're satisfied with the result. Read more about reed marks on page 152.

Heddle eyes too big

One student of mine threaded a lovely supplementary warp pattern with the warp threads being very close together, not only in the reed, but also in the heddles. Her heddles were the inserted eye type and were too big to pass one another when lifting the shafts. It was impossible to get any of the sheds. The entire warp had to be re-threaded on another loom. A solution could have been to eliminate threads and open the sett, but it would have changed her design considerably.

Crossed threads in heddles

If there are many crossed threads within the heddles, they can prevent the sheds from opening. The only thing to do is uncross them all. Read about crossed threads on page 114.

Cords to treadles crossed

If the cords to the treadles are crossed, pressing on one treadle will also press on the crossed treadle and can prevent a shed from opening cleanly.

Cords on loom need adjusting

On countermarch looms, the cords may need adjusting. Read about adjusting these looms in Book #2 in the chapter on adjusting looms.

Shaft bars tied together

During threading, you might have tied the shafts together at the tops of the shafts (most likely on counter balance looms). If they are still tied together, they certainly will prevent the shafts from moving and forming sheds.

Inspect area around shafts

Check all around the shafts—above, below and at the sides. Lift one shaft at a time to identify a problem. Try pushing the shafts back and forth—they may be hung up somewhere. It could be that a shaft is jammed against the frame of the loom. Look for any inconsistencies; for example, some looms have cords above the shafts going over pulleys; check that all the cords' paths are identical. Consider a problem as a physics problem to solve. Be sure the lease sticks are not too close to the back shaft—they will prevent the shed from opening.

The lams could be caught, too.

Shed too small

If the sheds are too small, try weaving closer to the shafts where the sheds are the deepest. Try raising the treadles higher.

Sheds not clean

Check the height of all your shafts—if some are higher or lower, they will make unclean sheds. Adjust the offending shafts to match the height of the others. However, the shafts on looms with many shafts may not be meant to be level; the back shafts are lower than the front ones in order to make clean sheds.

An un-sleyed warp

A threaded but un-sleyed end will hang down between the shafts and the reed. It soon will be caught into the adjoining ends, preventing these from making clear sheds. The reed has to be re-sleyed to make room for the missed end. See Figure 225.

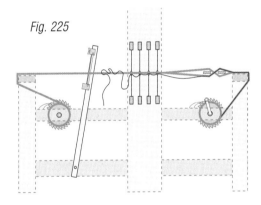

Fig. 225

Warp tension uneven

If the tension on the warp threads is uneven, you can still get a shed, but some warps may sag in the sheds. The shed isn't "clean." Re-tension the warps in the bundles on the cloth apron rod. If you beamed the warp tightly and carefully, there shouldn't be uneven tension further back at the warp beam. Read more about tension problems on page 141.

Loom needs adjustment

Cords can stretch over time, and may need adjusting so the shafts all make clean sheds. Treadle cords can stretch, too, making the shafts rise and fall unevenly. Knots in the treadle ties should not come undone or loosen if proper snitch knots are tied. See Figures 226a and b. Read how different

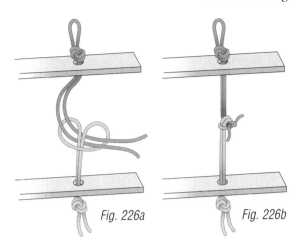

Fig. 226a   *Fig. 226b*

looms work in the Adjusting Looms Chapter in Book #2, beginning on page 111.

Sheds have loose and tight threads

This problem is seen on some jack looms, especially table looms. When the sheds are open, the threads on the bottom of the shed are loose; those on top are tight, because the shafts are too high when they are at rest. They should be at a level such that the heddle eyes are below a line drawn from the breast beam to the back beam. Lower the shafts if you can. Otherwise, build up the warp on the back beam by putting a dowel or smooth board under the warp and clamping it to the back beam. If you don't do something, the cloth can develop ridges. Read more about adjusting jack looms in Book #2 in the chapter on adjusting looms.

Beater won't move

If the beater won't move, the warp threads are too close together and probably sticky. Re-sley the reed, using one with larger spaces, if you want to keep the same warp sett. You might have to open the sett, however. Read about sticky warps on page 118.

Section of warp goes slack

If you find a whole section of the warp getting loose, it's probably that one of the bundles tied onto the cloth apron rod has loosened. If

121

you haven't woven too much, you can retie the bundle. If it happens later, you have an uneven warp tension problem. Try weighting the loose section of warp at the back of the loom. See Figure 232 on page 132. I don't like to do it, but you may have to pack something in the loose areas to take up the slack and tighten the warp. It might be as small as a pencil or lease stick or as big as a wad of yarn or cloth. However, first see if you can weave past the area and resume getting good-enough sheds. If that method fails, pad the cloth or the warps on the back beam, or wherever it will do the job of getting tension on the threads in the affected area.

The problem may be caused by the mixture of yarns you have in the warp. Tension problems are created when unlike yarns are used in *sections* in a warp. If different threads are intermingled among each other, the tension will stay uniform. If you want a stripe, and the threads in areas go slack or get tight, you'll have to weight one type of yarn separately. That might be by putting one of the yarns on a second warp beam or weighting those threads separately with weights. See page 8.

The problem might be *tight* threads in an area and you only notice the slacker ones. Look to see if the knots or straps on the cloth beam are protruding into the cloth and making bumps in the cloth. If so, they are causing the warp threads that are going over them to become shorter and, therefore, tighter. Pack the cloth beam with sticks. See page 28.

Twists in raddle groups

A few twists

There will be a few twists in the threads within the raddle groups, naturally, but they shouldn't slow down your weaving. A few twists can get hung up on the lease sticks, but you can push the twists back by working them toward the back beam during pauses in your weaving.

If this process seems like a chore to you, you can remove the sticks, and let the twists work themselves out between the back beam and the heddles. The extra distance and the action of making sheds gives the twists more space to get straightened out and feed properly into the heddles. True, you sacrifice the benefits of leaving the lease sticks in during weaving, but the twists may only work themselves out in this way.

Otherwise, try using the Swedish method of beaming the warp mentioned in Book #2, on page 14. Basically, this method uses a helper, with the thread-by-thread lease sticks worked through the warp while it winds onto the warp beam. This approach is used with yarns that twist naturally on themselves, unbalanced yarns. Read about severe twists below and in the sidebar on page 138.

Severe twists

If there are severe twists in the raddle groups, it may be that the raddle spaces were too large and too many threads were in each raddle section. Another reason is that the warp yarn is unbalanced and twists on itself. In Book #2, I discuss the problem on pages 38 and 176. Briefly, the warp needs to be beamed with the thread-by-thread lease sticks left in to prevent the yarns from *severely* twisting on themselves. With most threads, you can beam the warp with groups of threads in a raddle, but not with unbalanced yarns. Beaming warps with the lease sticks in is generally a bad idea because it can rough up the yarns as they are forced to go over and under the sticks.

A better method with these unbalanced yarns is to use a fine raddle so there is just one thread per dent. With this raddle, you have the thread-by-thread lease (cross) to keep the threads from twisting on themselves, but not the lease sticks in to rough up the yarn during beaming.

You can tell if a yarn is unbalanced because the yarns naturally twist and roll around each other when not under tension. See Figure 227. Read more about unbalanced yarns in the sidebar about kinks in yarns on page 138. Commercially made raddles (called warp combs or drawing-combs) can be made quite fine, say, 24 dents per inch for a warp that is 24 ends per inch.

Fig. 227

Cloth or Pattern Doesn't Look Right

Incorrect threading

Even when all the threads seem to be making good sheds, the order of the threading may not be exactly correct according to the threading draft. Check all the heddles/shafts/threads in the location of the problem carefully, with the threading draft.

Crossed threads

Threads crossed in the heddles or between the heddles and the reed can prevent the warp threads from doing what they were intended to do. Feel in the open shed for tight warps or look in the shed from the side and see if any threads are in the middle of it. See page 114.

Tie-up is reversed

It could be that the pattern you expected to see is on the underneath side of the cloth. If it is the case, your tie-up is reversed. Some tie-up drafts indicate shafts lowered rather than raised, or you might have a loom with shafts

that go down instead of the more common jack loom with shafts that go up. The solution is to tie up the empty spaces in the tie-up draft, rather than the filled ones. It will put the pattern on the top. Read more about tie-ups in the chapter on drafting.

Tie-up is wrong or hooks have fallen off

The tie-up may have been made incorrectly, or some of the treadle hooks may have fallen out. See page 1.

Wrong treadling sequence

Check the treadling draft carefully and make sure you're following it in the correct sequence. Sometimes, beginners look at the tie-up draft instead of the treadling draft when they are weaving. Experienced weavers know that the tie-up draft only gives the combinations of shafts that are to be used for the particular pattern. The *sequence* that these combinations are to be used is given in the treadling draft. See the chapter on drafting.

Out of proportion

To make the pattern square, you may have to change the size of your weft yarns to get a proportion that works with your warp threads. Too large wefts make the pattern elongated. Too fine wefts make the pattern units squished or not tall enough. Read about squaring the pattern on page 24.

Change the sett or the beat if changing the size of the yarns doesn't work. See page 24.

Colors disguise the pattern

It may be that the colors aren't working to make the pattern visible. Experiment to find colors that work with the pattern. Try colors of different values in your initial experiments. Use a very dark weft yarn, and then try something very light and then a medium value. Be sure to weave enough so you can really see what's happening with the cloth—a few inches will do, but 1/2" isn't enough.

Cloth doesn't look like the sample
Wefts don't beat in enough

The wefts might not pack in as much as in your sample. If your sample was small, narrow, or woven on another loom, you can't expect the same sett (epi) to work for a large piece of cloth. The wefts won't beat down the same because there's so much more friction, or resistance, on the beater from all those many more threads in the warp. The solution is to widen the sett (have fewer ends per inch) for the wider cloth.

 I suggest you make your final sample on the "real" warp; then, you'll know if the beat and the sett are O.K. You can wash that sample to know all you need to know about shrinkage and/or colors running. You can change the sett now and know how much longer to weave your design because you know how much the cloth will shrink. See page 39 about allowing for shrinkage. Then, you can weave your large piece without worrying about how it will turn out. Weave your sample at the beginning of the warp and make a two-stick heading (see page 4), so you can cut off the sample. With the two-stick heading, you won't waste warp yarn when you cut off the samples because you won't have to re-tie all the knots to get the warp back on tension. You also might be able to change your beat to achieve what you want. See page 24.

If the weft won't pack down well enough, it could be that the shed isn't open enough at the fell. If the shed doesn't open cleanly at the fell (dense or sticky warps might be the cause), weave closer to the shafts where the shed is taller.

Wefts pack in too much

The wefts may be too thin for the warp or the warps are too far apart for the weft. It may be that you're beating too hard. Read about beating on page 24.

Warps are too far apart

If the warps are too far apart, the wefts can pack in so much that the warps don't show at all. Try using a thicker weft. I would try doubling the weft or quadrupling it. A thicker weft will fill in the spaces, so both the warp and the

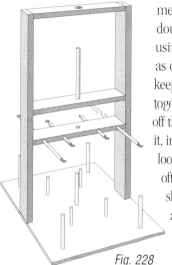

weft show. Use a commercial or homemade doubling stand when using multiple threads as one weft. This device keeps all the threads together as they come off the shuttle. Without it, individual threads get loose, and you must stop often to take up the slack. See Figure 228 and page 67. Another solution is to re-sley the reed so there are more warps per inch.

Fig. 228

Warps are too close

If the warps are so close that the wefts can't pack in, try using a thinner weft, or opening the sett.

Puckers in the cloth

Varying sizes of warps can cause puckers in the cloth. See Figure 229. Also, bands of thin wefts next to bands of thick wefts can cause the thin-weft area to pucker into the thick bands.

Fig. 229

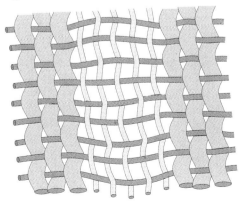

124

It might not show up until after finishing! Stripes of different textures or fibers can shrink differently in finishing and cause the cloth to pucker. Intermingling different yarns will eliminate puckers.

Weave structures look different

When different weave structures are woven across the warp, they takeup the warp differently and cause some areas of pattern to be too short and other areas to be too tall. It's the same idea as different sized yarns causing puckers. Where the warp is tighter, the wefts will pack in more, which will shorten the pattern. You may need to weight one of the structure's warps separately (see page 8) to keep the tension on the warp even.

Cloth too stretchy or shifts

Spun or reeled silk threads must be sett and beaten closer than other yarns. Otherwise, they shift, and the fabric becomes distorted and stretches out of shape Silk yarn should be sett closer than another yarn of the same size. Beat the wefts in close, too. The same number of picks per inch as ends per inch will give a balanced weave, which you may or may not want. Just be sure, in any case, to beat the wefts in tighter than you would for other fibers.

Unexpected tiny diagonal lines

After finishing or washing, your cloth may change character completely. The plain weave (tabby) that you wove now has millions of twill-like lines all over it, helter-skelter. This effect is called tracking or crow footing. It can happen when the cloth gets wet and is manipulated. It won't happen if the cloth is steamed or dry-cleaned. Usually, only plain weave tracks. The fibers swell and move around in the cloth. If a cloth is dense, there won't be room for the movement, and crow footing is less likely. It doesn't show up in pattern weaves. Worsted yarns are especially susceptible. If you don't want crow footing on

worsted—don't wet the cloth—steam or dry-clean it, instead. Read more on how to prevent this effect in the chapter on finishing, beginning on page 157.

This possibility is something you would learn from your sample and a good reason to support sampling and finishing the sample before proceeding to weave the whole cloth. You can make changes beforehand, so you won't have problems with the "real thing."

Colors run

Read about this problem in the finishing chapter, on page 164.

Getting stripes, borders to match

Read the section on measuring, beginning on page 37.

Shafts Don't Move Correctly

When the shafts do not move up and down easily when weaving on a counter balance loom, check that the loom cord has not slipped off the pulleys at the top of the loom, and that the lower bar of the shafts has not moved to one side so that it catches on the side of the loom or in among the string heddles of another shaft.

On other looms, see the section, "Inspect Area Around Shafts," on page 120.

Shafts tip

Keep a few empty heddles at each end of each shaft to stabilize the shafts and to prevent them from tipping. This problem is most likely to happen with a narrow warp where there aren't any heddles with warp yarns in them near the ends of the shafts. For shafts that don't have actual frames, just two bars connected by the heddles themselves, it is particularly important to have some heddles at both edges of the shafts.

Troubleshooting
...Broken Warp Threads

With strong, smooth yarns, you probably won't have many broken warp threads in your weaving life. But what about the threads that aren't quite that strong? Read how to choose a suitable warp yarn on page 127.

Read how to repair broken warp threads on page 109. Read why threads break, below.

Broken ends take time to repair and disrupt your weaving rhythm, so eliminate them as soon as possible. The sooner you repair them, the less mending you'll have to do later. A broken end left unattended behind the shafts will tangle with the nearby warp threads, and eventually, will cause them to break.

It's a good idea to see why an end breaks, especially, if the same thread breaks more than once. If it's at the selvedge, check the selvedge chapter for solutions. Otherwise, check the threads in the heddles and at the back beam, looking for threading errors, knots, etc. Be observant; see if you can solve the problem and prevent more breakage. See why threads break, below.

Why Warps Break During Weaving

Where the threads break can indicate the cause

When ends break during weaving, you can often discover the reason by observing at what point it happens.

> Advance the warp more often than usual if the warp threads are fragile, to reduce the abrasion on any one spot on the yarn from the heddles and reed.

For instance, broken ends near the fell of the cloth usually indicate that the *warp tension is too tight*, particularly if the yarn is soft and vulnerable to abrasion.

Breaks near the reed are often caused by a *poor shed opening*, which doesn't give the shuttle a clear path through the shed. Also, a burr in the reed could abrade and break a warp thread. See page 131.

Broken ends in the shafts can be due to damaged, or *rough heddles*. String heddles are the most gentle for silk and fragile yarns, but wire heddles work, too. The older, flat-metal heddles can fray and cut silk threads. If there are only a few offending heddles, you can tie a tiny bit of yarn around the top of the heddle eye to cushion that point of the hole. See page 130.

Broken ends in the shafts can happen if the lease sticks have been allowed to move too close to them, causing a bad angle for the shed opening.

Yarn not suitable for warp

It may be that the yarn itself isn't suitable for a warp yarn. Some yarns are just not strong enough to be warp threads. There are two qualities to look for in a warp yarn: it must be strong enough not to pull apart when the warp is on tension, and it must resist abrasion from the heddles and reed.

The strength of a yarn is relative. It depends on the type of fiber (cotton, wool, silk, etc.), the amount of spin (twist), and the thickness. Many weavers forget the first two factors and rely on a medium or thick yarn to be strong enough for a warp. Fine yarns can be very much stronger than a thicker yarn of the same material if the spin is tight on the fine one and loose on the thick.

How to tell if a yarn is strong enough

To test a yarn for strength, take a length of the yarn 10" to 12" long and break it with a snap. If it snaps when it breaks, it will make a suitable warp yarn. It shows that it will take a certain amount of strain before breaking. The yarn that does not snap, but slowly pulls apart is not suitable because there is not enough spin (twist) in the yarn to hold the fibers together. This kind of yarn will be all right for weft because the weft yarn is never under as much tension as the warp. Once the cloth is woven, the threads support each other, there's no strain at that point on either the warp or the weft.

Fragile yarns (thin, softly spun, etc.) can be used for warp, but they must pass the strength/snap test. Even after passing that test a thread can still be considered fragile if it would suffer with any abrasion in the heddles and in the reed.

Add your common sense to this test in choosing yarns for a particular type of cloth. A sheer curtain would certainly take a different type of yarn from upholstery fabric.

Yarn frays and breaks

If you want to use a yarn that frays and breaks, avoid any friction that can cause abrasion on the yarns. Advance the warp often, so no one area of the yarn rides too long in a heddle or in the reed and becomes abraded.

Change the sheds when the beater is against the fell of the cloth to help prevent the reed from abrading too much.

Lift one shaft at a time when making the sheds. See page 119.

Move the beater as short a distance as possible, with the fell close to the shafts. Swing the beater gently, and do not beat more than once.

The sett may be too close and/or the reed may be too fine. You'll need to use a reed with wider dents and/or open out the sett. For a given warp density (sett, ends per inch, or epi), a reed with wider dents and more threads per dent will cause less abrasion on the yarns than a finer reed with just one thread per dent.

Do not drag the warp through lease sticks during beaming. It causes abrasion and strain on the warp threads.

Be aware of, or repair, or deal with a rough heddle or reed wire. See page 130.

Warp the loom back-to-front

Warp your loom back-to-front, using a raddle, to allow you to handle the yarn as little as possible. This way of warping is the subject of my Book #2. Briefly, the process is to put the warp into a raddle as soon as it has been taken off the warping board or reel. The raddle guides the warp threads onto the warp beam. After the warp has been beamed on the warp beam, the heddles are threaded, the reed sleyed, and the warp tied onto the cloth apron rod. The process begins at the back of the loom and ends at the front. A raddle is shown in Figure 230. Figure 231 shows that the warp is beamed onto the warp beam before it is threaded in the heddles.

Fig. 230

Fig. 231

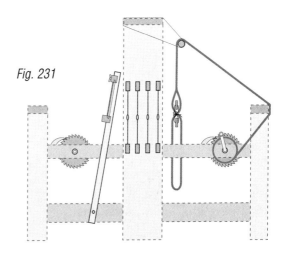

Yarn pills

If the warp yarns pill, they are getting too much abrasion. These little, innocent-looking pills can cause serious problems, especially with fragile and fine warps. The pills actually join threads together as though they were knotted. It is almost impossible to separate the threads if the pills are allowed to fully form and to become very tight balls. If there is *any* fuzz around a warp thread, get rid of it immediately, before a pill can form. Get up very often and look at the warp threads behind the shafts and pick off any fuzz. You must be diligent.

A tightly twisted yarn pills less than one that's loosely twisted.

One reason yarns may pill is that the reed may have rough wires. See page 131.

Using fuzzy yarns

The fuzz on some yarns can be roughed up in the heddles and in the reed.

There are lots of things to spray on the yarn to smooth out the fuzziness. Make sure anything you use will wash out completely. See a list of sprays and how to use them on page 119.

If very fluffy yarns are used in the warp, they should be spaced fairly far apart (fewer ends per inch). If they are too close together, the yarns will chafe each other during weaving, when the sheds are made. They may break or even disintegrate during weaving. You might use them as a supplementary warp, with a foundation warp thread that is finer and stronger, for example, and a fluffy yarn after every 4 warp threads.

Warp yarns with slubs

Some slub yarns can be used as warp threads. To test a yarn, pinch the yarn at the slub with your thumbnail and the nail of your index finger. Scrape your thumbnail and forefinger along the yarn. If the slub doesn't move along the yarn, it is stable. If the slub moves along the thread, it is not stable and can break or tangle with other threads causing them to break, too.

Sizing Yarns

Sizing preparations (sometimes called warp dressings) can be used to strengthen warp yarns and smooth down any loose fibers to make them more resistant to abrasion. They are applied to the warp before or after the loom is dressed, and washed out after the cloth is woven. Therefore, any sizing you buy, or recipe you use, must be water-soluble, so it can be completely washed out. It is employed on yarns that fray, pill, or break when used as warp yarns. However, if there are slubs in the yarn that drift apart under the tension of the warp, don't rely on sizing to glue the fibers; they are still unsuitable as warp yarns. Plied and medium to heavy yarns usually don't need sizing because they are strong enough and can resist abrasion.

Personally, I loathe the idea of using sizing, it's messy and another step that I wouldn't do unless absolutely necessary. Fragile, handspun yarns that are well spun can be used as warp yarns without sizing. Read the section about yarns that fray on page 127, and ways to treat fuzzy yarns above.

Sizing preparations

You might try spraying the warp. See the box opposite for a list of sprays that can be found around the house.

A commercial preparation for fragile warps, made by Nilus LeClerc, and called "Clerco," is good. See the "Sources" section at the end of the book. I have used it with success when the humidity was high and a fine wool singles warp kept breaking. It is painted on with a brush.

A sizing made of gelatin can be used. It doesn't discolor and washes out. Put some gelatin in water—just enough until you feel it. Then, soak the skeins, or run the threads through the solution and dry them. While they are still damp, snap the skeins to free the yarns from sticking to one another, or "bang" the skeins by hitting them against the edge of your kitchen counter. (This is a common practice in yarn dying.) There can be problems with very hairy yarns because the threads that touch each other will stick together as they dry, and may fray when pulled apart. To keep the threads apart, after squeezing out the excess sizing, wind the damp warp onto the warping board or reel in such a way that the threads do not touch each other. From time to time, take the yarn down and give it a good snap, as you would do to open a skein (see page 69), and wind it back on the board to continue drying. There are many other sizing recipes—too many to cover here. Look for more information in the literature for handspinners.

How to apply sizing

Linda Heinrich suggests the following: "The least messy way is to paint the warp while it is on the loom. Before starting to weave, paint the front of the warp with a brush. Run your fingers under the warp threads to coat them as well. Wind the warp toward the cloth beam so that the warp in the harness (shaft) area is treated.

Things to spray on the warp that might be found around the house

Fabric finish

Spray sizing

Hair gel or conditioner

Static Guard

Spray starch

Hair spray

"No More Tangles"

Oil (not yellow which might stain)

Hair conditioner

White glue

Skim milk

"Once painted, the threads can be separated to dry by propping open a shed. After drying, close the shed and wind the warp back to its original position. Now paint the back of the warp, between the harnesses (shafts) and the back beam. Continue to paint the area behind the shafts as you weave and advance the warp.

"A surplus of sizing solution will cause the warp to sag. Mop up any excess with an absorbent towel. Some weavers weave while the sizing is still damp; others let it dry first. Either way is fine, but do be consistent, and always remember not to roll wet fabric onto the cloth beam.

"...Immersing warp chains into solutions may pose more of a problem. I tried immersing a warp chain once with a flaxseed size, and it was like trying to manage a jelly-bag. And worse yet, the sized chain dried into a solid rope making it impossible to separate the threads without either damaging or tearing them."[23]

Sizing weft yarns

You might wonder why one would size weft yarns since they are not under any tension or subjected to abrasion.

Mohair yarn can be very fuzzy and difficult to get off the shuttle; sizing can smooth down the fibers. Also, read how to wind mohair yarn onto bobbins on page 65.

Sizing the weft may help you to get a balanced weave. If only the warps are sized, un-sized wefts tend to pack down more. With both sized, it will be easier to get the same number of warps per inch and wefts per inch. If you don't size the wefts, be careful when beating not to allow the weft to pack in too much. Beat on a closed shed to impede the beater.

---

[23] Heinrich, Linda. *The Magic of Linen: Flax Seed to Woven Cloth*. Orca Book Publishers, Victoria, British Columbia, Canada. 1992. pp. 103-104.

Novelty yarns

Novelty yarns—ones with lots of texture—are usually composed of thin and textured threads spun to combine them into a single yarn. (The "threads" that make up a yarn are called plies.) The thin binder thread holds the component textured yarn(s) in place. If the binder breaks or stretches, or the texture thread slips when friction is applied to the tensioned yarn, it will not be a good yarn for a warp. Test the yarn by holding a short length under tension and rubbing it lightly but firmly between the nails of a finger and thumb. If the yarn slips, frays or breaks, it will not be a suitable warp yarn. See "Warp yarns with slubs" on page 128.

Weak yarns

Some yarns are just not strong enough to be used alone as warps. See page 126. Intermingle stronger threads among them in a warp, or only use them for weft.

Inferior warp yarn

Once in a while, I get a cone of yarn that has weak places in it, and the warp threads break. It might have gotten abused in the dye process. Black yarn at a bargain price often has been weakened by over-dyeing an outdated color or a bad dye lot black. You may not know you have a bad lot of yarn until the warp is already on the loom. You may be able to repair all the breaks, or you may have to discard the yarn.

 Advancing the warp often to prevent as much abrasion as possible in the heddles and reed can help keep the threads from breaking.

Weak place in the thread

In the spinning process, an occasional weak place in the yarn may crop up. It shouldn't happen more than once for a yarn. If it does, you have an inferior yarn. See above.

Warp tension too tight

Too much tension on a yarn that is soft and vulnerable to abrasion can cause it to break, often at the fell of the cloth.

Poor sheds

If the shed isn't clean, the shuttle won't have a clear path and can break yarns as it goes through. Look to see if there are loose threads hanging down in the shed (see page 114) or if a shaft(s) isn't raised (or lowered) as much as the others. Look to see how the shafts work and adjust them so the distances they travel make clean sheds. For a reference on adjusting looms, see Book #2.

 When you need to put more threads on some shafts than others, use the shafts closest to you for the ones that will have the most threads because it will take less strain to lift them.

Rough heddles

Breaks in the threads in the shafts probably mean that the heddle eyes are not smooth. If a heddle has a rough spot on the top of the eye, it can cut the warp thread or abrade it until the thread breaks. The rough spot is usually at the top of the eye because metal heddles are usually used on jack looms. At rest, the shafts pull the warp threads down, and the threads lie at the top of the eyes. Of course, a rough spot on the bottom of the eye would do similar damage when the shaft lifts the heddle. Tie a tiny bit of yarn around the end of the heddle eye to cushion the point of the hole. If that trick solves the problem, you know it's a bad heddle: cut out the heddle, now, and make a repair heddle (see page 107) in its place, so that heddle is completely out of commission and won't harm future threads. It's the older, flat-metal heddles that generally fray and cut silk and fragile threads. Read about rusty heddles on page 144.

String heddles are the most gentle for silk and fragile yarns, but your loom may not be able to use them because some looms depend on the weight of the shafts to hold the bottoms of the sheds in place.

Burr or rust on reed

If a thread or threads break consistently, it may be that there is a rough place in the reed (or heddle, see above paragraph).

A burr on the wire(s) or rust can abrade a thread and cause it to break. Use a fine grade of emery cloth, found in hardware stores, to "file" down a rough reed wire. If it's a pretty big job, start with a courser grade and end up with the finest grade. The cloth can be torn into strips, so you can "floss" the wires to smooth them. Read about rusty reeds on page 144.

Roughed up warps

If one area of the warp breaks, see the paragraph above. If an area is roughed up or gets fuzzy, it's probably rust (or burrs) on the reed. It may or may not show up right away when you begin weaving, but it will get worse and worse as the threads continue to be abraded. Use emery cloth--see the paragraph above.

You can pick out the fuzz that accumulated before you smoothed the reed when the cloth is off the loom—*before* finishing.

Picking off the fuzz while the cloth is on the loom can break your rhythm, but it might be easier to do it then, with the cloth on tension.

Some tight warps

If the tension on the warp is uneven, the tighter threads could break. Read about warp tension problems on page 141.

Knots in warp threads

In a coarse or a fragile yarn, it is better to cut out a knot that gets hung up in the reed as you beat, and treat it as a broken end. If you

don't, it will prevent the reed's movement and will stretch the warp thread until it breaks.

If the knot is small, and you've used a reed sleyed two ends per dent, it probably can pass through the reed without hanging it up. You can continue weaving, mending the cloth later, before finishing. Mending the cloth is called burling.

Shed changed too soon

Changing the shed before the weft is beaten against the fell can be hard on the warp threads and cause fragile threads to break at the selvedges, because it makes the warp narrow in. Remember, change the shed while the beater is at the fell of the cloth.

The tension on the threads in the heddles is relaxed as the beater hits the fell of the cloth. Therefore, it is useful to start the shed change at that time to take advantage of the relaxed tension. It saves strain on the yarn.

Shuttle thrown too soon

If the shed isn't completely open when you throw the shuttle, it could bump against the threads in the shed and break them. Pointed shuttles will deflect the threads rather than break them. If this situation is a problem for you (perhaps with double weave fabrics), prop a full-length mirror beside your loom in a position to show you that the shed is clear before throwing the shuttle. It might need to be a little distance from the loom, say, 12-20 inches

High humidity

Wool gets weak when wet and also when the humidity is high. The warp threads can break repeatedly. Sizing may be required. Read about sizing on page 128. If the humidity is breaking your threads, it might be necessary to relax the tension on the warp when you leave the loom for any length of time. Remember to beat in the last weft when you tension the warp again and resume weaving.

Low humidity

If cotton thread is breaking, put it in the freezer for a couple of days. As it defrosts, moisture is absorbed into the fibers. Cotton yarns are stronger when wet.

Shed too big

There is more strain on the warp threads, the larger the shed is. In fact, the biggest strain on the warp threads is in making the sheds. Ideally, the sheds are just big enough for the shuttle to go through. Any more than that is adding extra stress on the threads. Treadle with less pressure or re-tie the treadles so they travel shorter distances.

Sudden treadling

Too big sheds, plus forming the shed to quickly, can cause severe strain on fragile yarns.

Beater moves too fast

Moving the beater too fast can break fragile yarn.

Lease sticks have crept near the heddles

When threads break in the shafts, it could be that the lease sticks are too close to the back shaft. This position can create an undesirable angle of the warps to the sheds and cause excess strain on the warp threads.

Strain on the back shafts

There is more strain on the warps on back shafts because they have to rise the highest distance. The shafts with the most threads should be at the front of the loom to put the extra strain on as few threads as possible. Put your weakest yarns on the front shafts, when possible.

Loose threads

Threads that are loose hang down in the shed and can be snapped when the shuttle passes through it. Weight each loose thread individually or draw the slack thread forward and wind

it around a pin like a cleat. Figure 232 shows weighting individual and small groups of threads. To weight large sections of warp, see "Weighting Warps Separately" on page 8.

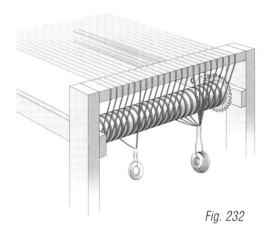

Fig. 232

Too much strain on warps

The strain from the change in tension on the yarn when beating and making the shed might require you to weight the yarns separately and not to beam them on the warp beam at all. Sometimes, I've beamed a warp and then un-beamed it to weight the threads separately. This process is called "warp weighting." Read about it on page 8, in the Preliminaries chapter.

Warp too dense: too many heddles on a shaft

If there are too many heddles on a shaft, the threads on that shaft are too close together, which can cause wear and tear on the threads. Abrasion leads to breakage. Advance the warp often so the chafing doesn't work on any one area of a thread very much. A general rule is never to have more than 20-25 ends per inch on a shaft—for any type of thread.

Troubleshooting
...Problems While Weaving Along

Preventing difficulties

I like to do everything ahead of time to make the weaving go well and without problems. I carefully determine the sett, how the selvedges should be handled, which yarns for warp and weft will not cause any trouble. Problems during weaving slow you down, but more importantly, they interrupt your rhythm—and an even rhythm is the most important factor in good weaving.

Check for knots in the warp threads or bits of fuzz, periodically—not once a week—but every time you pause to take a break or to move the lease sticks back. To avoid broken warp threads, make repairs; remove all hints of fuzz or pills as soon as you discover them. See page 128.

Fatigue can cause any number of mistakes: treadling mistakes, beating mistakes, and mistakes that come from not paying attention (e.g. throwing the shuttle into a shed that isn't completely open). Come to the loom when you are fresh—not at the end of the day when you're tired. You can become fatigued if you weave too long, as well.

Set a timer and stop and stretch or do some aerobic exercises periodically. Read about body mechanics on page 9. These breaks reduce brain and eye fatigue and thus, weaving errors. I like to stop at the computer every 1/2 hour, but at the loom, perhaps every hour is more appropriate to allow you to get your rhythm established.

Setting goals helps, especially when there's a lot of yardage to weave. Don't get up until the timer rings or until a certain amount has been woven. Then, stretch; go back to the loom fresh, and work toward the next goal. You might decide on an amount you plan to weave

in a day. Remember, a goal is just a goal—if you don't accomplish it in one day, start the next weaving session with a new goal for the day—don't think of yourself as being "behind." Negative thoughts can cause mistakes.

Listen to music; think about how nice the cloth will be in the end, or any good thoughts while weaving. Put negative thoughts or worries outside the studio during your weaving session.

Un-weaving Techniques
Why not to unweave

You may want to unweave to correct an error—whether it's a few rows or a few inches back from the fell of the cloth. You may think that's all there is to it—just unweave. But serious problems can occur if you unweave the cloth weft-by-weft. Un-weaving by reversing the order of the sheds abrades the warp threads as the beater goes back. As the wefts are dragged out of the not-so-open sheds, they can fluff up the yarns (especially soft wools) and affect the appearance of the cloth after finishing. (You might not notice any difference until after the finishing is done.) Un-weaving can rough up fine wool warps to the point of breaking them.

Un-weaving can change the twist in the warp yarns, changing the appearance of an area of cloth. It's entirely likely that you won't notice it until after finishing.

Some weaves are almost impossible to unweave because their treadling sequences are so complex. Double weave is especially hard to unweave because you can't see the bottom layer and may not treadle the correct shed for the weft to pull out. I find almost all unweaving to be tedious. I do un-weave a row or two, but usually, not more. Instead, I cut out the wefts.

Cutting out the wefts

Cutting out the weft threads puts no extra abrasion on the warps. It's also quick to do—quicker than making all the sheds necessary and passing the shuttle through them to unweave. I usually discard the wefts I've pulled out. Read about wefts that are too precious to discard, below. Read how to mend them in that paragraph, too.

Generally, I wouldn't cut out the wefts for more than a few inches—more than that and it would probably be easier to correct the mistake later when the cloth is off the loom. See when not to cut the wefts, below.

Sometimes, it's easier to cut the weft if the tension on the warp threads is increased a *little* bit. If you do increase the tension, be sure to put it back to "normal" when you resume weaving. With the shed closed, I cut the wefts at each side of the warp, about an inch in from the edge. If the warp is very wide, I might cut it at more places. Use your judgement as to which works the best for you in a given situation. At the place where I'm going to cut, I spread apart the warps a bit and snip the weft that's at the fell of the cloth first, and then succeeding ones, working back into the cloth for about an inch. As I work, I'm continually pushing the warp threads apart so I can get the points of my scissors in to cut the wefts, but *not* the warps. I use pointed scissors, have good light, and am fresh enough that I don't get lax and make mistakes and cut a warp thread by mistake. See Figure 233.

After cutting the wefts an inch in from each edge, I pull out the wefts, one-by-one, from the middle of the warp. I like to use a crochet hook or a tapestry needle

to grab, pulling it a little bit toward the reed. Then, I can grasp it with my fingers and pull it out. The wefts still at the selvedges can be removed by plucking at them a bit.

Check carefully that you've pulled out enough wefts and then, carefully, begin weaving again, watching that your pattern is accurate. Sometimes, I pull out one or two wefts beyond the error, so I can check the treadling sequence and be sure I start up again in the right spot.

When not to cut out the wefts

When cutting isn't efficient, I wouldn't cut more than a few inches. More than that and it may be easier to correct the mistake later, when the cloth is off the loom. Use your judgement, because, considering your weave, it might be too hard to repair the error when the cloth is off the loom, and you really must stop and cut back to the error.

If the weft yarns are too precious to cut and throw away, I leave the error in and darn in a new weft after the cloth is off the loom. That way, only the errant weft will be thrown away. In any case, precious or not, I do not recommend *un-weaving* for the reasons above. Read about darning, below. Again, make sure that the error can be repaired with fixing only one errant weft.

Un-weaving a single weft

It's often hard to un-weave the row where the problem weft is, because if you just slide your shuttle through the shed, the shed won't be clean (because of the mistake), and the thread from the shuttle gets hung up on the problem warp threads that didn't make the shed correctly in the first place. In that case, with the regular shed opened, lift up the weft where the

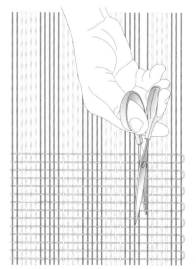

Fig. 233

errant threads are, and make a mini shed, so your shuttle can slide through the problem area. Then, take the shuttle through the remainder of the shed. It's easier than it sounds and saves a lot of time jockeying the weft out of the wrongly-made shed. See Figure 234 .

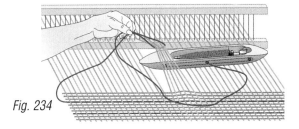

Fig. 234

Fixing flaws while the cloth is on the loom

If you notice a flaw in your cloth while weaving, it is often easier to stop and repair it while it is still on the loom, because the warp is under tension. On the other hand, you may decide that stopping to fix it will interrupt your weaving rhythm. Here are some reasons why you would or wouldn't stop weaving to fix a flaw.

Methods of correcting flaws begins on page 162, in the section about repairing mistakes after the cloth is off the loom.

Fixing Flaws a Few Rows Back

If the error happened just a few rows back, cut out the wefts to the mistake and begin weaving again. Read how to un-weave on page 134. Sometimes, another error occurs while fixing the first one. Be watchful for the next few rows that you have made the correction perfectly.

Fixing Flaws a Few Inches Back
Small flaws

For a flaw that occurred a few inches back, you can decide to stop and fix it now, or wait until after the cloth is off the loom. If the flaw is a small weft float over or under the cloth, you might fix it now. If you decide to fix it now, you may not need to un-weave to that point. You can thread a piece of the weft yarn in a tapestry needle and darn (weave with a needle) what should have been woven—extending your darn at least 1/2 inch beyond each end of the flaw. See Figure 235. Read more about darning repairs on page 162. Then, cut out the float, using rough cuts, if possible, or if needed. Read about rough cuts on page 34.

Large flaws

If a flaw is all across the warp, and the warp is wide, it's best to unweave back to that point and correct it. It would be a big job to mend such a long expanse, and it might still show up after the cloth is finished because the tension on your darned-in weft might be tighter or looser than all the other wefts. Be sure to read how to unweave, on page 134, so another flaw isn't created in the process. Read about darning a long weft after the cloth is off the loom, in the section on darning weft yarns, on page 162.

Weaving is crooked

If the woven cloth is higher on one side of the warp than the other, it may be that the beater was pulled against the fabric with more pressure on one side than the other. Or, it may have been set in the wrong position on one side of the loom, or have worked loose.

One half of the warp may have a different warp tension from the other. Check that the warp apron stick has not jammed on the side of the loom or on the ratchet wheel when advancing the warp.

It may be that the end stick is pulling away from the warp apron stick because the ties are failing or they weren't tied together evenly before the warp was beamed. See page 101 for a solution to this problem.

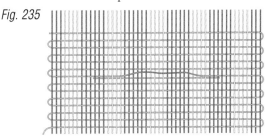

Fig. 235

Apron rod bows

When you tie on the warp, slip off any lashing that extends beyond the width of the warp. If you don't, the apron rod may bow under the tension of the warp. You can easily slip the lashing back on the apron rod for a wider warp at a later time. See Figures 236a and b. More details are in Book #2, beginning on page 61.

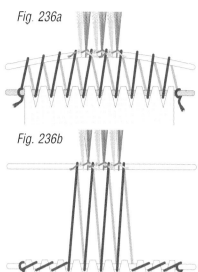

Fig. 236a

Fig. 236b

Packing sticks bow

On narrow warps, long packing sticks are needed to span the cords on the cloth beam. If the packing sticks bow up at the ends, tie them down at each end. See Figures 237a and b.

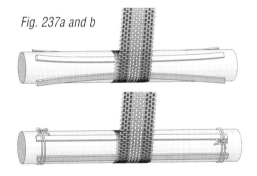

Fig. 237a and b

Basket weave not right

If your basket weave doesn't look like it should, with pairs of warps lying side by side, it may be that you didn't sley the reed in a special way—making sure that the pairs are not in the same dent in the reed. This method will keep the threads lined up and from rolling around each other and looking like there is just one thread instead of two next to each other. Rather than stopping to re-sley the reed, see if you can raise other pairs of warps in place of the usual shafts. Instead of lifting shafts 1and 2 against 3 and 4, make your basket weave with shafts 2 and 3 against 1 and 4.

Vertical flaws

Vertical flaws run in the warp direction. The most common cause is a mistake in sleying the reed. Read about it on page 116. It could be a threading error, as well. See page 114. A vertical flaw could also be caused by a broken warp thread that was never replaced, leaving a gap and showing more of the weft yarn in that vertical line.

A loose warp or a tight one can cause a flaw to appear in the cloth. A tight warp thread will appear slightly lighter in color than the other threads. It may be tighter because it was pulled too tight when repairing it. Loose threads will loop up and re-tension themselves unless they are very loose. In that case, adjust them by pulling the loop up on the surface of the cloth and pinning it into place at the right tension, using the pin like a cleat. See page 114.

Sometimes, these flaws don't show up until after the cloth is finished, when there is nothing that can be done to correct it!

Flaws in the warp should be corrected as soon as possible because there will be less mending (burling) to do once the cloth is off the loom. If the flaw occurs at the start of the warp, cut the offending end between the tie-on and the woven picks, pull it out of the cloth and pin it at the correct tension, or undo and retie the group which contains it. Use the pin like a cleat. See page 109.

Horizontal flaws and weft problems

Horizontal flaws run in the weft direction. The most common cause is that a shed was mistreadled or the shuttle skipped some threads in the shed. When you repair this flaw depends on how far back the mistake was made. If it was just a few rows back, I recommend un-weaving to that point and correcting the error. Learn the special techniques for un-weaving, beginning on page 134.

If the error is really far back in the cloth, my first choice is to mend it after the cloth is woven. However, if it is a wide warp and a serious flaw, the correction might be less visible if the cloth is unwoven and the weft put into the correct shed. Un-weaving, if not done properly, can show up in the cloth by abrading the warps or leaving fibers in the sheds. Read how to un-weave on page 134. Read about mending in the section on darning, beginning on page 162. Read about yarns too precious to cut and throw away on page 134.

Weft skips

A weft can skip over or under warps if the shed isn't clear or if you don't keep the shuttle on the shuttle race and it dives under or rides over unwanted warp threads. It's a very common flaw.

Weft streaks

An open space can appear if a weft wasn't beaten in closely enough. The best solution is to unweave to that point and begin weaving again. Read about un-weaving on page 134. Streaks often disappear during finishing, but if you see a streak, go back to it as soon as you can. It can be hard to repair this flaw by darning. If you darn in an extra weft, it won't be in the same sequence as the rest of the cloth. For example, in plain weave, you'd have to darn in two wefts to keep the odd-even sequence of the weave structure.

If you don't notice variations of beat until the cloth has been taken off the loom and held up to the light, you can disguise the variations by pushing the wefts around with a tapestry needle. Do it before finishing. The finishing process itself will help with the disguise, too.

Wefts not straight

Read about wavy wefts on pages 29 and 140.

Wefts that don't beat in straight could be caused by the beater not being square with the loom. Tighten the nuts and bolts on the beater. It also could be that your floor is uneven, which is making the beater not square. Prop up the low end as though it were a wobbly table in a restaurant. Use something strong enough to shim the loom so it's level.

Tangles in boat shuttles

Tangles in boat shuttles can be avoided by throwing and receiving the shuttles without jerky motions. Also, take the yarn from under the bobbin. Read much more about boat shuttles, beginning on page 60.

Sticky wefts

Sticky wefts, such as mohair, can be almost impossible to get off the bobbin. See page 65 for a way to tame these wefts. See Figure 237.

Fig. 237

Tangles and kinks

Only one kind of thread can't tangle: one under tension. If your yarn, in any situation, is a little tangled, give it a tug or put some tension on it.

Try spraying tangles with a silicone spray. Kinks in weft yarns can cause lots of problems. Read about them in the sidebar on page 138.

Kinks can appear in a skein of normal-looking yarn after washing or dyeing. Read how to block yarns in the "Handling Over-Twisted Yarns" section, in the sidebar on page 139.

Kinks in Yarn

Kinks in yarns form when the yarn is over-twisted and when it is not on tension. It's more of a problem for weft yarns than warp yarns, which are held under tension. As the yarn comes off the shuttle, it can kink, or curl up on itself, forming twisted loops of thread, which can become woven into the cloth and need to be removed. If you catch the kinky loop right away, you can open up the shed again and pull the kink out by tugging on the thread. If it's too far back, you'll have to cut out the kink after darning in a repair. Un-weaving a kinky weft thread is very tedious. Read about darning in repair threads on page 135.

Weft kinks are likely to appear in the middle of the cloth, not at the edge where the shuttle entered the shed, because there is some tension on the yarn at that point.

You might be adding the extra twist yourself in the way you're winding the pirns or bobbins, or the yarn might have been over-twisted to begin with. See below.

Test for over-twisted yarn

To check a yarn to see if it's unbalanced (over-twisted), hold it as in Figure 238a, a yard or so in from the cut end of the yarn on your spool or cone. If it twists on itself, as in Figure 238b, the yarn is over-twisted. If the yarn doesn't twist (Figure 238a), wet it and see if it kinks or twists on itself. If the yarn is in a skein, you usually can see the kinks because the yarn is not under tension. Read more about unbalanced yarns in Book # 2, on pages 38 and 176.

You might be putting in the kinks

Winding pirns and bobbins

Weft kinks can form as you wind your pirns or bobbins if you are taking the yarn off the top of the yarn package. If your yarn is on a spool and it happens, turn the spool upside down, and your problem will be eliminated. You add or subtract twist when you take the yarn off the top of a package of yarn. By turning a spool upside down when the yarn kinks, you can subtract some twist. Read about twist on page 50.

If you take the yarn from the side of a spool, you aren't changing the twist at all, so your yarn might not kink in the first place.

Yarns on cones are meant to be taken off the top end, so taking the yarn off the side isn't very workable. If it kinks, wind the yarn onto a spool or tube, and then take it off the end of the spool that subtracts twist. To conveniently take yarn off the side of a cone, stand it up it on a Lazy Susan, and pull the yarn off the side. See Figure 239.

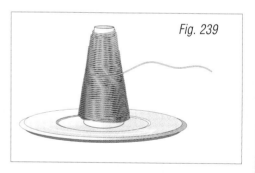

Fig. 239

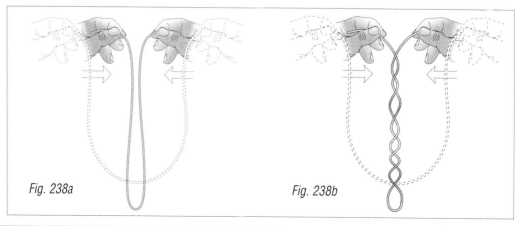

Fig. 238a

Fig. 238b

End-delivery shuttles

End-delivery shuttles change the twist in the yarn because the thread is taken off the end of the pirn, not the side. Read how to add or subtract twist to your yarns on pirns on page 50.

Boat shuttles

The yarn comes off the side of the bobbin in boat shuttles, so there is no twist change. If you're getting kinks with another type of shuttle, change to a boat shuttle, and the kink problem could vanish.

Balls of yarn

An old fashioned ball, wound by hand, won't change the twist in the yarn as it skitters around while being unwound. A ball made by a ball winder (Figure 240) lets you add or subtract twist depending on whether you pull the yarn out from the center or off the outside of the ball. See Figures 241 and 242. The amount of twist added or subtracted depends on the circumference of the yarn package. One twist is added or subtracted for one circumference of the package. Therefore, more twists per inch are added or subtracted with a smaller circumference than a larger one.

Fig. 240

Fig. 241

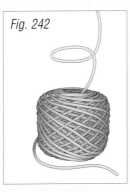

Fig. 242

Now, let's translate this twist/circumference information to balls wound on a ball winder. Yarn at the center of the ball, where the circumference is tiny, will have more twist added or subtracted than that at the outside of the ball, where the circumference is bigger. You can change the direction of the twist by turning the ball itself upside down, just like upending a spool or a tube!

Handling over-twisted yarns

The first line of action is to subtract twist by taking the yarn off one end or the other of the yarn package—Read "You Might Be Putting in the Kinks," above. You can subtract twist twice by taking it off the end of a spool and then winding it onto a pirn in a way that will subtract twist again as you weave. Read the sidebar on twist on page 50. If the yarn is on a cone, wind it off onto a spool or tube so you can take the yarn off the end and subtract some twist that way.

A kinky skein of yarn can be "blocked" to set the twist. That is, put the skein in water with a few drops of liquid detergent; then, hang it to dry with some weight on the skein to hold out the kinks. Use just enough weight to hold the skein out straight; or wind slightly damp skeins onto cones or spools to accomplish the same "unkinking" as drying the yarn in a skein under tension. A drastic measure is to take out some kinks by using a spinning wheel. Spinners know how to do it.

I did a lot of interesting projects using over-twisted yarns purposely. In the cloths, they "collapsed" (puckered) after they were wetted. Keeping the yarn under constant tension was the rule, and warping the loom back-to-front. See page 127.

Using the shuttles

In the chapter on shuttles, I tell a lot about putting tension on the weft thread. In end-delivery shuttles, the tensioning device accomplishes it. In boat shuttles, you can put your finger(s) on the bobbin as you remove the shuttle from the shed to put some tension on the weft. Read about ways to slow down the bobbin on page 65. You might use more tension than usual on kinky wefts, but don't use so much that you cut in at the selvedges and the selvedge threads break. You might need to use a temple to prevent the selvedge threads from breaking. Read about temples on page 94.

It's possible that the pirns or bobbins weren't wound tightly enough. Kinks form when there isn't enough tension on the threads.

Knots

Almost every situation with a knot is different, so you will need to use your own judgement. There's no one rule for getting rid of knots in the warp or weft.

Knots in warps

A knot in the warp can be mended later if it doesn't get hung up in the reed. If it does get caught in the reed, it's best to fix it right away, because the yarn will stretch and stretch and, eventually, break. Fix it just as you would a broken warp thread. See page 109.

Knots shouldn't catch in the reed if you sleyed the reed 2 ends per dent. However, if your warp thread has a lot of knots that are catching in the reed, you might consider lowering the reed a bit—the wires are more flexible in the middle of the reed than at the top and bottom. (I use this principle especially when I'm entering my sley hook while sleying the reed.) Try opening the sheds one shaft at a time to ease the knots through the reed.

An obvious solution is to re-sley the warp in a reed with larger spaces. You can maintain the original sett by putting more warps per dent. With wider spaces, the threads (and knots) can pass by one another and not be impeded by the reed wires. Be sure to read about reed marks on page 152.

Knots can catch in the heddles. Knots in the warp threads can prevent the sheds from opening or cause breakage if the heddles are very close together on the shafts. The solution is to spread the warp out on more shafts, if possible, to allow the heddles to pass by one another even if a warp knot happens along. A rule of thumb: never have more than 20 ends per inch on a single shaft. Read about heddle density on page 119.

Knots in wefts

You can cut out a knot in the weft and continue weaving as though you were just changing wefts. See page 32. Sometimes, I unpick the knot and use the ends of the threads that were tied together for the darns. Because the ends of the yarns are so short, I weave a tapestry needle into the cloth first, then thread it and pull the little short thread through the cloth. You can also decide to continue weaving, leaving the knot woven in to be mended after the cloth is off the loom, so you don't interrupt your rhythm. Read about darning on page 135.

Fell is wavy, concave, or convex

If the fell is wavy, and it doesn't show up until a fair amount of weaving has been done, it's probably that there are lumps or knots underneath, where the cloth is rolling up on the cloth beam. Unroll the beam and put in packing sticks to span the cords, making a smooth roll for the cloth to wind up on. See Figure 243. The lumps make the tension on the warp uneven. Where the humps are, the warp threads are tighter, and the weft packs in more closely, making little valleys in the fell. Where the warp tension is less, little hills occur. The fell becomes wavy, with hills and valleys. It must be corrected or it will get worse and cause warp tension problems. See below. If the warp is narrow and the packing sticks flare up at the ends, tie them down flat. See Figures 237a and 237b on page 136.

Fig. 243

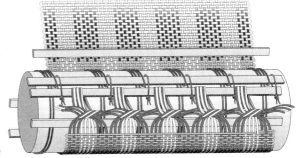

If you notice that the wefts are wavy right at the beginning of weaving, the warp tension isn't even. See Figure 244 and page 29.

If the fell is concave, see page 99; if it is convex, see page 100.

Fig. 244

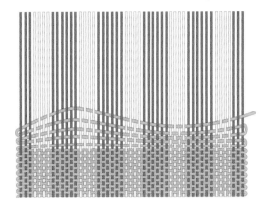

Warp rises above the shuttle race

On a jack loom, the warp tension could be too high if the warp rises above the shuttle race. If the tension is not the problem, see if you can raise the race by adjusting the beater height.

Another solution to getting the warp to sit on the shuttle race is to weave with the fell farther away from the shafts (closer to the breast beam).

Shafts float up

Many looms have a hard time holding just one shaft down when almost all the other shafts are raised. The one that should stay down floats up because so many threads around it are being lifted. Some looms have springs under the shafts to hold them down when making the sheds. Increase the tension on the springs if the shafts float. Note that if floating shafts is not an issue, have as little tension on the springs as you can, so the shafts are easier to lift. This problem generally occurs when the warps are dense. Try lifting one shaft at a time; see page 119.

Tension Problems

Read more about warp tension in the chapter on weaving, on page 29.

Poor beaming

Winding the warp over compressible materials

such as corrugated paper, heavy aprons, or straps can cause variations in tension. The best warp foundation is a bare wooden beam. Beams with a groove for the end stick don't require any aprons or cords. Read about them in Book #2, on page 25, and about a temporary apron on page 26. If there are straps, etc., or anything on the warp beam that may cause the warp to go on unevenly, you must use packing sticks to span them, so the warp is even on the warp beam. See Figure 245.

Fig. 245

Figure 237b on page 136 shows packing sticks for narrow warps with long packing sticks. Read more about packing sticks on the warp beam in Book #2, on page 34.

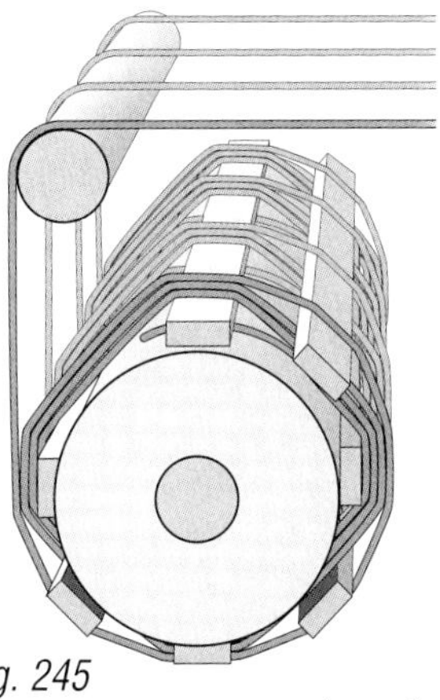

Warps on the warp beam may slip off at the edges.

Those edge threads will be looser or tighter than the other warps. Use packing paper or sticks to keep the edge threads evenly rolled on with the rest of the warp. See Figures 245 and 246. The warp should build up on the warp beam with edges like cliffs. See Figure 194 on page 105.

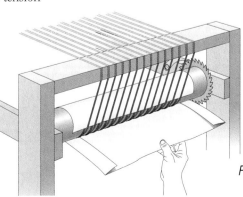

Fig. 246

Warp threads that bite into lower layers on the warp beam will cause uneven warp tension. It won't happen if you beam your warps on tight, tight, tight. See page 8.

Solutions

Pack sticks into the soft areas of the warp to even out the tension—you might have to re-beam the warp. To do it, pull the warp forward beyond the breast beam—keeping it in the heddles and reed. Then, re-wind the warp putting a lot of tension on it. Use the crank-and-yank method, that is, crank one revolution of the warp beam and yank 2" sections of the warp to tension what has just been wound onto the beam, then crank and yank again. If you have a helper, you tension the warp, and the helper turns the crank. Use paper or packing sticks as needed to keep the edges from slipping off the roll of warp. The edges should look like Figure 194, on page 105.

Warp beamed on too loosely

When a heavy weaving tension is applied to a loosely wound warp it can cause uneven warp tension. You can tell if it has happened if your warp looks snaky or wavy on the warp beam after you've woven off some of the warp. The outer layers slip around the beam and tighten up. On a long warp, friction stops the slip a few layers down, and the layers below become compressed. Yarns can't compress endways; instead, they buckle and take a snaky path around the beam. This problem won't affect the weaving until a few turns of warp are woven, and some of the buckled ends start to straighten out. They show up in a random fashion, a bunch here and a bunch there, and the carefully wound warp is suddenly uneven.

Different tensions on threads in warp

When using different kinds of threads in the warp, the tension should stay constant if the various threads are intermingled. However, if a group of one type of thread is next to a group of another type, the tensions in the different yarns may change differently as you weave along. If there are just two types of warp yarns, putting one of them on a second beam allows them to be under equal tension. If you don't have a second beam, or have more than two types of threads, weight them separately. Read about warp weighting on page 8.

Sectional beaming problems

The warp in each section on a sectional beam should be flat. If the warp curves upward at the dividers, the warp is too wide as it enters the section. If it curves down at the pegs, the warp is too narrow in the section. See Figure 247. A tension box with a pivoting reed solves the problem because you can slightly adjust the width of the warp by pivoting the reed. More details are in Book #2, beginning on page 95.

Fig. 247

One side of warp is slack

It sometimes happens that a warp becomes progressively slacker towards one side. It is generally caused by a badly placed end stick. Read Peter Collingwood's suggestion of a way to correct it, on page 101.

Threads soft on one shaft

This problem might only happen to a linen warp. The back shaft's threads might get soft if a shaft is a little low and it causes the threads on that shaft to stretch. Then, because they are longer, they will not be pulled as tight as the others and will sag down into the shed.

Automatic warp tension system-tension loosens

On looms with the automatic warp tension system (see below), you must beat lightly. If you beat hard, the tension will go soft. If your fabric requires a heavy beat, and/or you can't get yourself to beat softly, switch to the ratchet tension system. More details about how the tension system works are on page 8.

Another problem may be that the rope doesn't slip on its roller, and when you crank the warp forward, the tension just gets tighter and tighter. The cord on an older loom may have absorbed some of the finish from the roller, making the roller slippery. There needs to be some friction on the roller for it to work, so rough it up with sandpaper, just so the finish on the roller is removed. Replace the cord with sash cord or nylon cord. See Figure 248. If it's a new loom, and you need to help the cord slip to release the warp sometimes, reduce the tension on the cord and/or contact the loom manufacturer. They will know what material the roller is made of and what to do.

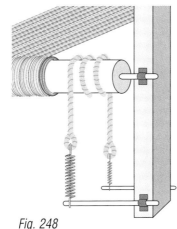

Fig. 248

No tension at all

If you can't get any tension on your warp, probably, you wound the warp on the warp beam the wrong way. Looms vary, with some winding one way and some the other. See Figures 249a and b. Check that it is wound correctly by engaging the brake and pulling

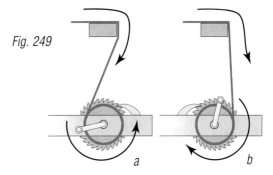

Fig. 249

a   b

on the warp or apron rod. If it doesn't hold, you know you've wound it the wrong way. The entire warp will need to be pulled forward in front of the reed and then rewound properly on the warp beam. You won't need to remove the warp from the heddles and reed, but you probably should wind up the excess warp you pull forward on one or more kitesticks so the threads stay on tension somewhat and don't tangle. See Figure 250.

A second alternative is to chain the warp sections like in crocheting instead of winding them on kitesticks. It isn't a good idea to just roll it up temporarily on the cloth beam, because it would be difficult to keep all the threads equally tensioned.

143

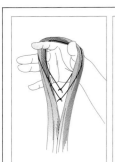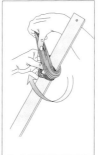

Fig. 250

Loom Problems

Shafts tip

Narrow warps on many looms need to have some empty heddles out at the ends of each shaft to keep them from tipping. So you don't have to worry, whether your warp is narrow or wide, always keep some there to stabilize the shafts.

Treadles uneven

The cords tied to treadles stretch with use and might need adjusting, so the sheds can all open cleanly. If you tied proper snitch knots (see page 2), the ties will be easy to re-adjust.

Treadle hooks come off

On some looms it is a huge and annoying problem. Sometimes, you don't notice until you've woven quite a bit that hooks have come off the treadles. Try not to "bang" the treadles or press them hard or suddenly; or use Texsolv cords rather than the hooks. See page 1.

Packing sticks slip

In Book #2, on page 34, I explain how to put in packing sticks so they won't slip as the warp is woven off. Briefly, it says to stagger packing sticks on the warp beam while beaming the warp.

Loom squeaks

Paraffin is good on the wooden parts of the loom. Listen to find out where the squeaks originate and what's rubbing or needs lubricating. Silicone spray lubricates metal and wood.

Stains on the warp

The warp can be stained from rust on the reed, see below. If it is a new reed, the oil on it should be removed before weaving by "flossing" it with a cloth or thick yarn in all the dents. If you don't remove the oil, make your warp longer to allow the oil to be absorbed by the excess warp threads passing through during weaving. You'll have to discard the cloth if the stains don't wash out. If your warp doesn't "clean" all the dents because it isn't as wide as the reed, you'll have to remove the oil on the unused reed wires when you use it to weave a wider warp. It's much better to take care of the job at the beginning

Rusty reeds

In a damp climate, the extra cost of stainless steel reeds (non-rusting) is well worth it. Rusty reeds are disgusting to look at, and if the rust isn't removed, it stains and abrades your warp threads.

Lay the reed on newspapers, dip a stiff-bristled scrub brush in powdered pumice and scrub vigorously, first on one side, then the other. Collect the pumice that falls onto the newspaper and use it over and over—it doesn't take much pumice. As the pumice gets rustier, the reed gets shinier and smoother. You can buy pumice at hardware stores. Finish the job with an oily cloth, WD-40, silicone spray, or Scotchgard Ultra Water Repellent With Mildew Block. Remember to wipe the reed down with a terrycloth rag to remove any oily residue to prevent staining warps; see above.

One of my students has a friend who sand blasted her rusty reeds for her—it worked fine, but the paper or tape on the top and bottom had to be replaced.

Rusty heddles

Rust on heddles can be removed with CLR (calcium, lime, rust remover), purchased in hardware stores or in the cleaning section of the supermarket. Place the heddles in a plastic container and pour in the full-strength liquid to cover. Check them every hour to see if the rust can be wiped off. It might take 3-4 hours—not overnight. Rinse, dry and rub them firmly between your fingers. To preserve them, spray with Scotchgard Ultra Water Repellant with Mildew Block. CLR is strong and very effective. Spraying with a silicone

Removing Rust Stains From Cloth

My modern stain pre-wash preparation doesn't get out rust stains. So, I've included the remedy from a 1959 U.S. Department of Agriculture pamphlet on stain removal. **Note**: Oxalic acid is a bleach for wood and is available in hardware stores.

Oxalic-acid method. *Moisten stain with oxalic acid solution (1 tablespoon of oxalic acid crystals in 1 cup warm water). If stain is not removed, heat the solution and repeat.*

If stain is stubborn, place oxalic acid crystals directly on the stain. Moisten with water as hot as is safe for fabric and allow to stand a few minutes, or dip in hot water. Repeat if necessary. Do not use this method on nylon.

Rinse article thoroughly. If allowed to dry in fabric, oxalic acid will cause damage.

Precaution: *Oxalic acid is poison if swallowed. Oxalic acid is used for rust and other metallic stains. Sold in crystalline form at hardware stores.*

As an acid, it weakens cellulose (plant) fibers and must be flushed from the fabric with more water than you think necessary. Then, just to be safe, make a paste with a little baking soda and water and spread it on the spot, rub it in and then wash the previously stained cloth.

Cream-of-tartar method. *Boil stained article in a solution containing 4 teaspoons of cream of tartar to each pint of water. Boil until stain is removed. Rise thoroughly.*

Lemon-juice method. *Spread the stained portion over a pan of boiling water and squeeze lemon juice on it.*

Or sprinkle salt on the stain, squeeze lemon juice on it, and spread in the sun to dry. Rinse thoroughly. Repeat if necessary.[24]

---

[24] McLendon, Verda I., *Removing Stains From Fabrics: home methods.* Home and Garden Bulletin No. 62. U.S. Department of Agriculture, 1959.

spray can also waterproof the heddles, so they won't rust again.[25]

Another suggestion for preserving heddles from rust is to rub them with beeswax. It also allows heddles to move freely on their frames. Sprays are, on the whole, easier to use, and they coat all surfaces in the heddles without missing spots, if used carefully.

Metal heddles won't slide

Spray metal heddle bars with a light coating of silicone spray. Use sparingly, wait, then wipe it off or it will get gunky. Beeswax or other candle wax is good, too. Don't use a bar of soap, because the soap attracts water from the air and causes rust.

To remove rust on metal heddle bars, scrub with Orange Hand Cleaner (with pumice). Rinse with water and dry. You can seal the metal with bluing, which is usually available at gun shops.

String heddles won't slide

Be sure to push string heddles around in their upright position—not on a slant, which would cause them to bind and not slide. Beeswax or paraffin on heddle bars makes the heddles slide better.

End stick pops out

Your loom may have a slot in the warp beam for the end stick. It is ideal because it allows you to wind onto a hard wood surface. When the stick is about to pop out of the beam slot, put in a temporary apron. Figure 251. Be sure

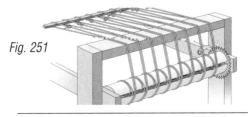

Fig. 251

---

[25] Friedel, Lynda, "Cleaning Old Heddles," *Handwoven.* Interweave Press, Loveland, CO. March/April 1997.

the loops of cord are long enough that the warp's end stick can advance all the way up to the back shafts, plus enough to wind around the warp beam about 1 ½ times. Wind the temporary apron onto the warp beam; then, tie your end stick with the warps on it to the free stick of the apron. Wind up the remaining warp. Now, you can weave almost to the end of the warp; the back loom waste will be only as long as the distance from the back shaft to the midpoint between the shafts and the breast beam. Page 26, in Book #2 has details.

Uneven Cloth

There are only two reasons for uneven cloth: uneven warp tension and uneven beat. See page 141 for more details on tension problems. See page 24, "Beat and warp tension."

Uneven warp tension

The warp may not be beamed uniformly and tightly; see page 8.

The warp threads coming off different types and sizes of packages (cones, spools, balls, etc.) can cause unevenly tensioned warp threads. Remember to use like packages and like sizes of packages, so all the threads are coming off the packages at the same tension when they are being put onto the warping board or reel.

If a linen thread is stretched once, it will stay stretched forever, and the loose thread could show in the cloth. Read more about linen on page 150.

If the cloth becomes lumpy and the fell becomes wavy, it's that there are lumps on the cloth beam fouling the cloth and therefore, the tension. See page 28.

Different yarns in the warp can make the warp tension uneven and the cloth uneven. See page 142.

Different weave structures in a warp may take up differently and make the warp tension and

the cloth uneven. The wefts will pack in more where the weave structure has more warp take-up, making the warp tension greater in that area. Read about weighting warps separately on page 8.

The warp bundles might not have been tied on evenly, which will make the hills and valleys at the fell and in the cloth associated with uneven warp tension.

If the weft yarns are wavy, it is caused by uneven warp tension. The loose areas make hills in the fell of the cloth and the tight areas, valleys. See pages 28 and 29.

Uneven warp tension may affect the colors after dyeing or finishing.

Crammed and spaced warps

Special effects called cramming and spacing can be achieved by putting extra warp ends in some dents and fewer ends in others. On long warps, two beams should be used because the crammed areas will take up more than the open areas. If you don't have two beams, one set of threads can be weighted separately. See page 8. You can get away with one beam for shorter warps, up to 5 yards. Over that length, the tensions on the threads can vary so much that you might not get good sheds.

Table looms

Some table looms tension threads unevenly when making the sheds and cause ridges in the cloth. The threads in the bottoms of the sheds are loose and the threads on top are tight. The shafts at rest need to be at a level such that the heddle eyes are below the line from the breast beam to the warp beam. If you can't lower the shafts, raise the warp at the back beam by putting a dowel or stick under the warp on top of the back beam.

Uneven beat

Read more about beating in the weaving chapter, beginning on page 22, and about horizontal flaws on page 136.

When you stop weaving, leave the warp on tension. Otherwise, you could see unevenly beaten areas where you stopped and then resumed weaving. However, if your warp was beamed on too loosely, the threads could become even slacker when you resume weaving, so, in that case, it is better to release the tension between sessions.

The distance the beater travels should be consistent for the cloth to look even. A series of graduations of color from that of weft dominance to warp dominance is frequently due to the difference in the length of the beat. Advance the warp about every two inches to avoid this effect. Details are on page 27. What makes this unevenness is that there is more force from the beater when it travels a greater distance, so the wefts pack in more, making the cloth more weft dominant. The wefts are farther apart when the distance is less—making the cloth more warp dominant.

The same number of picks per inch should continue throughout the cloth. See the paragraph above and strategies for getting an even beat on page 24.

Shuttles fall down

An end-delivery shuttle can fall on the floor if the pirn isn't wound properly, especially when using the fly shuttle beater. Read the very important directions for winding pirns on page 56.

A heavy yarn needs higher tension on the shuttle. If the shuttle is too light, the yarn tension can pull the shuttle off the shuttle race. See how heavy your shuttle should be on page 51.

If the beater or shuttle race is twisted, uneven or not level, the shuttle can fly off the shuttle race and onto the floor.

Fly shuttle beaters need to be carefully aligned for the shuttles to stay on the shuttle race. See page 18.

At the beginning, before there is any cloth accumulated, there is no place to set your shuttles down in front of you. A hand towel pinned in place over the apron cords will provide the "cloth" you need. See Figure 64, on page 46.

Twists in raddle groups

Information on normal or severe twists in raddle groups is on page 122.

Selvedge problems

Problems related to selvedges are in the selvedge chapter.

Cloth is shorter

Cloth will relax after it's taken off the loom. One of my students wove a rag rug. When she took it off the loom and put it on the floor, it immediately relaxed and was significantly shorter than the on-loom-on-tension measurement. Stretchy warps (for example many knitting yarns) will relax or collapse, as will cloth made with fat weft yarns or rags. Read about calculating take-up allowance for stretchy yarns on page 149. I'm making the case for sampling first, so you'll know how much extra to weave.

Of course, cloth usually shrinks during finishing, so calculate your warp length to allow enough for shrinkage. Weave structures with many floats will shrink more than plain weave because of the potential for the yarns to move closer together. You'll know how much your cloth will shrink after you finish (wash) your sample. Read about calculating shrinkage allowance on page 39.

Warp runs out too soon

You might be surprised that you don't have enough warp left to finish your project. There might be enough yarn to eke out a few inches by loosening the tension to get a better shed. Here are some more suggestions if you're desperate to weave a few more inches:

147

Remove the lease sticks behind the shafts.

If the loom's back beam folds up, folding it might give you the inches you need.

Unroll the warp on the warp beam and weight the warp in sections. Tie cord extensions on the sections and weight each one separately.

If your loom has many shafts, and you are not using them all, let the end of the warp "into" the castle area a little rather than stopping when the end is at the last shaft.

If you warped the loom front-to-back and have knots in the warp threads on the warp apron rod, you may be able to "recapture" the length used in making the knots. Untie them and retie overhand knots in small bundles at the ends of the threads. Then, lace a cord through the bundles and around the rod—or weight them.

If you're absolutely desperate, tie new warp threads onto the old ones to extend the warp length. Then, weight the yarns for the warp tension. See page 8. This method will give you enough length for the required loom waste, and you won't have to weave past the knots and then repair them all after the cloth is off the loom.

You can weave a few extra inches close to the reed with a very long blunt needle that upholsterers use, or use a rib from an old umbrella.

Not enough loom waste allowed

You may not have allowed enough loom waste for your loom. If you have lots of shafts, the castle area will be deeper, and there will be more loom waste necessitated than for a four-shaft loom. Remember, your loom waste is the distance from the mid-point between the breast beam and shafts to the point behind the last shaft. See Figures 252 and 253.

Not enough allowed for take-up

You may not have allowed enough for warp take-up in your calculations, and the end of the warp has come before you expected it.

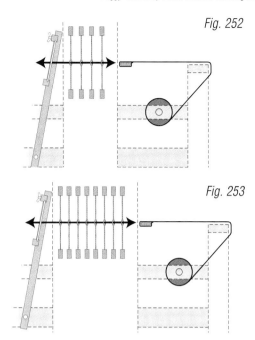

Fig. 252

Fig. 253

Large wefts take up more warp than fine ones because the warps need to bend more. You might need to allow 12" per yard for large wefts. See Figures 254 and 255. Note that weft-faced weaves take up very little; it's the wefts that do all the bending and the warps are left fairly straight.

You need only to allow take-up for the amount of the warp that will be woven—not for the beginning and end loom waste.

Fat *warps* will take up more then fine ones. See Figure 229, on page 124.

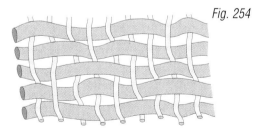

Fig. 254

Fig. 255

Some weave structures, such as leno, or gauze weave, take up a lot; again, try 12" per yard for warp take-up.

Warp-faced weaves will take up more, too, especially, with thick wefts.

Generally, I allow 10% for take-up when the yarn is neither large nor stretchy and for a relatively balanced weave. Linen is so inelastic that it doesn't take up as much as other fibers in weaving but shrinks in washing, so allow 10–15%. For a tapestry, the take-up is almost zero. The percentage of take-up could be as much as 50% for warp-faced cloths with large wefts. All these percentages are estimates. Allow more if it's really important, say 15% instead of 10%. If you repeat the project, you can calculate the actual take-up (see below) and use that number for the repeats.

Stretchy yarns can collapse or return to being un-stretched when they are off the warping board or reel. To know how much to allow for your calculation of take-up, experiment with a length of the yarn. Measure a yard when it is relaxed. Measure it again on tension and note the difference between the two measurements. This difference is the number of extra inches you should allow for every yard of your warp.

How to know actual take-up when the cloth has been cut off the loom

Keep track of how long the cloth is that you've woven as you go along. Be sure to measure what you wove for hems. It is easy to do if the cloth is all in one piece. If you have several pieces, be sure to add up all their measurements. Then, measure the front and back loom waste (the fringe at the beginning and end that can't be woven). Subtract this length of cloth and fringes from the length of warp you measured on the warping board or reel. The resulting number will tell you how much was "lost to take-up." To turn that information into a percentage, divide the smaller number (amount lost) by the larger number

(the length the warp was at the start). Move the decimal point over two places to the right to get the percentage. Say, your warp was measured at 9 yards (324 inches), and the cloth and loom waste came to 8 ½ yards (306 inches). The difference is 18". Divide 18 by 324 to get the percentage lost, which is .0555 or 5.5%.
(324 – 306 = 18; 18/324 = .0555; 05.55 = 5.5%.)

Not enough allowed for sampling

Perhaps the reason you are short of warp is that you wove too much for sampling at the beginning. I put the amount I'm allowing for samples on my warp planning worksheet and keep a record of what I've woven as I go along. Then, I know when I must stop sampling (or unweave some and sample some more). Figure 56, on page 41, shows a record sheet for keeping track of how much you've woven and how much warp is left.

Cloth looks ugly

It is a risk you take when you don't sample first. Nevertheless, I often find the cloth looks better after a day or two, or a friend says it looks great. Sometimes, there's what I call "post partum depression" right after you take the cloth off the loom. One weaver puts the cloth in a drawer and doesn't look at it for a week. After that time, he judges the cloth in two ways. First, did it do what I planned? Second, do I like the way it turned out?

If you're still not happy with it, give it more time—it might turn into another project completely. I hang pieces that aren't exactly O.K. in my bathroom; that way they aren't on a wall in the living room or in a gallery space, but I can still see them and think about improvements or ways to make them into something else.

One of the problems with the piece might be that you put in too many different things, so none stood out and shined; they all kind of negated each other. Read about ideas on page 155.

149

You might over-dye a cloth to save it. I saw a stunning set of quilts in a museum show years ago. The quilter had thrown all her beautifully crafted quilts into a black dye bath. It's pretty drastic, but they did relate because of all the shades and tones of gray.

You might cut up your cloth and use pieces of it for a project. All the pieces will be somewhat related because they were all on the same warp. If you really like one part of it, cut it out and mount it as a little wall piece; use it for a pocket, or a purse, or a pincushion!

Give it away, provided the recipient is worthy and appreciative of your work. Do not bad-mouth the piece to the public or non-weavers. They probably won't see what you are complaining about.

I had a student who un-raveled the whole cloth and used the yarn for something else! I couldn't believe it!

Linen fabric just off the loom often looks terribly disappointing—rough and almost like burlap. (Read more about finishing linen on page 192.) It's normal; it will soften and be beautiful after finishing. I have made beautiful linens by finishing them in the washing machine (normal cycle, warm water, regular detergent) and line drying them. While they are slightly damp, I iron them dry. For a hard press, I begin ironing them right from the washing machine, on a hard surface, one side and then, the other. I keep ironing and ironing, pushing the iron back and forth on the surface of the cloth, polishing it. Usually, I'm too impatient to continue until they are completely dry, so I hang the cloth carefully, so it doesn't wrinkle and so there is no mark from a towel bar. Later, I give it some more ironing to finish off the drying. Linen should be completely dry before handing or it will wrinkle and need ironing again. I've read about shocking linen to finish it by putting it in the freezer and then back into hot water a

few times. I've never had to give my cloth such severe treatment. Linen gets better looking the more it is used and washed; it gets softer and more supple. Inexpensive linen thread (tow linen) will never look as lustrous and supple as line linen; so if it's really rough, don't get your hopes up too high. Line linen is smoothly spun with long linen fibers and is more expensive than the rougher linen called tow linen. Wet spun tow linen can be smoother than dry spun, but never as smooth as line linen.

Linen problems

I've woven lots of linen fabric and not had much trouble, since I warp the loom back-to-front. Here are a few problems I've run into:

Some linen threads are unbalanced, and raddle groups can't be used in the warping process because the threads will roll up and twist on themselves. If it happens, it's impossible to weave. You'll have to unroll the warp towards the cloth beam and re-beam the warp with the threads in one-by-one order coming from the heddles. Read about unbalanced yarns on page 122.

Beam the warp on with a thread-by-thread lease (the cross), either with lease sticks in during beaming, or with a fine raddle with one thread per dent. A fine raddle is preferable to beaming with the lease sticks in because the yarns won't get roughed up or abraded going through the sticks. These raddles are called warp combs or drawing-in combs and are available from reed manufacturers. See Figure 252. More information about this tool is in Book #2.

Linen is not forgiving because it is not elastic. If a linen thread is stretched for any reason, it will not return to its original length. It will be forever stretched.

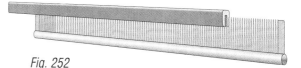

Fig. 252

A shuttle can hit a loose warp thread and snap or stretch it. So, if you have a sagging thread, repair it or weight it. To repair a loose thread, draw the slack forward and wind it around a pin like a cleat. Read about weighting on page 113.

Tying on a linen warp can be frustrating. Tie the warp bundles onto the cloth apron rod, as usual, mist the bundles and warp threads with water and begin to weave immediately. All the threads will work together and form an even tension. If you don't do the water treatment, some threads will loosen and some will tighten during the weaving. You can be re-tensioning them over and over. With the mist, there should not be any re-tensioning.

Slippery yarns

Read more about slippery yarns on pages 53 and 65.

On cones

If the yarn is slippery, sometimes, the outside turns of yarn drop to the bottom of the cone and get caught underneath it making it impossible to get the yarn off the cone. My favorite solution is to put a plastic baggie or a sock over the cone. I put the baggie upside down over the cone with a hole punctured into its bottom (now at the top of the cone) and draw the thread up off the cone through this hole. I tuck the top of the baggie (now at the base of the cone) snugly under the cone and tape it securely. A similar alternative is to put a sock on the package of yarn. I like to use a knee-high stocking. See Figure 107, on page 65. Socks for cones of slippery yarn are commercially made, and are called "bras." Check out a store where sergers and sewing machines are sold.

You can also set the cone of yarn on a piece of sheepskin (wool side up) or in a shallow dish filled with grains of rice.

In knots

Tying two slippery threads together can be a challenge. Use "Jim's Fisherman's Knot,"

explained in detail in Book #2, on page 165. The illustrations for tying the knot are shown here in Figure 253.

Another suggestion is to add in a fuzzy yarn with the slippery threads when tying the knot.

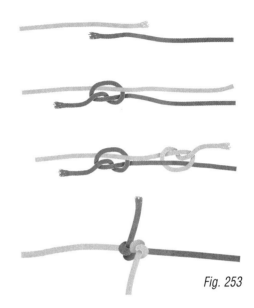

Fig. 253

Hard to see what you're doing
When threading

Good light is invaluable when you're threading. Threads may be hard to see because they are back-lit or because they blend with the rest of the warp coming from the warp beam. Rig a cloth or paper backdrop in a contrasting color to help the threads stand out clearly. Put it just behind the lease sticks wherever you can on your loom. See Figure 254.

Fig. 254

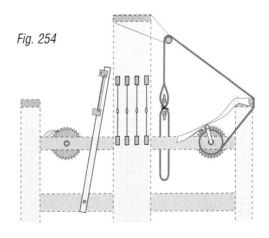

I thread from the right to the left, so I want a light at my right side where it shines on the heddles and the lease (cross).

Jim Ahrens had two sets of lease sticks, one painted white and one black. He used the light ones with dark warps and the dark ones with light warps. It made it easier to see the lease (cross).

Also, you can have special eye glasses made with the focal point set just for threading.

When weaving

If it's hard to see your cloth because it is very narrow or because all the loom apron cords are distracting, put a piece of paper from the cloth beam to the breast beam. It will hide all the cords under the area where you're weaving, and it will make it much easier to see the edges as you go along. Use a color of paper that contrasts with the color of the warps and cloth.

Slits in the cloth

Yarns can slip in the cloth making slits. If a weft is a slippery silk, you might see vertical slits in the cloth where the warp threads slid apart from one another along the slippery wefts. Reeled or spun silk needs to be woven with a tighter sett and beat, because it loosens up. If you want an open weave in silk, be prepared for some slits, which you can remove by tugging at the cloth on the bias as they appear. Another solution is to incorporate some rough yarns in the weave, periodically, to prevent the slippage. Tow linen or dry spun line linen are good choices for open weaves, because the roughness holds the threads in place and prevents shifts in the cloth.

Lint problems

Some threads shed a lot during weaving—tow linen, for example. Check under the loom to see if lint is accumulating there. Know that it's probably in the air, and you are breathing it

in. If you begin to cough while you are weaving, stop immediately and put on a mask to filter out the particles in the air! A surgeon's mask is comfortable. It hooks around your ears or ties at the back of your head. They are much more comfortable than the molded ones available at hardware stores. See Figure 62 on page 45.

If you work a lot with yarns (especially linens) that shed, you may need to wear goggles, as well.

When using a yarn that sheds a lot, vacuum around the loom, as needed. To reduce some of the fuzz or lint from tow yarns, dampen the warp from the breast beam to the heddles with a damp washcloth or a mister.

The reed's abrasion will cause the yarn to shed. Use reeds with larger spaces to reduce the lint, and be sure to remove the fuzz when it clogs the reed, because it will cause more wear on the warp threads.

If a lot of lint forms on the warp, balls of it can slide up and down on the warp threads caused by the movement of the reed and shafts. These balls can get woven into the cloth and cause warp breakage. See page 128. Remedy this situation as soon as the problem is discovered, because it will only get worse as you weave along, with the pills causing warp yarns to stick together and, eventually, break. Most of the pills will be just behind the shafts or in between them. Use hair spray (see page 129). Read about yarns that pill on page 128. Repair lint caught in the cloth by darning in a new weft. See Figure 235 on page 135.

Slippery bench

Cover your bench with rubberized "cloth" made to line shelves. It comes by the yard.

Reed Marks—Vertical "lines"

Vertical lines or streaks regularly spaced all over the cloth are called reed marks. They are the spaces between the warp threads where the wires of the reed were. They are more obvious the more threads there are in a dent, because those threads tend to draw together as they are crowded in between the wires. Using a reed with two warp ends per dent usually prevents these marks. Generally, reed marks disappear during finishing. However, if the dents were really crowded with fine threads, the marks may never come out. Reed marks in wool yarns will wash out better than those in inelastic threads, such as linen.

I like the reeds for my projects to have two ends per dent to give enough space between the wires for a knot in the warp to pass without hanging up in the reed. It also prevents reed marks. You can order a reed for any density you like, say, an 11-dent reed if you found 22 epi (ends per inch) was just perfect for a line of items you planned to make lots of and sell. Reeds are costly, so I wouldn't buy one until I determined the perfect sett from the reeds I already have. There is a reed substitution chart on page 60, in Book #2, which tells what to do if you don't have the exact size reed for your sett (1/2 your sett for 2 per dent).

Nevertheless, sometimes, you need more than two threads in a dent in a reed with larger spaces. For example, double cloth requires wider spaced dents because the warps are crowded by the nature of the weave.

Flaws in double cloth

Mistakes made on the bottom cloth in double weaving often go unnoticed. Attach a rearview mirror from an auto supply store to the loom, so you can see what the bottom of the cloth looks like as you weave along. Make repairs as needed. Otherwise, they will all have to be made after the cloth is off the loom, before finishing. It can be a daunting and depressing job if there are a lot of errors. Correcting them when the warp is on tension is usually easier.

The layers will be stitched together if you make any mistakes in treadling or if the sheds aren't clear when you enter the shuttle. Put a full-length mirror to the side of you to look in to be sure the sheds are absolutely clear before entering the shuttle. Another precaution: every time you advance the warp, lift up the top layer to be sure the layers are completely separate and nothing is stitching the layers together. If there are any unwanted stitchers, they should be corrected by un-weaving to them and correctly re-weaving. Tie up a special treadle to raise the whole top layer.

Double width problems

Start weaving with the bottom layer because the angle at which the beater hits the fell is better. The beat will be more regular, and the angle of the beater will even out the fell as you weave along.

A thick line at the fold of cloth woven double width can be avoided. In her articles, Margaret Gaynes tells how to treat the fold-side of the warp so the warps don't draw in, as they would tend to do. If there are loops at the fold, the warps were too far apart.[26] Here are her tricks for perfect folds. She supplies much more advice in the article.

"To provide an invisible fold, my trick is to thread a taut fishline with each of the last two warp threads at the fold edge. Use two lengths of 25-pound-test fishline about one yard longer than the warp. Tie them onto the front apron rod and sley them both through the same dent as the two warp threads. Thread each fishline through a separate heddle on the same shaft as the corresponding warp thread. Add a weight of about two pounds to each fishline. Use milk or bleach bottles filled with water or sand—or use cooking pots as I do!"

[26] Gaynes, Margaret, Double-width Blankets on Four Shafts. *Handwoven Magazine*, Interweave Press, Loveland CO. January/February, 2002.

She says to make sure the wefts turn snugly against the fishline, leaving no loops, and to begin and end weft threads on the selvedge side. You take out the fishline after the cloth is woven.

There are other ways to hide the fold, such as making a warp stripe begin there. You might be able to remove 2 threads at the fold if they are really crowded together. Usually, the warps get denser at the fold edge, where the selvedge would be. If you made some other areas of the warp denser, they would look similar to the one at the fold.

Put the fold on the edge where you usually have better selvedges.

You might ask, "Why would I weave double width if I have a wide enough loom?" Because your arms might not be long enough! It's more efficient to weave longer and narrower than wider and shorter.

A double thread at the fold in double-width cloth can happen if there are an odd number of warp threads in the warp. With an even number of warp threads, the fold can be on either side of the warp. If there are an uneven number of threads, the fold has to be on the side with the complete threading repeat to prevent the last two warp threads from weaving together at the fold. If that is the case, change the fold to the other side. Read on for another way to eliminate the double threads.

Another way a double thread at the fold can be eliminated no matter how many ends are threaded. You need to change the sequence of sheds. It doesn't matter whether an even or odd number of threads are threaded, what matters is the *sequence*. If you're getting the double threads, skip a shed and proceed. It will change which shed follows which in relation to the shuttle movement and correct the problem, like getting back in step with a half-step in

marching. Unlike moving the shuttle to the other edge as in twills, in this case, you skip a shed and continue weaving. Do it immediately when you begin, so the skip in the sequence doesn't mar the cloth.

A double thread at a fold in a tube can usually be eliminated if there are an uneven number of warp threads. Either add or remove one thread. However, even with an odd number of threads you can get the doubled threads. It's a sequence problem; see above. Start weaving from the side that has the missing or added thread.

The bottom layer may become narrower than the top layer if not enough weft diagonal was allowed in the sheds weaving that layer. Usually, there is enough diagonal from the fell to the shuttle race if you advance the warp often.

One layer is looser than the other. One layer stretches more when the cloth goes over the breast beam when you advance the warp. The way to avoid this condition is to put in a row or two of temporary wefts before you advance the warp. These wefts stitch the layers together so they can't slip when going over the breast beam. They are to be removed later, so use a smooth yarn and one that is thin enough that it doesn't leave a space when removed. Remember, you'll be using a specially-made shed or two for these wefts, not one of the regular sheds for the project. It is only a problem when the layers don't exchange often, say, when there isn't an exchange in layers for 3-4 inches or so.

One side usually looks better, but after finishing, they should both be alike.

The cloth narrows in too much in some places. When there are a lot of layer exchanges, more slack in the weft is needed, or that part of the cloth will tend to draw in.

Other problems

Aches and pains

Get yourself immediately to the section of this book on body mechanics, starting on page 9.

Bad streaks of color

A space-dyed yarn is dyed different colors along its length. An unwanted streak can sometimes occur where the colors cross one another. In that case, thread a section of the yarn with a better color, darn it in over the wrong-colored yarn, and cut out the offending yarn.

Stains in cloth

If a yarn is stained, follow the same procedure for bad streaks of color, above.

Slubs

Repair bumps in the yarn by darning in a new thread in that place and cutting out the defective thread.

Lint in the cloth

Sometiomes, a hair or piece of lint was accidentally woven into the cloth and doesn't just pull out easily. It should come out if you pick at it with tweezers or your tapestry needle. Do this before finishing or you might not be able to remove it.

Time problems

I have found that after a person retires, she has less time for weaving than when she was working. One student was a pediatrician and a caregiver for her elderly mother. She wove before breakfast every morning and made beautiful fabrics for coats, suits, and blankets. It was triple the amount of weaving that any of my retired students accomplished.

If I have a project going, I can manage to find time to work on it. It's the inertia beforehand that I have to overcome. Even if it's just tidying up in the studio, I count it as having my hands on the threads. Having a goal is an enormous help; make one and try to stick to it.

Problems with ideas

There are two types of ideas problems: too many and too few. I find I get great ideas when there's no chance I can get to my loom, and no ideas when I can.

I keep a box or a bin in my studio called "Weaving Ideas," and I throw all the scraps of paper with my ideas and other things that inspire me in it. I can sort them out later and combine some of them in a project. Usually, the ideas that I weave are current ones—not old ones, but sometimes, I see a theme, and often, it relates to an idea I've had over time. I pin the ideas up on the wall in my studio and try to put like thoughts together in groups. I can always add to them. The truth is, that there are getting to be too many ideas on the wall, and many just get pinned up haphazardly. My wall is not much different from my "Weaving Ideas" bins and boxes.

Nevertheless, it gives me a sense of ease knowing I *could* go into the studio and pick up an idea. You'll never run out of ideas—you just need to know where they are when you want them.

My idea boxes contain pictures, magazine articles, color ideas, project ideas, and weave structures I'd like to try. Someday, I should sort them or throw them out, but who listens to "shoulds"?

You might get yourself going by designing a present for someone or for some place in your home or wardrobe. Then, you can select and reject your ideas according to whether or not they are appropriate.

I get ideas from the weaving guilds I belong to, and it helps to bounce my ideas off fellow weavers. Having an audience helps me get something together for "show and tell," and the feedback is very helpful. The Handweavers Guild of America (HGA) has a list of guilds around the country.

155

156

5 *Finishing*

A cloth isn't finished until it's finished.

My teachers told me that when the cloth came off the loom, it was only half done! I could understand hems and fringes and any other sewing needing to be done, but I didn't realize that finishing the cloth was a process, as well. For our beginning projects, "finishing" meant washing the cloth in some way, not because it was dirty, but because it would relax the threads and make them curve around each other. The cloth off the loom looks flat and a little stiff, while finished cloth is soft and supple. Our teachers had warned us not to beat our cloth too hard because, "after it is washed, it will shrink and the threads will draw together some, and if you start out with a very dense cloth, it will turn into cardboard after washing."

Your common sense might tell you that, in some cases, no finishing is needed. It is important to finish samples, so you will know the best process to use, because the wrong finishing technique could ruin your project.

In this chapter, I write about the nuances of a variety of finishing techniques and when to use them. This book does not cover rugs and tapestries or other thick textiles that aren't thought of as regular cloth.

The Difference Between Finishing and Finishes

Finishing

Finishing is anything done to a fabric after it's woven to change the appearance (what you see), the hand (what you feel), and the performance (what its purpose is). It can stabilize the cloth, as well. In industry, the unfinished cloth is said to be in the "greige," "gray goods," or "loom" state.

Finishes

Finishes are often materials applied to a cloth as a method of finishing. A finish could be fireproofing, for example. Finishes added to a cloth are discussed beginning on page 201.

Finishes can refer to hems, fringes, edge treatments, etc. The section on these finishes starts on page 201.

How To Know What Finish To Use

Yarns

Different fibers require different methods. Read about the way to finish different fibers in the section about fibers. Generally, when there is a mixture of fibers in a cloth, the finishing technique to use is the one for the most delicate fiber.

The way the fibers were made into yarn can also make a difference. Woolen and worsted wool fabrics are finished with strikingly different methods. Chenille yarn is finished in a special way.

Weave structures

Some weaves require finishing because the yarns must move into different positions to attain the effect the weave is meant to achieve. The yarns are crossing at right angles on the loom, but with tension off and the fabric washed, the warps and wefts can move into very different positions. Two examples are waffle weave and M's & O's. Waffle weaves look flat when they come off the loom and have three-dimensional cells after washing. The yarns in the M's and O's structure move to create curved lines.

Appearance

The surface can change dramatically depending upon the finishing technique. A soft, fluffy cloth is finished differently from a hard, flat cloth.

Hand of the fabric

The "hand" or "handle" of a fabric means how it feels—whether it is it supple and drapey, or stiff, for example.

Purpose

There are finishes designed for special uses: brushing a cloth for a blanket, fireproofing a wall hanging for a public space, or finishing upholstery fabric to reduce staining, for example.

Sampling

Finishing a sample will guarantee that you won't have any surprises when you are ready to finish your final project. You might try several finishes on several samples before deciding what is best for your situation. Read more about sampling starting on page 164.

A new weaver made a baby blanket. Because she had washed a sample, she knew that it would be O.K. to wash the final product. She knew just how much it would shrink and that the cloth wouldn't fall apart. She knew whether she could put it in the washing machine and on what cycle and for what amount of time because she had tried different settings on different samples. She knew whether or not it would go in the dryer, or dry flat, or hang over a shower bar. Also, she practiced different hems and fringes on her sample pieces, so she knew which she would use on the blanket itself.

Steps for Finishing Cloth

Step 1. You must do something so the last wefts don't unravel. See page 44 and below.

Step 2. Do any mending or correction of errors. See "burling" on page 162.

Step 3. Sample different finishing methods to determine the best method for your project. Read about sampling on page 165.

Step 1: Prevent last wefts from unraveling

Hand-sew or machine-stitch the cut edges of the cloth so that the last wefts cannot unravel during finishing. See Figures 255 and 256. Read more about what to do with the cut edges on page 44.

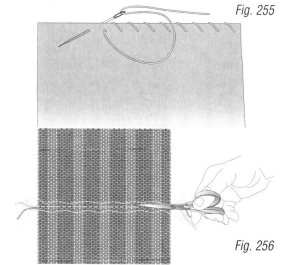

Fig. 255

Fig. 256

Many weavers hemstitch on the loom where the cloth is going to be cut. See below.

Fray Check™ is a commercially made liquid, which can be applied to a cut edge to prevent raveling. It doesn't survive washing, so use it before stitching or binding an edge. Try it on a sample first to be sure it doesn't hurt the fabric and so that it will be strong enough to prevent raveling when applying the finishing method you plan to use. You can make a similar preparation by combining a one-ounce tube of Duco cement with a three-ounce bottle of nail polish remover—use the regular type only, not the type with conditioners. Acetone, the necessary ingredient, can be purchased at a hardware store along with the Duco cement.

Machine stitching hints

I usually machine stitch the edges when I know the stitching will never show—when the stitching is enveloped in a hem, or cut off. You can use a serger or a regular sewing machine using zigzag or straight stitches. I make my lines of stitching a bit wavy so the stitches catch different wefts, because if the stitches go along one weft, during washing, the entire weft, stitching and all, can come off the cloth completely and expose the next wefts to raveling. See Figure 256.

Try different types of stitches on your sample to see what works best. Some zigzag stitches can ruffle the edge, so wavy straight stitches might be better.

Remember, these stitches are not going to show on the finished project. Don't use machine stitches if you think you might want to remove them because that can be tedious, and can disfigure the cloth if you're not extremely careful.

Machine stitches that show on a finished project can disfigure the project—making it look amateurish. If a machine-stitched edge is needed for security—say, for a dishtowel—machine stitch the edge before turning the hem and then stitch the final folded edge of the hem with hand stitches. I like an invisible stitch called a slipstitch seen in Figure 284, on page 205. Read about hems on page 205.

If you prefer to machine stitch where it would show on the finished project and there are color changes along the hem, you might change colors of thread so the stitches are less visible.

Hand stitching

An overcast stitch (See Figure 255) is a stitch I often use immediately after the cloth is cut off the loom when I want to protect the wefts temporarily, or when the edge is too delicate for machine stitching. I use a contrasting thread (but not a color that could run), so it is easy to see to remove later. I also overcast the edges when machine stitching would show on the finished project or would disfigure the edge. It can remain and be enclosed in a hem. This stitching isn't "for show" but to protect the last wefts during the finishing process.

Hemstitching on the loom

See Figures 257a-d and 258a-e (next page).

This hand sewing is done while the cloth is still on the loom and is easy to do while the warp is under tension. Many weavers prefer to do it then because they don't have to hand- or machine-stitch the cut ends after the cloth is off the loom (and before finishing the cloth). They may or may not cut off the stitches later, depending on what the edge is to look like when the fabric is complete. It's a big time saver when you want to have fringe on the edge because there is no knotting of the fringe needed—all you need to do is to leave enough unwoven for the fringe(s). Note: The instructions for hemstitching at the beginning of the cloth are a little different from those for the stitching at the end of the cloth.

When you are weaving several pieces, hemstitching the edges to be cut later saves a lot of time because neither hems nor additional stitching needs to be done. Placemats, for example, can be hemstitched on the loom and then cut apart and finished right after they are off the loom. Hemstitching the edges of your samples on the loom can save time too.

Use a size thread that will be unobtrusive for the hemstitching. Often, the weft thread is all right to use, but I've seen hemstitching that was too bulky because the thread for the stitches was too heavy.

How to hemstitch[27]

Many stitches are called "hemstitches." Besides different ways to do the stitching, the stitches themselves can be different. Here is one that does the job of holding in the wefts and is quick and easy. See Figures 257 and 258.

The process is only slightly different at the beginning of the fabric and at the end of it. The instructions are given for right-handed people who will always work starting at the left selvedge and work toward the right. Work from the right toward the left if you are left-handed.

_____

[27] Sharon Alderman method

At the beginning

Fig. 257

To hemstitch the beginning of a fabric, on the first weft of the fabric, leave a long tail of weft hanging from the left edge of the cloth. The tail should be 2½ to 3 times the width of the warp. It will be threaded into a tapestry needle and used to do the stitching after a few more rows of weaving are completed. See Figure 257a.

After weaving an inch or a bit more, thread the weft tail into a tapestry needle. The blunt point on the needle prevents you from pricking your finger and piercing the threads. Some methods prefer to pierce the threads to make the stitching more secure. See Figure 258e.

Begin stitching by holding the weft taut at the selvedge with the left hand. With the needle in the right hand, hover over 1/4"–3/8" worth of warp threads, then go straight down between the warps and come out at the selvedge. Tug this stitch so that it wraps around the warps and cinches them up into a bundle.

Point the needle straight up (away from you) along the selvedge for 3 wefts, take the needle down through the cloth there, and come out again through the opening you just made by cinching up the warp bundle. Read below for what to do with slippery threads.

Continue on with the next stitch. Hold the weft in the left hand taut and go around the next group of warps (coming out again in the previous opening), tug the stitch to make a bundle, go straight up three wefts, poke the needle down through the cloth, and come out at the opening you just made by cinching up the bundle. Repeat until you reach the right selvedge.

 My left hand holds the weft taut and does the tugging. It is engaged at all times while the right hand works the needle.

At the right selvedge, darn (needle weave) the tail into the cloth 1/2", so it doesn't show, and cut off the remainder of the tail flush with the cloth.

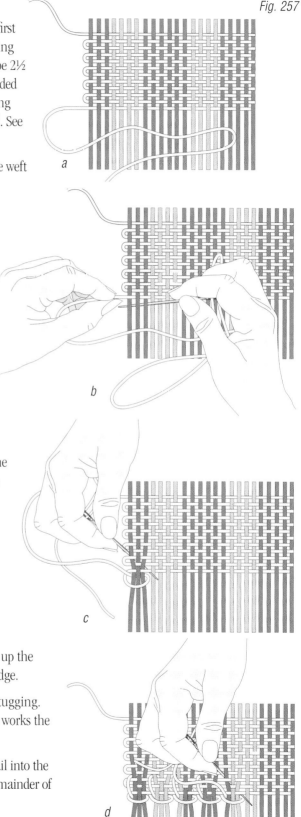

a

b

c

d

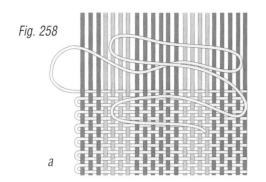

Fig. 258

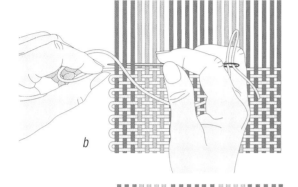

a

b

c

d

At the end

At the end of the fabric, make the last weft come out at the left selvedge. Leave a long tail on the last weft (2½ to 3 times the width of the warp) and thread it through the tapestry needle. (Figure 258a).

Begin stitching by holding the weft thread tail taut in the left hand, and with the right hand, go around 1/4"– 3/8" worth of warps, coming out at the selvedge as you did at the beginning of the fabric.

Point the needle straight toward you, for 3 wefts into the cloth; then poke the needle down through the cloth and come up in the space just made when you cinched up the bundle of warps. Notice that now you'll be poking your needle into cloth, which will be toward you. When you were stitching into the cloth at the beginning of the fabric, the cloth was away from you. See Figures 257 and 258.

For slippery threads, stagger where you dig in your needle, to make the stitches more secure. If they always go in after the third weft, the whole hemstitched edge could fall off during finishing. You can dig your needle in alternating between the third and fourth wefts—it looks deliberate, and the stitching doesn't pull out.

161

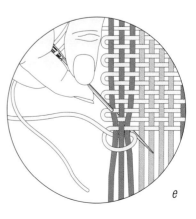

e

Step 2. Burling: Mending the cloth

After the cloth is taken off the loom, it has to be checked for errors and mended (called "burling" or sometimes "perching," in industry). It should be done before finishing the cloth so the mends will be less visible after washing.

Fixing flaws encountered during weaving begins on page 135. Errors that show up when you first start to weave are discussed on page 115. The effect of careful mending can be quite rewarding, so don't be discouraged if there is a lot of it to do. A cloth with many threads dangling can turn into a lovely, perfectly "woven" cloth.

Checking for flaws

Look at your cloth carefully and closely—on both sides—checking for any flaws. Do it when you have a fresh supply of energy. Holding the cloth up to the light from a window or a lamp is a great way to discover flaws. Put it over an ironing board, or over a light table like photographers use. Run your fingertips over the cloth. Surprisingly, touch reveals flaws you might not otherwise see.

Check for knots, bunches of threads, thick or thin spots, warp or weft floats and any flaws in the weave, and tails from repairs and weft joins.

☞ Be sure to check *both* sides of the cloth.

When to make repairs

Read the section on darning, below, for information on how to make repairs.

☞ Make all repairs before washing the cloth. They will settle into the cloth during finishing and be less visible. It is harder to darn in yarns after the cloth is washed because the threads and fibers blur the exact intersections of the threads. When making repairs, be sure to make rough or feathered cuts to your threads to make them less visible. Also, tapered cut ends are less likely to come out of the cloth. If the cloth is to be scrutinized, and any tiny flaw would show, leave the tails about an inch long and cut them flush with the cloth after finishing. I use rough cuts if blunt-cut ends are likely to show. Read more about cutting the tails on page 163.

Darning repair threads

Darning is another term for needle-weaving or mending. Most weavers use a tapestry needle for repair, because it has a blunt end and a large eye. Tapestry needles come in a variety of sizes. Basically, you'll weave by sewing your matching thread over a mistake, at least 1/2" beyond it in both directions, so your darned-in thread overlaps the correct weaving a little bit. See Figures 259, 260, and 261. Examine the path the warp (or weft) travels in the cloth,

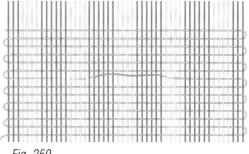

Fig. 259

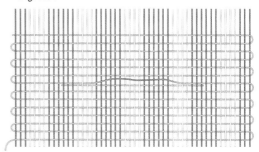

Fig. 260

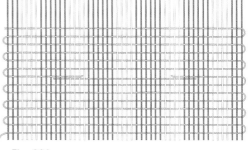

Fig. 261

162

and with your needle and thread, sew over and under the threads in the path that ought to have been taken, including the overlaps. Then cut out the incorrect yarn.

Be careful to put the right amount of tension on your darning, or splicing thread. Usually, my thread is loose while I'm darning, then I tension it. If it is too tight or too loose, you are likely to see the repair after finishing. When I'm repairing, I'm concentrating on the precise path my needle should be taking. After the darning is done, I tug on the new yarn so it lies smoothly in with the rest of the cloth. Then I tug the cloth on the bias (diagonally) in both directions, if it is off the loom, to settle the mend in place.

Sometimes, I untie an offending knot in the yarn and use the short threads themselves for the darns. Untying the knot gives me enough thread to overlap them a bit at the cut. Because the ends of the yarns are so short, weave the tapestry needle into the cloth first and then thread it and pull the little short strand through the cloth. For thick yarns, taper, or rough cut the yarns and pull just fibers into the cloth with the needle, for invisibility. See Figure 47 on page 35.

A latch hook is a handy tool for darning because you don't have an eye to thread. There are small ones that machine knitters use. They are available in the notions section of fabric stores. You work the hook like a needle into the cloth, then, put the thread into the hook, and with the latch closed to hold your darning thread, pull it into place. It is very helpful for short threads. See Figure 49 on page 35.

Cutting yarn tails

I have two ways of cutting off the tails of the darned and the corrected threads. Which I use depends on the threads, the cloth's structure, and its purpose. The first method is fail-safe. The second has worked for me, but has potential problems. The absolutely safest way

is to try both methods on a scrap of the fabric and wash it before working on the whole cloth. If your cloth will be scrutinized up close, don't take chances; use method #1. A fine, white silk scarf would show the tiniest flaws–a textured or multi colored cloth would not show them so much.

Method #1: Cut the tails about an inch long. Then, after finishing (washing), cut them flush with the cloth using rough cuts (feather the cut end of the yarn). Tapered cut ends will be less visible than a blunt cut; the thicker the yarn, the more important this method is. It allows the threads to do any shrinking into the cloth that they want to during washing. Rough cuts are less likely to come out of the cloth. Thread any fibers left on the tail into a tapestry needle and pull them into the cloth, so the cut is completely invisible. See Figure 48 on page 35.

Method #2 : Sometimes, I just blunt cut the threads flush with the cloth as I go, but always before finishing, and I cut the ends with rough cuts, only if necessary. Note that if your overlaps aren't long enough, and you cut the tails flush now, before washing, they can shrink into the cloth and cause unwoven places. Rough or feathered cuts are less likely to come out of the cloth. Just be sure your overlaps are about ½" long.

Cut off weft tails

The threads dangling from wefts can be cut flush with the cloth now, or cut 1" long to be cut flush after finishing. When you cut them flush, use ragged or feathered cuts rather than blunt cuts, especially, if the yarns are thick.

Warp or weft darns?

When I'm mending a mistake after the cloth is off the loom, I decide whether to darn the warp or the weft, depending upon which seems easier. For example, if a warp is errant over several picks, I fix the warp thread rather than all the wefts affected by it.

Warp repair darns

Fig. 262

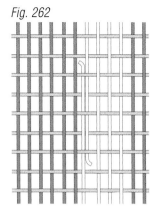

If you made warp repairs and wound the threads around a pin, darn the tails in so they overlap at least 1/2" and make the cuts rough or tapered, not blunt, now, or after washing. Read about cutting the tails, above. See Figure 262.

A loop in a weft

You might discover a kink or a loop in the weft. Work the excess yarn over to an edge with a tapestry needle, cut it on one side of the loop close to the edge and darn in the longer cut tail. If it is too far from the edge, cut the loop and darn the two threads into the cloth overlapping them a little. Read about darning, above.

A tight weft

Cut the weft at a selvedge and release the tightness, allowing it to slide into the cloth until it is smooth with the rest of the cloth. Darn in a new strand where the thread was released and pulled into the cloth.

Worming and snags

Any snags or loose threads hanging off the cloth must be mended, probably by darning. Chenille fabric, however, has a tendency to "worm." Its threads seem to work themselves out of the weave and look like snags. There's nothing you can do at this point except to poke the loops through to the back of the cloth. The problem is that the cloth was woven too loosely or in a weave structure with too many floats. Weave chenille tightly, with both warps and wefts close together.

Variations in beat

Sometimes, variations of the beat can be disguised before finishing by pushing wefts apart or closer with the tip of a tapestry needle. After finishing, the variations will become more disguised.

Step 3. Sampling

You probably need to have a few samples to try different finishing methods on to determine the best one. If you have given a piece of cloth very harsh treatment, such as a hot machine wash with lots of agitation and high dryer temperatures, the results cannot be reversed. So, if you tried that method on your only sample and didn't like the shrinkage and hand of the cloth, you are stuck with no more samples on which to try something less drastic. On the other hand, if you first tried some very gentle treatment, say, hand washing in cool water with no agitation and dried flat, you cannot reverse the result, but you can try something stronger on it—perhaps warmer water and a little more agitation. I hope you get the picture: there are so many variables to choose from; several sample pieces of cloth are needed, so you can compare the results.

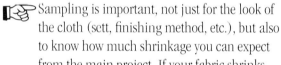Sampling is important, not just for the look of the cloth (sett, finishing method, etc.), but also to know how much shrinkage you can expect from the main project. If your fabric shrinks more than you like, try a gentler finishing method to see if the shrinkage is less and looks better to your eye.

Check if the colors run

Before experimenting on my samples, I check to see if the colors of the yarns will run. If they do, then I know that I can't wet finish my cloth unless I take certain precautions.

I only do this test if there is a high contrast in the colors in the cloth–especially, if black, navy, red, or very dark colors are used in a cloth with white yarns.

To check for colorfastness, wind off about a yard or so of all the yarns in your project. I wind the yarns around my fingers to make a tiny skein and then twist the skeins together so all the yarns are in contact with each other, especially with the white yarn. Then, I put them in a glass jar with hot soapy water. I shake the jar to agitate the yarns and let it stand until the water is cold. If there is any color in the water, you know that some color is running. If the white yarn stays pure white, you know the colors won't be absorbed into the yarn.

☞ If there is color in the water, but not on the yarn, take this precaution with the final cloth: Blot out excess water immediately and dry the cloth flat. If you hang it dripping wet over a line, the colored yarns might deposit color on the white areas as they drain through the cloth.

If the colors do run, you can try washing the yarns (and subsequently, the cloth) with Synthrapol SP, a scouring preparation that helps prevent excess dye from bleeding onto other yarns. Try it first on your woven sample, of course. If the colors run, avoid washing your project; dry-clean it instead.

Harry Linder suggests that if you test your yarns before weaving and find that the colors bleed, wash the yarns first to get rid of the excess dye. Make good skeins—that is, use a metal skein winder (Figure 116 on page 68), a yarn blocker that spinners use to block their handspun yarns, or your warping board. Do not use an umbrella swift (Figure 115 on page 68) because the rounds of yarns in the skein will not all be the same length and the yarns can tangle making unwinding the skein later tedious. Tie the skeins carefully in four places. Tie the skein once more with a rag to hold onto while dipping the skein in the wash and rinse baths. Dip the skein up and down in the soapy or detergent water until the loose dye is dissipated. Do not wring or twist the skein in any way, but gently squeeze out the water. Rinse until the water is clear and hang to dry in the shade. Harry says it's not a good idea to wash skeins in the washing machine because the yarns tangle terribly.[28] (Figures 118-120 on page 69)

---

[28] Linder, p. 13.

The samples

Sometimes, people make a warp especially for sampling. They might do this because they are planning a project that will be much larger, say, for yardage. Before taking the time and expense of making the big warp, it makes sense to be sure you know what you're getting.

I often do not repeat a warp, but sample on the warp itself. I allow a yard for samples. That way I can try out my ideas and make any adjustments needed before weaving the real project. I cut off the samples and finish them in various ways before going ahead and weaving the rest of the warp. Then, I know how much to allow for shrinkage as well as what the cloth will look like in the end. It may be that I need to change the sett, or some yarns, etc. All this information comes from sampling. If you have to open the sett, your warp will be wider than planned, and if you make the sett denser, the warp will be narrower.

I like to have at least 4 pieces to sample on. For a big warp, let your samples be about 8" x 9". Samples can be smaller if you don't intend to repeat the project, or to make a larger one using the results. In that case, make your samples at least 4" square, or so—no smaller.

One piece I will steam only—the mildest treatment. I choose what methods to try depending on the fiber content and sometimes the on the weave structure if it is one that requires special finishing, such as waffle weave or honeycomb. I may finish one with the harshest method and the others midway in the scale of gentle to heavy finishing. It depends on the look you want as well as the fiber content.

Fabrics shrink a bit, and some shrink a lot when washed. The wet finishing process also takes care of shrinkage problems by pre-shrinking the fabric before it is cut or hemmed and laundered later.

Fig. 263

Textile Finishing Process Record

Project: Date:

Description	Width in Reed	Woven				Finishing Method		After Finishing		Amount Lost		% Lost		Total % draw-in & shrinkage
				Width Draw-in		Machine	Hand			←Due to Finishing→				
		Weft Width	Warp Length	Amount Lost	% Drawn-in	Cold Warm Hot Gentle Reg. P. Press Det. Fab. Soft Time / Dryer Air Iron	Cold Warm Hot Soak Gentle Det. Fab. Soft / Steam Air Iron	Warp Length	Weft Width	Warp Length	Weft Width	Warp Length	Weft Width	Width
Washing Notes							Drying Notes							
Comments														

Keep records

Figure 263 shows how I keep my records for my finishing samples. I record the sample number, the before and after measurements, and the finishing process I used. Then, I calculate the percent of shrinkage (See page 39) and list any comments. I like to keep the samples clipped to the record sheet that goes into the folder with all the other records and notes for the project. While I'm working on the project I keep everything in a notebook. When the project is completed I staple all the pages together and make a file folder for the records and notes. It's surprising how many times I've referred to those folders.

Tracking

If, when you wash your samples, your plain weave has changed to look like some sort of twill, with tiny diagonal lines and/or diamonds going every which way, you are seeing what is called tracking, crazing, crow's foot, or cockling. Figures 264a and b show plain weave before and after tracking has occurred. It happens only with plain weave and after the cloth is in water. It doesn't appear in pattern weaves or in twill. If you like the effect, wash your project fabric just like your sample that tracked. (A light steam pressing will help smooth out the cloth, but it won't remove the

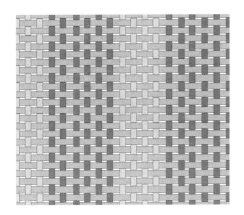

Fig. 264a

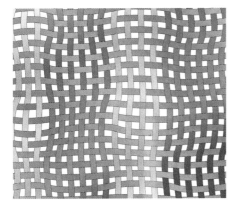

Fig. 264b

tracking.) If you want a smooth fabric, you must "crab," or set the fabric, before washing, or dry-clean it. (Dry cleaning does not use water.) See below.

If you plan to "full" your fabric, tracking won't be an issue—the tracks will blur with the fulling process. Read about fulling on page 178. If you plan to brush your fabric, the effects of tracking will also be blurred, so there is no point in setting the cloth before fulling. If the warp and weft are different colors, and you want them to stay fairly discrete, set the cloth before fulling. See below.

When does it occur?

Not all cloth will track. It happens more readily in finer yarns, especially worsted and singles yarns. Singles often track even if they are medium or heavy. Unbalanced yarns that

are overtwisted will track or collapse (pucker) with an open sett for plain weave or with weaves having floats, such as twill. Plain weave worsted fabric will certainly track if not crabbed first. The farther apart the yarns are in the cloth, the more room there is for them to move around and "track."

When you don't want tracking

Prevention

 If your sample tracks—and if you don't want tracking—it is better to prevent it than to try to remove it. Remember, if you dry-clean the cloth it won't track because water won't be involved. Removing tracking can be extremely tedious and take a lot of concentration and energy, and does not always provide complete removal of the tracks. See page 169. Two methods for preventing tracking are crabbing and blowing.

 For cloths that tend to track (results of sample experiments), the cloth must be set before washing to prevent it from tracking. In industry, when this set is accomplished by boiling in water it is called crabbing, and when it is done by blowing steam through the cloth it is called blowing.

Crabbing is a term many weavers use for both crabbing and blowing. Boiling the cloth isn't usually possible in a home studio, so most handweavers steam their fabrics. The industry method is described on page 169, and is sure to prevent tracking forever and ever.

Preventing tracking (setting the cloth)
Crabbing

 The cloth cannot be wet before the crabbing (setting) process. It's the water and agitation that cause the tracking, and you want to set the cloth now, so it can be washed later.

As long as any subsequent washing does not subject the cloth to a greater heat than that given during crabbing, the crisp, clear appearance of the plain weave will be maintained.

Note: After the crabbing has been completed the cloth can be washed.

If your fabric looks fine for the first washing after is was crabbed, but it tracks after the next washing, read how to remove the tracks, below.

Crabbing is actually a shrinkage process that sets the warp and weft by relaxing twists inherent in the yarns.

The principle is this. Your fabric will not track again on subsequent washing if it is never subjected to water hotter than that used for crabbing. In industry, they boil the fabric, assuming that no one will ever use water hotter than that for laundering. If you wash the fabric in water that is the same temperature as the crabbing, tracking will return, but it will be less strong. It will continue to track less and less as it is washed again and again.

An easy method for fabrics that track well (for example, worsted yarns and 8/2 unmercerized cotton) and aren't too big, setting (crabbing) is done in the washing machine. (For large pieces, try the same method in the bathtub.) Fill the tub of the washing machine with very hot water. Put a wetting agent in the water (dish detergent) to help the cloth absorb the water. If you suspect or know that a particular color will run, use Synthrapol SP for the wetting agent. Lay the cloth on top of the water and let it sink. Do not agitate the cloth in any way. Let the cloth sit in the water until the water is cold. (Note: You can open the door of some front-loading washing machines when the tub is full—check to be sure, if you are buying one.) When the water is cold, take the cloth out and drain the tub. Fill it with hot or warm water (depending on the fiber) and detergent, and wash the cloth as you would normally. Iron it dry.[29]

Crabbing by Blowing

An adequate crabbing job can be achieved at home by placing the fabric between two damp cloths on a fairly hard ironing board, pressing it with as hot an iron as is safe without scorching, and leaving the iron in position until all the steam has risen. It is important to lift the iron clear of the cloth before placing it in the next position, rather than sliding the iron across the surface. To maintain the warp and weft at right angles to each other, the cloth should be held out taut by pins inserted regularly up either selvedge and attached to the ironing board. If you mark the correct finished width of the cloth on the ironing board, you can stretch the cloth to fit that space each time it is moved forward over the board. Crab across the width of the fabric until it is dry, and move on in a similar way along its length.

Moving the cloth is easier to do if it is rolled from one cardboard tube to another as you go along, keeping it stretched so the edges are always even. Be sure to work on both sides of the fabric.

 The cloth should be pressed until it is completely dry. This means you might have to go over it several times. If it isn't dry, it can track.

This job can be time consuming but is necessary for the clear look of plain weave on cloths that will track otherwise. Be fresh when you begin this job, take your time and do it carefully.

Heavy steaming is needed to prevent tracking and permanently set the weave. Lighter steaming may set the cloth so it won't track but only if washed gently later—if washed with warmer water, the tracking will reappear.

Sampling to see if your blowing (crabbing) will prevent tracking is imperative. I knew that I should steam a worsted cloth, and it still tracked on my first sample. After that, I knew that my steaming had to be heavier. Steaming professionally at the dry cleaners is stronger than the steam one can usually achieve at home, and that much steam may be required to prevent tracking. Then, of course, to prevent it's return, the care of the fabric should be dry cleaning or wet finishing with water that is not very hot.

Removing tracking

If tracking occurs when the cloth is washed, the tracks can be smoothed out if the cloth is pressed while it is still damp. Sometimes, even if you already set the fabric by crabbing, and it was washed without tracks occurring, they will appear after a subsequent washing. Taking out tracking takes time and attention, so choose a time when you feel fresh and unhurried. (After each washing the tracking will be less and less.)

The fabric should be quite damp or moderately wet. Pull the cloth in the warp and weft directions to straighten the yarns and press to hold them in place. Press, that is, lift the iron to change positions; don't slide the iron over the cloth. Press on both sides until the fabric is dry.

☞ To avoid having to do this process again, never wash the cloth again—dry-clean it instead.

Permanent crabbing

Read about prevention of tracking, above and an easy method to prevent tracking, on page 168.

To make sure that crabbing is permanent, the cloth has to be boiled while it is on tension. As long as the finished fabric is never heated to that high temperature again, tracking will never reappear. Geraldine St Aubyn Hubbard describes an adaptation from industry that production weavers can use. The description shows how precise the process should be, ideally.

Most handweavers can't have this arrangement in their studios and have to rely on steaming for crabbing. This description helps explain why the steaming must be *heavy steaming* to last for subsequent washings. (Of course, dry cleaning will prevent tracking from returning.)

"To crab the cloth, take two solid rollers made of sycamore (it doesn't stain the cloth) of between 10 cm and 15 cm (4 inches and 6 inches) in diameter, grooved down the length. Fix the cloth in the groove of one of the rollers with a rod [Figure 265], roll the cloth round the roller and fix the cloth again. Immerse in a bath of water, heated to between 60 degrees and 70 degrees C (140 degrees to 160 degrees F), and revolve the roller for ten minutes, by using a piece of cord. This relaxes the fibres into a plastic state.

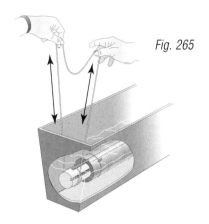

Fig. 265

"Remove the first roller from the bath, and while still hot, re-roll the cloth onto the second roller. The tension of warp and weft that you give the cloth as you roll it onto the second roller while the fibres are in this plastic state will determine the final look of the cloth (the more tension, the more the tracking will be eliminated). Roll the fabric directly from one roller onto the other, to avoid cooling. Again immerse in water, this time at boiling point 100 degrees C (212 degrees F) and revolve for ten minutes. This sets the fibres in position. Remove from the water. Allow to cool while on the roller, and keep turning to avoid water marks. When it is completely cold, re-roll the cloth onto the slatted drying roller, as for woolen cloth [Figure 267 on page 176]."[30]

30 St Aubyn Hubbard, Geraldine, *The Craft of the Weaver.* Lark Books, Asheville, North Carolina, pp. 100 and 103. 1983.

Wet Finishing

Wet finishing is a specialized way of washing fabric. Most fabrics should be wet finished. (See below for exceptions.) The wet finishing process is not the same process as that used in laundering the fabric. It is similar to just washing clothes, but all the steps are more extreme. Hotter temperatures, more agitation and more compression are used for the initial washing, or wet finishing, of the cloth. After a fabric has been wet finished, it can be washed to remove soil in warm, not hot, water, gently agitated by hand or in a gentle machine cycle, and very lightly ironed or not ironed at all. A wool fabric might never be washed again but only dry-cleaned.

Wet finishing precautions!

1. Tracking. Plain weave fabrics can show tracking after agitation in water! Check your sample—if tracking occurs, you know it will happen on the final project so you must decide if you want that effect or not. If you don't want this effect, you *must* set the fabric. Setting is done by crabbing, see above. Tracking is difficult and can be impossible to remove once the fabric has been in contact with water. Crabbing sets the yarns in their perpendicular state so they don't wander and "track" during washing. Read more about tracking beginning on page 167.

If the fabric is to be fulled or felted, setting the yarns (crabbing) isn't done. Read about woolens and fulling on pages 178 and 189. Felting is the most extreme stage of fulling.

2. Wringing and the spin cycle. Never wring cloth in wet finishing. It can permanently crease the cloth! Spinning in the machine can set creases in cloth, as well. Roll the cloth in towels and squeeze, don't wring. If spinning in the machine, read the precautions on page 181.

3. Different yarns. Cut off any headings you may have made if they were woven with yarns other than those in the fabric itself.

4. Shrinkage. Usually the cloth shrinks some and often a lot, so be sure to finish the fabric before cutting it and sewing it into a garment! Experiment with your samples to determine what process shrinks the cloth to your satisfaction.

When not to wet finish

Most, but not all, textiles should be wet finished. Some exceptions are tapestries and rugs, which may be only steamed or blocked. Read about blocking on page 175. Other exceptions might be wall hangings, and fabrics with colors that bleed (See page 164) or fabrics that track (See page 167). Sometimes curtain or upholstery fabrics are not wet finished, but they may be given a special finish to make them fireproof or anti-static. However, some drapery or upholstery fabrics require shrinking by steam pressing or dry cleaning by a professional cleaner (who can also apply stain and water repellent finishes).

Dry cleaning is not wet finishing. (There is no water in the dry cleaning process). It is a legitimate method of finishing cloth. Tracking will not occur as long as the fabric is dry-cleaned.

Steaming. Even though the fabric is not going to be wet finished, it usually needs to undergo a "setting" process (steaming). Read how to steam-set a fabric in the section on blowing, on page 168. It is a process that takes time and care, but is important to give stability to the cloth and prevent bagging and slippage of threads.

Rolling. Sometimes, a fabric can be finished by simply rolling it, under some tension, on a tube for a period of time. The yarns relax over time and flex nicely around themselves.

What is wet finishing?

Be sure to read the wet finishing precautions on the preceding page.

There are three stages of the process.[31] Most fabrics require all three stages, but there are exceptions and variations in the process depending on the fiber, yarn construction, and weave structure. These variations will be described separately by fiber content beginning on page 185.

Scouring is the first stage to get out any dirt or oil from processing the yarns. It will affect the color, soften the yarns, and make them more resilient.

Agitation is the second stage to relax the yarns and let them flex and settle into the cloth.

Compression is the final stage to flatten the yarns and lock them into place. There are times when this stage isn't used—when a lofty or textured surface is desired such as for blankets and chenille fabrics. It can give luster to fabrics such as silk and linen. It can give a nice, hard, flat finish to wools and other fibers. Sampling is the key to achieving the very best look and feel for a particular textile.

Stage 1: Scouring (washing)

Remember, since this process uses water, tracking can occur with plain weave fabrics. If the sample you washed shows tracking—and you don't like that effect—you must set the yarns before entering them in the water for scouring. Read about crabbing above.

Scouring is washing the cloth to get out any "dirt" that may be in the yarns because of the method used to manufacture the yarn. Even if the cloth doesn't look dirty, you should scour, or wash it because it will look brighter and the hand, or drape, of the cloth will be nicer.

The scouring process also "wets" the fibers. It's similar to shampooing your hair the second time when it takes only a little shampoo to make a lot of suds. The first shampooing got your hair "wet" and receptive to accepting the second application of shampoo more readily.

Soap or detergent?

Whether you use a detergent or soap will make a difference in the final hand, or feel, of the cloth. If your water is "hard," with calcium, magnesium and iron salts, these minerals will combine with soap and leave a scum on the cloth, which dulls the look of it and is hard to remove. If the water is hard, use a detergent instead of soap. A mild detergent is one you might use to wash dishes; one that is kind to your hands will be kind to the wool. Laundry detergent with no additives can work for more aggressive fulling, rather than for simply scouring. If a detergent is harsh, dilute it by using more water.

 Beginning on page 186, read the instructions for the specifics on scouring each fiber—for how hot the water should be, the type of soap or detergent to use, etc.

The process

 Be sure to use plenty of water, so the cloth can slosh around. Not enough water will contribute to shrinkage of wool fabrics.

The soap or detergent shouldn't have any additives in it. Different fibers require different pH's, but if the detergent is dissolved in lots of water, the pH of any detergent shouldn't hurt a fiber. If the pH is still too high for a fiber, dilute it with more water. Here's how to tell how much detergent to use: you want no more than 1/2" – 3/4" of suds on top of the water. Note, however, that some detergents (such as Synthapol SP and Orivus Paste) don't suds much, so 1/2" of suds would be much too much. Fill the tub or machine with water, add your detergent, and agitate the water to dissolve the detergent. Check for the amount

---

[31] Fry, Laura, *Magic in the Water: Wet Finishing Handwovens.* Fry Weaving Studio, Prince George, BC, Canada, 2002, p. 8.

of suds on the water and add more detergent, if necessary. The water should feel slippery. You want a lot of water, so the fabric can move freely in it. Then, enter your fabric.

Here's how Kati Meek scours her wool tartan fabric. "...I fill the washing machine with lukewarm water and a teaspoon of Synthrapol SP, a scouring agent that helps prevent excess dye from bleeding onto other yarns. I layer the cloth in loose folds and immerse it. After a five-minute soak without agitation, I spin it gently to extract the water (a hard spin sometimes sets permanent creases). I rinse three times (adding white vinegar to the second rinse), removing the cloth after each rinse to let water of the same temperature refill the tub. Throughout the finishing, I do not let the cloth agitate–the washer is just a convenient tub."[32]

It might take a few washings in the soap/detergent to get out all the spinning oils, etc. When the bubbles have disappeared from the surface of the water, it's time to change the water and repeat the process with clean water and soap or detergent. Another way to know when to change the water is to check the "look" of the water. Change it when it looks colored and/or milky. When it's time to change the water, remove the cloth before draining out the dirty water (you don't want to sieve the dirty water through the cloth), and fill the tub with clean water. Then, re-enter the cloth. In general, do not change the temperature of the water from bath to bath. The water will have cooled with the cloth in it so use that new temperature for the next bath, etc. Wool is particularly sensitive to temperature changes. Read about wool beginning on page 185.

You know when the cloth is "clean" when the suds don't disappear but stay on the surface of the water with the cloth in the bath.

Stage 2: Agitation

After the cloth has been entered into the scouring water, different amounts of agitation will bring different results. It can be gently agitated by hand. Washing machines can give gentle or harder agitation according to the setting and duration chosen. How much you agitate the fabric depends on the fiber, weave structure, and the look desired. Read what different fibers require under the heading for that of your fabric.

Agitation precaution

Agitation can cause certain fabrics to shrink greatly and to "full" or "felt" (extreme fulling). Read about fulling beginning on page 178. Agitate your samples in different ways to determine what you like best. Wool and hair fibers shrink and full especially.

What agitation does

Agitation along with scouring actually relaxes the yarns and fibers and allows them to move into place. I think of them settling in and curving around one another—a change from the straight, perpendicular crossings of the warps and wefts on the loom. Some weave structures, such as honeycomb and waffle weave, require that the yarns migrate after they are off the loom to give the effect the weave demands.

A certain amount of shrinkage happens with the relaxation of the fibers. Your samples will tell you how much. You can experiment with various amounts of shrinkage on your samples by trying different amounts of agitation and water temperatures. The sections about the fibers give suggestions and recommendations.

Agitation can minimize or eliminate reed marks—the spaces where the wires in the reed were between the warps. The yarns move to the places of least resistance. If there are spaces between clumps of threads in one dent in the reed, the yarns move into the spaces and eliminate some of the reed marks.

---

[32] Meek, M. Kati, *Handwoven Magazine*, Interweave Press, Loveland, CO. September/October, 1996, p. 103.

Nevertheless, don't depend on agitation to solve all instances of this problem. One student put 6 or 8 thin cotton threads in a dent, expecting the cloth to show none of the reed marks after wet finishing. That situation was too extreme, and the threads stayed crammed in little vertical lines making very obvious reed marks. It depends upon the yarns whether they can migrate or fluff up some to obscure any reed marks. Hard yarns like the cotton above (and worse yet, linen) couldn't obliterate the reed marks, but a soft cotton or wool might if there were only up to 4 or so yarns in a dent.

Front-loading washing machines give agitation as well as compression; See below.

Rinsing the fabric

After agitation is complete, rinse the fabric. Rinse several times in waters of similar temperatures—until the water is clear. Remember, do not wring or use the regular spin cycle of your machine to remove excess water. Roll your fabric in a towel and squeeze, don't wring. Read precautions about spinning in the machine on page 170.

A liquid fabric softener or vinegar in one of the last rinses can put the wool fibers into a more favorable pH state. Wool does not like alkaline conditions, which is what most laundry detergents provide. For wools, rinse three times, put fabric softener in the second rinse and white vinegar in the last rinse to neutralize any alkalinity.

Stage 3: Compression

This part of the process can be as time consuming as weaving, or setting up the loom. You want to allow plenty of time and to feel rested.

One important effect of compression is the flattening of the yarns that curve over and under each other in the cloth. The rounded curves are flattened into facets. These facets make the cloth more lustrous because light reflects more on the flat areas. Different fibers are compressed differently, so check the section on your type of cloth.

Compression also locks the yarns into place after they have been relaxed and moved around. This process stabilizes the cloth so it holds its shape. It will also help the cloth to wear longer.

The processes

There are several ways to accomplish compression, and which you use depends upon the fiber, yarns, weave, and the look desired. Read which methods are recommended for specific fibers in the sections given for each fiber. The processes are: hard press, cold mangling, and intermittent compression.

Hard pressing

Start with the cloth fairly damp after rinsing. It can have been in the dryer a bit, but it needs to be quite damp. Hard pressing is usually done with a regular iron that is as hot as the fiber content of the fabric can take. Try it on a sample first. If it isn't hot enough, it will take longer for the cloth to be ironed dry. If it's too hot, it can scorch or burn the cloth. (Synthetic fibers will melt.) Read how to remove scorch on page 195.

The ironing board should be fairly hard or only lightly padded. It could be a board with a piece of flannel covering it or a light towel. If one side of the cloth has a texture to be maintained, do all the pressing on the reverse side.

When I want to really hard press something, I iron on a wooden board, and between passes of the iron, I roll a rolling pin over the cloth, using a fair amount of pressure. Normal hard pressing doesn't need such extremely hard surfaces. The heavier the iron, the more efficient the pressing.

Lay the cloth out on grain—that is, with the warp and weft yarns going parallel and perpendicular, or at right angles.

Then, press by holding the iron down hard on

173

the cloth, in one position, for a few seconds. Laura Fry presses with her body weight and counts 6 seconds or so. Lift the iron and press it down hard again, this time overlapping the first place where the iron was. Continue this pressing over the entire cloth, front and back. Do one side, then the other, and maybe, the first side again. You can slide the iron across the cloth after the first flattening on both sides has been done to make drying the cloth easier and to add more sheen. The cloth should be almost or completely dry and flat, to avoid wrinkles.

Sometimes, I hang the almost dry fabric on a shower rod for awhile and then give it some more ironing (sliding the iron) until it is completely dry. If you hang it on a rod, be sure to move it frequently so a fold mark doesn't appear where the rod was.

To complete the drying, lay the cloth flat, roll it on a slatted roller, (See Figure 267 on page 176) or Z-fold it to air dry. (Figure 266.) It is important that the cloth be thoroughly dry before it is handled. It is still rather plastic and will not be actually "set" until it is completely dry.

If your piece is long yardage, read more about

Fig. 266

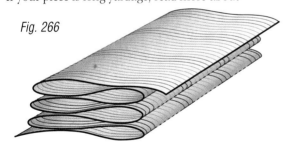

drying using a roller, on page 176.

Compression is always easier if the cloth is damp–rather damp, not just faintly damp. If your fabric is dry, dampen it before the ironing. If it is yardage, wrap the yardage on a roll between two sheets that are wet and let it absorb the moisture for a day or so, or sprinkle water on the fabric, roll it up, and let it sit several hours.

Cold mangling

Read about this process in the linen section beginning on page 194. It's a fascinating subject that most Americans have never heard of.

Intermittent compression

Read more about this treatment in the section on fulling, beginning on page 180. When you knead a fabric, you are applying "intermittent compression." Front loading washing machines give intermittent compression, as well, when the clothes fall from the top of the tub down into the water below. It can be done strongly with your feet or with hammers. Read about intermittent compression in the fulling section before trying it on your samples to see when it is recommended.

Ironing, Pressing, and Steaming

When ironing, you slide the iron over the fabric. It restores a finish to the cloth and smoothes out wrinkles. It can make the surface more soil resistant because it is smoother. Ironing can be done after hard pressing to finish drying the cloth and to polish it. It will not set the yarns in place as crabbing and hard pressing do.

When pressing, you hold the iron in one place and then pick it up and move it to another place. Pressing is done in the crabbing process with steam (See page 168), in hard pressing, and on other handwoven cloth at different times.

When steaming, you put a wet (cotton, wool, or linen) cloth between the fabric and the iron as you press. A piece of woolen cloth holds a lot of water and produces a lot of steam. Hold the iron in place until the steam stops rising. Test your sample to be sure that you won't scorch the cloth. Then, count or watch a second hand to know how long to keep the iron in one place.

Since you are setting the cloth, be sure it is exactly on grain.

Steaming

Heavy steaming with a soaking wet cloth will set the cloth so it won't track. Read about crabbing on page 167.

Light steaming is used to remove wrinkles that are not severe. Use a damp cotton or linen cloth and a medium warm iron. Press the cloth quickly, and then very lightly beat it with the back of a clothes brush (or a tailor's clapper) until the steam has evaporated. This treatment helps to keep the wool from becoming flat and dead, as it would if it were pressed with a heavy hand. [33]

There are times when you might steam or press a fabric, such as a blanket, even though you don't expect it to be ironed in its life as a blanket. The pressing should be light steaming with a steam iron or a damp cloth, not wet as for heavy steaming. You can just leave the iron in place, without applying any pressure, a second or two before moving it. It isn't compression, but it does set the yarns and can improve the hand and appearance of the fabric.

Steaming professionally can be done at a reputable dry cleaner. They have much stronger steam than you can get at home. Make sure they keep the cloth on grain each time before they apply steam. Be sure to have the fabric tested first by the professional. Tell the cleaner the fiber content so the correct amount of heat and pressure can be applied. For example, a fabric containing mohair should be pressed with medium heat (and no pressure for a fluffy surface).

Professional steaming can accomplish the shrinking and pressing processes.

Drying or Blocking the Cloth

Fabrics need to be completely dried for the setting process to be permanent. When the cloth is stretched out or laid out to dry with all the warps and wefts at right angles, it is called blocking. Various methods can be used; all are based on the principle of not wrinkling the cloth until it is completely dry. If the fabric doesn't track, the drying can set the yarns in the cloth and eliminate the need to hard press. Steaming or ironing after the cloth is dry may improve the hand of the cloth.

First, extract water out of the cloth. It's best to do this by blotting the cloth between towels. Do not wring or use the spin cycle of the machine because it can make permanent creases. Read the precautions about using the spin cycle on page 170.

Drying flat

Drying flat is ideal if you have the space. I dry my linen placemats and "iron" them in one operation by drying them flat on the clean kitchen counter. Put the right side face down on the counter for the smoothest finish.

Some people make frames to dry their handwovens. Some use small drying racks or racks made for drying sweaters.

Of course, fabrics dry faster if air can get to both sides of the fabric.

You can dry the fabric with the whole piece laid out flat on a board covered with a sheet to prevent staining. A large piece of foam-core board is ideal. Strong rust-proof pins placed every inch along the selvedges hold the cloth straight even while it dries. Avoid direct sunlight. Drying can take a few days. Dry one side and turn it over to dry the other. Read how to make a drying rack on page 177.

Line drying

You can hang fabric on a clothesline. If the clothesline is likely to make folds in the cloth,

---

[33] Mudge, Christine S., "Finishing Wool and Linen," *Shuttle, Spindle, and Dyepot*, Summer, 1978. p. 41.

you can slide PVC pipe over the line. Move the cloth every 30 minutes or so to prevent hard creases from forming where the cloth rests on the line or PVC-covered line. If you have a very long piece to dry, use two or more clotheslines parallel to each other. Drape the cloth over each line with cloth draping down between each line. Use the PVC pipe if necessary, and be sure to move the cloth every 30 minutes or so to prevent folds forming. Use a timer to make sure you move the cloth often enough. Move the cloth at each line about 6" so that the cloth is supported at a different point. Be sure that the clothesline follows a weft so that the grain of the cloth is not distorted.

Small lightweight pieces, such as scarves, might be able to be hung from a selvedge. Hang them from the edge, not over the line, to prevent fold marks. Use many clothespins, close together, to keep from having multiple peaks along the edge. The dripping provides the weight to "iron" the cloth as it dries.

Draping the fabric over several clotheslines gives more support to the cloth.

You can dry the cloth by draping it over a shower rod. Be sure to move the cloth occasionally, so a fold mark doesn't appear where the rod is. Blot out the excess water in towels before hanging it over the rod to dry.

You can make a drying closet with closet poles for drying racks. A heater with a fan can speed the drying process greatly.

Drying on rollers

Rollers to dry cloth can be solid wood, cardboard tubes, thick rolls of newspaper, or rollers with slats. See Figures 267a and b.

Fig. 267

a

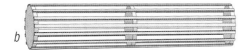

b

A slatted roller should be at least 15 inches in diameter and long enough to hold your widest cloth. A drying roller also can be made with rolled up screening, covered with muslin.

☞ Drying on a roller can replace the laborious hard pressing process as long as the fabric doesn't have tracking. If tracking needs to be prevented, the yarns *must* be set by crabbing before any water is applied to the cloth.

☞ Basically, you want to put the cloth onto the roller with tension fairly tight, to prevent wrinkling. Also, be sure the cloth is perfectly on grain, with the weft lying at right angles and straight across the width, and the cloth stretched out to its proper width. Some stretching might be needed. The cloth has to be on grain to set the yarns properly. When dry, there is no need to iron the fabric, but steam pressing can soften it.

A clean sheet or muslin prevents staining from the tube and makes it easier to get the rolling started. Read how Kati Meek rolls her fabric, below. Put the face, or the right side of the cloth, inwards toward the roller to make that side the smoothest.

Figure 268 shows how a stick can anchor the cloth to the roller at the beginning to get it started rolling tight and even. Also, see Figure 265 on page 169.

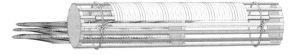

Fig. 268

Stand the roller on an end for drying. It should be turned over onto its opposite end periodically to ensure even drying. For a long length, the whole piece may need to be unwound, and rewound starting with the end that was outermost.

Here's how Kati Meek dries her tartans: "To dry wool tartan slowly without wrinkles, I roll it on a length of 4" cardboard tubing from a roll of carpet. Along its length, I've stapled one edge of a piece of muslin. I spread a sheet on the floor and accordion-fold the damp tartan onto it. Rolling most of the muslin around the tube so that one end of the handwoven overlaps the last 6", I now ask for another pair of hands to hold the other end of the tartan while I roll. Gripping the selvedges just in front of the roll, I stretch the cloth crosswise. Then gripping the roll, I pull back against my assistant's tension and roll a few inches tightly onto the tube. Then I stretch the cloth from selvedge to selvedge again, pull, and roll up a little more. With each quarter turn of the tube, I stroke the cloth roll from the center outward, keeping the cross-stripes of the cloth square on the tube. Stretching, pulling, and stroking the damp wool builds a hard, smooth roll of cloth. A few brass or stainless steel pins secure the edge. Propped on the roll end, it begins to dry.

"I check the cloth a couple of times a day, and when the outside layers feel dry, I find my assistant and re-roll the cloth starting with the dry end. It may take three or four re-rollings and several days for the cloth to dry, but it comes off the roll pressed and ready to cut and sew or wear."[34]

This step follows her scouring method. See page 172. You can see that this process takes time and patience, but is well worth it since no crabbing or laborious hard pressing has to be done.

Stretchers

Fabric can be stretched to dry on old-fashioned curtain stretchers.

Folding the cloth

The final drying can be done with the cloth folded loosely in a Z-fold, as in Figure 266, on page 174. Make sure there are no creases at the

---

A Custom Drying Rack

This rack by Linda Lemon was described in the guild newsletter for the *Contemporary Handweavers of Texas*, Inc., Volume 43, Number 2, December 1991. It breaks down and can be stored easily. Linda puts the PVC sections in a "stuff sack" (available at sporting good stores) along with the bungee cords, and she uses a mailing tube to store the screen mesh. It all fits in one sack.

1. Measure your bathtub enclosure length and width.

2. Buy at your hardware or building supply store:

   ½" PVC pipe (enough for two lengths and five widths of the tub enclosure)

   6 T connectors for ½" PVC pipe

   4 L or corner connectors for ½" PVC pipe

   1 roll of plastic mesh window screen. It comes in several sizes. Use the tub width and length measurements plus a margin to determine the size to buy

   3 short bungee cords about 18" long

   2 long bungee cords about 36" long

3. Saw the PVC pipe into pieces for lengthwise and width-wise fit. Be sure to figure allowances for the connectors. See Figure 269.

4. Using lengths and connectors, assemble the frame according to the illustration.

5. Unroll the plastic mesh screen over the frame, and cut to fit, leaving a margin of several inches all around the edges to fold under.

6. Using bungee cords, hook on one edge of the frame, securing the mesh (don't hook the mesh). Run across on the underside and hook onto the opposite edge. Use the short cords width-wise and the long ones lengthwise. See Figure 270.

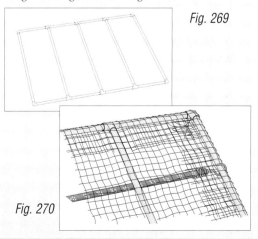

Fig. 269

Fig. 270

---

folds, so the cloth will not have any fold marks in it. It is not blocking, but a way to complete drying.

Blocking

By stretching and pinning a textile you can sometimes alter its shape a bit. Pin or tack the textile to its desired shape on a board or frame, pulling out slightly tight areas and/or easing in wide sections. Then thoroughly wet the fabric and leave it to dry. Slow natural drying will set the yarns to the blocked shape. Extreme buckling will not be cured but can be improved if the cloth is steamed on the blocking board. After blocking, careful washing or dry cleaning can be done, as needed.

Fulling

Most wool and other hair fibers can be fulled. With heat, moisture, and agitation the scales on the fibers swell and open, and the fibers migrate and move closer together, which causes the cloth to shrink in size and become thicker and narrower. The weave structure becomes blurred; the more fulling, the more blurred the weave. The cloth is also less flexible and is warmer to wear.

Because of the scale-like structure of the fibers the action of agitation in a warm alkaline environment encourages the wool fibers to move toward their cut bases. As you continue the fulling process, the fibers migrate closer and closer together and tangle on one another, and the scales become locked together. Once the fibers have locked together, they cannot be "unlocked"—the process is irreversible. However, it does take place incrementally, and you can stop the process at any point when you've reached the fabric look and feel you desire. If the oils are not removed from the yarns first, by scouring, the fulling process will take much longer to occur.

Be cautious. Fulling starts very slowly and then happens fast toward the end. Once you notice that fulling has begun, be very vigilant. Stop before it is as fulled as you want in the finished cloth, because rinsing will take the process further.

Experimenting on samples is crucial because of the irreversibility.

Fine fibers full more readily than coarse ones. Fine and coarse fibers come from different breeds of sheep and different locations on a sheep's body. Loosely spun yarns full more than tightly twisted yarns. The more open the weave structure, the more easily the fabric will full. Weaves with fewer intersections of warp and weft such as basket weave and twills allow the yarns to move more, tangle, and shrink more than plain weave. Even so, because fulling has to do with the openness of the weave, a loosely woven plain weave will full more easily than a tightly woven basket weave, or twill. Different effects are possible by controlling temperature, degree and duration of agitation, pressure, and the use of soap or detergent.

Once the weave has closed up by the expansion of the yarns, and the cloth has the thickness and hand for your intended purpose, the cloth is removed from the soapy bath and rinsed—to stop the process.

Worsted fabrics can be fulled somewhat, but usually aren't because fulling blurs the crispness of the weave and the luster of the fabric. For that reason, worsted warps are sett closer than woolen ones.

Woolen fabrics can be fulled from a little bit to a lot. The more open the sett (ends per inch), the more the cloth can full. In other words, if you want a cloth to full greatly, sett the warp threads on the loom to be quite open to allow for the shrinkage. There must be space between the wefts, as well.

The amount of shrinkage (fulling) of a given yarn or fabric will vary according to the amount and heat of the water, the amount of agitation, and the drying method.

The fulling process

The water

After the fabric has been scoured and all the oil removed, the fulling process can begin. Use hot, soapy water. Using less water in the bath encourages more shrinkage (fulling), faster.

Water temperature

The hotter the temperature, the faster the fulling process will take place, so start with warm or tepid water if you're not sure how much fulling you want. Start with water that is about 100 degrees F, which feels warm, not hot.

Soap or detergent

Fulling can take place with soap or detergent—you don't need much—just a light layer of bubbles on the surface of the water. Read about using soaps and detergents in hard water on page 171. In soapy water, the fulling takes place by agitation.

Agitation

Agitation can be done in the machine or by hand. It's the same as agitation in washing, just more of it and more controlled. Read about fulling by hand or in the machine, on page 180.

If you want a lightweight fabric do not agitate the fabric much as you move it around in the wash water. If you want a thick fabric, like for a woolly blanket, agitate it more—maybe using a machine's agitation. Fulling will continue as long as the agitation does, and can be stopped by stopping the agitation. Remember, the process is not reversible, so go in stages, increasing the agitation for more and more fulling. Here, your samples are crucial. If you pass the point you want for your fabric, you'll be happy it was on the sample and not on the whole piece of your good cloth.

When the cloth begins to narrow in, fulling is starting, so watch carefully and stop the agitation when the cloth is almost fulled to the degree you want.

To check on the progress of the fulling, stop the machine, pull up a handful of cloth, squeeze out the water with your hands and compare it to your finished sample.

Rinsing

Rinse the cloth when the fulling is complete or to check if it is complete. The temperature of the rinse water should be the same as the temperature of the cloth or you will encourage further shrinkage. Rinse the same way as other wool cloths until the water is clear. It will usually take several rinses to completely remove all the soap or detergent and oils or "dirt." The way to tell that you've rinsed enough is to check the water. It must look clear.

 Further fulling can take place in the rinsing by using more agitation. There will be some agitation in the rinsing, so be sure to allow for it when you stop the agitation in the soapy water.

A liquid fabric softener can be used in the final rinse.

Drying

It is important not to wring wet wool because the fabric is very "plastic" or vulnerable to distortion. You can spin it out in a washing machine or pile it up and allow gravity to pull the water to the bottom of the cloth and gently squeeze. Read more about drying methods beginning on page 188, in the worsted section.

Continue drying as for worsted fabrics and hard press (page 173) the cloth when it is still damp, unless you plan to brush the fabric. Read about brushing on page 182.

When is it done?

Basically, the fulling is done when you decide the cloth looks and feels right for your project. You can get a good enough idea after the cloth has been spun dried but is still damp. If you want more fulling, make a new soapy bath and agitate some more.

Laura Fry checks the stability of the cloth by pulling the cloth out of the water and running her fingernail across the threads–from beneath the cloth--to see how easily the threads shift. If you can poke through the cloth, it probably is not done. "The desired stability of the cloth will depend on the function the cloth is to perform–a shawl need not necessarily be as stable as fabric used for garments or upholstery, for example." If you plan to brush the fabric later, it needs to be very stable.

☞ It is better to stop the process too soon than too late. Stop a bit short of the desired end result because more changes can occur while rinsing and compressing. Remember to rinse the cloth in water that is the same temperature as the cloth.

Fulling by hand

Hand full folded layers of cloth in soapy water. The wet cloth can be kneaded in a tub or on a flat surface or on a laundry scrubbing board. You can also walk on the fabric in a bathtub.

☞ Turn the cloth over continually during the process so that all parts get the same degree of fulling. This is called intermittent compression. Read about compression on page 173. It can be a time consuming process if heavy fulling is desired. You can speed up the process with hotter water and slow it down with cooler water. Since the process is irreversible, unless you have experience, it is wise to begin with tepid water. You must check the fabric often once the fulling begins so you can stop the process when you have the desired effect. Experimenting on your samples will tell you what you can achieve with various amounts of fulling.

To save your knuckles, put a piece of foam in the bottom of the tub.

Add more soap dissolved in water if the suds become exhausted.

It can take a rather long time for the fulling to begin. It could start in a few minutes or

not until 10 minutes after you start working the cloth. You can continue for several hours if you want a particularly dense, thick cloth. In that case, keep the cloth warm and soapy throughout the time.

☞ You can tell when the fulling is just beginning because the width of the cloth narrows. From then on, fulling can take place rapidly, so you'll want to check the cloth often.

Another way to tell fulling is beginning is that the size of the bubbles begins to get smaller. You can feel a change in the cloth as you are kneading as well—it becomes more resistant to your kneading and has more substance.[35]

Fulling in a washing machine

The same fulling principles apply as for fulling by hand, above. Use the machine when you want significant fulling. For less fulling, use the gentle cycle and take the fabric out sooner. See below.

☞ For fulling, less water is used than for regular agitation when you want the cloth to slosh around. Less water enhances the shrinkage. To control the amount of water in a machine, use the setting for a small or medium load.

☞ You must, must, must check the fabric during fulling–more often once it has begun. So, stay by the machine until this process is completed. Remember, fulling cannot be reversed, and your cloth could be ruined by too much fulling. Different machines agitate more and less, so watching the activity is crucial.

Prepare fabric for top-loading machines

Prepare the fabric so that the fulling will take place evenly over the entire cloth and the edges won't ruffle. Read about ruffling below.

Protect the last wefts on the raw edges with a zig-zag stitch or by serging. See page 158.

---

[35] Fry, p. 21.

Fold the fabric lengthwise (warp-wise) and stitch the selvedges together with hand stitches. See Figures 271 and 272. Use a contrasting color thread that will not full or bleed, for example, smooth cotton or silk, so the stitches can be removed easily later.

Then, fold the length in half and handsew the ends together to make a large ring, or donut shape. See Figure 273.

Front-loading machines

Front-loading machines don't need the cloth to be prepared by folding and sewing. The raw edges must be stitched or serged, however.

Ruffled edges

If the cloth isn't prepared as above, more fulling will take place in the middle of the cloth and less at the edges, thus the ruffled edges. You may have to cut off the ruffles if the difference in fulling is too great. You can flatten the ruffling, but remember, it will not make them fulled enough to match the center of the cloth. If the ruffles won't press out, you can try dampening the edges and flattening them by placing weighted boards on top and letting the cloth air-dry. Avoiding ruffles by preparing the cloth is better.

Agitation

Put the ring of cloth around the central agitator in a top-loading machine. This type of machine applies agitation only. Front-loading machines apply intermittent compression; the cloth is put into them in no special way.

Rinsing

Rinse as for worsteds and other wools, making sure that the temperature of the rinse waters are the same as the temperature of the cloth, to prevent damage to the fibers.

Sharon Alderman warns. "If you have used a washing machine's spin cycle, be sure that there will be no point in the cycle where the machine sprays the fabric with cold water; many of them are programmed to rinse at

Fig. 271

Fig. 272

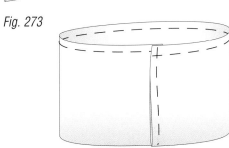

Fig. 273

a lower temperature and cool their contents with a cold spray which could be ruinous for your handwoven woolen cloth." Remember, you don't want to shock your cloth with temperature changes.

When spinning out in the machine, just spin out the excess water until the cloth is no longer sopping wet. Do not use the whole cycle, or permanent wrinkles may occur.

Using a clothes dryer

(If you prefer not to use the dryer, read about drying in the worsted section, beginning on page 188.)

More fulling can take place if the damp cloth is put into the dryer, but you must check the cloth often—every few minutes—because once the fulling (shrinking) starts, it happens quickly. Use a low temperature and check the cloth every few minutes. Remember, you can tell when fulling is beginning when the cloth begins to narrow. Take the cloth from the dryer when it has fulled the amount you want for the purpose of your fabric. It's better to take it out too soon (and put it back again), rather than too late when all the fibers are felted together and your cloth is ruined and can't be used for its intended purpose.

Rotate the fabric during the drying so creases do not appear.

Pressing (compression)

Read about hard pressing beginning on page 173.

Protecting fringe

Fringe can get hopelessly tangled and matted (felted) during fulling. The best idea is to loosely weave the areas where you want fringe when weaving the cloth. Use a weft that is smooth and won't full, or strips of dry-cleaner bags. Do not use wool. After fulling, these threads will be removed, leaving the fringe.

If you didn't weave where the fringe is to be and have loose warp threads, wrap them up in socks and secure them with rubber bands during the finishing process.

More details

Make a sample warp about 12" wide and about 18" long, and weave plain weave, twill, and the weave structure you are considering for your project. Check the results after wet finishing and/or fulling. You might have to change the sett to be more open if you want more fulling and shrinkage to take place. Start with a sett that is ½ the number of wraps of the yarn on a ruler.

Sampling is all-important before you begin to full your project. Full one of the samples *too much*—you might really like the result.

With significant fulling, plain weave will be stiffer and twill more drapey. (More drapey than plain weave, but less drapey than before it was fulled.)

Felting

Felting is fulling to the extreme. The weave structure is completely obliterated, and the fibers shrink to the maximum. Felt is thick because of all the shrinkage. You can avoid felting by stopping the fulling process before it gets to this state. If your goal is felting, use extreme fulling methods from the outset, and be prepared for the process to take quite some time.

Wadmal[36]

Wadmal is woven fabric that has been felted so the weave structure is no longer apparent. The "cloth" is very thick and dense and makes good jackets. It is too stiff for a fuzzy blanket.

Loosely spun wool and an open sett are basics. For the fabric to shrink so extremely, it must be woven with much space between the yarns. Yarns that are loosely spun will felt easier than those that are tightly spun.

Fulling takes place in the machine with the fabric folded and hand sewn as described on page 181. The wash cycle is repeated as many times as necessary. To increase the fulling, change the water temperature from hot to cold several times, removing the cloth when the washer is filling and draining, as usual.

After washing, rinse the cloth and put it in the dryer on air, with no heat, to fluff up the cloth, and then air-dry. If there is no ruffling at the selvedges, remove the hand stitches and open out the fabric to dry. If the fabric remains folded, rotate the fabric during the drying period, so creases do not appear at the fold.

If you plan to brush the fabric (See below), you'll get a heavier nap if you brush it when it is damp. Remember, wool is weaker when wet than dry.

Brushing

Fabric is brushed to give it a fuzzy surface. The fabric may have been fulled or not before doing the brushing. The fulled cloth may

———————————————————————————————————————

[36] Snover, Susan, *Wadmal Workshop Instructions*.

look somewhat rough and dull, and brushing can make it more lustrous, with a soft pile. Brushing roughs up the surface to disentangle the fibers and make them into a thick or thin pile or "nap." Sometimes "brushing" is called "napping" in industry.

The purpose of brushing is to raise a nap to provide warmth, softness, and beauty to a fabric. It can also give water and stain repellency to fabrics.

What can be brushed?

Woolen cloth is often brushed to raise some or a lot of nap. Mohair is the best fiber for a luxurious, lofty nap that wears well and stays good looking for a long time. Wools that resemble mohair—long staple length, high luster and good body are ideal. (Staple means the length of individual fibers.) Loop yarns brush up more readily than smooth yarns.

The best results occur when the weft yarns are made of low-twist yarns with a long staple length, or any staple fiber. Cotton, rayon, wool, or acrylic fibers can be brushed.

Depending on staple length and fiber content, a heavy nap can be raised on 2/2 twills or weft face twills. Plain weave, basket and other twills can be brushed, as well. Boucle yarns should be woven in plain weave to be brushed to a full nap.

Linen and other plant fibers can also be brushed, each giving its own effect. Even glazed cotton can be brushed![37]

What not to brush

Be careful with long floats in the weave because the yarn may snag during brushing and the brushing will hide the weave structure. Loose and lacy weaves and overshot weaves aren't recommended for brushing. The fabric needs to be stable—you should not be able to

easily poke your little finger into the cloth. You might need to full the fabric some more to make it stable enough.

The brushes

Traditionally, Fuller's teasels were used for brushing, and they still are today. Be sure you use Fuller's teasel (Dipsacus sativus); the spines of the common teasel (D.fullonum) are straight and aren't satisfactory for brushing fabric. See Figures 274 and 275. Suede brushes or pet brushes or anything similar can be used. A stiff bristle nylon hairbrush works better than a natural, too-soft bristle brush.

Heavy wire brushes for removing house paint, or wool carders can be used by the experienced only, and if used carefully.

When to brush

The cloth must be stable before it can be brushed. If it is a loosely woven piece meant to be fulled, it must be fulled first or it won't stand up to brushing. If the cloth is stable enough, it can be brushed while on the loom.

Read how to brush on the next page.

183

Fig. 274

Fig. 275

---

[37] Compiled by Irwin, Bobbie, "Fuzzy Stuff: Finishing the Fuzzies," *Handwoven* Magazine, January/February 1990. p. 51.

"If you are planning on brushing up a nap, you need to decide at this point if you will brush it before hard pressing, after hard pressing, and/or after the cloth has dried completely.

"Brushing before hard pressing will generally develop a much loftier nap which may be desirable for blankets or afghans. Brushing after hard pressing will raise a shallower nap. Brushing after the cloth has been completely dried will usually result in the lowest nap. 'Dry' brushing is done after the cloth has been allowed to dry completely, and then is spritzed with water, which acts as a lubricant."[38]

Full the fabric well before brushing. It will bring a lot of the fibers to the surface. Brush when the cloth is nearly dry from the fulling (including rinsing). Steam the cloth with a steam iron or a steamer and brush while it is hot and steamy. "It is important not to brush the fabric while it is dripping wet because the wool fibers are somewhat weaker then. Likewise, you will obtain better results if you brush the fabric before it is fully dry, because the brushing has to be more severe to raise a nap in a dry woolen fabric."[39]

Professional brushing

You can send out your fabric to be brushed. Ihana Brushing Service has an industrial machine with Fuller's teasels that can brush large pieces of cloth. For more information, see the Sources section. Be sure to check to see what the end result will be like and also, what the requirements of their machines are for your cloth.

How to brush

It's easier to brush large pieces when they are stretched on a frame. Brush small pieces on an ironing board by using one arm to clamp down the fabric while the other does the brushing.

Usually, both sides of the cloth are brushed.

Brushing on the loom

When brushing the fabric while it's on the loom, Ann Sutton brushes sideways (weftwise), so she doesn't distort the warps, and only the last stroke goes warpwise.[40]

Increase the warp tension before you brush. The other side of the cloth will be brushed after it is off the loom. Read more in the section about brushing dry cloth, below.

You can brush in only one direction or in both the warp and weft directions. Try various ways on your samples to decide what you like best. Whatever you do, brush with the grain—either or both ways—but never brush at an angle to the warp and weft because that can pull the yarns out of their positions.

Brush gently—this process, like fulling, is not reversible. And remember you are just raising some nap, not distorting the cloth.

For an all over fuzzy surface, brush the fabric in all four directions (parallel to the yarns). For a directional nap, brush in a single direction. The four directions are explained in the section about brushing dry cloth.

Brushing dry cloth

For dry fabric, lay the fabric flat on a table and hold it down with heavy weights. Dampen the brush by dipping it in water before use. Brush the cloth systematically in one direction (e.g., to the right), along its length. Re-dampen the brush frequently. Once the total area has been completed, the process must be repeated, but this time, brushing in the opposite direction (to the left), in order to produce an even texture.

---

[38] Fry, p. 22.
[39] Alderman.
[40] Sutton, Ann, Lecture notes from workshop. December 1997.

Brushing damp cloth

Cloth can be fluffed up in the dryer with no heat to help raise the nap, then brushed when almost dry.

Brushing wet cloth

For lofty blankets, Christine Mudge does her brushing just after the fabric has been fulled, while it is quite wet, before the rinsing process. She brushes with a stiff brush in both directions. When enough nap has been raised, she rinses it in progressively cooler rinses. After rinsing and squeezing out the excess water—or carefully and briefly spinning it in the washer—she brushes the blanket in just the warp direction and dries it on a frame or air-dries it. When it is dry, she brushes it yet again.[41]

Care of brushed fabrics

Dry cleaning brushed fabrics is recommended by Ihana Brushing Service with light brushing with a clean hairbrush to rejuvenate a worn nap. A heavily matted nap may need rebrushing. You could try to fluff up the nap in the dryer for 3-4 minutes with no heat.

If you wash your brushed fabric gently, you'll need to brush lightly to restore the nap.

Wool: Woolen and Worsted

Woolen and worsted fabrics are finished differently. They are woven differently, too, mainly because of the amount of shrinkage anticipated in the finishing process.

Just knowing the fiber content of your cloth is wool is not enough. Woolen cloth looks woolly–soft, lofty, opaque, and fairly thick. The weave structure can be blurred or even completely disguised in the finishing process.

The surface of worsted fabric has a hard finish. It is smooth and rather flat—not woolly at all. Think of fine wool fabric for suiting. Traditional tartans are also worsted fabrics. It is sometimes called the "cool" wool because the spaces between the threads are not filled in and the air can circulate from the body to the outside air. This cloth is set closer on the loom because it is not meant to shrink in the finishing process. It gives a clear finish that shows off the luster of the fiber and the weave structure.

The differences between woolen and worsted occur because of the way the fibers are spun into yarn as well as the length of the fibers and the breed of the sheep. Woolen fibers can be short and curvy. Worsted fibers are longer and smoother/straighter. Wool-spun yarns require a lot of finishing after the cloth is woven. Worsted fibers are processed to a greater degree during spinning, so less finishing is done to the woven fabrics.

Woolen yarns are composed of shorter fibers, are carded to make a lofty mass, and then drawn out and twisted during the spinning process. Usually, an oil, spinning oil, is used in the carding process to help the drawing out of the yarn. These yarns are wooly and smell of the spinning oil. The oil must be removed in the finishing process.

Worsted yarns are spun from longer fibers that are combed, so that the fibers lie parallel to each other, and then the fibers are drawn out and twisted. The yarns are smoother, don't smell of the spinning oil, and don't need as much finishing as woolen yarns do to get rid of the oil.

Where the fibers in worsted yarns are smooth and parallel, the fibers in woolen yarns are tangled and fuzzy. See Figure 276.

Whether woolen or worsted, the finest wool fabrics need to be washed gently, because the

---

[41] Mudge. Ibid.

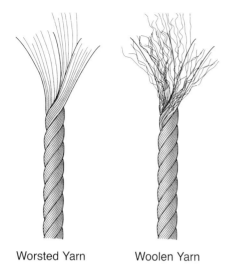

Worsted Yarn   Woolen Yarn

Fig. 276

finer the fibers, the more likely the wool is to felt. Read about felting on page 182.

☞ Both woolen and worsted fabrics woven in *plain weave* must be crabbed first, before they are wet finished, because water and motion in the finishing process will produce tracking in the fabric. If you want a true, worsted look, you will not want the tracking. Read about tracking and crabbing on page 167. Read the section on worsted finishing, below. Many worsted fabrics are not woven in plain weave, so they don't encounter the tracking problem. Twills, basket weave, and pattern weaves do not show tracking; only plain weave (tabby) does.

Finishing woolen vs. worsted

The beauty of woolen fabric lies largely in the finish of the cloth; and of worsted fabrics, in the weave. Worsted cloth, when taken from the loom, looks much as it will in the finished piece. Woolen cloths are often coarse and rough and require wet finishing to remove the spinning oil and sometimes, more finishing processes, such as fulling or brushing. Read about fulling, beginning on page 178. Fulling woolen cloth can often obscure imperfections in the weave, but any imperfections in worsteds will remain.

The wet finishing processes are about the same for woolen and worsted, but when worsted fabrics are fulled it is only to soften the weave, while the object in woolens is often to obliterate the weave.

Finishing Worsteds

☞ A worsted fabric should be set by steaming before it is scoured (washed), to retain the flat, clear, non-fuzzy surface of the cloth. It is especially important with *plain weave* worsteds, because tracking will occur if the fabric isn't set before washing.

Finishing by a professional dry cleaner

Test one of your samples to see if dry cleaning provides the desired look and feel of your worsted cloth. The cloth doesn't need to be set or wet finished in that case, because there is no water in the dry cleaning solution (There is liquid, but it's not water.) The dry cleaner may only give the cloth a heavy steaming—with or without pressure—for your finishing process.

Be sure to explain exactly what you want done, including how you want it pressed. For example, do you want the surface fluffy, soft, or hard? The dry cleaner can use lots of pressure, little pressure, or just steam with no pressure. The cloth will come back very flat without any texture if you don't say how you want it. Some weavers think dry cleaning doesn't produce as nice a cloth as wet finishing.

Setting the fabric

Read how it is done in the section on crabbing, beginning on page 167. Remember, it takes a heavy steaming on both sides of the cloth to prevent tracking, so practice on your samples until you find the process that results in a flat finished surface that shows up the plain weave structure rather than tracks. Read more about tracking, beginning on page 167.

After the fabric has been set, it can be washed or scoured.

Washing (scouring and agitation)

Worsted fabrics don't require much cleaning because oils are not used in the spinning process. Therefore, they won't need much soap or detergent.

☞ Be sure to use plenty of water. Not enough water can cause the cloth to shrink. (It is the rubbing of the fabric on itself that causes the shrinkage, which happens more if there isn't much water.)

For a flat "worsted finish" you don't want to full the cloth, so use only a little or no agitation in the scouring process. Fulling is explained on page 178. Worsted cloth can full if the finishing process is too strenuous. You can tell when fulling is beginning to take place—the width starts narrowing. Once it begins, it shrinks in a hurry, and the wool fibers migrate and can't be returned to their original places. This effect is a good reason to experiment on your samples—you can know when your finishing technique has gone too far.

Use a mild detergent—one that is kind to your hands, because wool is susceptible to alkalis and has only a fair resistance to acid. Read about soaps and hard water on page 171. If you use soap, or your detergent is strong, it probably is too alkali and can harm the wool. Putting white vinegar in the last rinse will neutralize the fabric.

☞ Dissolve the detergent in the water before entering the cloth. Use enough water to cover—that is, plenty of water.

☞ Always lift the cloth out of the tub when you fill it with the wash and rinse waters. Lift the cloth out in a bundle; don't pick it up by an edge, because wool is weaker when it is wet. Lift the cloth when the water is draining out of the machine, as well, to prevent loose fibers from settling on its surface.

Many weavers use the washing machine as a tub because it makes it easier to fill and drain

the machine, as needed. See page 172 for Kati Meeks method of washing tartans.

Water temperature

Wool will felt, or shrink greatly, if it is shocked by water temperatures that vary greatly, or if much agitation is used. You can enter wool into a fairly hot bath as long as you don't agitate it or suddenly put it into cooler water to rinse.

Soaking the cloth

Use water that is about 100-110 degrees F., which will feel pretty hot. First, just soak the fabric for about 15 minutes to wet the fibers and relax the yarns. Fold the cloth to fit the basin and submerge it with your fingers. Then, gently push the cloth back and forth in the water to clean (scour) it. You can gently squeeze the cloth in the water to make sure it is completely wetted. You are never agitating the cloth, just moving it gently.

After soaking

"I work the cloth while it is under water by pulling it on the bias in both directions and moving it between my hands; I work on a section of cloth about a foot to a foot and a half square and then move on to the next section. I never scrub the fabric against itself; if I did, I would raise a nap on the surface and cause the wool to full, which would defeat the reason for using a worsted yarn. After the entire length of the fabric has been manipulated, the washing water is drained away and replaced by water of the same temperature for the first rinse."[42]

Rinsing

Drain the cloth 1/2 to 1 hour by letting it sit in a heap between the wash and rinses. This position lets gravity extract some of the water

---

[42]Alderman, Sharon, and Wertenberger, Kathryn, *Handwoven, Tailormade*. Interweave Press, Loveland, CO. 1982, p. 60.

before you enter the cloth into the new bath water. Don't be tempted to squeeze the cloth; let it drain. Re-fold the cloth for each rinse and gently push it back and forth in the water as you did when scouring.

As usual, do not shock the wool with extreme temperature changes. Each rinse water should start out at about the same temperature as the previous one ended. One rinse might remove all the detergent (you didn't use much), but a second rinse should ensure that it is all removed. If the fabric feels too scratchy, use a liquid fabric softener in the second rinse. Use 1 tablespoon for a large capacity, top-loading washing machine if full, and 1 teaspoon for a front-loading machine. Don't use too much, or the cloth will feel sticky or gooey.

Drying

Extracting the water from the cloth can be tricky. Your washing machine can extract the water if it doesn't spray water on the cloth as it spins. Be careful: too much spinning can permanently set wrinkles into the fabric. A gentle spin speed is recommended, but watch the process often so that the cloth doesn't become wrinkled. If you can blot the cloth between towels, that would be ideal.

You can also hang the dripping wet cloth from a clothesline and let the water and gravity stretch the fabric. Hang it with the selvedge of the cloth just up against the line, not folded over it. Clothespin every 3 inches, then push the pins and cloth together so that the clothespins touch each other. Use your judgment to decide if the cloth is strong enough to be hung by the selvedge.

Liz Williamson hangs her scarves to dry while they are still full of water, because it seems to give less creasing that way. Hang from one selvedge if it is large, over a line in the middle of the scarf if it is small. Water drips down and out the other selvedge. She turns the scarves after 5 minutes, then every 10 minutes or so until nearly dry, so they will dry evenly. She removes them from the line when they are just damp and presses them until they are dry.[43]

Alderman drapes her damp, not dripping, cloth "over clotheslines, out of direct sunlight, so that the fabric loops over several lines. As I hang the fabric, I grasp it by the selvedges—right across from each other so that I preserve the grain—and pull outward smartly so that the fabric snaps a little bit; it isn't a destructive jerk, more a shaking out of the creases. This snapping removes most of the wrinkles before the fabric begins to dry; I smooth it with my hands and straighten the selvedges. From time to time, as it dries, I move the fabric so that the same places in the fabric aren't in contact with the lines all the drying time. When the fabric feels almost dry, it is time to press it."

Read about other drying techniques beginning on page 175.

Drying sets the yarns in place, so be sure the cloth is always on grain and smooth until it is totally dry.

Pressing (Compression)

Pressing (See Ironing, Pressing and Steaming on page 174) stabilizes the worsted cloth. (The stabilizing comes from fulling in woolen cloths.)

In pressing, use plenty of steam and a good press cloth (wet). The best press cloth is a piece of woolen fabric, because it keeps your cloth from becoming shiny.

If you want the shine, hard press the damp wool directly on the surface of the cloth rather than using a pressing cloth. The shine that develops can be removed by a simple steaming

[43]Willliamson, Liz, Finishing Lecture, Convergence, 1998.

188

if you don't like it. Read about hard pressing on page 173. Traditionally, one tries to avoid putting a shine on worsted fabrics.

Depending upon the look you want, use more or less pressure on the iron.

Liz Williamson uses a hot setting of the iron, with no steam, and presses both sides without a press cloth. If she can't press her scarves while they are still damp from the clothesline, she puts them in a plastic bag (without wrinkling) for up to a day or so, to keep them damp enough for pressing.

When you have pressed both sides of the cloth, it still may not be totally dry, which is necessary to complete the finishing process to prevent shrinkage and wrinkling. Lay the cloth flat; roll it on a slatted roller (Figure 267b on page 176); hang it so the air can circulate around it; or Z-fold (page 174) it until it is completely dry.

When the cloth is dry

If the cloth is dry, it can be dampened again by wrapping it in a wet towel or between two wet sheets for a few hours. It's much better if the cloth is damp from washing because it will be evenly damp throughout the cloth.

Maintaining worsteds

Read the section on maintaining woolens on page 190.

Finishing Woolens

Woolen cloths are allowed greater shrinkage and fiber movement, so they are usually not set or crabbed. However, you would crab a woolen cloth if you wanted an open weave or to prevent tracking. In that case, after crabbing you would scour the fabric very gently. You wouldn't want to full the cloth because that would shrink it and close up the openness you desired in the first place.

Woolens: To full or not to full

Fulling is a process that opens the fibers in the threads until they touch each other, filling in the spaces between the threads in the cloth as it was woven. Some shrinkage occurs when the threads close in on each other. Heavy fulling shrinks the fabric a lot. It is also called "milling." It takes place in the scouring stage of wet finishing. Read more about fulling, beginning on page 178. The more vigorous the fulling process, the more fulling (shrinkage) takes place and the thicker the cloth gets. Extreme fulling completely obscures the weave structure and is called felt or wadmal.

The sett, or ends per inch, for woolen fabrics is usually more open than for worsteds to allow for the shrinkage in finishing.

The finishing process is usually more rigorous than for worsteds to achieve the shrinkage and the desired hand.

Woolen yarns generally felt (extreme fulling) easily because their fibers are crisscrossing. Worsted yarns with their parallel fibers felt less easily. See Figure 276 on page 186.

 Warning! Fulling is cumulative and cannot be reversed. At first a little fulling takes place, and if you stop the process there, that is what the finished cloth will look like. You can change your mind and full it more, but you can never reverse the fulling that has already taken place. If your fabric turns into felt from extreme fulling, you can never change it back to the way the original cloth was.

Fulling takes place when the wool is agitated with soap or detergent and shocked by temperature changes.

Woolen cloths are usually fulled at least a little bit. (See page 178.) How much fulling you do depends upon the look and the hand of the fabric you want.

Scouring woolens without fulling

You can wash woolen cloth without allowing it to full or shrink. The main principle is not to change the water temperature extremely or to agitate the fabric very much.

☞ If you want an open or distinct *plain weave* and no tracking you must set the cloth (crabbing) before scouring. Read about this process beginning on page 167. Experiment on your samples to determine the look you want to achieve.

Woolen yarns are spun with lots of oil, which needs to be washed out of the cloth in the scouring process, even if the cloth is not to be fulled. Hot water and soap or detergent are used. Some weavers prefer to soak the fabric before beginning the scouring process and some don't. Delicate fabrics should be soaked less than heavy, oily cloths which can be safely soaked overnight. Start out with hot water and let it cool naturally. Use the scouring process described for worsteds, beginning on page 187. Since there is more spinning oil to be removed in woolens than in worsteds the scouring needs to be done more thoroughly with more washes. Because there will be more loose fibers floating on the surface in the washing water, be sure to remove the fabric before the water is drained to keep the fibers from settling on the fabric.

Remember not to agitate the cloth in the soapy water very much. Also, do not shock the wool with changes in the temperature of the wash and rinse water. If the cloth cools to room temperature, use water at room temperature to continue scouring.

Maintaining Woolen Fabrics

The degree of fulling that you have on your cloth can be maintained through subsequent launderings by using gentle washing or dry cleaning. If you wash the cloth again with hot water and agitation, you can increase the degree of fulling (and shrinkage). The

principle is: Once the fabric has been processed to its intended final state, great care must be taken to apply no more heat or agitation during future cleanings.

In other words, wash your wool garment (providing the linings, interfacings, etc. are washable) as if it were a fine wool sweater.

Animal Fibers

Mohair, alpaca, cashmere and angora fabric are finished in the same way as worsted fabric. Some mohair fabrics are brushed in the finishing process. They ought to be brushed while they are steamy, just as woolen fabrics are.

Cotton

> **Sample first**—you may get tracking. Read about this phenomenon, beginning on page 167.
>
> **Test the yarns for color fastness** before washing. See page 164.

Unlike wools, where the finishing process treats the fabrics in a gentle way, wet finishing cotton resembles regular laundering methods for cotton. Finish the textile the way it will eventually be treated.

Cotton cloth shrinks in the initial washing, and it may shrink more in a second one. You may need to pre-shrink your freshly handwoven fabric by washing it two or three times before using it. Wash your sample and measure it to see if it continues to shrink after the first washings. When it no longer shrinks, you can plan that it won't shrink any more on subsequent launderings—provided you use the same washing method, or something gentler.

Besides pre-shrinking, finishing cotton makes the colors brighter and gives a more lacy look for lace weaves, and a three-dimensional effect for waffle and honeycomb structures. For plain weaves and twills it allows the yarns to curve around one another and fill in the spaces for a softer, more "finished looking" cloth. Reed marks and some irregularities in the weave can be ameliorated, and the cloth will look and drape much better after finishing.

The first washing (scouring and agitation)

Don't let wrinkles get permanently set in your cloth in the first washing. The important thing to remember is to not allow the newly washed fabric to dry wrinkled. Use the regular cycle for washing in the washing machine but be sure to use the gentle *spin* cycle for drying, and remove the fabric as soon as the cycle is finished. Iron it dry (except for waffle weave) or hang it to dry after shaking it out and pulling at the selvedges to remove any wrinkles. Of course, you could hand wash it, but don't wring it, which would set in permanent wrinkles. Instead, blot it between towels to get rid of excess water and to allow it to dry without any wrinkles.

Use hot water for white cotton, warm water for colored fabrics, and soap or a strong laundry detergent. Cotton fibers can benefit from alkalis (which are in detergents) but are damaged by acids. You wouldn't put vinegar in the last rinse for cotton because vinegar is an acid. If natural cotton cloth floats on the surface, read about scouring it, below.

Drying and compression

Cotton fabric can be machine or air dried until damp and then given a hard press until completely dry (unless you don't want a smooth surface). The fabric can be stretched out to dry when a smooth surface isn't the goal. Iron both sides of the fabric—or just one side if you don't want a shiny or smooth surface. Read more about hard pressing, beginning on page 173.

Cotton can need strong heat, and the "cotton" setting on irons is quite high. Be sure not to

hold the iron down in one place too long or the fabric will scorch. Read about removing scorch on page 195 and sample first to know how long is too long to hold the iron in one place.

Scouring natural cotton

If the fabric just floats on the surface during the first washing, probably the yarns still have their natural waxy coating, which needs to be washed out (scoured).

Cotton can be scoured in hot water with washing soda. That is usually enough but if not, boil it in water with washing soda (found in stores near the laundry detergents).

The Linders, in *Hand Spinning Cotton*, recommend using one tablespoon of washing soda for each ounce of cotton fiber, plus soap, in soft or softened water and boiling for two hours. Unlike wool and silk the natural cellulose fibers can be boiled with no ill effects.

Bleaching

Chlorine beach is safe on cottons; be sure to follow the instructions for the particular bleach you will use. Note that chlorine bleach will ruin wools and silks.

Preventing shrinkage

It may be that you don't choose to pre-shrink your cotton fabric—perhaps there is too little material to allow for shrinkage. (It will shrink if you ever wash it in hot water, however.) You can finish the fabric in cold water by hand or machine (gentle cycle). Remove the cloth from the final spin-dry cycle after one minute so that wrinkles do not get permanently set. Dry flat, on the line, or on a tube, and iron it before it becomes completely dry. If you use a tube, reroll it several times as with wool. See page 177. Cotton can mildew; so don't let it stay on the tube too long. Remove it before it is completely dry and iron it.

I think it is safer and better to pre-shrink the cloth—then, you'll never have to worry that it might shrink after the garment is made. If there isn't enough fabric, use a contrasting fabric for the hem or for a band or for the pieces that won't fit on the original cloth. This situation can force you to be creative to find a solution that works for you and the amount of cloth you have.

Care of cotton

Care of cotton is usually the same as the finishing process. You can expect that the shrinkage has taken place during finishing and that the cloth won't change with laundering. Hand or machine washing and drying, and ironing—if needed—are the usual methods for cleaning cotton. Dry clean if you have made a garment with interfacings, etc., which require dry-cleaning.

Usually, ironing on one side of the cloth is all that is necessary whether or not the fabric was hard pressed during finishing. If ironing makes a shiny surface and you don't want it, iron on the wrong side of the cloth.

About mercerization

Mercerized cotton, held under tension, has been treated with caustic soda. This process increases its strength, luster and absorbency. Better absorbency means that it takes dye better than unmercerized cotton, and the colors look brighter. These yarns and cloth have a sheen, whereas unmercerized cotton has a matte or dull appearance.

Which is better for dishtowels is a controversy. Mercerization increases absorbency, but since it is usually tightly spun, its absorbency can actually be less than that of unmercerized cotton. If the yarn weren't tightly spun, a mercerized dishtowel would be so absorbent that it would get sopping wet. I have dishtowels woven of both types of cotton and the ones made of mercerized cotton seem to get a little wetter than the unmercerized ones, but it is not a detriment in any way.

192

Linen, Ramie, and Bast Fibers

"'New' bast fibers are stiff and not very pliable. The application of pressure, or alternating hot- and cold-water baths, is an effort to break the fiber down somewhat in order to enhance pliability and increase drape. It is accepted wisdom that linen improves with age. The fiber softens with use and laundering."[44]

In the loom state, linen cloth looks rather rough, less refined, and can look quite coarse. After finishing, it can be soft and lustrous. The amount of luster you can expect depends upon the type of linen yarn as well as the finishing process used. The smoothest is line linen that has been wet spun. Line linen is made from the longest linen fibers. Tow linen is made from the shorter fibers, which are removed when the long fibers are extracted during the processing of flax into linen. Tow linen won't be as lustrous because the fibers are short to begin with. Wet spinning smoothes out linen fibers, so wet spun tow linen is more lustrous than dry spun tow linen. Wet spun line linen is more lustrous than dry spun line linen.

Finishing linen is much like that for cotton— washing or scouring by hand or by machine. Hot water can be used for white or unbleached yarns and warm water for colors. Many weavers feel that exposing linen to extremes in temperatures helps soften it and make it more lustrous. They put their linen in alternating hot and cold environments in the wash or rinse water, or take it from the freezer to a hot iron. The big difference in the finishing of linen is in the compression stage. I've gotten very lustrous linens from the compression process, never exposing it to hot and cold extremes. The softening comes from breaking down the pectin that's in the unfinished linen. It can be

44 Fry, p. 12.

done in several ways: by repeated laundering, by extreme temperature changes, by hard pressing, and by beetling (See page 195).

Scouring and agitation

Wash and rinse as for cotton fabrics.

 Be sure not to wring the cloth or spin it in the washing machine at any stage of the wash cycle, because permanent wrinkles could form and spoil the look of the cloth. (I spin my linen fabric gently and then iron it while it is still wet, straight from the machine.) Use lots of agitation. You can wash linen with bath towels and tennis shoes to achieve the needed agitation.

Ordinary laundry detergent can usually be used. If in doubt, use a mild detergent.

Check the lint trap in the washing machine. Once I washed some loosely woven *tow* linen cloth and its lint stopped up the drain.

Tow linen

If your linen yarn is hairy and not very smooth, it is likely to be tow linen. If it is, and you're not careful in the finishing process, you can end up with lint rather than a nice fabric. You will never end up with the smooth, lustrous fabric that you can get with wet spun and line linen.

The water temperature should be warm, not hot. Hand wash or use the gentle machine cycle because too much agitation will break down the waxy substance, which holds the fibers together and gives it the luster. Use a light hand with the detergent, as well.

Temperature extremes

There are several ways to accomplish shock in temperature on linen. One is to place the cloth into alternating boiling- and ice-water baths. Another is to freeze the cloth after scouring it. You can figure out other ways. The purpose is to increase the softness and luster. I never had to do it with the linens I wove, which were mostly line linen.

Compression

Compression can be done by hard pressing or cold mangling. I've always used hard pressing, but Laura Fry prefers cold mangling because it softens the fabric without unduly damaging the fiber itself. It gives more luster and a stiffer fabric. See below. Hard pressing softens the fiber, but the cloth will not have as high a luster.

Hard pressing

I hard press the cloth when it is damp from scouring. I put the cloth on a large breadboard and iron with a lot of pressure, sliding the iron back and forth warp wise and weft wise. I iron an area, then roll a rolling pin on the area before moving on and ironing and rolling the next area. I iron both sides alternating one side then the other until the cloth is completely dry. If I am impatient and the cloth isn't perfectly dry, I hang it or lay it flat without disturbing it, so it can dry on grain, and the cloth won't wrinkle. Ironing gives the luster to linen.

Cold mangling

The Swedes use this method on their traditional linens. They have huge mangles weighing hundreds of pounds. No heat is involved—instead great pressure is applied to the cloth.

Laura Fry describes the process in her book and article.

Cold mangling is achieved by rolling the damp cloth around a dowel and applying consistent pressure.[45]

Hand mangling

This method can be done by hand, using a hand mangle, which is a large dowel about 2 1/2 - 3 inches in diameter and a flat board often with a handle. The cloth is wrapped around the dowel, and then the flat board is

---

[45] Fry, Laura, "All About Wet Finishing," *Handwoven Magazine*, Interweave Press, Loveland, CO. Jan/Feb, 2001, p. 29
Fry, p. 12.

placed on top of the dowel at right angles to it. The dowel is pressed down hard and rolled back and forth using the board. See Figure 277. This rolling is done until the fibers flatten and the cloth surface becomes shiny. Fry has used a rolling pin or a glass bottle with straight sides.

Be sure the cloth is wrapped tightly on the dowel or rolling pin. As the mangling takes place, the cloth will loosen up and need to be rewound—so it is tight—to prevent wrinkling. Continue the process until the amount of pressing you want is achieved. The cloth will still be damp and will need ironing to polish the surface.

The cold mangle

"A large cold mangle has a flat bed often made from a large slab of stone, several large dowels (approximately 10 cm or 4 inches in diameter) and a top slab that rests on the dowels. The top slab rolls the dowels back and forth. See Figure 278.

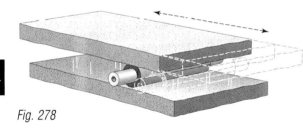

Fig. 278

"The damp cloth is rolled tightly around <u>one</u> of the dowels. A length of fabric covers the cloth being mangled, separating the layers and protecting it from the stone slabs. There must be no creases or folds in the cloth or these will be permanently set into it.

"The dowel is inserted into the mangle between the two stone slabs, and the top stone is lowered onto the dowels. The top stone begins to roll back and forth applying extreme pressure to the cloth.

"As the dowel rolls back and forth, slack begins to develop in the rolled cloth as the

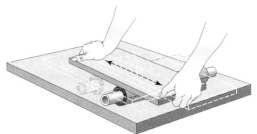

Fig. 277

compression flattens the fabric. The dowel is removed from the mangle, the cloth removed and re-rolled onto the dowel from the ***other*** direction and mangled again. [Figure 278 shows the cloth-wrapped dowel between the slabs in position to be rolled.]

"The process is repeated until the desired compression has been achieved. ...The cloth will still be damp and can be ironed to polish the surface and further develop the shine."[46]

Ironing

Hard pressing in general has been described, above. However, use a well-padded ironing board for lace weaves (which are often woven with linen). Place the textured side down on the padding and iron with pressure on the wrong side. The last side to be ironed will be the shiniest; the other side will be more textured. A thin press cloth provides additional protection when ironing open work or delicate lace.

For delicate linens, use the cotton setting on the iron—it is hot but not as hot as the linen setting. Too hot an iron can scorch or burn the fabric. Read about scorch below.

Heavier fabrics can be ironed with the hotter setting, but be sure to keep the iron moving. Holding it in one spot will cause it to scorch, for sure.

---

[46] Fry, pp. 13-14.

If the fabric is dry, dampen it by sprinkling water on it and roll it up without wrinkling for a couple of hours.

A friend told me how her mother taught her to "iron" linen hankies without an iron. She smoothed out the wet cloth on the bathtub to dry. It dried flat and crisp. Put the right side next to the tub. I've "ironed" damp placemats that way by putting them out flat on the kitchen counter to dry. You don't get the luster you would from ironing, but the cloth dries wrinkle-free.

Removing scorch marks

Scorching means that the surface has been charred a bit. Severe scorch (damaged fibers) can't be removed. If you have a scorch mark on a washable fabric, immediately try to sponge it with cool water. If it remains, work a little detergent into it, then rinse. If a stain remains after the detergent treatment, use hydrogen peroxide for a light stain or chlorine or sodium perborate bleach for a heavier stain. Try these chemicals on an inside seam to be sure that the color will not be damaged. You might have to repeat the process. To apply the peroxide or bleach: dampen a cloth with the chemical, lay it over the scorched area and sponge lightly. Never use bleach on wool or silk. Use hydrogen peroxide instead.

For surface scorch on heavy fabrics you may be able to remove the damaged part with very fine sandpaper.

Drying

I don't recommend drying linen in the dryer because it can put in permanent wrinkles and not allow you to iron the fabric while damp to get the sheen and totally wrinkle-free surface. Also, it's easier to iron out all the wrinkles when linen is damp. Iron until it's dry or almost dry, and finish drying, carefully, without wrinkling.

Stiffness

If the cloth is stiff after drying, you can roll it onto a tube and gently squeeze it until the whole cloth is more pliable. Or, you can put it in the dryer with no heat, and iron out any wrinkles. They should iron out because the cloth was dry when you put it into the dryer.

Care of linens

You can launder linens just like cotton and, while damp, iron or cold mangle them. Remember that linen gets softer and more lustrous with many washings. If a garment has interfacings, etc., that require dry-cleaning, it should be dry-cleaned.

Store flat or on rolls. If you fold the fabric, change the location of the folds periodically because, if you don't, the fibers (the cloth) will break at the fold lines.

Mildew

Linen is susceptible to mildew, so never store linen cloth damp. Be sure to iron it until it is completely dry or air dry it after ironing until it is completely dry. Undyed, gray linen contains pectins that have been mostly removed in off-white, bleached and dyed linens. These pectins will cause gray linen fabric to be more subject to mildew and rot if it is left damp in a dark place.

Remove mildew as soon as it is discovered. Pre-treat stains with a paste of soap or detergent, and chalk. Wash at once. Dry in the sun or under a sun lamp. If stain remains, bleach in the sun with paste of lemon juice and salt or sodium perborate bleach. (If fabric is colored, test a corner first.) Rinse thoroughly and dry.

Traditionally, linens were spread out on grass to bleach in the sun as they dried.

Beetling

The process of beetling is done to flatten the yarns and close them together to produce a smooth surface and bring up the natural luster of the fiber. In the eighteenth century, beetling engines were introduced which pounded the cloth, creating a flowing, flossy, sheen akin to silk.[47] Now-a-days, that effect is accomplished by cold mangling or hard pressing because they are easier to do. Beetling is noisy, tedious, and physically demanding. It would be almost impossible to beetle a large piece of cloth. However, a lovely, silky small piece might be worth the effort.

We think of it being done by women placing the cloth on a large flat stone beside the river and beating it with a wooden club known as a "beetle."

Handweavers can do the process by hammering with a rubber mallet you can buy from the hardware store.

"1. Lay the damp cloth out flat (after rinsing) on a stout board (such as a chopping block).

2. Keep the cloth damp using a water spray, if necessary. Hammer with a loose wrist and a pounding movement, beating the cloth, a section at a time, over and over again.

3. When the whole piece has received an equal amount of treatment, mangle it, or use a wooden roller pressing as hard as possible as it is rolled backward and forwards over the cloth, always in a warp or weft direction, never diagonally.

4. Finally, press with a steam iron on a fairly high heat. Take care not to scorch the cloth. The heavier the iron the better. For a high sheen, press on the right side; to bring out the surface texture, press on the wrong side. Lay out flat to dry."[48]

Another method was presented at a weaving conference: "A stiff linen can be made to drape nicely for clothing. Place the fabric between layers of plywood. Using a hammer and a wood block, hammer the entire surface."[49]

Ann Sutton suggested using round beach stones for beating.[50]

Silk

Silk fabrics woven from spun silk yarns are likely to shrink during the finishing process. Fabrics made from filament yarns do not shrink noticeably.

If your sample is extremely stiff after you've washed (scoured) it, it probably has not been degummed and still contains sericin. See how to remove the gum, below. Most silks available to handweavers have already been degummed and need no special processing before scouring.

You are more likely to find sericin in tussah silks, which may be sold un-scoured because they are prized for their natural color and, therefore, are not dyed as often.

Washing (scouring and agitation)

You may prefer not to wash some silks. Read about it below.

Wash silk in warm water with a mild detergent and gentle agitation. Use enough detergent that you see a small amount of suds on the water's surface. (If you use soap, instead, put some vinegar in the last rinse to neutralize it.) Do not soak it in soap for a long time because the alkali will damage the fibers. Do not wring the cloth or permanent wrinkles will be set into the cloth.

---

[47] Baines, Patricia, *Linen: Hand Spinning and Weaving*. pp. 161-162.

[48] Ibid.

[49] *Secrets of the Loom*, Northern California Handweavers, Inc. Conference, 1983.

[50] Sutton, Ann, Workshop notes, December, 1997.

Washing by hand

Sue Hiley Harris[51] washes her silk scarves in 1/2" of water in the bath tub. She lays the fabric flat in the tub—with no creases. Then, she brushes her hand over the cloth, back and forth on the surface, working in sections of the cloth—first on one side, then the other. She never scrunches or creases the fabric. She is careful not to let the fringes (which have been tied and/or twisted) tangle.

She rinses the silk a few times by dipping it in and out of the water, holding the cloth to keep it from wrinkling when taking it out. She folds the fabric back and forth on itself when in the water, like the Z fold shown in Figure 266 on page 174.

Washing by machine

You can machine wash silk using the gentle cycle and warm water. Remove the cloth from the machine before the spin cycle has finished to prevent serious creases.

Hang the cloth for excess water to drain out if the piece isn't too large. Otherwise, blot it in large towels to remove most of the water. The cloth can be in a dryer for a few minutes, just to remove the excess water. Be sure to take it out of the dryer before it is thoroughly dry. Iron when damp.

If colors run

Don't worry too much if the colors run in the water. Wash the cloth only to finish it and then dry-clean it after that. Or let the fabric partially air dry before ironing. See page 165.

If you don't wash silk

Light ironing may be enough to soften the stiffness of silk fabric that is just off the loom. It can also increase the luster. Use a steam or dry iron with a dry press cloth and light ironing, or press with a damp cloth for a different effect. A steam iron, held above but

not touching the cloth, is a way to shrink the cloth without disturbing the surface. Use a moderate setting on the iron—between rayon and wool. Ironing directly on the cloth gives a sheen. If you don't want a sheen, iron on the wrong side of the cloth, use a press cloth, or hold the iron above the cloth.

Ironing (compression)

Silk can be steam-pressed while damp. When it is dry, after washing, press it lightly with a dry iron, or steam press it with a heavy pressing cloth. Pressing after the cloth is dry will increase its luster and softness.

When it is damp, iron on both sides until it is dry or almost dry to get a glossy sheen. Use a moderate (approximately cotton) setting on your iron. To reduce sheen, use a press cloth between the iron and the fabric.

Sue Hiley Harris irons the cloth when it is sopping wet with the iron temperature fairly hot—around the setting for cotton. She makes sure the iron sole plate is clean first.

Straighten the cloth and tug on the fringes to straighten them while the cloth is sopping wet. Flatten the fabric on the ironing board and square up the cloth so the warps and wefts are perpendicular to each other, so you can iron the cloth with the threads square. This ironing board does not have much padding.

The iron should hiss as it touches the fabric (she doesn't use a press cloth between the iron and the fabric). Move the iron around on the cloth as you go, sliding the iron warp-wise and weft-wise–not on the diagonal. Iron in sections until one side has been ironed, turn the cloth over and iron the reverse side. Turn again and iron the first side and then the second side. Keep ironing both sides until it is fairly dry. Hang to fully dry.

 The cloth may be stiff at this point.

To soften the cloth, when it is fully dry, put the fabric into the clothes dryer on the air-dry (no

197

51 Harris, Sue Hiley, Inlay Workshop, January, 2003.

heat) setting for 10 minutes. It will soften with wear even if you don't put it into the dryer.

Cut off any weft tails flush with the cloth and iron again with steam.

Re-comb the fringe, mist it with water, comb it again and trim it.

Laundering silk

The reason you might hesitate to wash silk is that the dyes may not be set for washing. Note that when the colors run, wash silks to finish them and then, dry-clean them.

Two views on ironing: iron damp with a steam iron, and iron with no moisture. In other words, experiment and see what works for a specific situation. Experiment on your samples or on an area that won't show.

If the finished project has no interfacings, etc., it can be hand washed, or dry-cleaned. Dry-cleaning is necessary if the interfacings, etc., require it.

Stiffness

After the fabric is dry, it may seem stiff. It will soften up if it is manipulated a little bit. You can slap small items against a smooth hard surface such as a tabletop to soften them. Five or ten minutes in the dryer with no heat will work too. Any folds in the cloth can then be ironed out because the fabric was dry when it went into the dryer.

Ironing the fabric can soften it up.Wearing it will do the same.

Degumming silk

Silk fabric or thread that is very stiff or crisp (sometimes called "raw" silk or "hard" silk) has sericin remaining in it and can be treated to remove the sericin and make the silk soft. The process is called degumming. It is surprising how a crisp silk yarn can become as soft as cotton candy. If you prefer the crispness, leave it the way it is.

To degum silk you need washing soda, which is available in the laundry detergent section of the grocery store. How much you use and how long you simmer the silk depends upon how soft you want the silk to be. If you simmer it too long it can get gummy, so you want to do some testing beforehand. This process is not reversible—you can degum more, but you can't get the crispness back again.

You can determine the amount of washing soda to use by taking a percent of weight of the silk to be degummed. One recipe uses 8-10% of the weight of wet silk, and another suggests using 25% of the weight of dry silk. Too much washing soda can degum more than you want, so sample first.

Dissolve the washing soda and an equal amount of soap in a small amount of water. Celia Quinn suggests grated Ivory bar soap, Kiss My Face bar soap, or a mild shampoo without conditioner.[52]

Gently heat the solution until the soap and soda are dissolved.

Add enough lukewarm water so that the silk can move around easily—about 40 times the volume of the silk is ideal. (Soft water helps.) Add the silk and simmer until soft, 20 minutes or longer, up to about 1½ hours. Check periodically (after 20 minutes), to see if the silk is soft enough by removing a sample and rinsing it. Check after that, as needed. (Remember, too much time can make it gummy.)

Rinse it while it is hot to remove most of the sericin, soap, and soda. Add about 1/3 cup of vinegar to a pound of dry silk to neutralize the alkalinity, and soak for 10 minutes. Then, rinse in clear water. (When rinsing for degumming, put the vinegar in the next-to-the-last rinse.)

---

[52] Quinn, Celia, Degumming Recipe, *Silk Tidings*, September 2002. Treenway Silks publisher.

Rodin degumming powder is a commercially available preparation to add to the washing soda and soap to help control the amount of degumming and to prevent too much degumming, even if you overcook it. See the sources section for more information.

Rayon

Rayon, available for handweavers, can vary greatly in quality, so it is very important to wash your samples in different ways to see what works best. It is very weak when wet and can be damaged if dried in sunlight. Handle a rayon fabric gently until you are sure it can withstand more vigorous treatment.

Washing (scouring and agitation)

Try machine-washing your sample in warm water, using a gentle cycle. If that process makes the cloth very limp, wash the next sample by hand and chose the better method for your "good" fabric. Use a laundry detergent and warm water for your first sample. A mild detergent may be required, but good quality rayon is not damaged by the alkalis that are in soaps and detergents.

Since rayon is weak when wet, do not let the cloth stay in the spin cycle for a very long time. The cloth can be severely creased in the spin cycle, and these creases can be very hard to remove.

Drying

Since rayon is weak when wet, do not hang a big piece of wet fabric on a single clothesline. Instead, drape it over several clotheslines, so the weight is supported. Hanging it on a single clothesline can damage the cloth where it folds over the line. Hang it out of sunlight.

To add further support, put plastic pipes on the clotheslines. To prevent them from spinning around the lines, cut a little notch in each end of the pipe.

Ironing (compression)

Press rayon fabric when it is nearly dry. Use a fairly cool iron at first to be sure the cloth won't melt or stick to the iron. Some rayons can withstand temperatures that are as high as those used for wool and silk.

Tencel (Lyocell™)

This fiber, new to the handweaver, is made from wood pulp, as is rayon. However, it comes from managed forests, and the processing is much more environmentally friendly. The fabric is distinguished after finishing by its very high drape and very soft hand.

Wash with warm water, a light soap or detergent, and agitation. When wet, the cloth feels very stiff. Hard press when damp. Polish the cloth by swirling the iron all over the cloth a few times for more sheen and drape.

Chenille

There are many ways weavers finish rayon or cotton chenille fabrics.

Some people mist the unfinished cloth and put it in a plastic bag overnight to dampen it. Then, they tumble it in the clothes dryer with medium heat for a short period of time, filling excess space in the dryer with towels if there is a small amount of chenille cloth. This process gives a softness to the cloth. Expect 10-15% shrinkage of rayon chenille with the misting method.

A variation on this method may give a more even and consistent dampness. Soak a bath towel in very hot water and spin the towel out in the machine or wring by hand just until it stops dripping. It should be very wet. Roll the chenille fabric in the towel, put the towel in a plastic bag, and let it sit for a few hours or overnight. Then, machine dry at a medium setting.

You can wash (scour) rayon and cotton chenille fabrics in warm water with agitation. Note that when you completely soak rayon chenille, it turns very stiff, but it will soften up dramatically when it is completely dry. You can hang the fabric to dry or dry it in the machine on a medium setting. Washing is harder on chenille than misting, and washed fabric will shrink considerably more than misted pieces. (20-25% with machine-washing compared to 10-15% with misting.) Some weavers prefer the drape of chenille fabric that has been thoroughly wetted and agitated to that of misted fabric.

Pressing (compression)

In order to preserve its plush surface chenille usually isn't hard pressed. Touch up areas with a steam iron by holding the iron as close as you can to the fabric without touching it.

Hard press the cloth with a moderate iron to get a satiny finish with a very high sheen and a nap in the direction you pressed. Try it on a sample first to see which look you prefer.

Maintain chenille fabrics by dry cleaning.

Mixtures of Fibers in a Cloth

Mixtures of wool and other fibers[53]

A cloth containing both worsted and woolen yarns is crabbed first, then scoured and fulled until the desired hand and look is achieved.

- Woolen yarn-combined-with-silk fabric is finished like woolens.

- Worsted-combined-with-silk fabrics need a worsted finish.

- Cotton or linen and wool require a woolen finish.

- Cotton and linen are best finished like linen.

Mixtures of other fibers

 The guiding principle is to gear the finishing process to the most fragile fiber in the cloth. Use a neutral pH or gentle detergent when unsure whether the combination of fibers can withstand alkali or acid conditions.

Identifying Fibers

There is much to be understood about the characteristics of all the fibers, such as wool, cotton, linen, silk, etc., but that is not the focus of this book. The information is well covered in the books, *Handwoven, Tailormade*[54] and *Fibre Facts*.[55]

Burn tests

Burn tests can indicate what fiber(s) a yarn is made of. Once you know what the fiber is you can read about its properties. For example, if you know your yarn is silk, the most important consideration is its slipperiness; it must be sett and beaten closer than other natural fibers.

One simple way to conduct your own burn test is to burn a fiber that you know and compare it to the unknown one.

You can use the chart on page 206 (Figure 287) to determine what a fiber is. The chart explains what each fiber should be like after burning.[56]

 With tweezers, hold a short piece of the yarn. Hold the yarn horizontally and feed it slowly into the edge of flame and observe what happens. Test a few times to confirm your results. Do not use a larger piece of fiber or fabric because you don't know how it will

[53] Halsey, Mike and Youngmrk, Lorre, *Foundations of Weaving*. David & Charles (Publishers), Great Britain. 1975. pp. 175-176.

[54] Alderman, Sharon D. And Wertenberger, Kathryn, *Handwoven, Tailormade*, Interweave Press, Loveland, CO, 1982. pp. 6-13.

[55] Hochberg, Bette, *Fibre Facts*, Bette Hochberg Publisher, Santa Cruz, CA. 1981.

[56] Roth, Bettie G. and Schulz, Chris, *Handbook of Timesaving Tables for Weavers, Spinners and Dyers*. 1991. p. 19.

flame up. Some novelty yarns are composed of more than one fiber—each strand in the yarn should be tested separately. Some fabrics have more than one type of yarn as well—look for differences in individual yarns.

Finishes Applied Professionally

In industry, many many finishes are applied to the cloth, both before and after it is made into a product. Some examples are: shrinking, pressing, sizing, bleaching, shearing, felting, napping, and texturizing. Most commercial finishers require minimum quantities of cloth—often more than the handweaver is prepared to produce—so aren't generally available to handweavers.

Some finishes are required for handwoven textiles, for example, fireproofing for work that is to be in public spaces and finishes for upholstery. Be sure to test a sample to ensure that the appearance and/or hand won't be changed in a way you don't want. Checking with the company before the cloth is woven to make sure you follow their requirements is essential—for example, providing the minimum width and length to fit their machinery.

Upholstery fabric can be backed for strength and endurance if the fabric isn't woven firmly enough. If you want a backing, stay away from latex, which crumbles and drifts to the surface, making "dandruff." Acrylic paint-on backing is better.

If 100% wool is used, fireproofing isn't needed. Not only does fireproofing often make the cloth stiff, some may be injurious to the cloth.

Stain repellent finishes are not permanent even if the cloth is immersed in the solution. It rubs off in use, and if a spot is blotted away, the finish goes away with it. That is the reason spots seem to return.

Besides simply cleaning them, a professional dry cleaner can shrink and steam textiles. Careful discussions with the dry cleaner are imperative, so you understand what can be done. Providing samples before doing the big project goes along with good communication with the dry cleaner.

Fringes

Whatever finish you choose for the ends and/or edges of your cloth, something must be done to protect the first and last wefts from sliding out from the cloth. The viewer must feel comfortable that the weaving is not going to unravel.

Fringes can be made by knotting, twisting, wrapping, knitting, braiding, and many more ways. Unwoven warp (or weft) threads become fringe. (Weft fringe is described on page 97.) They may be made from the loom waste or from areas left unwoven between pieces during weaving. To leave space for fringe between woven pieces, you can weave in 2" strips of cardboard from cereal boxes or strips of dry cleaner bags. Both will go smoothly around the cloth beam and come out of the fabric easily. The advantage of using plastic bags is that the cloth can be washed before removing them.

Some weavers work their fringe treatment before washing the cloth. Others wash the cloth first, then pull out the plastic bag strips as they go, when making the fringe. If the warp threads are loose during washing they can become terribly tangled. Wrapping the threads or fringe in socks and securing them with rubber bands is a way to prevent tangling.

If you hemstitched the first and last wefts of your pieces on the loom, it can be enough of a fringe treatment. If you prefer a knotted, twisted or other type of fringe, see below. Again, practice will tell you what is best for a given project. Projects with dense warps may need a different technique from that of a weft-faced project with sparse warps.

201

Some yarns disintegrate during washing (linen), and some are slippery and untwist. Twisted, braided, or wrapped fringes are advisable in these cases.

For dense warps, knots or twisted fringes can be too bulky. One solution is to tie square knots in pairs of warp threads, every inch or so apart. With this knot the tails will look more like the regular warp threads and won't show.

A technique I like to use for very dense warps is to needle-weave a warp back into the cloth about every inch or so and cut it flush with the cloth. The last weft is protected and the fringe looks un-interrupted. You can weave more of the warps back into the cloth, depending on the effect you want. See Figures 279a and b.

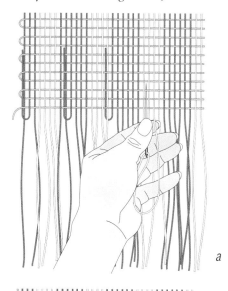

a

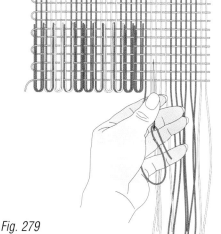

b

Fig. 279

Knitted Fringe

"A knitted fringe can be knitted in any yarn, wool, silk, or cotton. This can be used doubled, trebled, or quadrupled, according to the yarn used, and the weight of fringe desired. A cotton fringe is better quadrupled, which necessitates the simultaneous use of four balls of cotton, the four strands being held together and knitted as one.

Cast-on a number of stitches divisible by three. Nine stitches will make quite a deep fringe when unraveled, six a medium fringe."

Cast on 6 stitches.

Row 1: *K.1, Y.O., K. 2 tog. Repeat from *. (Note: Y.O. {yarn over} means throw the yarn over the needle. It will make a hole when used in conjunction with the K. 2 tog., without reducing the number of stitches on the needle)

Row 2, and all succeeding rows: Repeat row 1.

"Knit sufficient length to cover the fringed edge, and then cast-off as follows:

With six stitches on the needle, cast-off three stitches, and fasten off.

Unravel the remaining three stitches along the entire length of the knitted strip, until one side presents a fringe of even loops, while the opposite side has the appearance of a knitted braid.

Attach this braided side to the fabric with an overcast stitch.

To straighten the fringe, dampen it, allow it to hang straight, and to dry."[57]

---

[57] Thomas, Mary, *Mary Thomas's Knitting Book*, Hodder and Stoughton Ltd, London. 1938. p. 128.

For sparse warps, you might needle weave all of them back into the fabric. Or make the fringe fuller by hooking in more threads.

It's easier to work on the fringe if you place a weight on the cloth and work on the threads as they hang over the edge of your worktable.

To cut the ends of fringe evenly, hang the excess over the edge of the table and cut along the edge of the table. Another way is to use a rotary cutter and a cutting board. Align the edges with the lines on the mat. Comb the ends, lay a straight edge on the fringe, and cut.

Sometimes, it's nice to have tiny knots at the ends of the fringes. To get them at the very tips of the fringes, tie them close to the ends of the threads and trim away any excess thread. If the knot is likely to come out, put a drop of diluted white glue on the knot. Chenille threads will unravel in fringes during finishing if they are not knotted at the tips.

☞ Sometimes, the unwoven warps do not make a good-looking fringe because of their color. The color of the fabric with its mixture of warp and weft colors may not look "right" with the warp color alone. My friend, Helen Pope, knitted a separate fringe and sewed it over the warp fringe to hide it or modify the warp color. See the sidebar. Another solution is to loop in extra threads to modify the fringe color before knotting or twisting.

Knotted fringe

Fringe can be knotted with overhand knots up close to the last woven pick. Gradually undo the overcasting or strips of dry cleaner bags protecting the last weft as you work along the edge so the last weft doesn't wander out before you get there. Practice with different size bundles for the knots and with which side of the knot you want to be on the "right" side of the piece. See Figures 280 and 281. Read about trimming the ends above.

To get the knots up close to the last weft, keep them loose by putting a nail or something similar in the loop of the knot as you move the knot right up until it's snug against the weft. (Pull the tail of the warp thread with one hand, hold the nail with the other, and push the nail up close to the weft as you pull.) Then, remove the nail and tighten the knot in place.

Twisted fringe

Twisting tools are available from weaving supply shops. A battery-operated tool for twisting hair is available where hair supplies are sold. They can speed up the process a lot.

Experiment with the number of threads in each twisted fringe and with how many twists work best. A lot of variation can be discovered this way, and the twisted look can be loose or tight.

Basically, you'll take two warp ends or two groups of threads and twist them separately in the direction of the yarns' twist. (Read about S- and Z-twist on page 49.) Keep twisting them until they begin to kink up on themselves. Then ply these two groups together by holding them next to each other and twisting them together in the opposite direction. You may not have to do very much twisting; they will tend to twist on themselves. See Figure 282. Then

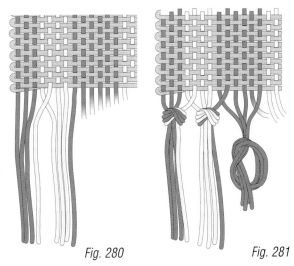

Fig. 280   Fig. 281

knot the ends with an overhand knot. Trim the excess threads and put on a drop of diluted white glue if the knots tend to come undone. Note that white glue comes out in washing.

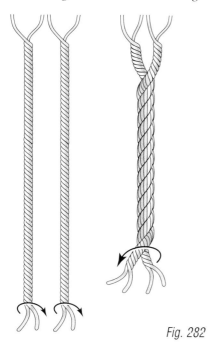

Fig. 282

Wrapped fringe

This method is a lovely way to enclose fringes with wrapped yarn. There is a trick to hiding the tails of the wrapping thread. See Figure 283.

Lay the thread that is to be used for wrapping on top of the bundle of fringe, making a loop at the end where the wrapping is to stop. The short tail from the loop should extend beyond where the wrapped area is to begin. See the illustration. With the long tail of the wrapping thread, wrap the bundle of fringe threads neatly, working towards the loop made at first. When the wrapped area is completed, take the working tail through the loop. Pull this tail out of sight and about halfway into the wrapped area by pulling on the short tail from the original loop. Trim the ends of the wrapping thread flush. You can leave the fringe itself or trim it as in Figure 283.

Braiding and other fringes

There are many other treatments for fringes given in the following books: Suzanne Baizerman and Karen Serle's *Finishes in the Ethnic Tradition*, Dos Tejedoras Fiber Arts Publications, St. Paul, MN. 1989, and Peter Collingwood's *The Technique of Rug Weaving*.

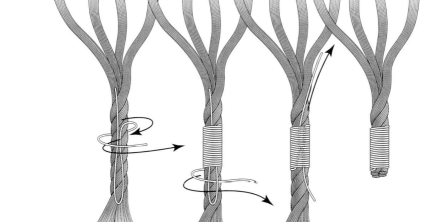

Fig. 283

Hems

Very often machine stitching that shows on a finished project is disfiguring. It might be sturdy, but it doesn't look good with the handmade cloth. Practice on a scrap to decide if you can make stitches that don't show. You might have to change the colors of the sewing thread (and bobbin) when you sew across different colors. For machine stitching to be acceptable, it *must* be perfectly done. No matter how beautiful the cloth is, it will be ruined if the hem's stitches aren't done with absolute perfection. If in doubt, don't machine stitch, hand sew the hems in an invisible or decorative stitch.

I often baste the turns in my hems by hand. It makes it easier to do the permanent hand or machine stitching. Use a contrasting color thread if it is to be removed.

The stitch I like to use for hems is a slipstitch because it is practically invisible. You slip the needle in the fold of the hem as you progress from stitch to stitch. See Figure 284.

Fig. 284

Another stitch is done inside the hem. I like it because the edge of the hem doesn't press into the body of the project, which can show as a ridge on the right side. It is especially good if the weight of the hem might tend to pull on the fabric. See Figure 285.

Sometimes, on art pieces, I don't make a hem at all—I overcast on the wrong side to hold the last weft in place. Then I cut the fringe

flush or almost flush with the cloth. Overcast stitching is shown in Figure 255 on page 158 at the beginning of this chapter.

Other times, I invent how the hems or edges should be treated.

Sewing books give details you need to know to make perfect hems. Poor hems on garments ruin the look of the whole garment. Sometimes that is the only way someone might know that you made it yourself. It would be worth it to hire a seamstress if you can't make perfect hems.

For heavy cloth, consider a facing of a lighter weight cloth, probably a commercially made fabric.

Hems can be decorative as well, using special hemstitching, fancy stitches and/or embellishments.

Seams

Seams in handwoven cloth need extra consideration. Often, "regular" seams are too bulky, so the edges of the cloth are butted together or overlapped. Seams that are disfiguring ruin the entire garment—learn from sewing books or hire a seamstress.

To sew a seam where the fabrics butt next to each other, without overlap, use a blunt needle and a thread that matches the weft and sew

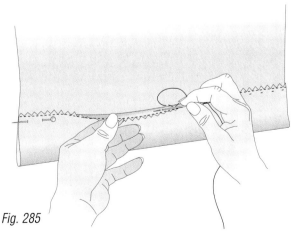

Fig. 285

the edges by alternately picking up weft loops inside the first warp thread of each edge. See Figure 286.

Attractive seams can be made with decorative embroidery stitches. See the book, *Finishes in the Ethnic Tradition*, mentioned above, for ideas.

For information regarding melting and burning of fabrics, refer to the table in Figure 287.

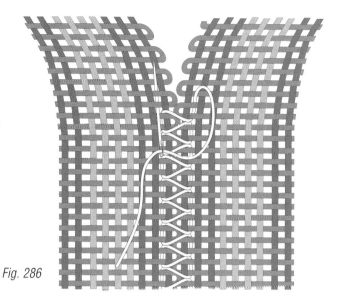

Fig. 286

Fig. 287

BURN TEST FOR VARIOUS FIBERS[*]

FIBER	MELTING	IN FLAME	LEAVING FLAME	ODOR	RESIDUE
COTTON	Does not melt	Ignites readily	Continues to burn Smokes, glows, smolders	Burning paper	Feathery gray ash
LINEN, other bast fibers	Does not melt	Ignites readily	Continues to burn	Burning paper	Fine gray or white ash
VISCOSE RAYON	Does not melt	Ignites readily	Continues to burn	Burning paper	Small amount of gray ash
WOOL	Scorches	Burns slowly	Self-extinguishing	Burnt hair or feathers	Bead, crushes to gritty black powder
SILK	Scorches	Burns slowly	Self-extinguishing	Burnt hair	Bead, crushes to gritty black powder
ACETATE	Melts away from flame	Ignites after melting	Continues to burn	Vinegar	Dark, solid bead
ACRYLIC	Melts	Ignites smoky	Continues to burn	Broiled fish	Hard, brittle
NYLON	melts in droplets	Melts before igniting	Self-extinguishing	Celery	Beige or gray bead
POLYESTER	melts in droplets	Melts before igniting Burns with black smoke	Self-extinguishing Continues to glow	Sweetish chemical	Hard, dark bead

NOTE: Animal fibers, such as wool, mohair, camel hair, vicuna, cashmere, llama, and alpaca cannot be distinguished from each other by burning.

[*] From Bettie G. Roth and Chris Schulz's *Handbook of Timesaving Tables for Weavers, Spinners and Dyers*. 1991. p. 19.

6 Drafting

Drafting in weaving is a system of notation that describes weaves so you will know the threading of the loom, the tie-up of the treadles, and the sequence the treadles are to be used. It's much easier to read a draft all along the way—while planning, or threading, or weaving—than to read words in paragraphs on several pages.

You will want to understand the drafts in the weaving books and magazines so you can either re-create projects, or use them as inspirations, varying them to suit your own ideas.

Drafts typically only give you the bare bones of the threads of a project. They do not give the color, texture, or size of the yarns, or how a weave structure works. This information is usually given in words. Many weave structures themselves have rules, which are explained in books on weaves and not given in a project's directions.

Sometimes, it's the other way around, you have an idea, and you want to make the draft yourself—to make the weaving easier to do and to see what the idea might look like. You might draft several ideas before choosing the best design.

By drafting out your ideas, you can predict, plan, control, abandon, create, and learn. Reading existing drafts lets you use "recipes" that others have created, so your projects can be successful.

Shafts and harnesses

What many weavers learned to call harnesses should really be called shafts. With people talking about more complicated looms today, it's important to wean oneself from saying "harnesses" when you are actually talking about shafts. Drawlooms and other complex looms have at least two sets of shafts. One set usually controls the ground weave structure and the other set(s) of shafts controls the pattern. The name for a set of shafts is harness! What we learned to think of as a 4-harness loom or an 8-harness loom is really a one-harness loom because it has just one set of shafts. Drawloom weaving isn't a subject of this book, but it is important for you to understand that "shaft" is the proper word for shafts. Figure 288 shows two shafts.

What this chapter will do

In this chapter, I explain how drafts are made and used. I will show you how to make your own drafts quickly. Of course, a computer can make them faster than a person can, but you can't ask a computer to do the job if you don't know what drafting is. I still enjoy drafting

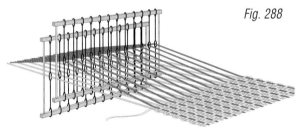

Fig. 288

207

with a pencil (and eraser) because I don't do a whole lot of it. If I did need to do a lot of complicated drafting, I'd certainly do it on the computer. There are several software programs available that do this work.

I think of drafting as puzzles. When I first learned to draft, the examples were so easy I could "see" the answers without thinking them through. Soon, I was over my head with harder drafts, which needed to be solved with a process, step-by-step.

It seems that drafting knowledge first comes into one's head and then, for some reason, disappears — simply going out of the brain. I will explain the process and give you some rules that will help you get started again whenever you come back to drafting. See page 211.

If you've had difficulty understanding drafting in the past, you might want to jump to the section on fabric analysis, beginning on page 228. In that chapter, you will make a draft from an existing cloth, which may help you understand the process.

How drafts are read

A weave draft is divided into four quadrants each one a different size. See Figure 289. The bold lines are the skeleton of all drafts and divide the whole draft into separate parts. Figure 290 shows the quadrants of a weave draft and a description of what each quadrant represents.

To interpret the drafts, read outwards from the bold lines in the directions the arrows show (Figure 291). In other words, in the upper left section, read the draft from right-to-left. Read from left-to-right in the upper right section, and so on. It can be confusing, sometimes starting from the right and sometimes starting from the left. The key is to *see* that everything works outward from the bold lines.

Each part of a weave draft can be called a draft. That is, a threading draft, a tie-up draft, a treadling draft, and a drawdown draft complete a weave draft.

The threading draft shows how the strands are to be threaded in the heddles on the shafts. Once the threads have been put into the heddles, they will not normally ever be changed for the entire warp. The tie-up draft and the treadling draft tell which shafts are to be lifted and when. They can be changed anytime along the way. The drawdown area shows the results from the other parts of the draft. Examples follow. Refer to this illustration as you read along.

208

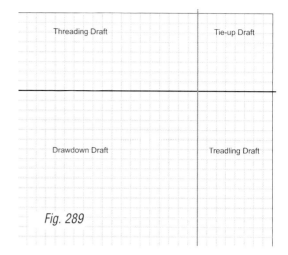

Threading Draft — Tie-up Draft

Drawdown Draft — Treadling Draft

Fig. 289

3. **Threading Draft:** The way the warp threads are entered in the heddles on their respective shafts

2. **Tie-up Draft:** The combinations of shafts needed

4. **Drawdown Draft:** The result of the other three quadrants

1. **Treadling Draft:** The sequence in which the combinations are used

Fig. 290

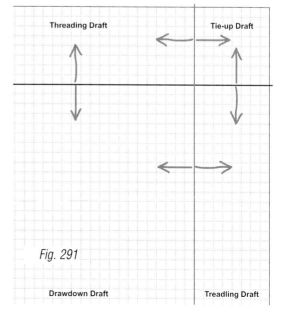

Threading Draft — Tie-up Draft

Fig. 291

Drawdown Draft — Treadling Draft

Understanding weave drafts

To understand weave drafts, you need to understand each part's contribution to the whole, or to the drawdown.

The threading

Look at Figure 292 to get an idea of what a weave draft will tell you.[58] The vertical threads, which are the warp threads, are coming out of rings, which represent the heddle eyes on the loom. Each heddle itself is hanging from its shaft. This illustration shows the threading of the loom in the order that the yarns are threaded on the shafts. Note that the threading is read from right-to-left, reading outward from the bold vertical line of the draft. Thread #1 is on shaft 2, thread #2 on shaft 1, thread #3 on shaft 2, etc. In drafts made in America today, the bottom row of shafts is always shaft #1. It is the one nearest the weaver on the loom.

☞ More threading details are on page 222.

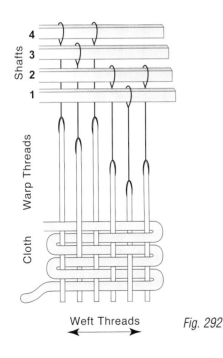

Weft Threads ←——→   *Fig. 292*

---

[58] Adapted from: Sutton, Ann; Collingwood, Peter; St Aubyn Hubbard, Geraldine; *The Craft of the Weaver*, Lark Books, Asheville, NC, 1983, p. 89.

The cloth (drawdown)

Now, look in the lower part of the illustration. The horizontal threads are the wefts interlacing with the warp, making the cloth. Do you see how a shaft lifts a warp thread so that the weft can go under it?

Concentrate on the top weft (here the top weft, as it would be on the drawdown) and see that some warps were lifted for it to pass underneath. Note that the cloth (drawdown) is read from the top down, reading from the bold horizontal line in the draft. Which warps are over the weft? Those warp threads were lifted by the shafts. Note which shafts. You should have said that shafts 2 and 3 had to be raised. Look at the second row of weaving and see which warp threads were lifted and the shafts on which they are threaded. The answer is shafts 3 and 4.

Just to check that you understand so far, look at the bottom weft (the last one in the illustration). What shafts were lifted to raise up the warps, which are on top of that weft? I hope you said shafts 1 and 4.

Note that where the *wefts* are on top, the warps were not lifted. Therefore, the weft will show wherever a warp thread is not lifted, and a warp will show wherever it is lifted.

☞ Another way to show the drawdown is described on page 211.

The tie-up

Look at Figure 293 and see that more has been added to the previous illustration. The upper right hand quadrant (the tie-up draft) has some circles in the squares of the graph paper. Think of the circles as bubbles, because bubbles rise and the circles indicate shafts that are rising or to be lifted. (In many books, filled-in squares are used instead of bubbles, but they mean the same thing: shafts that are to be lifted. Read about other types of tie-up drafts on page 221.) Reading the tie-up draft outwards from the bold vertical line, and

Fig. 293

of the graph paper. Since the treadling tells the *sequence* of the combinations of shafts to be lifted, it is under that combination (2 and 3) in the first column of the tie-up, above.

When you are weaving, you will first look in the treadling draft and then look up above the X to see which combination of shafts is indicated for that particular X (row of weaving).

Some treadling drafts use slash marks instead of X's. I'm using X's because they're easier to read. Either works just fine.

The X in the second row of the treadling draft indicates the second row of weaving. Here, it's just down and to the right of the first X. Now, look up directly above this X to see which combination of shafts is to be lifted for this row—it's 3 and 4. Notice that the third row of weaving asks for the same combination as the first row, so the X is put in the same column as the first, under the same combination (2 and 3). You don't need to write a combination more than once. The combinations for the draft are given once, and the X's are positioned underneath them, as indicated.

upward from the bold horizontal line of the draft, see that the first combination of shafts to be lifted is shafts 2 and 3. Again, shaft one is on the bottom line of the draft just as in the threading section. Read the next column to the right to see that the second combination of shafts to be lifted is 3 and 4, next, 1 and 4, and the last combination given for this particular weave is 1 and 2.

Figure 294 shows the relationship of the tie-up to tying up the combinations of shafts to the treadles.

You might be able to see the relationship between the tie-up draft and the "cloth." In the cloth, two shafts were lifted for each row of weaving (each weft). The combinations that were lifted for the cloth are given in the tie-up.

☞ More tie-up details are on page 220.

The treadling

The treadling draft is indicated in the lower right corner of weave drafts. (Figure 293, above.) Sometimes, it is called the lift plan. It is the place to look when you are weaving. It is read outward from the vertical and horizontal lines of the draft, that is, left-to-right and downward. The first X is in the top row of the left-most column. Notice a dot in that square

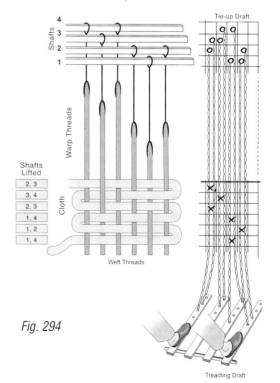

Fig. 294

The fourth row's X is under the combination of 1 and 4, and the fifth row's X is under the combination of 1 and 2. The last row of weaving uses a combination previously listed in the tie-up draft, shafts 1 and 4, and is in its previously used column.

You can write the combinations of shafts for each row of weaving, row-by-row, beside the cloth draft—another way to indicate which shafts are to be lifted for each row. The written-out combinations for every row is called a peg plan and is shown in Figure 295 above. More about peg plans is on page 227. Sometimes, the peg plan is called the lift plan.

More treadling details are on page 224.

A complete "real" draft

Figure 295 shows a complete draft, the way it is usually written. The threading is indicated in the threading draft. It shows that the first thread is on shaft 2, the next on 1, etc. You can read the threading as follows: 2,1,2,4,3,4. It is one repeat of the threading for the weave structure or pattern.

The drawdown draft shows the "cloth." The "threads" are represented as squares rather than little dashes, which would be more like threads, but the drawdown does show the results from the other 3 parts. Squint your eyes, and you can see that it is easier to see the

<table>
<tr><td colspan="2">**Drafting Rules**</td></tr>
</table>

Drafting Rules

These rules can help you when you zone-out and forget what you're doing, or when you want to draft after not doing it for awhile.

Rule 1: Begin in the treadling draft.

Rule 2: All filled-in squares represent warps lifted.

Rule 3: Everything relates horizontally and vertically.

Rule 4: Work outwards from the bold lines dividing the quadrants in the draft. Sometimes, you'll read right-to-left (as in the threading and drawdown) and sometimes, left-to-right (as in the tie-up and treadling).

Rule 5: Work row-by-row, top to bottom; bottom to top is O.K., too, as some drafts put the threading at the bottom of the drawdown.

Rule 6: Work counter-clockwise when starting in the treadling draft (treadling draft to tie-up draft, to threading draft, to drawdown draft).

Rule 7: Work clockwise if beginning in the drawdown (drawdown draft to threading draft, to tie-up draft, to treadling draft.)

weave in the drawdown than in the "cloth" illustration on its left.

Note that filled-in squares represent warp threads lifted.

Read the steps below to see how the squares in the drawdown were filled in. Note the drafting rules, above.

Summary: Reading drafts

1. Start in the treadling draft.

2. Look up above the X for the combination of shafts to be lifted.

3. Look over to the threading draft and find all the threads threaded on the shafts indicated.

4. Look down from the threading draft to the top row of the drawdown draft and find the filled-in squares. Here, 2's and 3's are to be lifted.

Fig. 295

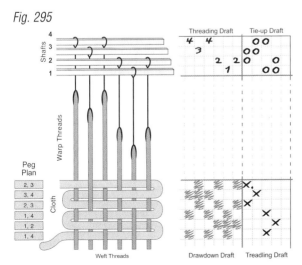

Drafting the color order

Figure 296 shows drafts for the order to be used for the colors of warps and wefts. The color order for the threading may be above or near the threading draft, or somewhere in the text describing a project. The color order in the example is read this way (from right to left): 8 ends (warp threads) of green warp, 2 ends of black, 10 ends of brown, 2 black, 8 green, and 2 black, for a total of 32 ends.

The weft color sequence is usually given to the side of the treadling draft. The weft color order reads (from top to bottom): 8 picks (wefts) of green, 2 picks black, 10 picks brown, 2 picks black, 8 picks green and 2 picks black. This illustration shows the color order for the warps and wefts for the draft in Figure 332, on page 226.

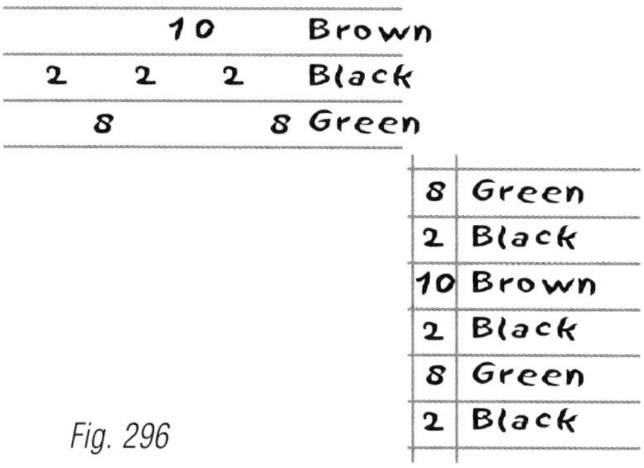

	10		Brown
2	2	2	Black
	8		8 Green

Fig. 296

8	Green
2	Black
10	Brown
2	Black
8	Green
2	Black

Making an Original Draft

Remember that I said my first drafting exercises were so easy I could see the answer without having to work it out? For that reason, I'm going to suggest nonsense threads in the parts of the drafts.

Step 1: Create a threading draft.

Arbitrarily, I chose numbers for the threading, 4,1,3,1,2,1,4,3,3,4, and entered them in the threading draft. See Figure 297.

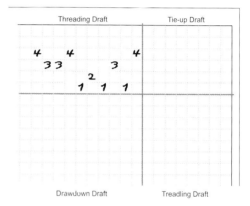

Fig. 297

Step 2: Create a tie-up draft.

Again, by chance, I chose the combinations 2 and 4; 1 and 2; 1,2,3; 3; 1; 2,3,4 for a total of 6 combinations. Note that a single shaft can be lifted by itself. (Figure 298.)

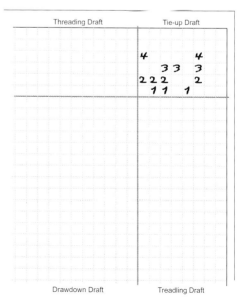

Fig. 298

Step 3: Create a treadling draft.

I scattered X's under the combinations in the tie-up draft for 15 rows of weaving. (Figure 299.) Now, look at Figure 300 and, for a check, see that the first X is indicating that for the first row of weaving the combination of shafts 2 and 4 should be lifted.

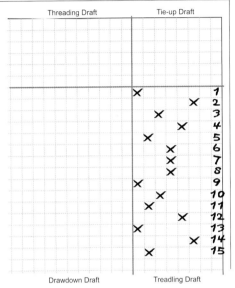

Fig. 299

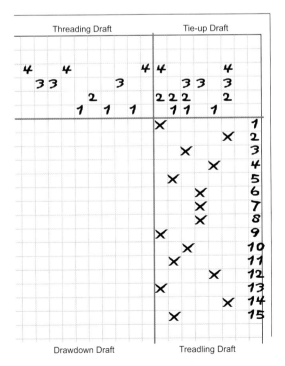

Fig. 300

Step 4: Using the three parts given, fill in the drawdown draft.

See Figure 301. (Note the fast way below.)

- Start in the treadling draft (find the X for the row you are working on)
- Find the combination of shafts to be lifted, above. (In the first row, the combination is 2 and 4.)
- Find all the threads on 2 and 4 in the threading draft and fill them in on the first row of the drawdown draft.

Continue, working row-by-row, always starting in the treadling draft.

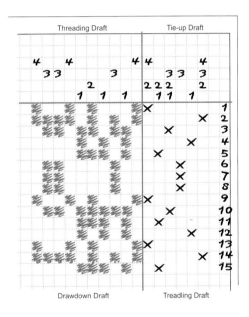

Fig. 301

213

A fast way to draft with a template

You can speed up the process of creating your drawdown drafts.

The idea is to make a template for each different combination of shafts indicated in the tie-up draft. In Figure 302 there are six different combinations. I make my templates one at a time as I work down the treadling draft, row-by-row. You can make them all at once, if you prefer. Look at the first row of weaving in the treadling draft and see the combination indicated is 2 and 4. Then,

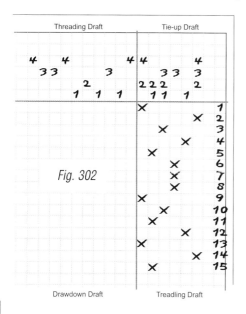

Fig. 302

the treadling draft and wherever there is an X in that same column for the same combination in the tie-up draft, use your template to fill in the squares for those rows. Here, the first row of weaving is repeated in Rows 9 and 13. (See Figure 301.)

Now that Rows 1,9, and 13 are filled in, look at the second row (in the treadling draft) and see what combination is directly above that X. It is shafts 2,3,4. Take a new card, and lining

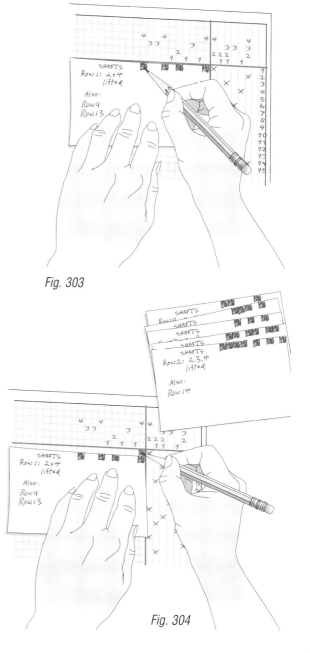

Fig. 303

Fig. 304

look in the threading draft, take a card like an index card and mark on it where all the squares should be filled in for that row. It's important—very important—that you always line up your templates at the intersection of the lines of the weave draft—the upper right corner of the drawdown draft—when you're making the cards. See Figure 303. Make one card for each combination. Write on the card which shafts are to be lifted, the first row that this combination is used, and the numbers of all the other rows that use it.

Fill in the squares on the drawdown for the row by copying the marks from the card (template). See Figure 304. Now, look down it up accurately at the upper right corner of the drawdown draft, fill in all the squares indicated for that row—first on the template, then on the graph paper. Look to see if there are any more rows with the same combination of shafts lifted. Row 14 is identical, so fill in the squares matching your template for Row 2 on Row 14. See Figure 301.

Go on as above for all the other combinations.

Now, the whole draft is filled in. It's much easier using a template than working out each row one at a time, because as you get farther and farther from the threading draft, it's harder to see exactly which square should be filled in. The important thing to remember is to always line up the template accurately—for obvious reasons.

Practice basic weaves

Practice reading the drafts for some basic weaves in Figure 305. Remember where to begin? Notice that since all the threadings are identical, all these weaves could be woven on one warp, which would be a good beginning sampler. Read more tie-up details on page 220.

Fig. 305

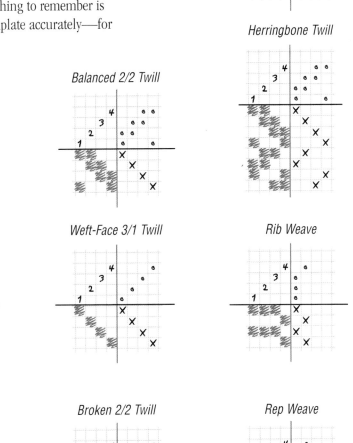

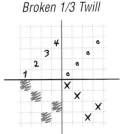

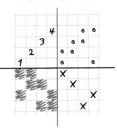

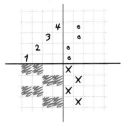

You can figure out the tie-up and the treadling drafts in Figure 306, now. This time, begin in the drawdown draft, look up above the squares for a given row to see which shafts were lifted. (Remember filled-in squares show warps lifted.) Can you see that for the first row, shafts 1 and 2 were lifted because the squares underneath all the 1's and 2's were filled in? Put bubbles (or numbers) for shafts 1 and 2 in the first column of the tie-up draft and put an X below that combination in the first row of the treadling draft. Continue, working row-by-row, beginning in the drawdown and ending in the treadling draft. The "answer" is given in Figure 325, on page 225.

When you fill in the drawdown for Figure 307 you will be surprised to find no pattern. I call it my "snowflake" draft because the warps are scattered and don't make a recognizable pattern. I took a threading that is very regular and scattered the threads during weaving by changing the tie-up draft. Some experienced weavers will recognize that the tie-up draft is actually a satin weave draft. The "answer" to this draft is in Figure 317, on page 220.

Figures 308a, b, c, and d are related puzzles. Work out these drafts and check the "answers" in Figures 327-330 on pages 225 and 226. This group of drafts is meant to show how, if part of a weave draft changes, the result (drawdown) will change as well. Here, in 308a, b, and c, the threading remains the same, but the treadling or tie-up changes.

Notice that the treadling draft in Figure 308a was substituted for the threading draft in Figure 308d. Substituting the treadling for threading, and vice versa, is called "turning a draft" See that the image in the drawdown is turned on its side. Read about turned drafts on page 225.

216

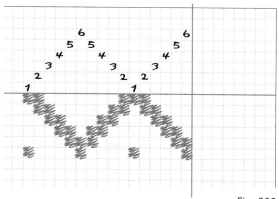

Fig. 306

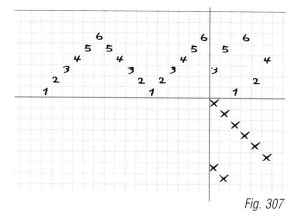

Fig. 307

Fig. 308

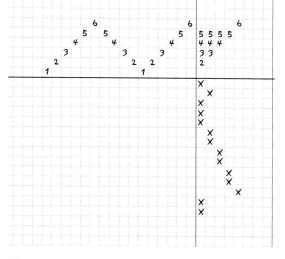

a

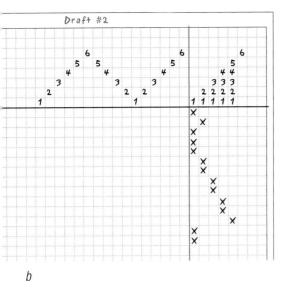

b

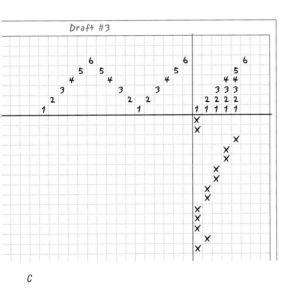

c

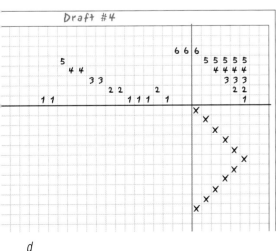

d

What about repeats?

Usually, weave drafts show one repeat of the weave, and you can repeat it over and over as much as you like. A repeat can be given in the threading draft as well as in the treadling draft.

Two ways to repeat

There are two ways to repeat a design or a draft: straight and point (mirror image).

A **straight repeat** means that when you come to the end of a section, you start again at the beginning of the repeat.

A **point repeat** reproduces a section in mirror image. That means, you begin again at the end of the section and work backwards to the beginning.

The houses in Figures 309a and b are repeated in the two ways. Figure a shows them repeated in a straight repeat and Figure b shows them in a point repeat, or mirror image.

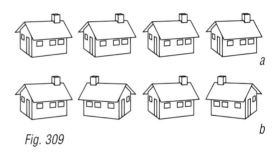

a

b

Fig. 309

When you are weaving along, you can decide which type of repeat to weave every time you come to the end of a section.

Repeats in the threading

A straight repeat of 1,2,3,4 is called a straight draw. It would be 1,2,3,4; 1,2,3,4; 1,2,3,4.

You could make a point threading like this: 1,2,3,4; 3,2,1; 2,3,4; 3,2,1, with the repeat being 1,2,3,4.

You can make your repeat as long as you like—that is, the basic unit, which is to be repeated. Say, you wanted a large repeat or

design. Your repeat could be 1,2,3,4;
1,2,3,4; 1,2,3,4, and then, you could
make a point repeat: 3,2,1; 4,3,2,1;
4,3,2,1.

Practice

Straight repeat: Make a weave draft
with a threading draft that has a
straight repeat of 1,2,3,4. Make a
straight repeat in the treadling draft, as
well, as shown in Figure 310. Make up
a tie-up of your own or use the one in
the illustration.

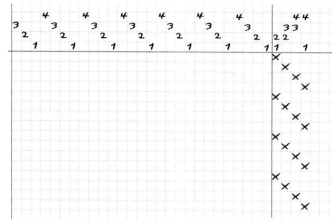

Fig. 310

Point repeat: Make two more drafts,
this time with a point threading for
the repeat of 1,2,3,4. For the treadling,
on the first draft, make a point repeat,
and on the second, a straight repeat.
Do about 12 rows of each, all on the
same page under the threading, or
make two separate drafts. Use a tie-
up of your own, or use the one in
Figure 311.

Make an original draft: Now, make
an original draft. Choose a repeat
unit, that is, a unit to be repeated.
Remember, it can be of any length.
For the threading draft, repeat your
unit in one or both ways (straight,
or point). Make at least 30 threads in
your threading. Make up your own
treadling draft. It could be the same
as your threading draft (called "tromp
as writ," see page 226), or it could be
a completely different repeat, and the
unit repeated in either or both ways.
Make your treadling draft as long as
you like. The tie-up draft can be of
your choice, or the one in the previous
drafts.

More practice

Figure 312 shows drafts that could be
either threading or treadling drafts,
and tie-up drafts. Copy them on graph paper,

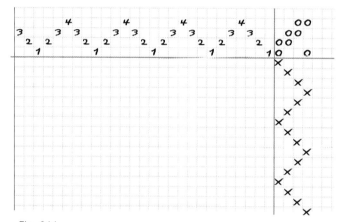

Fig. 311

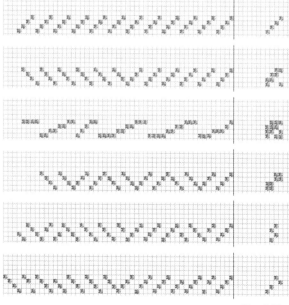

Fig. 312

218

mixing and matching them for more drafting practice. Notice how straight and point repeats affect the drawdown drafts—when they are in the threading and treadling. What effect does "tromp as writ" have in the drawdown? Try different tie-ups. If one doesn't work well, choose another. Make up your own tie-ups. Notice that weaves often have some sort of system that is apparent.

Make more drafts!!! You might take one of the drafts in the illustration as a threading draft and make many drafts with that threading, but using all the other drafts for treadling drafts. Be sure to include the draft you chose for the threading as one of the treadling drafts. Draft several rows of each treadling, so you really can see what the weave looks like and how each one differs just by changing the treadling. I suggest using the threading with the point repeat in the middle. Use any of the top three tie-ups.

Then, you might take your threading and use it for the treadling with the different tie-ups. Draft enough rows for each tie-up so you see how they influence the drawdowns. Use the top three tie-ups for this exercise.

The twill circle: A design tool

Sometime you might want to have a certain number of warp threads threading in one direction, say in the S direction (read about S and Z on page 49), and then a certain number of threads in the Z direction, and to repeat them over and over for a threading draft. You do not need to have a multiple of 4 threads for 4 shafts, or 8 threads for 8 shafts, etc. Say, you want to have 6 threads going S, and then, 12 going Z, and reversing (or making a point) after each number of threads. The threading would be 6 threads in the S direction, 12 threads in the Z direction, then, 6 in S and 12 in Z for as wide as your draft (or cloth).

Using the twill circle can help you greatly. Make a circle with as many points on it as

shafts you are planning to use. For 4 shafts, number the points 1,2,3,4 as shown in Figure 313. Now, working clockwise on the circle and also on your threading draft, begin with 1,2,3,4, and repeat the numbers until 6 threads are indicated on the threading draft. You'll stop at shaft 2: 1,2,3,4,1,2. Next, reverse the direction of the threading (make a point and reverse directions), and work counter-clockwise on the circle. You'll stop at shaft 3: 1,4,3,2,1,4,3,2,1,4,3 for 12 threads. Since the point thread "goes with" both directions, count it as a thread in each direction. (Note that for the 12 threads, the 2 from the first set of threads is counted as thread number 1, and there are only 11 new threads written in.)

The circle can be helpful in making a treadling draft, as well. I find it quite useful when I'm drafting twills, and at other times, too.

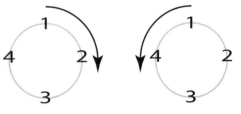

Fig. 313

A special kind of point

There's another kind of point that is nice to know about because sometimes the regular point discussed above can look a little odd at the tip. It just isn't crisp or sharp because of the floats of threads. If this phenomenon happens with point twills, beat the wefts at the points more gently than usual to avoid the wefts from packing in too close together there.

A broken point can solve the problem and create very sharp points. Again, it can be used in either threading or treadling drafts, or both. At the point, there is a "hitch" in the threading. To find out how to make the hitch, use the twill circle. When you have enough threads going in one direction (S or Z), go directly across the circle and begin going in the opposite direction with that number. In Figure 313, with 4 shafts, if you stopped at shaft 3, working clockwise, you would go across the circle to shaft 1, and work counter-clockwise to determine the threading or treadling.

Figure 314 shows a twill circle for 8 shafts. If you had stopped at shaft 5, the next shaft to use for a broken point would be shaft 1. If the last shaft before the direction change were 7, the next shaft would be 3. Figure 315 shows a broken point threading on 8 shafts.

Fig. 314

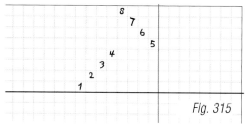

Fig. 315

More about tie-up drafts

A different tie-up can dramatically change the resulting cloth–even when the threading and treadling are identical.

You can see the effect of the tie-up in Figures 316a, b, c. All three drafts have identical threading and treadling drafts; what makes them different is the tie-up. In the tie-up in Figure 316a, see that 2 shafts are always lifted (and two are not lifted or are down). Because half the shafts are up and half are down, the weft will show just as much as the warp, as you

can see in the drawdown. We say it is a balanced weave when the warp and weft show equally. This twill is called a 2/2 twill. The number above the line in the fraction tells the number of shafts that are up, and the number below the line, the number of shafts that are down.

In Figure 316b, the tie-up indicates that only one shaft is lifted at a time. Only one warp, but three wefts will show on the cloth. It means that the weft will predominate in this weave. This twill is called a 1/3 twill, or weft-faced twill.

A warp-faced twill (3/1 twill) is seen in Figure 316c. The warp predominates in the drawdown because for every shed (row of weaving) there are always 3 warps up and only one down.

You can see the dramatic effect the tie-up had on the drawdown in my "snowflake" draft. See Figure 317. The tie-up in that draft is the weave structure for satin weave where the threads are meant to be scattered. Read about this interesting weave in several weaving books on structure.[59] When I was learning to weave, I thought the threading was the most important, if not the all-important, part of the draft.

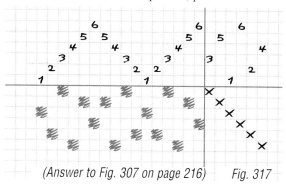

(Answer to Fig. 307 on page 216)   *Fig. 317*

[59] Alderman, Sharon, *Mastering Weave Structures*, Interweave Press, Loveland, CO, 2004, and van der Hoogt, Madelyn, *The Complete Book of Drafting for Handweavers*, Shuttle Craft Books, Coupeville, WA, 1993.

Balanced 2/2 Twill   *Weft-Face 1/3 Twill*   *Warp-Face 3/1 Twill*

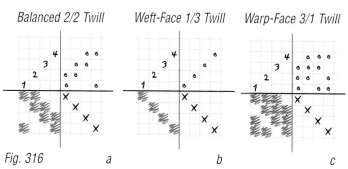

Fig. 316   *a*   *b*   *c*

Now, I would say all three parts are equally important.

Read about skeleton, standard, universal, and direct tie-ups in Book #2, on page 72.

Tie-up drafts in other books

Some books use another system for the tie-up drafts. In these, the marks in the tie-up indicate shafts that are to be lowered. If you don't know it is the case for a given book, any draft that you weave from that book will have the pattern on the underside of the cloth instead of on top. It is not the end of the world, but it's hard to enjoy the design while you're weaving.

Books and magazines give the key to their drafting systems—usually at the beginning of the drafting section. The convention is that if X's are written in the tie-up draft, they indicate which shafts are *to be lowered*. You cannot rely on that convention, however. If the book is not a new one, look carefully for the explanation of the drafting system.

A Handweaver's Pattern Book was written a long time ago and is still used today by thousands of weavers. All the tie-up drafts in the book indicate shafts to be lowered. Here's what it says in the "Explanation of the Drafts" section: "In the instance of this illustration, [a tie-up draft] the first cross at the right means that the rear harness is to be lowered."[60]

Swedish books often show warps lowered in the tie-up drafts and the wefts (where warps are lowered or not lifted) as the filled-in squares in the drawdown.

Converting tie-up drafts

To convert a tie-up draft that indicates shafts to be lowered to a rising shaft draft, raise all the shafts that are not marked.

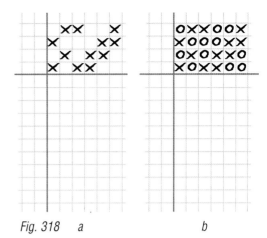

Fig. 318 a b

Figure 318a (above) shows a draft with X's in the tie-up draft.[61] Put bubbles in all the blank squares to convert the draft for rising shed looms. See Figure 318b.

Counterbalance looms: Sometimes, counterbalance looms are referred to as sinking shed looms because when you press on a treadle, it pulls its shafts down. To convert a "regular" tie-up draft with rising shafts to a tie-up with lowering shafts, which is required for counterbalance looms, treadle the blank squares. In other words, if you want shafts 1 and 2 to rise, pull down shafts 3 and 4. Figure 318b shows a draft with both bubbles and X's, where the bubbles show rising shafts and the X's lowering ones.

To learn more details about counterbalance looms, see the chapter on adjusting looms in Book #2.

Countermarch looms: Countermarch looms need tie-ups that indicate both which shafts are to be lifted (bubbles) and which are to be lowered (X's). Figure 318b is a countermarch tie-up. Read about tying up the treadles on page 1. To learn more about these looms, see the chapter on adjusting looms in Book #2.

221

---

[60] Davison, Marguerite Porter, *A Handweaver's Pattern Book*, Marguerite P. Davison, Publisher, Swarthmore, PA. 1944, p. xii.

[61] Davison, "Jefferson's Fancy" draft, p. 115.

More about threading drafts

Drafts usually give just the basic repeat units and how many times to repeat them. Figure 319 shows part of a threading draft. It indicates the number of times each particular section should be repeated in the threading draft. For example, the first section (reading from right-to-left according to the convention of reading threading drafts) shows that 48 threads (12 x 4) will be threaded on the shafts according to what that section indicates, which is: 1,2,3,4. The next section has only one thread: to be threaded on shaft 1. The third section tells you to thread 4 x 4, or 16 threads in the sequence indicated: 4,3,2,1. By the way, treadling drafts do the same: tell you how many times to repeat each section.

The twill circle can help you design your threading drafts and repeats.

Threading drafts in other books

In Swedish books, shaft #1 is given to the shaft farthest away from the weaver, and in the drafts, will be on the top line, rather than on the bottom line as in American books. Some drawdowns show wefts, rather than warps, as the filled in squares.

Fig. 319

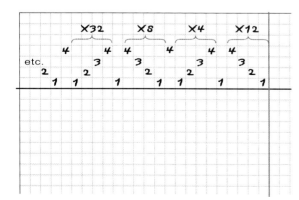

Threading drafts vs. profile drafts

Sometimes, every thread is indicated in the threading draft. Figure 320 shows a thread-by-thread threading draft and the complete drawdown draft that results. Other times, groups of threads are indicated according to a design. The actual threads to be threaded aren't given in the threading draft. They are indicated in words that tell which weave structure is being used. Each weave has its own rules, so only the design is shown because the weaver is expected to understand the weave and its rules. They are called profile drafts. They are for working out designs as opposed to patterns.

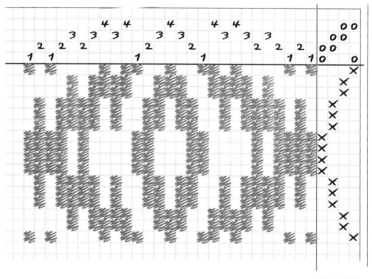

Fig. 320

Profile drafts: Figures 321a and b are profile drafts. The threading draft only shows sections of threads, not individual threads, and the drawdown shows the resulting design of the fabric. The treadling draft is not shown, but would be a profile, as well, and the sequence the blocks are treadled is the same as the threading sequence (often called "tromp as writ," see page 226).

The bottom line of the threading draft is called Block A, and the next line up is Block B. Succeeding blocks going up away from the bottom of the threading draft will be C, D, E,

Fig. 321

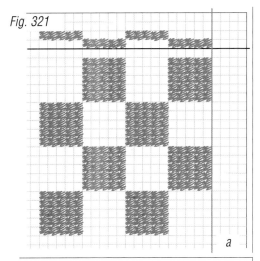

a

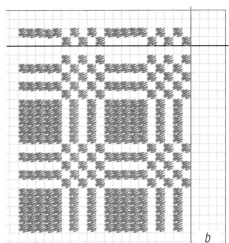

b

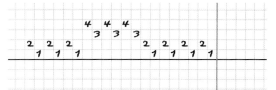

Fig. 322

of the threading (1,2) or 2 threads. You will thread 10 threads because there are 5 squares filled in for the first A Block.

Block B, in Figure 321a, would also have 10 threads, threaded: 3,4,3,4,3,4, etc. Notice that in that draft all the blocks are equal in width—so each would be given 10 threads in this example of monk's belt weave.

In Figure 323, the blocks are different widths: the size of the first block is very small—only one repeat—so only 2 threads would be threaded in the first Block A section. Figure 323 shows the actual threading for that profile draft.

Summary: Substitute the threading for your weave structure into the profile draft. Each structure has its special threading and weave. (Figure 366, on page 246, shows some different weave structures.) There are books that explain this method thoroughly.[62]

etc. Read more about blocks beginning on page 241. The chart in Figure 366, on page 246, tells how many blocks are possible for various weave structures.

How to use profile drafts: Let's say the weave structure you want to weave is "monk's belt," where Block A is threaded on shafts 1 and 2, and Block B on shafts 3 and 4. See Figure 322.

The threading draft would read: 1,2,1,2,1,2,1,2, etc., for as many threads needed for the width of the block indicated in the profile draft. In Figure 321a, each square on the graph paper is equal to one repeat unit

Fig. 323

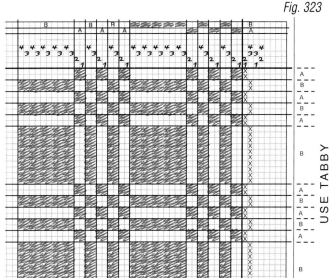

USE TABBY

[62] Alderman, van der Hoogt, Chandler, Deborah. *Learning to Weave*, Interweave Press, Loveland, CO, 1995.

223

More about treadling drafts

Much information is given in words or extra numbers in the treadling draft. See Figure 324. It is important, and the drafts assume you know how to interpret them. Read on.

"Use tabby"

When "use tabby" (Figure 324) is given in the treadling draft or nearby, it means that in between every weft indicated in the treadling draft itself, you should put a tabby weft. Since there are two sheds needed to make a tabby

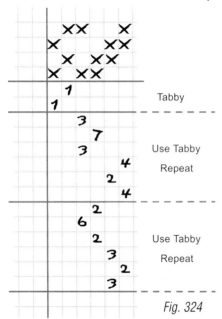

Fig. 324

(or plain weave), you must keep track of which tabby shed should be used as well as which row you are on in the treadling draft. It is much easier than you might think.

Different weave structures have different ways of accomplishing the tabby weave. Don't think that tabby is always lifting shafts 1&3 and 2&4. For example, in the structure called "Summer and Winter," one tabby shed is made by lifting shafts 1&2, and the other shed is made by lifting all the remaining shafts.

Where you put your tabby treadles is important, so it will be easy to keep track of which tabby shed you are to use.

Remember, to weave efficiently and to save your back, you should tie up the treadles so you can "walk" them, or use them with alternate feet. If the draft says, "use tabby," then every other shot (pick) should use one of your tabby treadles, and would be operated by one foot. Here's how you would treadle: left foot, pattern; right foot, first tabby; left foot, pattern; right foot, second tabby.

Keeping track of the tabby sequence is easy if you set up your two treadles to make tabby in this convenient way. The tabby treadles will probably be next to each other. When the tabby shuttle is on the left of the warp, use the left tabby treadle. When the tabby shuttle is on the right, use the right treadle. You don't have to keep track of the tabby sequence at all, and you can concentrate on the pattern treadle sequence. That is easy, too, if you have tied up the treadles with the first treadle in the sequence on the outside treadle. Then, your pattern-treadle-foot will work its way from the outside treadle toward the inside. More on tying up the treadles is on page 1.

Numbers in the treadling draft

Figure 324 shows numbers in the treadling draft. The numbers indicate that you should use that treadle (combination of shafts) that many times. For example, the first numbers given in Figure 324 are 3, then 7, then 3, then 4, etc. They mean the treadle indicated should be used 3 times before moving on to the next treadle, which is to be used 7 times, and so on. (Since "use tabby" is also indicated in the draft, besides repeating the treadles as indicated, you will intersperse tabby treadles between each shot (pick).

Keeping track of your place. Weavers use a variety of ways to keep track of complicated treadling sequences. Some write the sheds (peg plan) on an index card and attach it to the loom, so they can see it. As they weave along, they move a paper clip down the card to show which row to use. Of course, if you have a computer operated loom, the computer can keep track of your place very easily.

Repeats

Treadling sequences can be repeated in both ways, just like in threading drafts: with straight repeats or point or mirror image repeats. Figure 310 on page 218, shows a straight treadling draft (and threading draft). Figure 311 on page 218, shows point repeats in both the threading and treadling drafts

If a draft shows one sequence of a treadling, such as in Figure 325, you can decide to repeat it as a straight or a point repeat, but if no more indication is given, it is assumed to be a straight repeat, since the treadling sequence given is one unit of a repeat.

Sometimes, a sequence in the treadling draft is given in a bracket, with the number of times the sequence in the bracket is to be repeated.

Turned drafts

You can put the threading draft in the treadling area of a draft and the treadling into the threading area. It's called a turned draft. You literally copy one draft into the other position, and vice versa. Figures 327 and 328 show how it can be done.

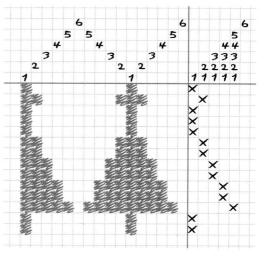

(Answer to Fig. 308b on page 217)   Fig. 327

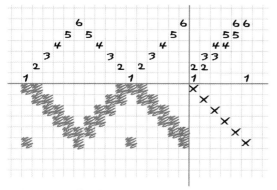

(Answer to Fig. 306 on page 216)   Fig. 325

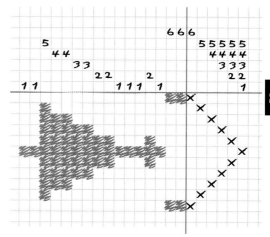

(Answer to Fig. 308d on page 217)   Fig. 328

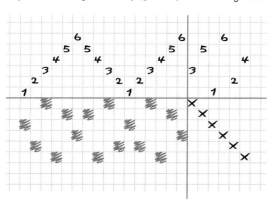

(Answer to Fig. 307 on page 216)   Fig. 326

I had fun with the pine trees, and turned them upside down as well as from positive to negative as in Figures 329 and 330. More information on turned drafts is in *Mastering Weave Structures* and *The Complete Book of Drafting for Handweavers*.[63]

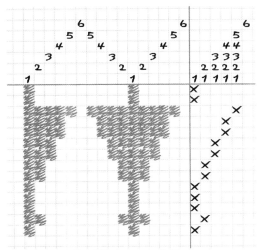

(Answer to Fig. 308c on page 217)   Fig. 329

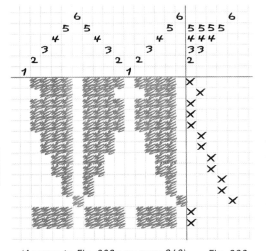

(Answer to Fig. 308a on page 216)   Fig. 330

Tromp as writ

When the treadling draft is exactly the same as the threading draft, we say the draft is treadled "tromp as writ." Sometimes, only the threading is given, and the words "treadle as written" or "treadle as threaded," tell you to tromp as writ.

Figure 331 is an example of a draft that is treadled tromp as writ. The profile drafts in Figures 321a and b, on page 223 are also treadled tromp as writ. You can tell because the blocks in the drawdown draft are squared. Figure 323 on page 223 shows the thread-by-thread draft for the profile.

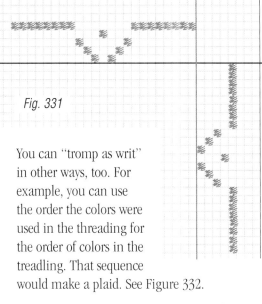

Fig. 331

You can "tromp as writ" in other ways, too. For example, you can use the order the colors were used in the threading for the order of colors in the treadling. That sequence would make a plaid. See Figure 332.

One way to go about it is to assign numbers to the treadles (the combinations in the tie-up). Remember, the first treadle would be the left hand combination, working outward from

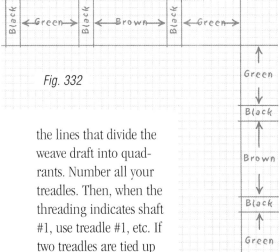

Fig. 332

the lines that divide the weave draft into quadrants. Number all your treadles. Then, when the threading indicates shaft #1, use treadle #1, etc. If two treadles are tied up for tabby and the rest for pattern, just number the

---

[63] Alderman and van der Hoogt.

pattern treadles (combinations). This method assumes there are as many shafts used as treadle combinations. If there is a discrepancy, check if there are blocks in the threading, and treadle them in the order they are used in the threading, as above. You can make any convention, but be consistent when you tromp as writ.

Peg plans

A peg plan can be used instead of a treadling draft. It is a list of the shafts that are to be lifted for every shed. Peg plans are ideal for looms without treadles and computer-driven looms. When a table loom is used, the levers are pressed for each shed, so a peg plan is easier to read than a treadling draft. See Figure 333.

Computers need to have the shafts for each shed entered, as well, so peg plans are used.

My beginning students find it easier to treadle the weaves on their samplers by making peg plans from the treadling drafts I've given them, as seen in Figure 334.

A weave draft written with a peg plan would not have anything in the tie-up quadrant of the draft, because no treadles would be tied up. Each set of shafts is lifted individually for each shed, or row of weaving.

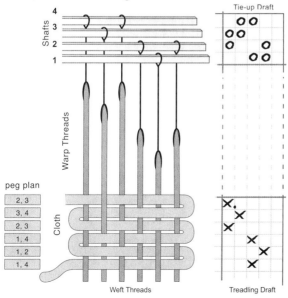

Fig. 333

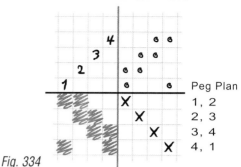

Balanced 2/2 Twill

Fig. 334

Peg Plan
1, 2
2, 3
3, 4
4, 1

More about drawdown drafts

Sometimes, the filled-in squares in a drawdown indicate the wefts showing, rather than the warps lifted. The wefts show where the warps are *not* lifted. Some Swedish drafts are written this way. By the way, in the Swedish books, shaft #1 is on the top line in the threading draft and indicates the shaft *farthest* from the weaver.

Color drafting

You can put the warp and weft colors into the drawdown draft and try out your colors before weaving them. First, assign colors to the warp threads by coloring in the squares in the threading draft accordingly. Then, in the drawdown, color over the filled-in squares, looking up in the threading draft for the colors to use. All the blank squares in the drawdown represent weft threads. Assign the colors in the weft along the side of the treadling draft and fill in the blank squares, row-by-row, according to them. Read about putting the color order for the warps and wefts in the draft on page 212.

Oelsner drafts

A Handbook of Weaves by G.H. Oelsner is a useful book sometimes overlooked by handweavers because it uses an industrial format. The diagrams are peg plans for straight draws (mostly) so the shafts to be lifted can be read directly from the diagrams. See *Mastering Weave Structures* (Sharon Alderman), Appendix B. If you have a first edition, go to: www.interweave.com for three corrections.

227

Drafting
...Anayzing Fabric

It's easy to work out the weave draft from a fabric. Sometimes, it's easier to understand weave drafting itself by analyzing a fabric.

What fabrics can you analyze?

Look for warp and weft threads that are perpendicular and big enough to see without a magnifying glass. You can work on finer fabrics after you have learned the procedure. A pick glass is a special magnifying glass for analyzing textiles. See Figure 34, on page 24. (It is a big help for seeing the threads in a textile. I always carry one in my purse and one in my weaving apron.)

For your first attempt, try something that you can see the threads and the weave structure easily— but not a twill, which you already "know."

Please don't take a multi-level, complex-structure fabric made by a jacquard loom, where every warp thread was lifted independently, and there are no shafts.

Finding the threading

We'll start with a picture of a make-believe piece of cloth as it was on the loom.

If you've read the previous chapters in this book, you will recognize some of the following material. Here, it is giving you a different angle on drafting.

I think the best way to find the threading is to use colored pencils to color in the warp threads in Figure 335. Before you begin to learn how to analyze, make a copy of the illustration (and one for a friend you will teach the process to).

The first warp thread in the illustration is the thread on the right side. Remember, threading drafts read right-to-left. Read how to read drafts and see Figure 291 on page 208.

Color in the first warp thread from the top, where it is in a heddle, all the way through the cloth diagram (under and over the wefts). Then, using the same color, color in all the other warps that go over and under wefts in exactly the same way as that first thread.

You should have colored in two threads—the first one (on the far right) and the third thread.

Now, with a new color, fill in the second warp thread and any others that are just like it. You will find that there isn't any other just like it, so you have only one warp thread to color with this color.

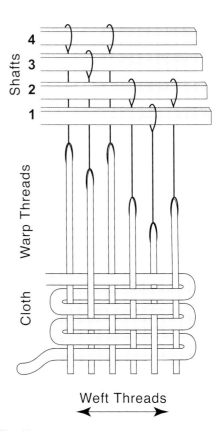

Fig. 335

With a third color, fill in the next warp that hasn't been colored in yet—warp number 4 (the 4th thread from the right). Again, color in all the others like it. There are two threads this time, thread #4 and the last one (the one on the far left).

There is one warp left uncolored. It is different from all the rest, so it should have its own color.

This part of the exercise was to show you how to look for identical warp threads.

Look up above the cloth where the warps are in the "heddles" or eyes, and to the "shafts" that the eyes are attached to. Read about shafts on page 207.

The illustration labels the shafts, #1 through #4, with shaft #1 being on the bottom, and shaft #4 on the top line. This is the way drafts are usually written–with shaft #1 on the bottom line and the last shaft on the top line. Shaft #1 is the one nearest the weaver on the loom.

Now, look at the colored warps you have and note that the ones of the same color are attached to the same shafts. That is, the first warp on the right and its mate are attached to shaft #2.

Look at the second warp—it had no one else like it—so there is no other thread on that shaft.

Warp threads that act identically will be on the same shaft.

To confirm that all the threads on a shaft act alike, look at Figure 288 on page 207.

Look at the pine trees in Figure 336. We are going to start looking for identical things in columns, that is, identical warp threads. The darkened-in squares represent a warp thread lifted, raised up—a warp over.

See if you see any warp threads that are always lifted the same—that is, they are alike along the vertical length of the warp threads.

Look at all the tree trunks. Whenever one tree trunk is up, so are all the others. If you look up and down the trunk (vertically), you will note that those trunk threads are lifted for the entire tree—forming part of the body of the tree and the tips of the trees. There are no other threads acting just as they are. Give them a shaft assignment, let's say, shaft #1.

Look at the little "branches" on either side of the treetops. The two threads on either side of the middle are lifted to form the branches sticking out. The same configuration is in all the trees and in the same position. In each tree, they are on either side of the middle thread.

Check out those two threads on one tree. Follow them vertically, up and down. Notice that they work as a pair. Working from the top down, see that they are up for the "branch", then, down for three squares, then, up all the way to the bottom of the tree.

One branch never acts independently of the other. Therefore, they are threaded alike and are on their own shaft.

Check the other trees for threads that match the ones in the original tree. Do they go up for the branch, down three spaces, and up for the rest of the tree? They do, so all those threads on the other trees are to be put on the same shaft as the first tree's branches: give that shaft #2.

You could assign any shaft number you want, you just need to give threads that act alike the same shaft number.

Don't worry that one thread is up forever, making a long float. It is not really weaving. This is only a puzzle at first to see identical vertical threads.

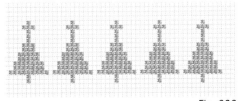

Fig. 336

Let's look for how the other threads will be assigned. Any identical threads will get their own shaft.

Continue working out from the center, check for warps on each side of the middle to see if they are alike. If they are, they get shaft #3.

Work until every warp thread has an assignment. You should get 6 different warps or six shafts. It's important to count the spaces, too, because there is "cloth" there–or a thread that is weaving something.

Where to write the shaft assignments

Write the shaft numbers above the trees–in the blank area just above them on the graph paper, in the threading section. Put #1's above all the tree trunk threads, on the bottom line of that section. Put #2's on the second line, over all the "branches" threads on each side of the trunk that match–there are 12 threads that are threaded on shaft #2–two per tree. Put all the #3's on the next line, above its threads, etc., until all the numbers have been transferred to their proper lines on the graph paper. See Figure 337. You should have the space filled above the trees with numbers going from 1 to 6. Now, you should be able to see that the threading is a point repeat on six shafts. (See page 217 for information on point repeats.)

Practice, practice, practice

Practice looking for identical vertical threads on some textured or patterned drafts that are not so recognizable, and give them their own shafts. See Figure 338. It's harder here to see the identical vertical warp threads.

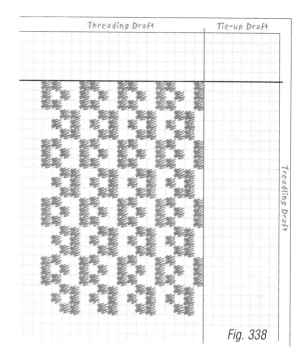

Fig. 338

At first, we are always looking for what the warps are doing–which ones are up.

☞ *The key: look for identical vertical columns.* All vertical columns that are the same represent threads on one shaft. So, looking across the cloth, whenever you see threads acting identically, they are being lifted together on one shaft.

Finding identical vertical columns is easy to do when you use a template.

Using a template

To find the threading draft for Figure 338, start with the column on the right, and working up and down along that column, mark the positions of the filled-in squares on one edge of the template. See Figure 339. Now, slide the template over to the left and notice all the other vertical columns that are just the same as the first one. Assign them shaft 1, and put 1's over them on the bottom line of the graph paper in the threading draft in Figure 338.

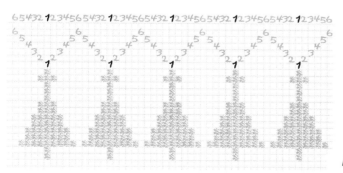

Fig. 337

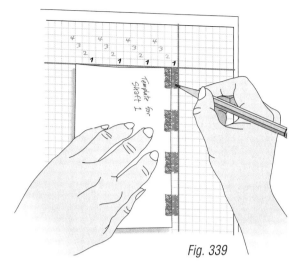

Fig. 339

Look for the next unique set of vertical columns by making another template. Assign those threads to shaft 2.

Complete the entire threading draft. Making the template takes all the scariness out —you just slide it along, and all the columns that match the template get the same shaft assignment. See the complete draft in Figure 340.

Read more about using templates for drafting on page 214.

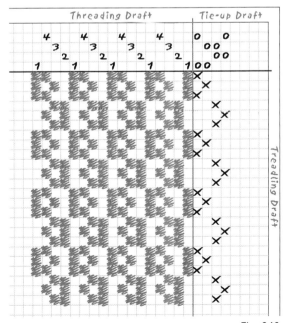

Fig. 340

Rule #1

To find the threading draft, look for identical vertical columns (or vertical threads). All threads that act identically are on the same shaft.

Threading Draft	Tie-up Draft

Fig. 341 Drawdown Draft Treadling Draft

Compete the threading draft in Figure 341. Remember to start with the right-hand thread and to follow rule #1. Your threading in the draft should be: 1,2,1,3,4,3.

Finding the treadling, and tie-up

We need to fill in what's missing in the weave draft for a weave analysis, because the threading alone won't give you all the information you need.

We work out the treadling and the tie-up drafts at the same time.

Remember : All the parts of the draft read *outwards* from the bold lines dividing the whole draft into quadrants. See Figure 291 on page 208.

- The *treadling draft* gives the sequence in which the combinations of shafts are used.
- The *tie-up draft* lists the combinations of shafts that will be used.
- The *threading draft* tells the way the warp threads are entered in the heddles on their respective shafts.
- The *drawdown draft* shows the result of the other three quadrants.

231

See Figure 341 on page 231. Put an X in the first, top, leftmost square of the treadling draft to account for the first horizontal row of weaving. (I put a dot in the square of graph paper to show where to get started.) The arrows in Figure 291 on page 208 show that we read the treadling draft from top to bottom. That means that the first row is the top row, as indicated by the little dot.

Look at the first row in the drawdown and see what squares are darkened, which warp threads are lifted. Then, note in the threading on which shafts they were threaded. In the tie-up draft, in the column directly over the X, put circles in the boxes corresponding to the combination of shafts lifted for that row. You should have marked 1 and 4. Reading up from the bold line, put 1 on the bottom line in the tie-up draft, and 4 in the top square.

The X for the next row of weaving goes on the horizontal line even with that row, and one square to the right of the X above it, because the drawdown draft indicates that the second row of weaving is different from the first row and a new combination of shafts will be needed in the tie-up. Note that now you are mainly working horizontally–row-by-row. The combination to put directly over the second X in the tie-up is 3 and 4, because the darkened squares were under shafts 3 and 4 in the threading draft.

Now, look at row three. It's a combination already given. 1 and 4 are to be lifted again, and that combination has already been written in the tie-up draft. The X should be placed directly under the combination of 1 and 4, already in the tie-up, next to its row.

You can work out the treadling and tie-up for the last three rows, now. Following the rules of drafting on page 211, begin in the treadling draft. Check the row of weaving to see if the shafts to be lifted for that row are the same

as any previous row. If they are, place the X for the row under that combination. If it is a new combination, place the X under an empty column in the tie-up and write in that column the combination of shafts lifted for that row. The fourth row should have the combination of 3 and 2, and the fifth row the combination of 1 and 2. The last row is a repeated combination, so place the X for that row under the combination of 2 and 3.

The "answer" for the *treadling draft* only is in Figure 295 on page 211. Take a good look at the drawdown in the illustration and compare it with the one you've just completed. The two drawdowns are exactly the same. The threading and the tie-up are different, but the resulting analyses are both correct. The difference is that in Figure 295, the threading draft was made from the drawing of the cloth and shafts. In Figure 341, the threading was worked out "from scratch." In real life, you wouldn't have an illustration of cloth and shafts to work from–you would either work from the cloth (more later) or from a drawdown draft.

Rule #2

To find the treadling and tie-up drafts, begin in the treadling draft and, from the drawdown work row-by-row, right-to-left, top-to-bottom. Place an X in the treadling draft on the row of weaving to be analyzed. All the shafts lifted for that row represent the shafts tied up to one treadle. Put all of those shafts in a vertical column in the tie-up draft. Put an X in the treadling draft under that combination every time it's used. All filled-in squares are warps lifted.

Practice

Fill in the treadling and tie-up drafts for Figure 338 on page 230, using the threading you already analyzed. The complete draft is given in Figure 340.

Summary

How to analyze a weave. (How to work directly from a cloth starts below.)

First, find the warp direction (See below).

1. To find the threading, look for identical warp (vertical) threads–they all go on the same shaft.

2. To find the treadling and tie-up, work row-by-row (horizontally) to see what shafts were lifted for each row. Put an X in the treadling draft for the row you are working on, and circles in the vertical column above the X in the tie-up draft for the correct combination of shafts.

3. You can write the information as a peg plan instead of as tie-up and treadling drafts. Read about peg plans on page 227.

How to analyze a real cloth

It is not hard to do, and is easier and more fun if you have a partner who can write down on graph paper what you see.

Ways to determine the warp direction

- Warp threads are likely to be plied and stronger than the weft threads.

- Hold the cloth up to the light, and you might see reed marks going in the warp direction. They show up as tiny vertical spaces between small groups of threads.

- Selvedges will indicate the warp direction.

- Commercial cloth will probably have more warps per inch than wefts per inch.

- There will be more color changes in the warps than in the wefts–in other words, it was woven with as few shuttles as possible.

After you've determined the warp direction, poke a pin into the cloth at an intersection of threads that is fairly easy to see. It will be your starting point, and you'll be coming back to that pin's location often. Do not begin at a selvedge where the threads are bound to be closer together making it impossible to see the threads.

 Plotting out the warp and weft threads on graph paper is easier if you use dashes and work on the lines of the graph paper as in Figure 342, because the lines or dashes look more like threads. Filling in the squares is confusing, especially when you need to look at wefts as well as warps.

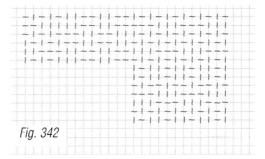

Fig. 342

Begin plotting the threads on the graph paper. Look up and down an individual warp thread, follow it and mark on the graph paper whether it is going "over or under" weft threads. A vertical line means the warp is up (or over a weft), a horizontal line represents a weft that is over a warp (the warp is under): hence, over, under. The first warp thread in the illustration, starting at the right, and working from the top to the bottom on the graph paper, is under, over, under, over, under, over three, under, over, under, over two.

You can follow a weft thread, it doesn't matter; you just want each warp-over and weft-over to be plotted out. Sometimes, I lose a warp thread; then, I work on the wefts for awhile, starting at the pin.

If you have a partner, you can call out the overs and unders for that thread to your partner.

The illustration shows a made-up-weave fabric so that you can understand the process and not be able to "see" what is coming next.

Plot out enough that you have a repeat in both the warp and the weft directions. Then, you're ready for the fun part—making the weave draft.

Cut a clean piece of graph paper as in Figure 343. Figure 344 shows how to place the cut-out paper over the paper with the weave plotted out on it. Line up the graph paper and tape it in place.

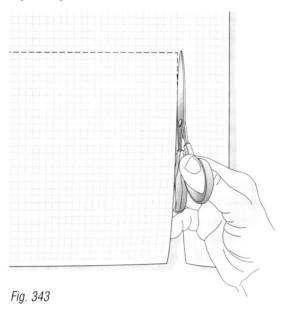

Fig. 343

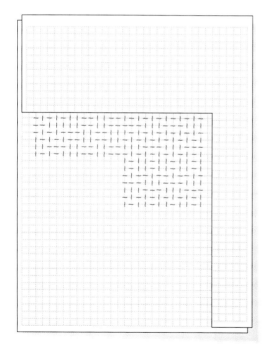

Fig. 344

Making the weave draft

See Figure 345.

Step 1: With a pencil, lightly extend lines from the warp threads up into the threading draft a little way.

Step 2: Put identical warp threads (vertical columns) on one shaft, as usual. I draw little X's at the intersection of the extended warp lines and the threading draft lines to indicate which shaft the thread is threaded on. For example, the first warp thread (the one on the right-hand side) is assigned to shaft 1—on the bottom line of the threading draft. Look across that row of weaving for all the other warps that weave identically to the first one. (They have the exact same pattern of overs and unders as the first warp thread.) In the illustration, the third warp thread is the same as the first, so it is also "threaded" on shaft 1. Following along that row, there are two more threads for shaft 1.

Using a template is a great help. Read about using them for analyzing on page 231.

Continue making the threading draft, as usual, putting the threads that weave identically on their separate shafts. Part of the draft is shown in the illustration. You can put in the threading for the remaining warp threads. Remember, this is a make-believe threading and shouldn't resemble any pattern or known weave structure.

Step 3: Lightly extend lines from the weft threads into the treadling draft.

Step 4: Work row-by-row in the treadling and drawdown drafts. Put the combination of shafts that lifted the warp threads into the tie-up draft, directly above the X for the horizontal row of weaving you are working on (in this case, row 1). Drawing a line vertically from the X in the treadling up into the tie-up makes it easy to tell which tie-up is for which X. The illustration indicates what shafts are tied to

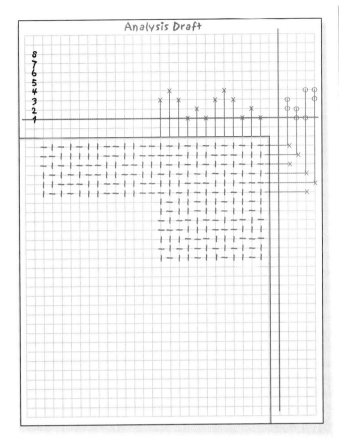

Fig. 345

the X's in the treadling draft. Put an X in the treadling draft for each different weft in its appropriate row, and in the same column for identical ones.

And you've done it!! You've made a weave draft from a make-believe cloth. That's all there is to it! Read the hints for making it even easier, below.

Fabric Analysis Hints

- Use a pin to mark the starting point. Be sure it won't fall out.

- Use 2 more pins to probe. (You will probably push the threads around a bit to see exactly how they are woven.) Hold one stationary, and probe with the second.

- Don't start at an edge where threads might be askew or worn.

- Don't start at an "odd" spot, for example, at an edge of a border. Do the main structure and work out to the edges, if necessary.

- Look at the back of the fabric for clues.

- Since you can only see one surface at a time, only draft one side of the cloth.

- Make your own grid if there is no graph paper big enough.

- Enlarge a grid. For example, wefts might be shown as even farther apart than the warps, if it makes it clearer. You might put the wefts on every other line of the graph paper, for instance.

- Work with a partner, one writing, one calling out the overs and unders. Make sure both of you are fresh and patient when you start out.

- Photocopy the textile and enlarge it on the copy machine.

- Look below or beside a float to find out how many threads are underneath it.

- If you see a plain weave, you know that there are two threads for each one you see in a single row (and two shafts were needed to make the plain weave).

235

Drafting
...The Basics of Multi-shaft Weaving

> "Multi-shaft" looms are referred to here as looms with more than four shafts.
>
> In case you're not sure what a shaft is, read about harnesses and shafts on page 207.
>
> In this section, we are always talking about shafts lifted. To convert to other types of looms, see page 221.
>
> If necessary, review "Understanding Weave Drafts" on page 209.

Why have more than two shafts?

When you can weave the most complicated designs and pictorial images, as are woven in tapestries, with two shafts, why would anyone want more? Of course, tapestries take a lot of hand manipulation, or weaver-control. When you have more shafts, there is less hand manipulation and more loom-control. Actually, the more shafts, the fewer options you have, and the more programmed your weave design is. That is, with only two shafts, you could, in theory, weave anything–if you manipulated the warps with your hands. With a loom-controlled weave, you are limited to that weave and variations on that weave.

Most weavers know the huge variety of things that can be woven using four shafts. There are 14 different ways you can combine the four shafts. There are no choices with only two shafts.

With eight shafts, the possibilities leap—there are 254 different ways eight shafts can be combined to weave. There are 65,000 different possibilities with sixteen shafts! This is the reason it can become overwhelming if you don't understand how to choose the combinations of shafts needed to do what you want to do.

It's O.K. not to use all your shafts

You absolutely do not need to use all the shafts on your loom—ever—if you don't choose to.

Multi-shaft weaves take more "work"

You need to realize that weaving with more than four shafts is quite different from weaving with only four in that it involves much more work.

It takes more work:

To thread—You have to sort out the heddles on perhaps eight or sixteen shafts.

To tie-up—The shafts must be tied in combinations to the treadles. A direct tie-up with one shaft to a treadle won't do—you don't have enough feet!

To treadle—You have more shafts to lift, so it's often slower to weave because more shafts are heavier. Some looms' shafts are heavier than others, making lifting many shafts at a time nearly impossible. It is a consideration in buying a multi-shaft loom.

Ways to use more than four shafts

There are lots of ways you can use more than four shafts.

Very dense warps

Very dense warps can be spread out on extra shafts. A clean shed is easier to make because the heddles are spread out more. To weave plain weave (tabby), thread the warp onto eight shafts, rather than on four. For one shed, lift 1,3,5,7 (the odd numbered shafts), and for the second shed, lift 2,4,6,8, (the even numbered shafts).

More layers

More layers can be woven with extra shafts. Since it takes only two shafts to make a layer, with eight shafts, you could weave four separate layers. You could weave six layers with twelve shafts, etc.

Figure 346 shows the tie-up draft for weaving four layers, with shafts 1 and 2 on top. *The tie-up changes whenever you decide to assign another set of shafts to be the top layer.* Read more about double weave in the books on drafting mentioned above.[64] Read more about layers in the book, *A Reference Book of 4 and 8 Shaft Double Weave,* by Paul O'Connor. It is available to view and print out only on www.haven.com/proc.

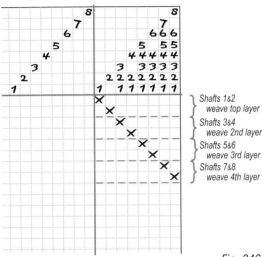

Shafts 1&2 weave top layer
Shafts 3&4 weave 2nd layer
Shafts 5&6 weave 3rd layer
Shafts 7&8 weave 4th layer

Fig. 346

In double weave, to weave a layer beneath the top, all the shafts for the layers above it must be lifted out of the way before you can lift the shafts for the particular layer you are weaving. In the tie-up (Figure 346), the first two wefts indicated in the treadling draft are to weave the top layer. First, shaft 1 is lifted and then, shaft 2 for the second row of weaving for the top layer.

The next two X's in the treadling draft are the wefts to weave the next-to-the-top layer. Shafts 1 and 2 are lifted up out of the way (they are tied to the two treadles used for the next-to-

the-top layer as shown in the tie-up draft for the third and fourth rows of weaving) and shaft 3 is added to weave the first shed of the second layer. Then, shaft 4 is added to shafts 1 and 2 to weave the second shed of the second layer. In summary, the shafts that are to be lifted for the next-to-the-top layer are: 1, 2, 3 (tied to one treadle) and 1, 2, 4 (tied to another treadle).

To weave the third layer (on shafts 5 and 6), lift up all the shafts for the layers above it (the first and second layers: 1, 2, 3, 4) and add shaft 5 to weave the first shed (this is one treadle) and add shaft 6 to those lifted out of the way to weave the second shed (this is another treadle). The fourth layer is woven with the shafts lifted out of the way for the upper three layers.

It may occur to you that lifting all those shafts with just two feet must be difficult, not to say heavy. Actually, you are only using one foot on one treadle for each shed. Each treadle has all the shafts needed for its particular shed. That's why it takes eight treadles—each treadle lifts out of the way the necessary shafts for the upper layers as well as the shaft needed to weave the layer itself. You can't *leave* shafts up—they are lifted with each shed.

All those shafts on a floor loom can get heavy. The bottom-most layer requires that seven shafts are tied up to each of the two treadles needed for the two sheds.

A table loom, however, has levers and is easier, perhaps, because you can leave the shafts up along the way—and it's easier to exchange layers with a table loom because you pull the levers for each shed—no combinations are tied up (locked to particular treadles).

☞ There, you have it! It takes eight wefts to weave the two sheds necessary for each layer. If you choose to make another layer for the top, middle, or bottom, etc., another tie-up draft for eight treadles is required.

_____

[64] Alderman, Chandler, and van de Hoogt.

Supplementary warps

Supplementary warps, or extra warps, can be threaded on some shafts while others are used for the ground warp. For more information, see Harriet Tidball's monograph and van der Hoogt's *The Complete Book of Drafting*.[65]

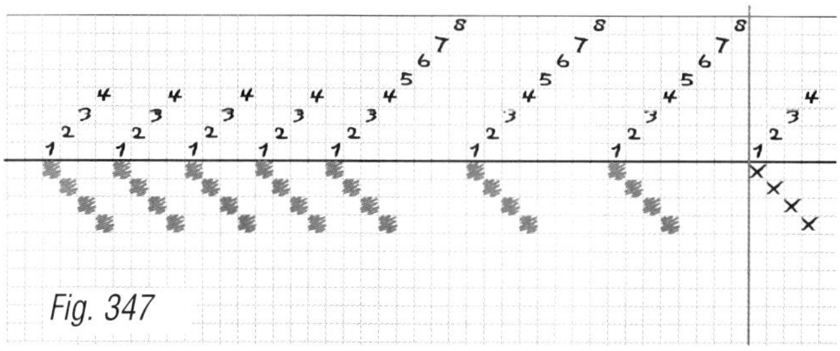

Large-scale patterns

Larger scale designs and patterns can be woven. The more shafts, the larger the patterns can be, and the more negative space between them. See Figure 347.

Complex patterns

With more shafts, more complex patterns can be woven. Notice in the books and magazines that the complicated patterns often are made on eight or more shafts.

Weave more than one "thing" at a time

Weaving two or more different weaves at once often requires extra shafts.

How to Weave Two Things at Once

Let's say you want to weave a design like the one in Figure 348. One weave is for the main part of the cloth, and a different weave is for a stripe.

To illustrate this example, I will use twill weaves that many weavers already know. To learn about them, read "More About Tie-up Drafts," on page 220. To review briefly, a balanced twill (2/2) shows an equal amount of warps and wefts in the weave. A warp-faced twill (3/1) shows more warps than wefts, and a weft-faced twill (1/3) shows more wefts than warps.

238

[65]Tidball, Harriet, *Supplementary Warp Patterning*, Shuttle Craft Monograph 17, HTH Publishers, Santa Ana, CA. 1966.

van der Hoogt, Madelyn, *The Complete Book of Drafting*.

Fig. 347

Here are the treadling (lift) sequences for these weaves:

2/2 twill: 1,2; 2,3; 3,4; 4,1

3/1 twill: 1,2,3; 2,3,4; 3,4,1; 4,1,2

1/3 twill: 1,2,3,4

Now, let's say the stripe in the middle should be 3/1 twill with the background being 2/2 twill. If I had only four shafts, I would have to lift shafts 1 and 2 and take the shuttle out of the shed where I want the special stripe. Then, I would lift shafts 1,2,3, put the shuttle in the new shed for the width of the stripe and take it out again. Finally, I would change the shed back to 1 and 2, enter the shuttle and weave to the edge of the cloth. It would be a nightmare, both weaving, and keeping track of the two lift sequences.

To solve the problem, it would be nice if we had another loom to put in place for the special stripe. That's exactly the principle I'll use. The "second loom" will actually be shafts 5,6,7,8.

The threading draft would look like Figure 349. See that the "first loom" is used for the background and uses the first four shafts. Most of the warp would be threaded 4,3,2,1 (or 1,2,3,4) because most of the warp is the background. It's only in the area where the stripe is to be that the "second loom" is needed—and it's only in that area where the threads are threaded on 8,7,6,5 (or 5,6,7,8).

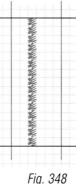

Fig. 348

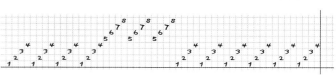

Fig. 349

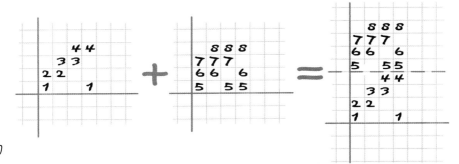

Fig. 350

It doesn't matter whether you thread 1,2,3,4 or 4,3,2,1. I just think it's easier to thread the loom 4,3,2,1.

Don't let the place where the stripe and background meet and the threading is 8,7,6,5,4,3,2,1 confuse you. It's really 8,7,6,5 and then, 4,3,2,1, where the first loom begins.

How do you get both weaves? It happens with the tie-up draft. Look at Figure 350. First, the tie-up is given for "loom 1," a balanced 2/2 twill. See that the combinations of shafts to be lifted are: 1,2; 2,3; 3,4; 4,1. The tie-up for "loom 2" is given in the second part of the illustration, for the warp-faced, 3/1 twill. Those combinations are: 5,6,7; 6,7,8; 5,7,8; 5,6,8. To make both twills weave at the same time, combine the two looms' tie-ups as shown in the third part of the illustration.

The treadling draft would show the first X under the combination, 1,2,5,6,7. The second X is under the combination: 2,3,6,7,8. Since there are 4 combinations used, four treadles will be needed.

Practice

Figure 351 shows another design. This time the background is to be weft-faced twill (1/3) and the stripes, 3/1 twill, again. The threading would show the background on shafts 1,2,3,4 and the stripes on the "second loom": 5,6,7,8. In this design, the stripes and the

Fig. 351

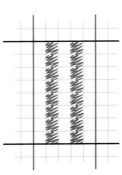

background areas are all the same width. In Figure 352a, "thread" the first loom for the number of threads necessary for the width of a stripe for the background. Then, assign an equal number of threads to the "second loom": 5,6,7,8. Continue across the remaining warp with threads for the background, then, threads for a stripe, and end with threads on the "first loom" again for the background. There should be a total of five stripes, 3 for the background on "loom 1," and two interior stripes on "loom 2."

Fig. 352a

Now for the tie-up, which will allow both looms to weave together. In other words, each shed will have threads on both looms lifted. In Figure 352b, put the tie up for the "first loom" in the tie-up draft with the lift sequence

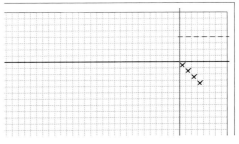

Fig. 352b

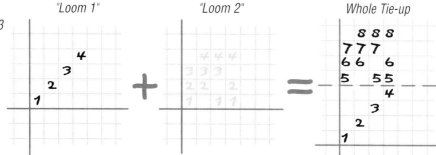

Fig. 353   "Loom 1"   "Loom 2"   Whole Tie-up

for 1/3 twill: 1,2,3,4. Notice in Figure 353 above, that I've indicated a dotted line in the final tie-up to separate the looms. Make the complete tie-up now, putting the lift sequence for the "second loom" on top of the tie-up for the "first loom," above your dotted line. Just as in Figure 353, I often write 1,2,3, and 4 very lightly instead of 5,6,7,8, at first. Then, I write the real shaft numbers of 5,6,7,8 over the temporary numbers, because it's easier for me to think of four shafts and two looms. The lift sequence you should put in the upper tie-up is: 5,6,7; 6,7,8; 7,8,5; and 8,5,6. See Figure 364, on page 245 for the "answer."

Remember that each treadle will lift shafts from both "looms," forming one shed. Since there are four sheds for this design, only four treadles are needed, as shown in treadling for stripes in Figure 355.

More practice

Figure 354 is a variation of the previous design. Let's say you want the stripes and a border all the way around the design. The threading wouldn't change because the two looms are in the same configuration of five equal stripes or spaces. To weave the border, the two looms will both act alike. Another set of treadles must be tied up to weave with both looms acting in another configuration (with both looms now acting alike). Working

in Figure 352a, first, put in the tie-up you made in Figure 353. Now, add four more combinations, or "treadle tie-ups" in the tie-up draft, as follows. The background weave doesn't change; it is still 1/3 twill. Put the tie-up for the 1/3 twill on the tie-up draft below the dotted line: 1,2,3,4. Now, put the tie-up for the "second loom" above it—this time, it is also a 1/3 twill. Put 5,6,7,8 in place. When these four treadles are used, both looms will weave 1/3 twill. When you've woven enough for the bottom border, switch to the other set of treadles until you are ready for the top border. (Notice I used the same weave that was already on the sides, for the top and bottom borders, to make a border all around.) Then, use the first four treadles again. You will be using eight treadles, 4 at a time. (Your treadling draft should have eight X's—4 under the combinations for the striped area, and 4 more for the borders.) See Figure 355.

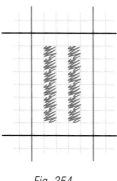

Fig. 354

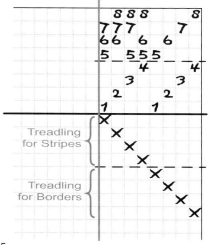

Treadling for Stripes

Treadling for Borders

Fig. 355

Using the "looms"

The special weave can appear and disappear, but it must stay in its position where it is threaded on its special loom, or its special set of shafts. In Figure 356a, b, and c, the two looms are threaded the same as in Figure 349, on page 238. The difference is that the special weave doesn't show all the time; it can come and go as you choose. When it doesn't show, the "second loom" is weaving the same weave as the "first loom."

Blocks

We can give the different "things" we are weaving a proper name. They are called blocks. Look at Figure 356a, b, and c. There are two blocks or two different "looms" or groups of threads that act alike as a group because they are threaded to work as units. If you want to understand blocks, be sure to read, "How to weave two things at once" on page 238, before reading on.

Counting blocks

To identify blocks, look for identical vertical columns.

All vertical columns that act alike are the same block. In Figure 356a, b, and c, there are two blocks in each illustration. Beginning at the right edge (as we do in reading threading drafts), assign the first area (or block) as "Block A." Move your eye (or template—see page 231) across to the left and when something else happens, that's a second block— "Block B." As you continue working across the warp toward the left, you come to a column that is identical to the right-hand column which was assigned as Block A. Hence this design has two blocks.

Any block weave could be used instead of the twill weaves I used here as examples. Read about different block weaves (Figure 366, on

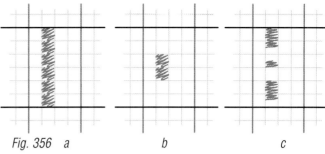

Fig. 356 a   b   c

page 246), and about using profile drafts on pages 222 and 243.

Practice

Count the blocks in Figure 357. Start at the right edge of the first illustration with Block A. Move to the left and see that there is something different: a new "thing"—a new block—Block B. Continue looking for identical *vertical* columns and see that the left side is exactly identical to the right side which was named Block A. You can name the sequence of the blocks, working from right-to-left: A Block, B Block, A Block; or A, B, A. Again, it is a two-block design.

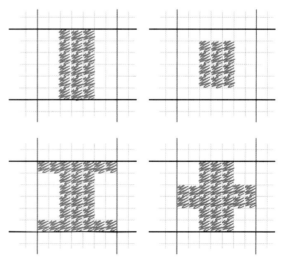

Fig. 357

Notice that all of the illustrations in this figure have the same configuration (A, B, A) and sizes of blocks. They could all be woven on the same warp because the "second loom", or Block B, is the same size and in the same position in all of them, as are the A blocks.

241

Identifying more blocks

Count the blocks in Figure 358. Remember, the key is looking for identical vertical columns. Vertical, because we are looking for how the threading will be. At the right edge is Block A, as usual—you can give it any letter, but usually, we start counting on the right and name the first section Block A. Move along until you get to a vertical column that is different; it is Block B. Moving along, there is some more Block A. The next column is one that is completely different from any so far, so that will be Block C. (So far, there are three blocks.) Moving along, there is some more of Block A. Then, there is a change again. Look at it carefully. Is it a block already identified, or something completely different? Is there any other place in the design where the vertical column is exactly the same? There is no other exactly identical column, so this must be called Block D. The left-hand edge is Block A again. How did you do? Were you tricked because Blocks B and D are the same shape and size? See that they are different by looking from the top to the bottom of the design in both areas—the vertical columns are different. Where Block B is showing, there is nothing special going on in the area where Block D is threaded.

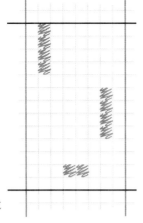

Fig. 358

The order of the threading of the blocks is: (reading right-to-left): A, B, A, C, A, D, A. Notice that there is only one C Block mentioned even though it occupies *two vertical* columns. The reason is that that block is twice the width of the other blocks.

Practice, practice. practice

How many blocks are in Figure 359? They can be read as A, B, C, D, A.

Fig. 359

242

Weave from the bottom up

If you are weaving a specific design, you need to weave it from the bottom up, because that's the way weaving "happens." To weave Figure 358, you would begin at the bottom of the treadling draft and weave as follows:

1. Weave the bottom border with the treadles that weave all the blocks alike in your chosen background weave structure.

2. Weave with the set of treadles used for Block C in pattern, and with all the other blocks weaving in background.

3. All the blocks are in background again; use the first set of treadles.

4. Blocks A, C, D are weaving background, with Block B weaving in pattern—another set of treadles is needed.

5. Weave with the first set of treadles for all background again.

6. Another set of treadles is needed to weave where only Block D is weaving pattern. You will need four sets of treadles: 1 set where all the blocks weave alike for the background, 1 set with just Block B in pattern, 1 set with just Block C in pattern, and 1 more set with Block D in pattern.

Treadling blocks

Multi-shaft looms often need a lot of treadles. One way to keep track of your treadles is to organize them so that when you are weaving, you alternate your feet, called "walking the treadles." I think beginning from the outside treadles and working in is a good idea, because your feet can always "feel" the outermost treadle without your having to look down at the treadles. So, the treadles for weaving all the blocks alike might be the far left one, then, the far

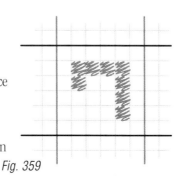

right one, then, the next-to-the-left, and the next-to-right one. If you had another set of treadles, say for borders, as in Figure 355, on page 240, put them on the outside and put the ones for the stripes or the body of the design nearer the middle of the loom. I try to put the treadles I will use more often nearer the center of the loom, so my feet don't have to reach so far for them. If possible, I like to leave a treadle down between my sets of treadles, so my feet can feel their way easier. Always try to set up the treadles so you don't have to look at them and can feel them with your feet. Walking your treadles makes keeping track of them easier.

Profile Drafts

Profile drafts (page 223) show the blocks and their sequences in both the threading and the treadling drafts. Often, there is a profile tie-up, as well. Figure 360 is a profile draft for Figure 358. Notice blocks are filled in the threading draft according to their size. Block A is on the bottom line, just as shaft 1 is on

the bottom line in thread-by-thread drafts. Blocks B, C, and D are on the lines above. The reason a regular threading draft for the shafts isn't given is that we don't know what weave structure is going to be used. There are many block weaves, and any one of them could be used for this design, if there are enough shafts on the loom to weave the number of blocks indicated. Figure 366, on page 246, shows how many blocks you can weave in several block weaves, depending on the number of shafts you have on your loom.

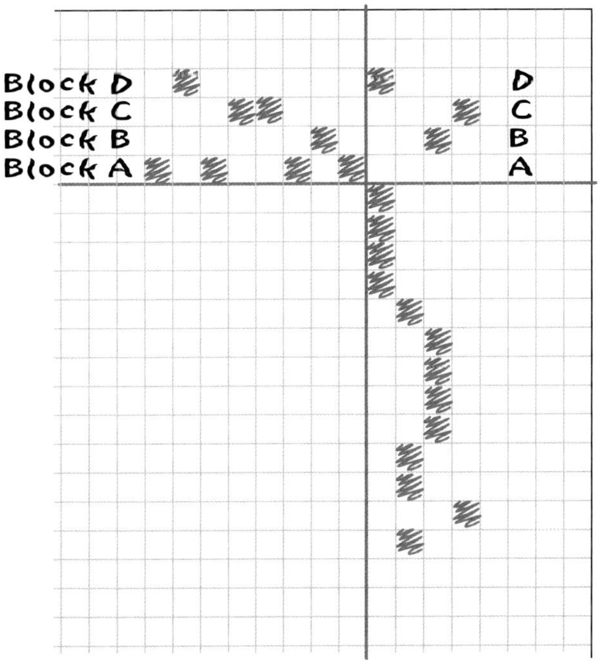

You set up your loom for your chosen weave structure, putting the blocks in place as though you had a loom for every block.

Each structure has its rules for what's needed for a block. Rules for various weave structures are given in the books listed previously.[66]

In this threading profile, see that it reads (right-to-left as usual): A, B, A, C, A, D, A, and see that the all the blocks but Block C are the same width. Look at the treadling and tie-up drafts. Beginning at the bottom of the treadling draft, look for the first filled-in box. It is in the second square to the right of the bold vertical line. Follow it up to the tie-up draft and see that, at first, no blocks are showing, only background is woven for 1 square's worth. Reading up to the next filled-in square in the treadling draft (the fourth square to the right of the bold vertical line), note that Block C is to be "woven" (or to show) 1 square tall. Then, only background is woven for the height of 2 squares. Then, Block B is woven to show 4 squares high. Then, background again for 1 square's worth, and last of all, 4 squares with Block D showing are woven.

Fig. 360

Block D
Block C
Block B
Block A

D
C
B
A

243

---

[66] Alderman, Chandler, and van der Hoogt.

Practice

Fill in the drawdown draft for the profile draft in Figure 361. The answer is Figure 359 on page 242.

Figures 321a and b on page 223 are profile drafts. Complete them by putting in the tie-up and treadling profiles.

How many blocks can I have?

Different weaves require different numbers of shafts for each block as well as different rules to weave them. Figure 366 on page 246 is a chart that can be helpful to tell you the number of blocks you can have for the number of shafts you have. When you read about these weaves, you will learn how the blocks are threaded and woven for each weave.[67]

Reading the chart, let's assume your loom has eight shafts. If you wanted to weave "crackle" weave, you could have eight blocks. If you wanted to weave double weave, you could only have two blocks. This discrepancy occurs because the two weaves require different numbers of shafts for each block. Double weave requires four shafts for one block, as do the twill blocks I used in the examples to explain blocks and multi-shaft weaving. Using "M's & O's" weave structure on your eight-shaft loom, the chart says you could have 4 blocks, the number of shafts on your loom divided by two. In other words, each block needs 2 shafts.

"Overshot" weave is very popular with weavers, and you can have four blocks with only four shafts. Figure 362 is a familiar pattern sometimes called Snail Tracks. The illustration shows the drawdown in a profile draft. You can make a profile threading, tie-up, and treadling draft. Remember to look for identical vertical columns to identify the blocks, and that a template (See Figure 339 on page 231) makes it easy to do.

[67] Alderman, Chandler, and van der Hoogt.

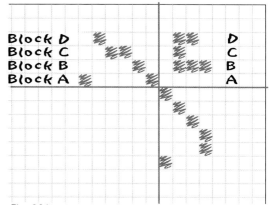

Fig. 361

☞ You can see that you can plug any weave structure that you like into your profile draft, providing you have enough shafts, and like the way the weave looks.

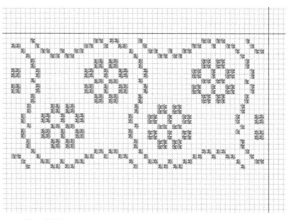

Fig. 362

"Two Looms" with Four Shafts

You can divide a four-shaft loom into "two looms", too, with two shafts per block. See Figure 363. For example, Block A can be weaving plain weave and Block B can be

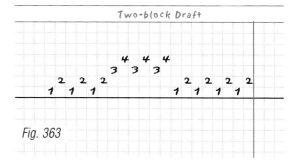

Fig. 363

floats, with no shafts lifted. Another way to divide the shafts into blocks is by color placement. In Figure 363, you could put the light threads on the odd shafts (shaft 1 in Block A and shaft 3 in Block B) and the dark threads on the even shafts. Then, you could choose to have the light threads up in only A, or only B, or in both blocks, or in no blocks. In other words, you have "two looms," and each one can act independently or like the other. Monk's belt, on page 223, is another weave threaded on two blocks on four shafts.

Mixing Weaves

You could use entirely different weaves on your looms. For example, with an eight-shaft loom and a threading that is a straight repeat (1,2,3,4,5,6,7,8), you could have a 5-shaft satin on shafts one-five, and a 3-shaft twill on 6,7,8. That threading could also be used as a one-block weave in a variety of ways, for example, an eight-shaft twill (and all the variations of warp-faced and weft-faced twills), or an eight-shaft satin. All these weaves can be woven on one warp with this threading. Just like with "two looms," they can act alike or different from one another.

Practice

Figure 364 shows a two-block threading, and the "answer" to Figure 352a on page 239. Using that threading draft, make up more tie-ups for different weaves in the two blocks.

Examples:

1. Basket weave in Block A, and 2/2 twill in Block B.
2. Basket weave in both blocks.
3. Plain weave in Block A, and basket weave in Block B.
4. Make up your own combinations of weaves.

More Practice

Work out the missing parts of the drafts in Figures 365a, b, c, d, e (on next page). All of them are related; so complete them in sequence. Notice the different types of repeats: straight and point (or mirror image), and notice the broken point in one of the threading drafts.

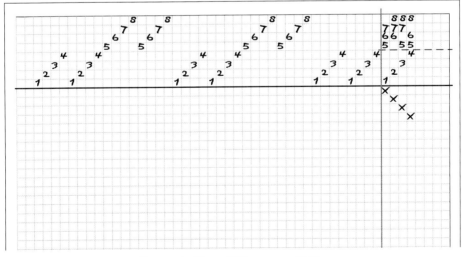

Fig. 364   *(Answer to Figure 352a on page 239)*

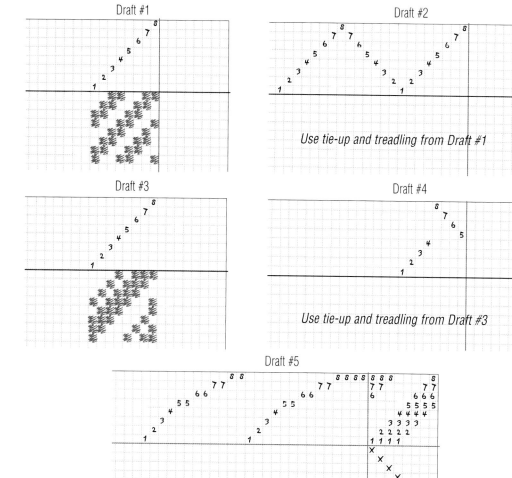

Fig. 365

WEAVE CHART

Weave Structure	# Shafts on your loom		# Blocks you can have
Crackle			=
Double Weave		Divided by 4	=
Lace Bronson		Minus 2	=
M's & O's		Divided by 2	=
Overshot			=
Ripsmatta		Divided by 2	=
Satin (5-shaft)		Divided by 5	=
Satin (8-shaft)		Divided by 8	=
Shadow Weave			=
Spot Bronson		Minus 1	=
Summer & Winter		Minus 2	=
Twills (4-shaft)		Divided by 4	=

Fig. 366

Sources

Brushing Service
Ihana Brushing Service
6400 W. 99th Street
Overland Park, KS 66212
913-648-1575

Clerco Sizing
Leclerc Looms
PO Box 4
Plessisville, Quebec, Canada G6L 2Y6
819-362-7207
www.leclerclooms.com

Degumming Powder
Habu Textiles
135 W. 29th Street, #403
New York, NY 10001
212-239-3546
www.habutextiles.com

Doubling Stand
Bruce Bannerman
Purrington Looms
Box 44
Scott Depot, WV 25560
304-743-5455
www.puringtonlooms.com

Hemostat
Fire Mountain Gems and Beads
One Fire Mountain Way
Grants Pass, OR 97526-2373
800-355-2137
www.firemountaingems.com

Lightweight Lease Sticks
AVL Looms
3851 Morrow Lane
Chico, CA 95928
800-626-9615
www.avlusa.com

Pick Glass/Linen Tester
Part #YAL 20A
Shop Tools, Inc.
892 Commercial Street
Palo Alto, CA 94303
800-300-8331
www.shoptools.com

Pirn Winder
Olympic Pirn Winder Co.
7120 Prairie Ridge Drive, NE
Olympia, WA 98516-1133
800-753-3896 #00
www.olympicpirnwinder.com

Rotary Temple
Fireside Fiberarts
1060 Olele Point Road
Port Ludlow, WA 98365
360-437-0733
www.firesidelooms.com

Synthrapol SP
Dharma Trading Company
PO Box 150916
San Rafael, CA 94915
800-542-5227
www.dharmatrading.com

Tension Box
AVL Looms, above
Purrington Looms, above
see weaving equipment

Texsolv Cord
Unicorn Books and Crafts, Inc.
1338 Ross Street
Petaluma, CA 94954-6502
800-289-9276
www.unicornbooks.com

Warp Comb (Drawing-in Comb)
Southern Loom Reed Mfg. Co.
226 Hyatt Street
Gaffney, SC 29341
800-782-8187

Sources for Weaving Equipment

(also mail order)

Halcyon Yarn
12 School Street
Bath, ME 04530
800-341-0282
www.halcyonyarn.com

Leclerc Looms
PO Box 4
Plessisville, Quebec, Canada G6L 2Y6
819-362-7207
www.leclerclooms.com

Lunatic Fringe
15009 Cromartie Road
Tallahassee, FL 32309
800-483-8749
lunatic@talstar.com

Schacht Spindle Co., Inc.
6101 Ben Place
Boulder, CO 80301
800-228-2553
www.schachtspindle.com

the handweavers studio
29 Haroldstone Road
London E17-7AN
tel. 181-521-2281
www.handweaversstudio.co.uk

The Mannings
1132 Green Ridge Road, PO Box 687
East Berlin, PA 17316
800-233-7166
www.the-mannings.com

Yarn Barn
930 Massachusetts Street
Lawrence, KS 66044
800-468-0035
www.yarnbarn-ks.com.

Bibliography

Ahrens, Jim. Production Weaving Class Notes. Berkeley, CA: circa 1975.

————————. Notes from Apprenticeship with Jim Ahrens. Berkeley, CA: circa 1976-77.

Alderman, Sharon. *Mastering Weave Structures*. Loveland, CO: Interweave Press, 2004.

————————. *Handwoven* Magazine Page 67. Loveland, CO: Interweave Press, Sept./Oct., 2003.

————————. Conversations with Sharon Alderman. 2004.

————————. and Kathryn Wertenberger. *Handwoven, Tailormade*. Loveland, CO: Interweave Press, 1982.

Arn-Grischott, Ursina. *Double Weave on Four to Eight Shafts*. Loveland, CO: Interweave Press, 1999.

Ashenhurst, Thomas R. *Design in Textile Fabrics*. London: Cassell and Co., Ltd., 1899.

Baines, Patricia. Linen: *Hand Spinning and Weaving*. London: B.T. Batsford Ltd., 1989.

Baizerman, Suzanne, and Karen Serle. *Finishes in the Ethnic Tradition*. St. Paul, MN: Dos Tehedoras Fiber Arts Publications, 1989.

Beaumont, Roberts. *Wool Manufacture*. London. George Bell and Sons, 1899.

Chandler, Deborah. *Learning to Weave*. Loveland, CO: Interweave Press, 1995.

Collingwood, Peter. *The Techniques of Rug Weaving*. New York: Watson-Guptill Publications, 1969.

Creager, Clara. *All About Weaving*. Garden City, NY: Doubleday & Company, Inc., 1984.

Cyrus-Zetterstrom, Ulla. *Manual of Swedish Handweaving*. Newton Centre, MA: Charles T. Branford Co., 1956.

Davison, Marguerite Porter. *A Handweaver's Pattern Book*. Swarthmore, PA: Marguerite P. Davison, Publisher, 1944.

Fannin, Allen A. *Handloom Weaving Technology*. New York: Van Nostrand Reinhold Company, 1979.

Frey, Berta. *Design and Drafting for Handweavers*. New York: Macmillan Company, 1958.

Friedel, Lynda. "Cleaning Old Heddles." *Handwoven* Magazine. Loveland, CO: Interweave Press, March/April 1997.

Fry, Laura. *Magic in the Water: Wet Finishing Handwovens*. Prince George, BC: Fry Weaving Studio, 2002.

Gaynes, Margaret. "Weaving with Sticky Yarns." *Handwoven* Magazine Jan./ Feb. Loveland, CO: Interweave Press, 1990.

————————. "Double-Width Blankets on Four Shafts." *Handwoven* Magazine, Jan./Feb. Loveland, CO: Interweave Press, 2002.

Gilmurray, Susan. *Weaving Tricks*. New York: Van Nostrand Reinhold Company, 1981.

Halsey, Mike, and Lore Youngmark. *Foundations of Weaving*. London: David & Charles Limited, 1975.

Harris, Sue Hiley. *Inlay Workshop Notes*. January, 2003.

Heinrich, Linda. *The Magic of Linen*. Victoria, BC: Orca Book Publishers Ltd., 1992

Hochberg, Bette. *Fibre Facts*. Santa Cruz, CA: Bette Hochberg, 1981.

Hooper, Luther. *Hand-Loom Weaving*. New York: Pitman Publishing Corp., 1920.

————————. *Weaving for Beginners*. London: Sir Isaac Pitman & Sons, Ltd., 1934.

Hoykinpuro, Anja. *Handwoven* Magazine. Loveland, CO: Interweave Press, Nov./Dec. 1994.

Irwin, Bobbie (Compiled by). "Fuzzy Stuff: Finishing the Fuzzies." *Handwoven* Magazine, Jan./Feb. Loveland, CO: Interweave Press, 1990.

Ligon, Linda, editor. *A Rug Weaver's Source Book*. Loveland, CO: Interweave Press, 1984.

Linder, Harry P. *Hints From Harry*. Sun City, AZ: Sun City Handweavers and Spinners Guild, 1991.

McLendon, Verda I. *Removing Stains From Fabrics: Home Methods Home and Garden Bulletin No. 62*. United States: U.S. Department of Agriculture, 1959.

Meek, M. Kati. *Handwoven* Magazine, Sept./Oct. Loveland, CO: Interweave Press, 1996.

Mudge, Christine S. "Finishing Wool and Linen," *Shuttle, Spindle, and Dyepot* Magazine, Summer. United States: Handweavers Guild of America, 1978.

Northern California Handweavers. *Secrets of the Loom*. California: Northern California Handweavers, Inc., 1983.

Oelsner, G. H. *A Handbook of Weaves*. New York: Dover Publications, Inc., 1952.

Osterkamp, Peggy. *Winding a Warp & Using a Paddle*. Sausalito, CA: Lease Sticks Press, 1992.

————————. *Warping Your Loom & Tying On New Warps*. Sausalito, CA: Lease Sticks Press, 1995.

Quinn, Celia. *Silk Tidings*, September. Canada: Treenway Silks Publisher, 2002.

Regensteiner, Else. *The Art of Weaving*. New York: Van Nostrand Reinhold, 1970.

Roth, Bettie G., and Chris Schulz. *Handbook of Timesaving Tables for Weavers, Spinners and Dyers*. Elk Grove, CA: Roth-Schulz, 1991.

Schacht, Barry. *Instruction Pamphlet for End-Delivery Shuttles*. Boulder, CO: Schacht Spindle Company, 1997.

Selk, Karen. "Ins and Outs of Weaving Silk for Clothing." *Threads* Magazine, June/July 1989.

Snover, Susan. *Wadmal Workshop Instructions*. Seattle, WA.

Straub, Marianne. *Handweaving and Cloth Design*. New York: The Viking Press, 1977.

Strong, John H. *Foundations of Fabric Structure*. London: National Trade Press Ltd., 1953

Sutton, Ann. *The Structure of Weaving*. Asheville, NC: Lark Books, 1982.

————————. *Lecture Notes from Workshop*. December, 1997.

Sutton, Ann, Peter Collingwood, and Geraldine St Aubyn Hubbard. *Craft of the Weaver*. Asheville, NC: Lark Books, 1983.

Thomas, Mary. *Mary Thomas's Knitting Book*. London: Hodder and Stoughton, 1938.

Tidball, Harriet. *Supplementary Warp Patterning*. Santa Ana, CA: HTH Publishers, 1966.

————————. *The Weaver's Book*. New York: Collier Books, 1961.

Tovey, John. *The Technique of Weaving*. London: B.T. Batsford Ltd., 1965.

————————. *Weaves and Pattern Drafting*. London: B.T. Batsford Ltd., 1969.

van der Hoogt, Madelyn. *The Complete Book of Drafting for Handweavers*. Coupeville, WA: Shuttle Craft Books, 1993.

Wertenberger, Kathryn. *An Introduction to Multishaft Weaving*. United States: Kathryn Wertenberger, 1988.

West, Virginia M. *Finishing Touches for the Handweaver*. United States: Charles T. Branford Company, 1968.

White, George. *On Weaving by Hand and Power Looms*. Glasgow: John Niven and Son, 1846.

Williamson, Liz. *Finishing Lecture*. At Convergence, 1998.

Woolman, Mary Schenck, and Ellen Beers McGowan. *Textiles: A Handbook for the Student and the Consumer*. New York: The Macmillan Company, 1914.

Index

253